Modern Full-Stack Development

Using TypeScript, React, Node.js, Webpack, Python, Django, and Docker

Second Edition

Frank Zammetti

Apress®

Modern Full-Stack Development: Using TypeScript, React, Node.js, Webpack, Python, Django, and Docker

Frank Zammetti
Pottstown, PA, USA

ISBN-13 (pbk): 978-1-4842-8810-8   ISBN-13 (electronic): 978-1-4842-8811-5
https://doi.org/10.1007/978-1-4842-8811-5

Managing Director, Apress Media LLC: Welmoed Spahr
Acquisitions Editor: James Robinson-Prior
Development Editor: James Markham
Coordinating Editor: Gryffin Winkler

Cover designed by FreePik
Cover image from Wirestock

Distributed to the book trade worldwide by Springer Science+Business Media New York, 1 New York Plaza, New York, NY 10004. Phone 1-800-SPRINGER, fax (201) 348-4505, e-mail orders-ny@springer-sbm.com, or visit www.springeronline.com. Apress Media, LLC is a California LLC and the sole member (owner) is Springer Science + Business Media Finance Inc (SSBM Finance Inc). SSBM Finance Inc is a **Delaware** corporation.

For information on translations, please e-mail booktranslations@springernature.com; for reprint, paperback, or audio rights, please e-mail bookpermissions@springernature.com.

Apress titles may be purchased in bulk for academic, corporate, or promotional use. eBook versions and licenses are also available for most titles. For more information, reference our Print and eBook Bulk Sales web page at http://www.apress.com/bulk-sales.

Any source code or other supplementary material referenced by the author in this book is available to readers on GitHub via the book's product page, located at www.apress.com/9781484288108. For more detailed information, please visit http://www.apress.com/source-code.

Printed on acid-free paper

Dedicated to the Xenomorph, the perfect organism.
Its structural perfection is matched only by its hostility.

(my wife may be right when she says I watch entirely too
many movies entirely too many times over and over again)

Table of Contents

About the Author

Frank Zammetti is a Principal Full-Stack Developer for a major financial firm with nearly 27 years of professional experience (plus almost 15 years of nonprofessional experience before that). He is an author of, including this one, 13 technical books for Apress. Frank has also authored over two dozen certification exams for SHL as well as several independent articles for various publications. He is also a fiction author (shameless plug: look him up on Amazon if you like sci-fi) and a musician of some renown (and here, "some" should be taken to mean very little). Frank has been married for 27 years (to the same woman even!), and they have two children together. When not doing any of the aforementioned things, Frank can be found sleeping, 'cause that's about all there's time for after all that, and not nearly enough of it either!

About the Technical Reviewer

Herman van Rosmalen works as a software developer
for De Nederlandsche Bank N.V., the central bank of the
Netherlands. He has more than 35 years of experience
in developing software applications in a variety of
programming languages. Herman has been involved in
building mainframe, PC, client-server, web, and mobile
applications. The last few years Herman has been mainly
involved in developing applications in BizTalk, .NET C#, and
Angular after working for 15 years with Java technology.

Herman lives in a small town, Pijnacker, in the
Netherlands with his wife Liesbeth and their children
Barbara, Leonie, and Ramon. Next to developing software,
he loves to read, travel, and hike. He is also an enthusiastic
soccer fan and supporter of Feyenoord!

Acknowledgments

I'd like to acknowledge the exceptional team at Apress for allowing me to write not one but thirteen books for them over the last decade or so (true story: in the first edition of this book, I actually had the wrong count – I don't even KNOW how many books I've written at this point!). I've worked with so many great people, and it's virtually impossible not to forget someone in a list like this, but among the crew for sure are James Robinson-Prior, Gryffin Winkler, Aditee Mirashi, Celestin Suresh John, Ami Knox, Arockia Rajan Dhurai, Beth Christmas, Dulcy Nirmala Chellappa, Chris Mills, Christine Ricketts, Dominic Shakeshaft, Douglas Pundick, Frank Parnell, Frank Pohlmann, Gary Cornell, Jill Balzano, Julie Miller, Katie Stence, Kelly Gunther, Kelly Winquist, Kevin Shea, Kim Wimpsett, Kimberly van der Elst, Krishnan Sathyamurthy, Laura Cheu, Laura Esterman, Leah Weissburg, Leonard Cuellar, Liz Welch, Louise Corrigan, Marilyn Smith, Michelle Lowman, Nancy Chen, Nicole Faraclas, Nirmal Selvaraj, Richard Dal Porto, Sharon Wilkey, Sofia Marchant, Stephanie Parker, Steve Anglin, Tina Nielsen, and Tracy Brown Collins.

As I said, I'm sure I've forgotten someone, but rest assured it was not on purpose! Thank you all for giving me a shot and allowing me to continue this journey. I most definitely could not have done it alone, and I thank you all, unreservedly!

Introduction

You know, when I started learning how to program, it was a piece of cake!

You'd turn on the computer and be greeted by a nice little "Ready" prompt. You'd start typing in some code (BASIC), and eventually, you'd type run, hit Enter, and watch whatever it was you put in there spit back something (my first program was a man drawn with various keyboard characters doing jumping jacks). You might save that program to a cassette – yes, kids, a *cassette*! – and hand it to your friends if you wanted to share.

But that was it. It was just that easy.

Nowadays, though, the story is *very* different.

Writing even a trivial application now involves layers upon layers of abstractions and complexities that you must mix together, like baking the world's most complicated cake, hoping it all works in the end. Then, should you want to distribute the technological terror you've constructed (sorry, Aldearan), you've got even more challenges to overcome.

How *anyone* learns to program from scratch these days, I'm not sure!

But I'm hoping to help there!

With this book, I'm going to look at the ingredients that go into baking a cake – err, building an application – these days. To be sure, it won't cover everything. And no one recipe is necessarily the same anyway – there are lots of choices available to a developer now. But I believe I've chosen the ones most commonly used to build modern full-stack applications.

What exactly is a full-stack application anyway? Well, simply put, it's an application that includes both a front-end "client," like a website, and a back-end "server," like, well, a *server*! We're talking about building an application that combines those two halves into a coherent whole. Most application development these days is web-based in some way (where "web" doesn't have to mean something available on the public Internet, but something built with web technologies like HTML, JavaScript, and CSS), so that's what we're going to be doing in this book.

To do this, we're going to use React, which is one of the most popular libraries for building clients out there today. And we'll use Node.js, which is a popular choice for back-end development. We're also going to use TypeScript, a language that enhances

JavaScript on both sides of the fence to make our coding lives better. We're going to touch on several other tools that relate to all of this including Babel and Webpack. We'll talk about some strategies for connecting the client to the server including REST and WebSockets. Then we'll "flip the script" a bit, if you will, and build our back-end code using Python and its popular framework Django instead, just because! Finally, you'll learn about packaging up applications using the very popular containerization tool Docker.

All this will be combined to build three full, real applications. This way, it's not just simple, contrived examples. No, it'll be real code, practical solutions to real problems encountered in building them, and real techniques for putting all these pieces together and making sense of all this complexity.

In the end, you'll have a solid foundation for building modern full-stack applications that you can go forward with on your own to create greatness.

I mean it'll never be as great as my guy doing jumping jacks written in BASIC and loaded off a cassette, but you gotta have goals.

So let's get to it. There's work to be done, learning to be accomplished, and, I hope, fun to be had!

CHAPTER 1

Server-Side Action: Node and NPM

Welcome to the book! I hope you've got a comfy chair under you, a tasty drink on the table next to you and perhaps a light snack (may I suggest some dark chocolate biscotti?), and your brain ready to soak up a ton of knowledge on modern web development, 'cause that's what the show is all about and the curtains are about to be drawn!

In this book, we'll be building three full apps that will demonstrate all the concepts that we'll be discussing along the way in a practical manner. Far from being just simple, contrived bits of code, these are three full apps which are functional and useful (and even *fun*, given that one of them is a game, which will provide you a whole new way of looking at coding). As we do so, you'll get insight into the thinking that went into them, their design and architecture, so you get a holistic picture of what's involved in building something like these three apps. You will even, here and there, get some notes about issues I faced and how I resolved them, things that will almost certainly help you achieve your goals as you charge onward into your own projects.

To start, we'll look at what is most usually (though not exclusively, as you'll learn!) the purview of the server side. Remember that we're talking "full-stack" development here, which means you'll be learning about coding clients as well as the server code they make use of in order to form a cohesive, whole application. In this chapter, we'll begin by looking at two extremely popular tools for developing servers: Node.js and NPM.

© Frank Zammetti 2022
F. Zammetti, *Modern Full-Stack Development*, https://doi.org/10.1007/978-1-4842-8811-5_1

Of JavaScript Runtimes and Building (Mostly) Servers

Ryan Dahl – that cat has some talent, I tell ya!

Ryan is the creator of a fantastic piece of software called Node.js (or just plain Node, as it is often written, and as I'll write it from here on out). Ryan first presented Node at the European JSConf in 2009, and it was quickly recognized as a potential game-changer, as evidenced by the standing ovation his presentation received (I presume Ryan is an excellent presenter generally as well).

Node is a platform for running primarily, though not exclusively, server-side code that has high performance and is capable of handling large request loads with ease. It is based on the most widely used language on the planet today: JavaScript. It's straightforward to get started with and understand, yet it puts tremendous power in the hands of developers, in large part thanks to its asynchronous and event-driven model of programming. In Node, almost everything you do is nonblocking, meaning code won't hold up the processing of other request threads. Most types of I/O, which is where blocking comes into play most, are asynchronous in Node, whether it's network calls or file system calls or database calls. This, plus the fact that to execute code, Node uses Google's popular and highly tuned V8 JavaScript engine, the same engine that powers its Chrome browser, makes it very high performance and able to handle a large request load (assuming that you as the developer don't botch things of course!).

It's also worth noting that, as weird as it may sound, Node is single-threaded. It at first seems like this would be a performance bottleneck, but in fact, it's a net benefit because it avoids context switching. However, this is a little bit of a misnomer in that it's more correct to say that Node is event-driven and single-threaded with background workers. When you fire off some type of I/O request, Node will generally spawn a new thread for that. But, while it's doing its work, that single event-driven thread continues executing your code. All of this is managed with an event queue mechanism so that the callbacks for those I/O operations are fired, back on that single thread, when the responses come back. All of this means that there is no (or at least minimal) context switching between threads but also that the single thread is never sitting idle (unless there is *literally* no work to do of course), so you wind up with that net positive benefit I mentioned.

Note   In later chapters, you'll see that Node isn't specific to the server side of the equation, and in fact, you don't always build apps with Node; sometimes, you use it to install and execute tools for various purposes on your own development machine. Hold on to that thought; we'll be coming back to that before long a few chapters from now.

None of these technical details are especially important to being able to use Node as a developer, but the performance it yields is what makes it no wonder that so many significant players and sites have adopted Node to one degree or another. These aren't minor outfits we're talking about, we're talking names you doubtless know, including DuckDuckGo, eBay, LinkedIn, Microsoft, Netflix, PayPal, Walmart, and Yahoo, to name just a few examples. These are large businesses that require top-tier performance, and Node can deliver on that promise (again, with the caveat that you as the developer don't mess things up, because that's always possible).

Node is a first-class runtime environment, meaning that you can do such things as interacting with the local file system, accessing relational databases, calling remote systems, and much more. In the past, you'd have to use a "proper" runtime, such as Java or .Net, to do all this; JavaScript wasn't a player in that space. With Node, this is no longer true. It can compete not only on performance but also in terms of what capabilities it provides to developers. If you can think of it, chances are you can do it with Node, and that wasn't always the case with JavaScript.

To be clear, Node isn't in and of itself a server. You can't just start up Node and make HTTP requests to it from a web browser like you can servers like Tomcat, Apache, or IIS. It won't do anything in response to your requests by default. No, to use Node as a server, you must write some (straightforward and concise, as you'll see) code that then runs on the Node "runtime." Yes, you effectively write your own web server and app server, if you want to split hairs (or potentially FTP, Telnet, or any other type of server you might wish to). That's a very odd thing to do as a developer – we usually apply the "don't reinvent the wheel" mantra for stuff like that and pull one of the hundreds of existing options off the shelf. Plus, writing such servers sounds (and probably actually *is*) daunting to most developers, and for good reason! To be sure, it absolutely would be if you tried to write a web server from scratch in many other languages, especially if you want it to do more than just serve static content files. But not with Node!

But remember, acting as a server is just one capability that Node provides as a JavaScript runtime, and it can provide this functionality only if you, as a developer, feed it the code it needs to do so! In fact, a great many developer tools, and other types of apps, use Node as their runtime nowadays. Node really is all over the place!

Note   As you'll see, three things – React, Webpack, and TypeScript – are the main focuses of the first two apps we'll be building, and they all themselves use Node to run and/or to be installed (well, NPM is used to install them if we're being accurate, but we'll get to NPM in just a moment). These are tools, not servers, which is the main point: Node is useful for much more than just creating servers!

Node allows you to use the same language and knowledge on both client and server, something that was difficult to accomplish before. In fact, aside from Java and some Microsoft technologies (see project Blazor, which seeks to do the same thing with C#, if you're curious), there never has really been an opportunity to do so until Node came along. It's a pretty compelling opportunity.

Another critical aspect of Node is a driving design goal of the project, which is keeping its core functionality to an absolute minimum and providing extended functionality by way of APIs (in the form of JavaScript modules) that you can pick and choose from as needed. Node gets out of your way as much as possible and allows you only to introduce the complexity you really need, when you need it. Node ships with an extensive library of such modules, but each must be imported into your code, and then there are literally thousands of other third-party modules that you can bring in as needed, some of which you'll see as we progress throughout this book.

In addition to all of this, acquiring, installing, and running Node are trivial exercises, regardless of your operating system preference. There are no complicated installs with all sorts of dependencies to manage, nor is there a vast set of configuration files to mess with before you can bring up a server and handle requests. It's a five-minute exercise, depending on the speed of your Internet connection and how fast you can type! There is also no required tooling to work with Node. In fact, a simple text editor is enough, in simplest terms (though that isn't to say you won't want a robust IDE with Node support later, but at least for this book I won't be assuming anything other than Notepad or some equivalent text editor).

All of this makes working with Node so much more straightforward than many competing options while providing you with top-notch performance and load handling capabilities. Moreover, it does so with a consistent technological underpinning as that which you develop your client applications.

That's Node in a nutshell!

Next, let's see about getting it onto your machine so that you can start playing with some code together and we can look at Node in a little more depth.

Note   If you aren't a JavaScript expert, don't worry, we won't be getting too fancy. Even when we get to the apps, I'll consciously keep things as simple as possible. It *is* expected that you have *some* experience with JavaScript though, but you don't need to be Brendan Eich or Doug Crockford (but if you have no experience with TypeScript, that's fine; we'll start from square one with it later).

First Baby Steps with Node: Installation

To get started, there's only one address to remember:

```
http://nodejs.org
```

That's your one-stop shop for all things Node, beginning, right from the front page, with downloading it, as you can see in Figure 1-1.

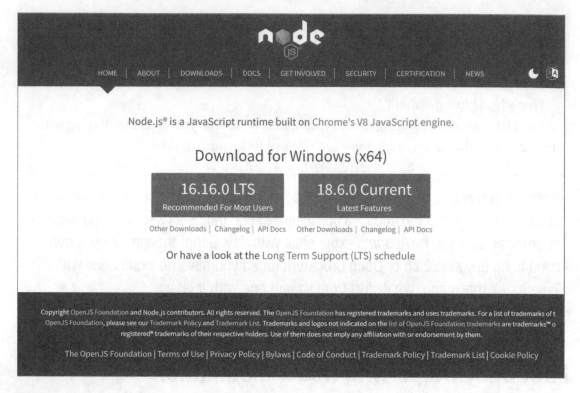

Figure 1-1. *Node has a simple website, but it gets the job done!*

Usually, I would tell you to install the latest version available, but in this case, it might be better to choose a long-term support (LTS) version, because they tend to be more stable. However, it shouldn't (he said, with fingers crossed) matter which you choose, for the purposes of this book. For the record, however, I developed all the code using version 16.16.0 LTS, so if you encounter any problems, I would suggest choosing that version, which you can get from the Other Downloads link and then the Previous Releases link (you'll be able to download any past version you like from there).

The download will install in whatever fashion is appropriate for your system, and I leave this as an exercise for the reader. For example, on Windows, Node provides a perfectly ordinary and straightforward installer that will walk you through the necessary (and extremely simple) steps. On macOS X, a typical install wizard will do the same.

Once the install completes, you will be ready to play with Node. The installer should have added the Node directory to your path. So, as a first simple test, go to a command prompt or console prompt, type node, and press Enter. You should be greeted with a > prompt. Node is now listening for your commands in interactive mode. To confirm, type the following:

```
console.log("Hello, you ugly bad of mostly water!");
```

Press Enter, and you should be greeted with something like what you see in Figure 1-2 (platform differences excepted- I'm a Windows guy myself, unashamedly, so that's where the screenshots throughout this book will be from, perhaps with a few exceptions later).

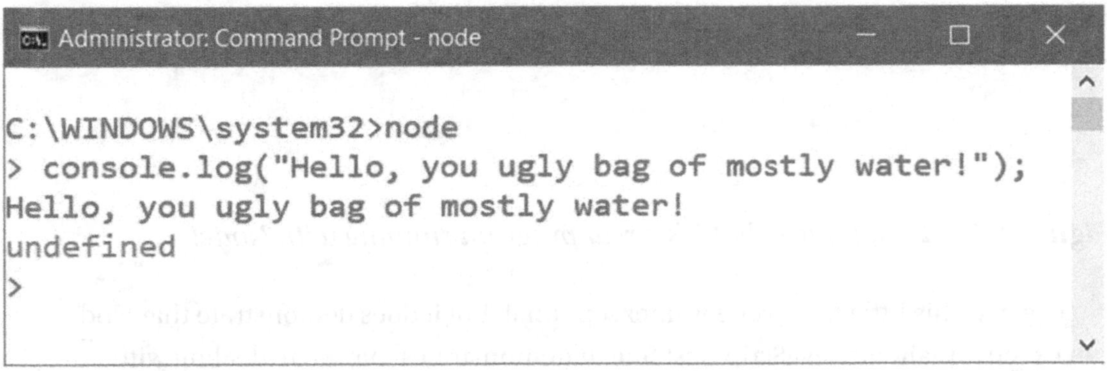

Figure 1-2. *The rather uppity (though technically accurate) first greeting, proving Node is alive*

If you find that this doesn't work, please take a moment and ensure that Node is indeed in your path. It will make things a lot easier going forward.

More Useful: Executing JavaScript Source Files

Interacting with Node in CLI (Command-Line Interface) mode like this is fine and dandy, but it's limited. What you really want to do is execute a saved JavaScript file using Node. As it happens, that's easy to do. Create a text file named test.js (it could be anything, but that's a pretty good choice at this point), and type the following code into it (and, of course, save it):

```
let a = 5;
let b = 3;
let c = a * b;
console.log(`${a} * ${b} = ${c}`);
```

To execute this file, assuming you are in the directory in which the file is located, you simply must type this:

```
node test.js
```

7

Press Enter after that, and you should be greeted with an execution, such as the one you see in Figure 1-3.

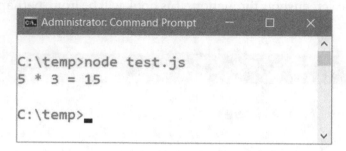

Figure 1-3. *It ain't much, but it's a real program running with Node!*

Clearly, this little bit of code is unexceptional, but it does demonstrate that Node can execute plain old JavaScript just fine. It demonstrates that we're dealing with at least the ES2015 specification as well, being more specific, thanks to the use of let and template literals (or string interpolation if you prefer). You can experiment a bit if you like, and you will see that Node should run any basic JavaScript that you care to throw at it like this. If you're not familiar with ES2015, these are specifications of something called ECMAScript, which is a standardized form of JavaScript. It defines the various language constructs that a JavaScript engine should implement. In the bad old days, JavaScript could vary greatly from browser to browser, causing all sorts of havoc for developers and users alike, and while there's still *some* of that, for the *most* part, browsers implement some version of ECMAScript, and the versions are called ESxxxx, where xxxx is typically the year the specification was finalized. At the time of this writing, ES2016 is probably the most commonly targeted specification, but there is already ES2017, ES2018, ES2019, ES2020, ES2021, and ES2022, though support for them will vary and you need to take care if you want to use features from them. When it comes to Node, the latest LTS supports all features of ES2022. For browsers, you'll need to consult docs online to see what each supports (at the time of this writing, Chrome was at version 103, which also has full support for ES2022 – and note that for the purposes of this book, I'm making an assumption that you're following along with Chrome, though all the code should work fine in any other modern browser like Firefox, Opera, or Edge).

Node's Partner in Crime: NPM

NPM, which stands for Node Package Manager, is a companion app that installs alongside Node (though it is developed separately and can be updated on a different schedule than Node). With it, you can download packages, which are reusable JavaScript modules (and any supporting stuff they might need) from a central package registry (or a private repository if you have one). The central repository you can find at

www.npmjs.com

You can visit it through a web browser and look through all the packages available, which makes finding exactly what you need easy.

Using NPM is simple: it's merely another command to run from a command prompt, just like Node is. For example, let's say you create a directory named MyFirstNodeProject. In it, you execute the following:

npm install express

Here, npm is the CLI program that is NPM itself, and install is one command you can issue to it. Then, express is an argument to that command, and this is the general form that most of your interactions with NPM will take.

Note   Most NPM commands have a shorter form as well. For example, rather than type install, you can just type i, and it will do the same thing. Consult the NPM docs for these shortcuts, or be pedantic like your favorite author and always type it long-form, err, for clarity or something!

If you execute that, you'll find that a directory called node-modules has been created, and inside it will be a lot of...well, a lot of stuff you typically don't need to worry about too much! In short, though, it's all the code that makes up the Express module (which doesn't matter right now, but is a JavaScript module, or package if you prefer, which we'll be using in the MailBag app a few chapters hence... but we'll get to that app in due time, we've got a fair bit of ground to cover before then, so for now suffice it to say it's one of the three apps we're going to be building with the technologies discussed over the first six chapters), plus whatever modules Express itself depends on (and whatever they might depend on, and so on). NPM takes care of fetching all those dependencies for you. You'll also notice a file named `package-lock.json` has been created, and for our purposes here, you don't need to worry about that except to know not to delete it as NPM needs it to do its job.

When you use the `install` command like this, the modules you name are installed in the current directory, and this is referred to as the *local cache*, or *project cache*. You can also install the module into what's called the *global cache* by adding an argument to the command:

```
npm install -g express
```

Now, Express will be installed in a location outside the current directory and will be shared by all Node projects – or, more precisely, it will be available to all projects, because, of course, a project won't use a globally installed module unless you tell it to. Let me make sure that's clear: if you install a module in the global cache, it'll just sit there, unused, unless and until you reference it in your code. But, if you *do* reference it, Node will be able to get it from the global cache transparently; you don't need to ever tell Node whether a module is in the global or local cache, it's smart enough to find it. And, if you happen to have a module installed in both local and global cache, the local cache version will be used. All that aside, note that usually, it's considered something of a best practice to install dependencies in the local cache so that different projects can use different version of a given module than other projects (there is always a single version of a given module in the global cache, if any are present at all).

A Few More NPM Commands

Aside from `install`, there are many other NPM commands, but you'll probably only use a subset most of the time. For example, to find out what modules are installed in your project, you can issue this command:

```
npm ls
```

Like on a *nix system, `ls` is short for list, and that's what it does: lists the installed modules. What you'll see is a textual tree that shows the modules and then the modules they depend on. In other words, more will likely be shown than just the modules you explicitly installed (some modules don't have dependencies, but in the NPM ecosystem, those tend to be the exception rather than the rule).

If you want to see what's installed in global cache instead, you can do

```
npm -g ls
```

In fact, keep that -g option in mind because you can add that to most NPM commands to differentiate between the local and global caches.

You can also update a given module:

```
npm update express
```

Just provide the name of the module to update, and NPM will take care of it, updating to the latest available version. If you don't provide a package name, then NPM will dutifully update *all* packages. And yes, you can drop a -g on it either way to target the global cache. You can also install or update to a specific version of a package by appending an at sign and a version on the end. So, for example, to install version 1.1.0 specifically of that Express package:

```
npm install -g express@1.1.0
```

Likewise, you can update (or downgrade even) to a specific version:

```
npm update -g express@1.1.0
```

You can, of course, uninstall packages too:

```
npm uninstall express
```

Execute that and NPM will wipe Express from the local cache, along with its transient dependencies (so long as nothing else that remains that depends on them).

These few commands represent likely the majority of what you'll need to interact with NPM. I refer you to the NPM docs for other commands (and note that just typing npm and hitting Enter at a command prompt will show you a list of available commands, and you can then type npm help <command> to get information about each).

Note   You will frequently hear horror stories about the node_modules directory. That's because when you install a package, NPM also installs all the other packages it depends on, and the packages each of those depends on, and so on. Before long, the node_modules directory becomes positively massive. Fortunately, you can usually just ignore it and let NPM do its thing for you. You may have to go digging sometimes, especially if you need to reference certain assets in a specific package in your code, but generally speaking, you shouldn't have to do too much of this. Note, however, that you almost never want to include the node_modules directory in your source control repository (Git most likely these days, but could be Subversion or Perforce or something else in some places). You don't want to include a large directory like that just for space purpose for one thing, but the whole idea is that someone can re-create your project – including the node_ modules directory – easily using npm, as you're about to find out, so there's no real reason to include it anyway.

Initializing a New NPM/Node Project

Now, in all of this, I did skip one step that clearly is optional but is, in fact, typical, and that's initializing a new project. With most Node/NPM projects, you'll also have a file named package.json in the root directory of the project. This file is the project manifest file, and it provides metadata information to NPM (and Node, at least indirectly) about your project that it needs to do certain things. It will tell NPM what modules to install if they haven't been installed yet for one thing (which makes giving a project to another developer very easy!). It will also contain information like the name and version of the project, its main entry point, and lots of other information (most of which is optional, but we'll look at that a bit more in the next chapter).

While you can write this file by hand or even go entirely without it, it's a good idea to have it, and it's a good idea to let NPM create it for you, which you can do by executing this command:

```
npm init
```

If you are following along, please make sure the directory you run this from is empty (delete `node_modules` and the `package-lock.json` file, which I'll talk about later, if it's present). This will trigger an interactive process that walks you through the creation of the `package.json` file, something like you see in Figure 1-4.

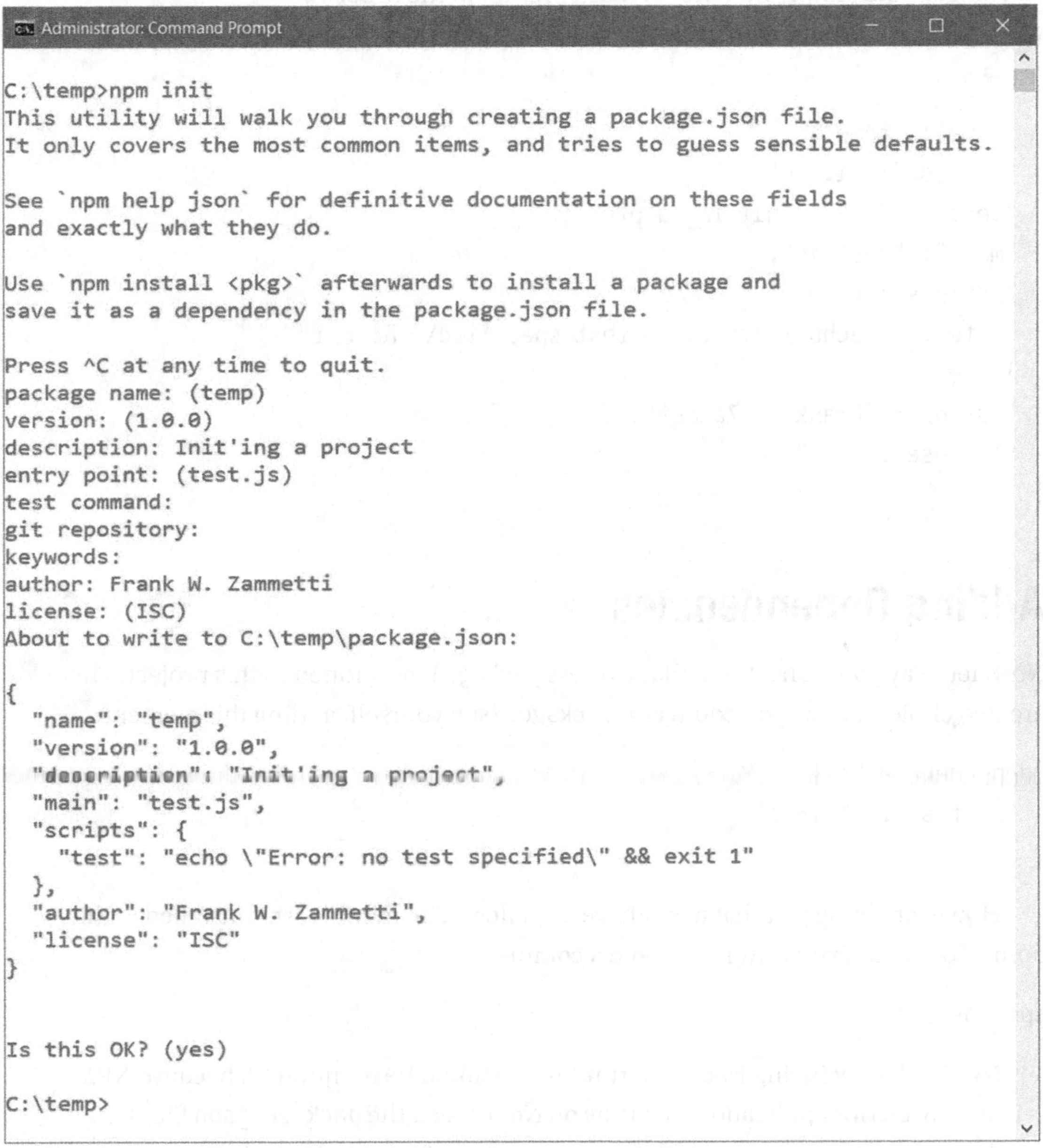
Administrator: Command Prompt
C:\temp>npm init
This utility will walk you through creating a package.json file.
It only covers the most common items, and tries to guess sensible defaults.
See `npm help json` for definitive documentation on these fields
and exactly what they do.
Use `npm install <pkg>` afterwards to install a package and
save it as a dependency in the package.json file.
Press ^C at any time to quit.
package name: (temp)
version: (1.0.0)
description: Init'ing a project
entry point: (test.js)
test command:
git repository:
keywords:
author: Frank W. Zammetti
license: (ISC)
About to write to C:\temp\package.json:
{
"name": "temp",
"version": "1.0.0",
"description": "Init'ing a project",
"main": "test.js",
"scripts": {
"test": "echo \"Error: no test specified\" && exit 1"
},
"author": "Frank W. Zammetti",
"license": "ISC"
}
Is this OK? (yes)
C:\temp>

Figure 1-4. *Initializing a project with NPM*

This will walk you through an interactive, step-by-step process wherein you can enter whichever information is relevant to your project, if any. You can just hit Enter on each option to use the default (or a blank value, whichever is applicable), or you can enter the values that are appropriate to you. For our purposes here though, you indeed can and should simply hit Enter on each prompt in the process.

Opening the generated `package.json` file should look something like this:

```
{
  "name": "temp",
  "version": "1.0.0",
  "description": "Init'ing a project",
  "main": "test.js",
  "scripts": {
    "test": "echo \"Error: no test specified\" && exit 1"
  },
  "author": "Frank W. Zammetti",
  "license": "ISC"
}
```

Adding Dependencies

Now, let's say you want to add that Express package I mentioned to this project. There are two choices. First, you could edit `package.json` yourself, adding this element:

```
"dependencies": {
  "express": "4.16.1"
}
```

However, doing just that won't have any effect. The module isn't installed at this point. To do that, you now must issue a command:

```
npm install
```

NPM will now (using Node as a runtime, it should be mentioned, because NPM is just a JavaScript application that runs on Node) read the `package.json` file, see the dependency listed, go fetch the Express package from the central repository, will determine all the dependencies it needs, and will download and install all of them in the node_modules directory under the current directory (which it will create if it's not already there). All these modules are now in the local cache (not global cache, it should be noted) and ready for you to use (normally, you wouldn't use the transient dependencies of Express directly, though you certainly could, but it's good form to declare all the modules you intend to use explicitly in package.json as dependencies).

Another alternative, and the one generally favored by developers, is not to edit the file directly and instead let NPM do it by issuing a command like this:

```
npm install express --save
```

This will cause NPM to add the dependency entry in package.json for you. This avoids the possibility of accidentally fat-fingering something and having a broken experience (or, worse, handing the project to another developer only to get the dreaded "It won't even start up!" call).

Note   You can also replace --save with --save-dev. This results in a devDependencies entry being added to package.json. The difference is that devDependencies are modules that you only need during development, but which your project code itself doesn't depend on. As you'll see later, two good examples of this are TypeScript and Webpack. Also, when uninstalling dependencies, --save and --save-dev can also be used to remove the dependency from package.json.

The reason this is all important is that, now, let's say you want to give this project to someone else. You typically do not want to provide them with all the dependencies your project requires, all the content of node_modules, if for no other reason that that directory can quickly grow to a large size. Instead, they can recreate it using the package. json file just by doing this:

```
npm install
```

That will cause NPM to read the package.json file and automatically install all the dependencies! Now, the person you're working with has the same development environment as you as far as project dependencies go for this project without having to do any leg work themselves! Pretty sweet, right?

As you can guess, there's quite a bit more to NPM than just what I've shown here, but these are the real basics.

A Quick Aside: Semantic Versioning

The dependencies section also lists the version(s) of each dependency, using a technique called semantic versioning (often called SemVer). SemVer versions are in the form *major.minor.patch*.

In this model, changes in the major number are meant to represent an update that contains breaking changes that would require changes to your code to remediate. Changes to the minor number are intended to constitute an update that is backward compatible but which provides new functionality and, optionally, contains old functionality that while still functional is now deprecated and will be removed in a future release (minor number changes can also represent major internal refactoring but which produces no outward-facing changes). The patch number represents bug fix changes only that are not expected to break your code.

On top of this, the tilde (~), caret (^), and asterisk (*) characters have special meaning. Tilde is used when dealing with patch versions, while caret is used when dealing with minor versions, and asterisk has the typical "wildcard" meaning you're probably familiar with in other contexts.

To give you a very brief overview, here are some of the most common dependency versions you might see in package.json, using Express as an example:

- **"express" : "1.2.3"** – NPM will grab this specific version only.

- **"express": "~1.2.3"** – NPM will grab the most recent patch version. (So, ~1.2.3 will find the latest 1.2.x version but not 1.3.x or anything below 1.2.x.)

- **"express": "^1.2.3"** – NPM will grab the most recent minor version. (So, ^1.2.3 will find the latest 1.x.x version but not 1.3.x or anything below 1.x.x.)

- **"express": "*"** – NPM will grab the newest version available. (There is also an explicit *latest* value that does the same thing.)

There's quite a lot more to SemVer than this (and there's also no shortage of criticism and folks who aren't exactly fans of it), but this should cover the most common features you're likely to encounter. Indeed, this should be all you will need for this book.

Note that when I wrote the first edition of this book, I specified most of the versions using ^. This is usually a safe thing to do since there's not supposed to be breaking versions in minor version updates. But, being humans who makes mistakes, it turns out that's not always the case, and a few version upgrades actually broke my code! Since then, I've come down on the side that thinks it's better to specify specific versions in package.json. What I then do is I globally install a package named npm-check-updates, or ncu for short. This handy app, which you can run simply with an ncu command at a command prompt, checks the dependencies in the current directory (or globally with -g) and tells you if any of them are outdated. Then, I can manually update the version numbers, and test to make sure nothing is broken, as I have time. I think this leads to more stable code, so in a sense, I don't use SemVer at all. You'll have to decide for yourself which approach you prefer. And, hey, you can do both! During development, it might be fine to use ^ or even *, since you probably do want the latest version all the time. But, when you're nearing the end of your development cycle, maybe then you lock the versions down to the current latest versions. Your call!

Note   The package-lock.json file sort of serves a purpose similar to specifying exact versions, but for dependencies. If you think about the packages that Express might depend on – the dependencies of Express – those could get updated even if Express itself isn't. The package-lock.json file maintains a dependency tree that contains all the versions used for a specific dependency in your package.json. So, the combination of package.json – especially if you lock your versions down – plus package-lock.json should ensure that every dependency, whether specific in your package.json file or whether a dependency of one of them, is the same for another developer as it is for you. As such, it's a best practice to always include package-lock.json in your source control system.

Fisher Price's "My First Node Web Server"

Now that you know a bit about Node and NPM, the very basics at least, let's write some actual code, beyond the simple example shown earlier, that is, and run it with Node.

When I say that Node makes writing server software trivial, that may well be the understatement of the decade! Perhaps the simplest example (that does something "real," at least) is this:

```
require("http").createServer((inRequest, inResponse) => {
  inResponse.end("Hello from my first Node Web server");
}).listen(80);
```

That remarkably small bit of code is all it takes in Node to write a web server. Even though it's not necessary, just for practice, go ahead and create a directory and use NPM to init it as a project (and this time, add a -y to the init command, which will use the defaults for all the prompts rather than making it interactive). Then, type that code into a file and save it as server.js. Now, at this point, you could start it up like so:

```
node server.js
```

But let's do one more thing first. Open the generated package.json file, and in the scripts section, add a new attribute to the object:

```
"start": "node server.js"
```

What this does is it effectively defines a custom command for NPM. The start command is one that already exists, but it's one that does nothing until you add this entry in package.json, so it may as well not exist! Once you add that entry though, NPM will look for that start key, take its value, and execute whatever the command is that you provide in it. The benefit of doing this is that every project you create with Node and NPM will be startable the same way. Without this, a developer would need to figure out what file is the main entry point to launch it with Node (and note that the main key in package.json may not be enough to tell someone this, as is the case here, since the default value of index.js would be wrong for this project, though you could of course always change it to accurately reflect the server.js file).

Once you add that, go ahead and start the app:

```
npm start
```

Yep, that's it! NPM knows what to do now and will launch Node and tell it to execute server.js.

Now fire up your favorite web browser and visit `http://127.0.01`. You'll be greeted with the text "Hello from my first Node Web server." Note, however, that if anything else on your system is already listening on port 80, then the app won't actually start; you'll get an error instead. In that case, simply change the `listen(80)` call to a free port, and you'll be good to go (and, naturally, add the port to the end of the URL in that case too).

If that isn't a little bit amazing to you, then you've probably seen the Flying Spaghetti Monster (FSM) travel one too many times around your neighborhood and have been totally desensitized to the amazing! (FSM – yeah, uhh, I'm not gonna even try and explain what the FSM is if you don't already know; here's a link: `www.venganza.org`.)

Obviously, this is a simplistic example, but it should get the basic idea across well enough. But what exactly is going on in that simple example at a code level? As it happens, quite a bit, and most of it is key to how Node works.

The first concept is the idea of importing modules. In the example code, `http` is a module. This is one of the core Node modules that Node comes with out of the box, and, as such, it is compiled directly into the Node binary. Therefore, you won't find a separate JavaScript file for it in the Node installation directory for it. This is true of all the Node core modules, all of which you can find in the Node documentation on the Node site. To import any of them, you just `require()` them by name.

Note   We'll look at some of the more commonly used modules in the next chapter.

You can create your own modules too just by adding other `.js` files to your project and `require()`-ing them. This gets a little more involved, with discussions of things like scope and exports, and we'll get to all of that in time. But for now, I wanted to mention it at least in case you really are entirely new to Node so that you can find the appropriate section in the Node docs to describe this if you want to jump ahead.

The `require()` function returns an object that is essentially the API provided by the module. This object can include methods, attributes, or whatever you want. In fact, it could conceivably be just a variable with some data in an array. More times than not, though, it will be an object with some methods and attributes. In the case of `http` in this example, one of the methods the object returned is `createServer()`. This method creates a web server instance and returns a reference to it.

The argument you pass to this method is a function that serves as a request listener, that is, the function executed any time a request is made to the server.

This function handles all incoming HTTP request. You can do anything you need to there, including such things as the following:

- Interrogate the incoming request to determine the HTTP method.

- Parse the request path.

- Examine header values.

You can then perform some branching logic on any or all of these, perhaps access a database or other durable storage mechanism, and return an appropriate and fully dynamic response for the specific request.

Creating a web server alone won't actually *do* anything. It's just the foundation. It won't respond to requests until you do a little more work – build the house, so to speak. As mentioned, the `createServer()` method returns a reference to the web server instance, which itself contains the method `listen()`. That method accepts a port number on which the server should listen and, optionally, the hostname/IP address on which to listen. In the example, the standard HTTP port 80 is specified, and by default, the local machine loopback address 127.0.0.1 is used if no IP address is specified, as is the case here. Once you call this method, the server will begin listening for requests (i.e., assuming nothing else is already using that port on your system!), and for each request that comes in, it will call the anonymous function passed to `createServer()`.

This callback function (callback functions being one mechanism by which Node provides nonblocking functionality, the others being Promises and `async/await`) receives two arguments, `inRequest` and `inResponse`, which are objects representing the HTTP request and response, respectively. In this simple example, all this callback function does is call the `end()` method on the response object, passing the response you want to send back. By default, an HTTP 200 response code header will be added automatically, so this completes the handling of a given request.

With just this little bit of code, you, in fact, know the basics of what you would require for writing a server for the MailBag app later! But, when we get to that app, we'll use something a little more robust (as it happens, we'll use that Express package I mentioned earlier), but this gives you a fundamental idea of what it takes.

Bonus Example

Let's take this web server code just a little further to roll in some more NPM goodness, just to use almost everything discussed so far.

To begin, let's add a dependency to our project. We're going to use the not-very-creatively-but-very-accurately-named *request* module, which will provide to our server an elementary HTTP client for it to use to make remote calls:

```
npm install request --save
```

With that done, copy that server.js file and name it server_time.js, then replace its contents with the following code:

```
require("http").createServer((inRequest, inResponse) => {
  const requestModule = require("request");
  requestModule(
    "http://worldtimeapi.org/api/timezone/America/New_York",
    function (inErr, inResp, inBody) {
      inResponse.end(
        `Hello from my first Node Web server: ${inBody}`
      );
    }
  );
}).listen(80);
```

As you probably recognize, it's the same code as before, but now with a bit more inside the callback function provided to createServer(). What we're doing now is firstly to import the *request* module and to give it the name requestModule (just to help disambiguate it from the inRequest object passed into the callback function). The API for this module is straightforward: pass a URL to the constructor, plus a callback, and a call will be made to the URL, and the provided callback will be executed when the response to that call comes back. The URL here is to the World Time API, which you can read about here: http://worldtimeapi.org. This particular form of the URL (the API provides a few) takes in a time zone, America/New_York here (though you should certainly feel free to replace that with a time zone you prefer – you can access http://worldtimeapi.org/api/timezone in a browser to see a list of available time zones). What we get back is a chunk of JSON, which is then written to the response that is returned to the browser.

The final step is you'll need to edit package.json to change that start value to indicate the new JavaScript file, after which you can launch the app and try it. The response you'll see now isn't necessarily pretty:

```
Hello from my first Node Web server: {"week_number":36,
"utc_offset":"-04:00","utc_datetime":"2019-09-06T17:22:45.406437+00:00",
"unixtime":1567790565,"timezone":"America/New_York","raw_offset":-18000,
"dst_until":"2019-11-03T06:00:00+00:00","dst_offset":3600,"dst_from":
"2019-03-10T07:00:00+00:00","dst":true,"day_of_year":249,"day_of_week":5,
"datetime":"2019-09-06T13:22:45.406437-04:00","client_ip":"12.198.42.69",
"abbreviation":"EDT"}
```

but it gets the job done (and, if like me, you have a browser extension that automatically "prettifies" JSON, then what you'll see will be, well, *prettier*!).

This is a good example not only of adding dependencies to a project and using them but also of the asynchronous nature of Node I talked about earlier. Here, the call to the World Time API takes some time, and the response to the request coming from the browser is queued up and awaits that response before executing the callback passed to the requestModule() constructor, which then produces the final response to the browser. But, all that time, Node was free to handle other incoming requests; work wasn't held up awaiting the remote request, that's the key thing.

Summary

In this chapter, we looked at Node and NPM and discussed the very basics of their usage. But, because Node and NPM are, conceptually, pretty simple things, these basics are, by and large, all you need to write real applications. You now know how to execute JavaScript code, how to create an NPM project, and how to add dependencies. You understand the difference between the global cache and the local (project) cache, and you even know how to write a basic web server!

In the next chapter, we'll continue looking at these two tools in a bit more detail, getting to some slightly more advanced stuff with them, to expand the foundation from which we'll build the first of our two apps later in the book (the third app will use a completely different server-side technology stack, just for giggles!).

CHAPTER 2

A Few More Words: Advanced Node and NPM

In the last chapter, we began looking at Node and NPM, and you even built a quick Node-based web server to demonstrate the concepts. I said then that you now have the basics you'd need in both things to start working on some apps. But, before we get to that, let's look at them both in just a little more detail.

Since Node got the pole position in the last chapter, let's flip the script for this one and give NPM the head start this time out of the gate (yeesh, how many metaphors can be mixed in one sentence?!).

NPM: More on package.json

In the last chapter, you learned how to init a project with NPM, which generates a `package.json` file. I said then that most of its contents were optional, and that's definitely true, but let's talk about what's available in that file, discussing each of the keys available (remember it's just a JSON file, which means it's defining a JavaScript object, which has *keys* and *properties*, the latter of which are sometimes called *attributes*, or even *elements* – all these terms are generally taken to be interchangeable in this context):

- **name** – We start with a simple one: the name of the thing you're coding! The name element's value must be no more than 214 characters, cannot start with a dot or an underscore, can have no uppercase letters, and must be URL-safe.

23

F. Zammetti, *Modern Full-Stack Development*, https://doi.org/10.1007/978-1-4842-8811-5_2

- **author** – The author is a single person and is defined by an object with three potential attributes: name, email, and url (where name is required, and both email and url are optional). Alternatively, you can make the value a single string in the form "<name> <email> (<url>)", and NPM will parse it for you automatically.

- **bin** – Some packages require executables to be installed to do their work and added to the path. That's where the bin element comes in. You can make the value an object (or map, which is probably the more appropriate term here) that maps a command to an executable, and NPM will take care of "installing" it for you when you install the package by creating the appropriate symlink.

- **browser** – Some modules are meant to be used in a browser, not in Node, and for those packages, you can use this element instead of the main element (coming up shortly!) to hint to the users of your package that it depends on primitives available to JavaScript that aren't available in Node.

- **bugs** – If your project has an issue tracker, then you can reference it with the bugs element. The value of this is an object with two attributes, url and email, and you can specify either or both (but you must specify at least one, or NPM will complain).

- **bundledDependencies** – Some projects need to preserve NPM packages locally or through a single download. For those, this element allows you to specify an array of package names that will be bundled with your package when you publish it.

- **config** – If you need to have parameters available in the environment when your package is used, then the config element might do the trick. Here, you can specify a value like "config" : { "port" : "8888" }, and then in your code you can reference npm_package_config_port as an environment variable to get the value configured.

- **contributors** – The contributors element is just like the author element except that this is an array of people who helped with the project.

- **cpu** – If your code is only meant to run on certain system architectures, you can specify which as an array of strings with the cpu element.

- **dependencies** – You saw the `dependencies` element in the previous chapter, but I'll also mention that in addition to specifying a package name and optionally a version to be pulled down from the NPM registry, you can also specify a URL to a tarball to be downloaded or a Git/GitHub URL or a local file system path.

- **description** – A freeform string that describes your package. It's as simple as that!

- **devDependencies** – Again, one I mentioned in the previous chapter, and it's simply the same as dependencies, but it names packages that are only needed during development.

- **directories** – This element allows you to describe the structure of your package, things like the location of library components binary content, man pages, Markdown documentation, examples, and tests. See the Common JS package specification for details on this.

- **engines** – This element allows you to specify what version(s) of Node your package works on. You can also use this element to define what version(s) of NPM is capable of properly installing the package.

- **files** – When your package is installed as a dependency, NPM will need to know what files to include. It will by default assume all, but if you want or need to be specified, then the `files` element will let you do that. It works a lot like a `.gitignore` file, but in reverse: anything listed in this element will be included, not ignored.

- **funding** – You can specify an object containing a URL that provides up-to-date information about ways to help fund development of your package, or a string URL, or an array of these items. Users can then use the `npm fund` command to list the funding URLs of all dependencies of their project, direct and indirect. A shortcut to visit each funding url is also available when providing the project name such as `npm fund <project_name>` (when there are multiple URLs, the first one will be visited).

25

- **homepage** – If your project has a website, then you can specify the URL of its homepage with this element.

- **keywords** – The keywords element is an arbitrary array of strings that can be used to help people find your package (more on this in the next section).

- **license** – The value of the license element is the license your package is released under. The value of this must be a currently registered SPDX license identifier (see spdx.org for a list). Alternatively, if you are using a custom license or one that doesn't yet have an SPDX identifier, then you can set the value to "SEE LICENSE IN <filename>" and place the <filename> license file alongside the package.json file. Or, if you don't grant rights to use your package to anyone (vis-à-vis, you want to make it private and/or unpublished), then you can use a value of "UNLICENSED".

- **man** – With this element, you can specify a single file or an array of filenames to put in place for the Linux man program to display for your package.

- **main** – This is the primary entry point to your package. For example, if your package is named super_duper_cool_package, then a user will expect to be able to do require("super_duper_cool_package") after they install it. To allow this, the main element must point to the file that exports your package's main export object.

- **optionalDependencies** – If your package has dependencies and NPM can't install them, then it will fail the installation of your package. If, however, you want to specify that some dependencies are okay to be missing and that NPM should go ahead with the installation anyway, then optionalDependencies is where you can list them.

- **os** – Just like cpu, if your package only works on certain OSs, then this element is where you can have an array of strings naming those it runs on.

- **overrides** – If you need to make specific changes to dependencies of your dependencies, for example replacing the version of a dependency with a known security issue, replacing an existing dependency with a fork, or making sure that the same version of a package is used everywhere, then you may add an override. Overrides provide a way to replace a package in your dependency tree with another version or another package entirely. These changes can be scoped as specific or as vague as desired.

- **peerDependencies** – Sometimes, a package will function as a plugin to others, and so you'll need a way to define what other packages yours is compatible with. The peerDependencies element allows you to do that.

- **peerDependenciesMeta** – When a user installs a package, npm will emit warnings if packages specified in peerDependencies are not already installed. The peerDependenciesMeta field serves to provide npm more information on how a package's peer dependencies are to be used. Specifically, it allows peer dependencies to be marked as optional.

- **private** – If you want to ensure that you can't accidentally publish your package, then set private to false, and NPM will refuse to publish it (more to come on publishing in the next section).

- **publishConfig** – This element is an object that defines many pieces of metadata that come into play with publishing your package to the NPM registry. This includes things like tags and such. This can get fairly involved, and we won't (for the most part) be worrying about any of it in this book beyond a few words in the next section, so I'll leave this one to the NPM documentation if and when you need it.

- **repository** – If you'd like to specify where the code for your package lives, whether GitHub or something else, whether public or private, the `repository` element is where you do that.

- **scripts** – As mentioned in the previous chapter, the scripts element allows you to specify a dictionary of commands that can be run at various points in the lifecycle of your package for various purposes. Like publishConfig, this can get a bit involved, so I defer to the NPM docs for details.

- **version** – This is the version of your module, and it must use SemVer as discussed in Chapter 1. The name and version values together form a unique "coordinate" to your package, an identifier that is assumed to be completely unique. If you plan to publish your package, then name and version are the most important elements in package.json (if you *don't* publish it, then they're a bit less important, but for your own sanity, you should probably make them meaningful anyway!).

- **workspaces** – The optional workspaces field is an array of file patterns that describes locations within the local file system that the install client should look up to find each workspace that needs to be symlinked to the top-level node_modules folder. It can describe either the direct paths of the folders to be used as workspaces or it can define globs that will resolve to these same folders.

You know, I said a few times that I'm deferring to the NPM docs on a few things, but that's true of *all* of those! This isn't meant to be a reference guide detailing every option and how to use them; it's just meant to be a survey of the elements, so you have a rough idea of what's available. If and when you need to use these, at least for the ones that aren't simple, single values, then the NPM docs at docs.npmjs.com are where you'll need to visit. There's a section dedicated to the contents of package.json that goes over every last detail you could need or want.

NPM: Other Commands

Although you've already seen the essential NPM commands, let's talk about a few more that you might find yourself needing to use from time to time. As with the previous section, this is not intended to be an in-depth reference guide, and it's not a list of every available NPM command. But, between what was shown in the previous chapter and what's in this section, I believe you'll have exposure to probably 95% of the commands you'll need a majority of the time (and there may be one or two more shown as we progress in later chapters as well).

Auditing Package Security

The sad reality is that, sometimes, packages you use will be discovered to have security vulnerabilities, just like any other software you use. But, being aware of this, the NPM team has constructed a useful command for dealing with this:

```
npm audit
```

Running this command will scan your `package.json` file (or global packages if you use -g) and submit the list of dependencies to the default NPM registry requesting a report on any known vulnerabilities in them. This report will also include information on how to remediate them. But, if you want the quick answer, execute this command:

```
npm audit fix
```

That will cause NPM to update any vulnerable packages with the newest available version that hasn't had the vulnerability reported in it.

If you'd like to see a detailed audit report, execute

```
npm audit --json
```

or, if you prefer plain text

```
npm audit --readable
```

Finally, if you'd like to see what `npm audit fix` would do but without literally doing it, you can use

```
npm audit fix --dry-run
```

Deduplication and Pruning

One of the complaints you'll commonly see about NPM and Node is that the size of the `node_modules` directory can balloon in a hurry. Fortunately, you rarely will need to dive into it, but it's still a question of disk space, and while disk space is cheap these days, it's still not *chic* to be wasteful!

NPM provides two commands for dealing with this situation, starting with

```
npm dedup
```

The dedup command searches through the tree of packages in node_modules and looks for opportunities where packages can be moved up the tree and shared between dependencies, thereby reducing redundancy and saving space. The package tree is built up as you install packages and as NPM installs the packages it depends on, and so on. Sometimes, packages will have dependencies in common, but being a tree, branches (read: packages) are mostly independent. This command attempts to reorganize those branches to make it more efficient.

The second command is this:

```
npm prune
```

This command will examine the installed packages and look for any that may no longer be needed. This typically happens when you uninstall packages and especially if you've done a dedup at some point. Any package that is not listed in the parent package's dependency list is considered "extraneous" and therefore subject to being pruned.

Note   In regular operation, prune will be run automatically any time you install something, so you shouldn't need to run this manually, but sometimes, as the saying goes, poo happens, so it's good to know about it anyway.

Finding/Searching for Packages sans Browser

It's easy enough to browse the central NPM registry for packages of interest via a web browser, but it's not your only choice. NPM itself provides a search capability, an example of which you can see in Figure 2-1.

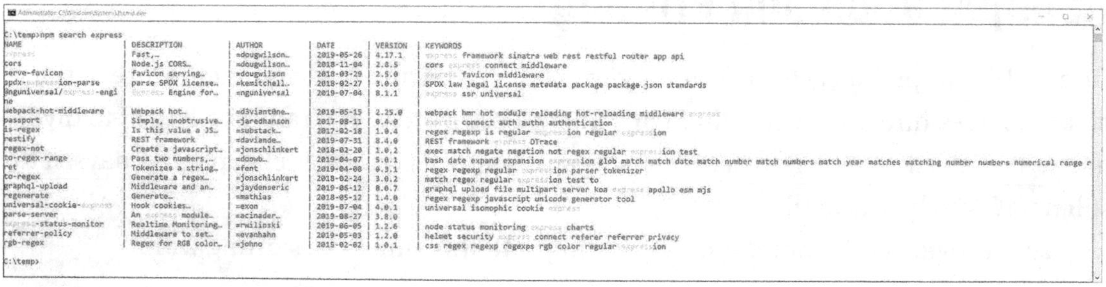

Figure 2-1.   *A simple NPM search for "express"*

You can use the search command in a few ways, but searching via description like this is perhaps the most common. In fact, this search will examine all metadata for packages, not just the description, which is why you see some name and keyword matches highlighted as well. Personally, I almost never use this command since I find the web interface on npmjs.org to be more robust and easier to use. But, it's always good to at least know a tool exists so you can decide whether it's something you want to use or not (and I can imagine those who live life at a command prompt might be more apt to use this than someone like me that generally prefers a GUI environment).

Updating Packages

Once you have a project set up, you may on occasion want to update the packages it depends on. This is very easy to do:

```
npm update
```

Yep, that's it! NPM will go off and update all packages to the latest version, respecting your SemVer settings. You naturally can stick a -g in there too in order to update global packages.

But, don't sleep on the ncu package I mentioned in the last chapter! Even if for no other reason than to know what's going to be updated *before* it's updated, it can be extremely helpful (it's not the only package like that by the way – here's a good chance to play with the npmjs.org website! – but it's the one I find to be most efficient).

Publishing/Unpublishing Packages

The final NPM topic I want to touch on is publishing (and optionally unpublishing) packages, usually to the central NPM registry at npmjs.org (though nothing says you can't have your own private registry to work with).

Publishing to a registry is quite easy! First, you'll need to, well, write your package! Gotta have something to publish, right? You don't need to do anything special, but npm init your project and cobble your code together.

Once that's done, create an account on the registry's website. Next, you'll need to log into that account from the command line:

```
npm login
```

This will prompt you for your username, password, and email address. Once you're logged in, publishing is a snap:

```
npm publish
```

As long as you're in your package's root directory (the one you ran npm init in and that now has your package.json file), it will be published.

Well, hold up, there's one thing that can go wrong: your package name could already be taken. It's always a good idea to do an npm search for the name first, but assuming the name isn't taken (or you've changed it after discovering a collision), then it'll be published and available in the registry immediately.

Tip   If the name you really want isn't available, NPM also lets you publish to a scope. This means, for example, you can change the name to @<username>/<package-name> (or do npm init --scope=<username>). You'll then also need to add --access public to the publish command. That way, as long as your package name is unique within the scope, then you're good to go; the name can be used in other scopes without issue (and no scope is effectively the default scope!). So, if, like domain names, the one you want is taken, there's a way around it in NPM land.

If you for some reason down the line decide you need to remove your package from the registry, it's as simple as

```
npm unpublish [<@scope>/]<package-name>[@<version>]
```

If you don't specify a version, then *all* versions will be removed.

Two important notes here: First, removing a package is generally considered bad form because others may be depending on it. The better thing to do is to use another command: deprecate. That will mark your package as deprecated, optionally applying a message you can specify about what happens. Second, it's essential to understand that even if you unpublish a package, the name and/or name-plus-version combination can never be reused. So again, if you want to be a good citizen, it's best not to unpublish but instead deprecate the package (better still not to publish something you later have to remove *or* deprecate – but it happens, so NPM has you covered in either case with these two commands).

Node: Standard Modules

Now that we've given NPM its due, let's swing back to the Node side. Here, we'll take a look at some of the modules that come with Node and that you can use at any time without having to install anything else. Again, let me say that this is in no way meant to be an exhaustive look at everything available. There are *many* more modules available, and you definitely should take a look at the Node documentation to see what they are. I'm just going to give you a quick overview of what, from my experience, will be the ones you'll likely use most often and then only briefly.

File System (fs)

The File System module is one of the more often used modules available. It provides you an API for working with the local file system in a pattern that closely matches that of the standard POSIX functions.

To use this module, you'll need to `require()` it:

```
const fs = require("fs");
```

This, in fact, is necessary for all but one of the modules described here (and it's true for *most* of the modules you'll find in the Node documentation). That's what the string in parentheses after each title is: it's the value you need to `require()` (you can, of course, assign it to a variable of whatever name you wish, though I tend to make the variable name and the `require()` value the same).

You can also import modules another way:

```
import * as fs from "fs";
```

or

```
Import { cat, dog } from "animals.js";
```

This form of importing is the ESModules form and is the more current and standard version (eventually, it will likely be the only form you ever deal with, but that's not today). When I wrote the first edition of this book, this was only just recently added to Node, and it wasn't yet widely available. At this point though, you can import most modules either way. However, one key thing to notice is that `require()` is a function call. That means that you can use it anywhere in your code, even inside an `if` statement, which is called a *conditional import*. You can't do that with the ESModules form.

Now that we have the module imported, what can we do with it? Well, here's some of what I think are the handier bits of functionality this module offers:

- `fs.copyFile()` – As you would guess, it allows you to copy a file. You supply to it the source file to copy, and the destination location where to put it and Node will send the request to the underlying operating system to perform. Note that as is the case with most of Node, this call will be asynchronous. Therefore, it allows you to pass it a callback function to execute once the copy completes. Alternatively, there is an `fs.copyFileSync()` method that is synchronous and so will block your code until the operation completes. This pattern, of passing a callback or offering a synchronous version of the function, is a pattern repeated in much of this module and even other modules when asynchronous operations come up, so keep that in mind as we proceed, though I won't mention it again. To be clear, it's not something you'll find available in *every* case, but in many, perhaps even most.

- `fs.readFile()` – Yep, it reads a file and passes the data from it to a function you supply, wherein you can do whatever you like with it. And yes, there is, of course, a matching `fs.writeFile()` method, with which you can do things like writing a JavaScript object that you `JSON.stringify()` to marshal into a string to a file.

- `fs.unlink()` – If you want to delete a file, you actually want to "unlink" it in POSIX-speak, so this module offers an `fs.unlink()` method. Pass it the path to the file, and thy bidding will be done! (You can also remove symlinks with this.)

- `fs.mkdir()` – Not only can you work with files with this module but you can work with directories too. The `fs.mkdir()` method allows you to create directories. I should also note at this point that all the methods so far also accept an object with various options. For example, this method allows you to pass a `mode` key in the options object to specify the permissions for the directory (although note that this is not supported on Windows). This is a typical pattern that repeats itself frequently in this module as well. To delete a directory, the `fs.rmdir()` method is provided.

- `fs.stat()` – If you're looking for information about a file or directory, things like its size, last access time, and when it was created, then `fs.stat()` is your friend. It returns an `fs.Stats` object, which is an object within the File System module, and it contains many pieces of information including the size of the file or directory (`size`) and when it was created (`birthtime`).

- `fs.readdir()` – This method allows you to read in the contents of a directory given its path and returns to you an array of filenames, an array of `Buffer` objects containing the names, or an array of `fs.Dirent` objects, one per file (which you get depends on the options you pass in, with an array of string filenames being the default).

In later versions of Node, starting around v10, a new subsection of the File System module was introduced: the Promises API. Basically, it provides methods matching the fs methods seen here and most of the others this module offers, but that return Promises. So, if you prefer a Promise-based coding style (or `async`/`await` on top of that), then have a look at the section on that in the docs. Other than different names (e.g., `fs.fsPromises.copyFile()` and `fs.fsPromises.readFile()`) and the obvious syntactic differences, they otherwise are mostly the same as the non-Promise versions.

HTTP and HTTPS (http and https)

Although Node isn't exclusively for writing servers, whether web servers or other kinds of servers, it is, in fact, best known for writing web servers (or, to be more precise, HTTP servers). As such, you'd reasonably expect to find one or more modules related to such activities, and you would be very right to do so!

The HTTP module is where you'll find most of what you need to write servers that use the HTTP protocol. If you're into the whole security thing (and, uhh, you *are* into the whole security thing...*right*?!), then there is also an HTTPS module.

You already saw the `http.Server` class, if only briefly, in the last chapter, because it's what you get back from the `http.createServer()` method, which is one method available in the HTTP package. You saw how to call the `listen()` method on that `http.Server` instance, but you can also find out if the instance is listening by interrogating its `listen` property (a simple boolean). You can also call the `close()` method on the instance to stop it from accepting requests. You can call `setTimeout()` on it to set how long a socket to a client lives for (two minutes by default), and you can set the maxHeadersCount property to limit how many HTTP headers your server will accept (defaults to 2000).

The HTTPS module builds on top of the HTTP module and provides the ability to create servers that use TLS to secure connections. The only real difference is some extra information about certificates and keys that you must provide when constructing the server:

```
const fs = require("fs");
const server = require("https").createServer(
  {
    key : fs.readFileSync("my_key.pem"),
    cert : fs.readFileSync("my_cert.pem")
  },
  (inRequest, inResponse) => {
  inResponse.writeHead(200);
  inResponse.end("I am protected by TLS!");
}).listen(443);
```

Aside from that, the API available is virtually identical.

But the HTTP and HTTPS modules aren't just about servers: they also provide the means for your Node-based code to *make* HTTP requests! Here is an example, using the http.request() method:

```
let finalResponse = "";
const request = require("http").request(
  {
    hostname : "www.some_remote_system.com",
    port : 80,
    path : "/someAPI",
    method : "POST"
  },
  (inResponse) => {
    console.log(`STATUS: ${inResponse.statusCode}`);
    inResponse.setEncoding("utf8");
```

```
  inResponse.on("data", (inDataChunk) => {
    finalResponse += inDataChunk.
  });
  inResponse.on("end", () => {
    console.log(finalResponse);
  });
  }
);
request.write("Some data to send to the remote system");
request.end();
```

Here, we build up an http.Request object, providing to it all the pertinent connection details in the first object passed to the http.request() method. Then, we send some arbitrary data string to the remote server and build up a response string. The on event fires every time the server sends back a chunk of data, so we add it to the finalResponse string, which is displayed when the end event fires, signifying the complete response has been received. We are, of course, free to do whatever we wish with the response at that point.

OS (os)

The OS module provides a set of operating system–level utility functions that allow your code to be aware of the environment it's running in and make any necessary allowances for it. Some of what it offers include the following:

- os.EOL – Provides you the end-of-line character the operating system uses

- os.cpus() – Returns an object array where each object gives you information about the CPU(s) in the system including information like their model, speed, and times (e.g., how long the CPU has spent in user mode)

- os.freemem() – Returns an integer value that is the number of free system memory available in bytes

- os.homedir() – Returns a path to the current home directory of the user running the process

- os.hostname() – Returns the machine's host name

- os.tempdir() – Returns a path to the default system temporary directory

You'll also find an os.constants property that is an object with several keys, things like SIGHUP, SIGFPE, SIGCHILD, and SIGSTOP. These are commonly used OS-specific constants for things like error codes and, as in these examples, process signals. These will, of course, change from system to system to at least some extent, but it's good to know such a collection of information like this exists and is made available to you thanks to the OS module!

Path (path)

You'll notice that in several modules discussed thus far, you need to reference file and directory paths. Node provides some additional functions for working with them housed in the Path module.

For example, the path.basename() method returns the last portion of a path:

```
path.basename("/my/path/index.htm"); // "index.html"
```

By contrast, if you want just the path portion:

```
path.dirname("/my/path/index.htm"); // "/some/path"
```

And if you just want the extension:

```
path.extname("/my/path/index.htm"); // ".htm"
```

Finally, the path.parse() method is handy for, in a way, doing in one call what all of those do, plus a bit more:

```
path.parse("/home/users/mydata/accounts.dat");
```

This will return you an object in the form:

```
{ root : "/", dir : "/home/users/mydata",
  base : "accounts.dat", ext : ".dat", name : "accounts" }
```

If you need to know the platform-specific path delimiter (; for Windows and : for *nix systems), then you can get the value from the `path.delimiter` property.

Then there is the path.join() method which joins path segments into a final form that uses the platform-specific separator automatically (this example is on a Windows system):

```
path.join("/my", "path", "index.htm"); // "my\path\index.htm"
```

Because it is common to have to build paths dynamically in code, and because that process can result in munged string easily, Node offers a helpful method to deal with such issues in the `path.normalize()` method:

```
path.normalize("C:////tmp\\/\\/dat.md") // "C:\\temp\\dat.md"
```

Here, assume that some logic produced the string passed to `path.normalize()`, and that logic has to take a lot of things into account, so it can wind up with some sequences as you see that need to be reduced down to platform-specific and valid sequences. That's what `path.normalize()` can do for you.

Process

Unlike the other modules, this one is a global, which means it is always available, and there is no need to import anything. You simply call methods on the intrinsic `process` reference or access its properties.

That, of course, is good to know, but what does this module do for us? Well, the answer is quite a lot! In short, it allows you to retrieve information and control the current Node process. Here are just a few of the items it offers:

- `process.abort()` – This method aborts the Node process, ending your program. However, that unceremoniously kills the process, so what you likely want to use is `process.exit()` instead, to which you can pass an exit code to return to the process that started Node.

- `process.version` – This contains the version of Node itself.

- `process.uptime()` – How long has the Node process been running for? This method will tell you!

- `process.mainModule` – Here, you can find the name of the `.js` file that was launched by Node. Note that Node also provides a handful of global variables that contain important information like this, `__filename` being the equivalent to this property (they generally all start with two underscores like that). For reference, `__dirname` will provide the name of the directory where the script was launched from, which tends to be an often-needed piece of information.

- `process.env` – This contains an object whose keys are user environment variables.

There's quite a bit more that the process module offers, but in my experience, much beyond these is a bit more unusual to use, so I'll leave its exploration as an exercise for the reader.

Query Strings (querystring)

When building HTTP(S) servers with Node, having to examine the query string is commonly needed (I mean that's not limited to *just* Node of course: dealing with query strings, either parsing them or creating them, is a big part of what web developers do!). The Query String module offers a handful of methods for such times.

When talking about query strings on the input side of the fence, `querystring.parse()` is the primary tool in your toolbox (assume this code is within a server event handler as you've previously seen, and the URL in the comment is the request that came in):

```
// "http://mysite.com/?account=36764&add=125";
let parsedURL = url.parse(request.url);
let parsedParams = querystring.parse(parsedURL);
```

Now, you're getting a bonus look-ahead here to the next module we'll be checking out: URL. The `url.parse()` method takes in a URL and returns an object like so:

```
{
    protocol: 'http:',
    slashes: true,
    auth: null,
    host: 'mysite.com',
```

```
    port: null,
    hostname: 'mysite.com',
    hash: null,
    search: '?account=36764&add=125',
    query: 'account=36764&add=125',
    pathname: '/',
    path: '/?account=36764&add=125',
    href: 'http://mysite.com/?account=36764&add=125'
}
```

All by itself, that's useful, but if all we're interested in are those query parameters account and add, then that's where the querystring.parse() method comes in. What you get back from that is an object:

```
{ account : "36764", add : "125" }
```

From there out, you can do whatever you like with the data. Note that there is also a querystring.decode(), which is just an alias for querystring.parse().

What about if you need to construct a query string? Well, that's where the querystring.stringify() method (and its querystring.encode() alias) fits in:

```
const qs = querystring.stringify({
  account : 36764, add : 125
});
// Returns "account=36764&add=125"
```

Finally, there are the querystring.escape() and querystring.unescape() methods, which are the yin and yang of encoding and decoding parameter names and values in query strings so that they are safe for inclusion in URLs. Note that you typically wouldn't call these directly as they're used by querystring.parse() and querystring.stringify() internally and automatically, but they are there if you need them.

Well, how about that. This is the first (and only) module where *everything* it offers is described here! It's not a big module, but it's a somewhat important one!

URL (url)

In the previous section, you saw the `url.parse()` method used, and that's just one thing the URL module offers. Some others are as follows:

- URL – Okay, this is going to sound weird, but the URL module exposes the URL class, and the URL class is where a large chunk of the functionality of this module resides. For example, the `url.URL.hash` property returns the fragment portion of a URL (e.g., `new url.URL("http://mysite.com/page.html#sectionA").hash` will have the value `#sectionA`). Similarly, you can get the `host` (which will include the port, if specified), the `hostname` (which will not include the port), the `username` and `password` portion of a URL (if specified), and the `port` or `protocol,` in the same way, all properties of a URL instance.

- `url.pathToFileURL()` and `url.fileURLToPath()` – Respectively, these methods ensure that a path is resolved absolutely and that the URL control characters are correctly encoded when converting into a file URL and that correct decoding of percent-encoded characters in a file URL is done while ensuring the result is a valid cross-platform path.

Utilities (util)

The final module we're going to look at briefly is a little bit of a catch-all, or maybe it's better to say it contains functions that support Node internally, but which also provides generic JavaScript functionality that might be useful to application code.

For example, if you want to format a string using a printf-like format, you can do

```
util.format("%s:%s", "aa", "bb", "cc") // "aa:bb cc"
```

What if you have an asynchronous function, like `fs.stat()` let's say, that uses the common pattern seen in Node where the callback receives an error object first and then a value object and you want to make it use Promises, but you don't want to have to rewrite the code? Well, then there's this:

```
const newStat = util.promisify(fs.stat);
```

Now, you can call it like so:

```
newStat("/home/fzammetti")
.then((inStats) => { console.log(inStats);
})
.catch((inError) => { console.log(inError);
});
```

Nice, right?

Do you have a variable and need to know its type? Then Utilities has you covered: `util.types.isArrayBuffer()`, `util.types.isBigInt64Array()`, `util.types. isBooleanObject()`, `util.types.isDate()`, `util.types.isMap()`, `util.types. isPromise()`, and `util.types.isUint32Array()` are available, just to name a few.

Finally, the `util.inspect()` method can be used to get a string representation of an object intended for debugging purposes. This method accepts a whole bunch of options, including being able to specify whether you want to show `hidden` fields, how far down into the object to go if it contains nested objects (`depth`), and if you wish to `sort` the keys in the stringified object that is returned. It's important to note though that this method's documentation states that the representation this produces can change at any time, so you, therefore, should never try to use this programmatically. Printing the string to the console is fine, but trying to parse it wouldn't be a great idea lest you find your code randomly broke at some point in the future after a Node upgrade.

The Rest of the Cast

As of this writing, the other modules Node provides, which we won't be looking at in detail but which I wanted to at least make you aware of, are as follows:

- **Assertion Testing** – The Assert module provides a simple set of assertion tests that can be used to test invariants.

- **Async Hooks** – The `async_hooks` module provides an API to register callbacks tracking the lifetime of asynchronous resources created inside a Node application.

- **Buffer** – This is, in fact, a class, not a module, and as such, it's in global scope. Either way, it's a class created before JavaScript offered the `TypedArray` that provides the ability to work with streams of binary data.

- **C++ Addons** – Node add-ons are dynamically linked shared objects, written in C++, that can be loaded into Node using the `require()` function and used just as if they were an ordinary Node module. They are mainly used to provide an interface between JavaScript running in Node and C/C++ libraries. This module allows you to work with them. The N-API module goes along with this and enables you to build them.

- **Child Processes** – The `child_process` module provides the ability to spawn child processes outside of Node.

- **Cluster** – A single instance of Node runs in a single thread. To take advantage of multicore systems, the user will sometimes want to launch a group of Node processes to handle the load. The `cluster` module allows easy creation of child processes that all share server ports.

- **Console** – The `console` module provides a simple debugging console that is like the JavaScript console mechanism provided by web browsers.

- **Crypto** – The `crypto` module provides cryptographic functionality that includes a set of wrappers for OpenSSL's hash, HMAC, cipher, decipher, sign, and verify functions.

- **DNS** – The `dns` module contains functions belonging to two different categories: methods that use the underlying operating system facilities to perform name resolution and methods that connect to an actual DNS server to achieve name resolution.

- **Events** – Much of the Node.js core API is built around an idiomatic asynchronous event-driven architecture in which certain kinds of objects (called "emitters") emit named events that cause Function objects ("listeners") to be called. The `events` module provides the ability for your own code to hook into and use these same capabilities at the application level.

- **HTTP/2** – The `http2` module provides an implementation of the HTTP/2 protocol. It's just like `http` and `https`, but newer and better!

- **Inspector** – The `inspector` module provides an API for interacting with the V8 inspector.

- **Net** – The `net` module provides an asynchronous network API for creating stream-based TCP or IPC servers and clients.

- **Performance Hooks** – The Performance Timing API, by way of the `perf_hooks` module, provides an implementation of the W3C Performance Timeline specification. The purpose of the API is to support the collection of high-resolution performance metrics. This is the same Performance API as implemented in modern web browsers.

- **Readline** – The `readline` module provides an interface for reading data from a readable stream (such as `process.stdin`) one line at a time.

- **REPL** – The `repl` module provides a Read-Eval-Print-Loop (REPL) implementation that is available both as a stand-alone program and includible in other applications.

- **Stream** – A stream is an abstract interface for working with streaming data in Node assertion testing.

- **String Decoder** – The `string_decoder` module provides an API for decoding `Buffer` objects into strings in a manner that preserves encoded multibyte UTF-8 and UTF-16 characters.

- **Timers** – The `timer` module exposes a global API for scheduling functions to be called at some later time.

- **TLS/SSL** – The `tls` module provides an implementation of the Transport Layer Security (TLS) and Secure Socket Layer (SSL) protocols that are built on top of OpenSSL.

- **TTY** – The `tty` module provides the `tty.ReadStream` and `tty.WriteStream` classes and deals with reading and writing output and input to the terminal.

- **UDP/Datagram** – The `dgram` module provides an implementation of UDP/Datagram sockets.

- **V8** – The v8 module exposes APIs that are specific to the version of V8 built into the Node binary.

- **VM** – The vm module provides APIs for compiling and running code within V8 virtual machine contexts.

- **Worker Threads** – The worker module provides a way to create multiple environments running on independent threads and to create message channels between them.

- **Zlib** – The zlib module provides compression functionality implemented using Gzip and Deflate/Inflate, as well as Broutil.

Note   There are a few other modules listed in the Node documentation, but I did not include any here that were marked for deprecation or that were experimental at the time of this writing.

Summary

In this chapter, we delved into just a little more detail on Node and NPM, talking about package.json in more detail and some other NPM commands you might need, and we took a look at the standard libraries that ship with Node, at least those that I believe most developers would find of most significant interest.

In the next chapter, we'll look at the next technology we'll need to build the two coming apps: React.

CHAPTER 3

Client-Side Adventures: React

In the previous two chapters, we talked about Node and its good friend NPM, two of the most popular tools for building server-side applications. Now, let's look at the client side of the fence.

The big joke – which is less a joke and more an observation really – is that there seems to be a new framework/library/toolkit for building web-based client applications every day. That is both the benefit and the curse of having such a vibrant development community! But, over the last couple of years, a few popular options have floated to the top of the pile, and React is one of them. That's what we're going to look at in this chapter and the next.

A Brief History of React

React (the logo for which you can see in Figure 3-1 because why not?), which is sometimes referred to as React.js or ReactJS (but I'll stick with React because, like the Dude, I'm into the whole brevity thing), is a product of everyone's favorite (or the exact opposite of favorite – there seems to be no middle ground) company: Facebook. React, in simplest terms, is a library for building web-based user interfaces.

F. Zammetti, *Modern Full-Stack Development*, https://doi.org/10.1007/978-1-4842-8811-5_3

Figure 3-1. *The React logo in all its React-y glory!*

It all started back in around 2010 when Facebook developers, who, despite any feelings about the company you may have, are quite talented, began to run into a lot of issues with code maintenance. That's nothing unusual in the modern web development world: especially when building Single-Page Apps (SPAs), it's easy to make a massive mess of things if you don't have robust architecture and disciplined adherence to it. As you bring more developers onto the team, doing that becomes exponentially more difficult.

Facebook faced this issue and found that their development velocity was slowing down immensely and their delivered quality was suffering for it, all of which are bad for a company trying to make a buck.

In 2010, the engineers introduced XHP into their PHP stack. XHP is an extension to PHP that augments the syntax and, so the argument goes at least, makes your PHP code easier to read. Perhaps the most significant thing it provides is the notion of composite components, which allows for an interface to be broken down into mostly independent but easily integrated units of functionality.

Then, in 2011, the first notion of what would become React emerged in large part based on some of the core concepts of XHP: FaxJs. This was a project created by an engineer by the name of Jordan Walke. FaxJs had several critical characteristics we now see in React, including the following:

- Views, which roughly means screens or sections of screens, are automatically updated any time their state changes. This is termed a *reactive* interface, and it essentially means that when the data the interface deals with changes, the interface will update appropriately to reflect it, all without the developer having to write code to do so explicitly.

- High performance is a key consideration right from the start. While FaxJs achieved this in large part thanks to a string concatenation approach, React instead uses something a little more robust: virtual DOM. I'll come back to this in the next section.

- Perhaps most importantly, FaxJs at a high level was based on the notion of components. Everything you did was a component, and then you composed these components into the interface seen by the user.

Possibly the big turning point in the history of React was in 2012 when Facebook started running into a lot of problems managing the ads displayed on the site. Since ads usually are served by someone else's server and you aren't in complete control of what they are, it's easy for them to break your site. So, the engineers at Facebook started looking for a solution, and FaxJs jumped out at them.

At that point, Jordan Walke started working on an initial prototype and, before long, React emerged.

But just creating React and even using it internally wouldn't have changed the world even if it helped Facebook tremendously. No, something else had to happen, and that something else was in April of 2012 when Facebook acquired Instagram. This was important because Instagram wanted to use React, but at that point, the library was tightly coupled, relatively speaking, to Facebook's site itself and its code. And, of course, it was entirely internal for Facebook and maintained by, for the most part, one (brilliant) person. No, if Facebook was going to let others, even a new acquisition, start to use React, they would have to open source it, and they would have to build a community around it to continue driving the ball down the field.

The primary driving force of this shift was a guy named Pete Hunt. Pete, along with Jordan, got React open sourced in May of 2013. Interestingly, at its initial release, there was a lot of skepticism about React, and many people, for various reasons, saw it as a bit of a step backward. It didn't take long, however, for the momentum to shift as people got a better look and some experience with it, and by the end of 2013, things were looking a lot better for React.

During 2014, several things occurred to shift the currents in React's favor. For example, React Developer Tools were released as an extension of Chrome Developer Tools, giving React developers a robust development toolset to use to develop and debug their React apps. A significant number of conferences and meetups were held to expand exposure to React. Many editors and IDEs begin to introduce native support for React. All of this began to take React mainstream.

2015 and 2016 are when it *really* started to go mainstream. Flipboard, Netflix, and Airbnb all using React most definitely helped a lot. Many more conferences and the release of more robust React tooling did too.

Since the end of 2017, React has continued to grow and is now one of, if not *the*, most popular libraries for building client-side web applications.

Note   I keep emphasizing the client-side nature of React, and that's primarily because that's how we're going to use it in this book. But it's worth noting that React can also render content on the server side. That's a whole other topic of conversation that I won't be covering in this book, but I wanted to make you aware of it. Should you wish to Google for it, the somewhat obvious term applied to this is Server-Side Rendering, or SSR. It's not *exclusive* to React, but React makes it considerably better.

Yeah, Okay, History Nerd, That's All Great, but What IS React?!

It's a library you use to build websites with! How's that for an elevator pitch? You might actually be surprised to see how little there fundamentally is to React. It doesn't ship with a bunch of interface widgets like grids and buttons and sliders and such as many more "robust" toolkits do. It doesn't provide a rigid structure to your application like many frameworks do.

At a very high level, the point of React is to make it easy to reason about the structure of your interface at any given moment in time. This is accomplished by way of *components*, which you can think of as self-contained pieces of the interface. Combine a whole bunch of components together and you have yourself a user interface.

Getting into a little more detail, but still in possibly simplest terms, React supplies just four things: the aforementioned components (more precisely, an approach for building them), props, state, and style (some might argue this fourth shouldn't be included since it's outside React itself, but I think it's reasonable to include it).

Well, you might consider there to be a fifth thing too, given that it's so fundamental to React, and that's virtual DOM.

You won't be using virtual DOM directly, but React will be using it extensively. Presumably, you know what the regular DOM is, but if not, it's the Document Object Model, which is to say the tree structure that the browser builds as it parses your HTML. All the elements, denoted by tags, in the HTML, become nodes in this tree.

Typically, when you do something that makes a change to the page, whether it be as a result of user action or programmatically, the browser has to perform some relatively intensive and expensive work, primarily to repaint the screen (any change that doesn't affect the flow of the page falls in this category, things like changing the color of text) and reflow (any changes that can affect the layout, say, inserting a new `<div>` element). This DOM, therefore, has a direct tie to what you see on the screen, and it offers an API to manipulate it with. All of this takes computing time obviously, and sometimes a lot of it – enough to impact the user experience.

So React uses the concept of a virtual DOM. This is, in essence, a secondary DOM that sits conceptually *on top* of the real DOM in memory. Rather than manipulate the real DOM directly, you instead allow React to mediate the changes that could occur to the page. React will update the virtual DOM and then will intelligently figure out, via a diffing algorithm, the least amount of real DOM work that can be done to accomplish the update. Most importantly, this allows React to batch up real DOM changes and apply them all in one go, which is much more efficient than doing each one individually. The result is better performance than can typically be achieved with direct DOM manipulation (there's always exceptions, but this tends to be generally true).

Putting virtual DOM aside, since it's in a sense just an internal React implementation detail, let's talk about each of the other four in turn, and in the process, let's build ourselves an elementary React app to see it all in action!

The Real Star of the Show: Components

Let's start things off by creating ourselves a plain old HTML document, like that shown in Listing 3-1.

Listing 3-1. A basic HTML document to start building our simple React app with (if you don't understand this already, then, Houston, we have a problem!)

```
<!DOCTYPE html>
<html>
  <head>
    <meta charset="UTF-8" />
    <title>Intro To React</title>
  </head>
  <body>
  </body>
</html>
```

Yep, that ain't exactly rocket science!

Now, to it, let's add two lines into the <head> of the document to bring React into the fold:

```
<script crossorigin src="https://unpkg.com/react@16/umd/react.development.js">
</script>
<script crossorigin src="https://unpkg.com/react-dom@16/umd/react-dom.
development.js"></script>
```

Here, I'm using a CDN to download the main React code (`react.development.js`) as well as the react-dom package, which you can think of as the bridge between React itself and the browser's DOM. React can talk to different renderers, which are the bits of code that produce the visual output. It might be possible to have a renderer that produces, say, bitmap images for display in a desktop operating system, allowing you to write desktop apps with React. The react-dom package is that but targeting the browser DOM and HTML. Note that for both, I'm specifying the development builds rather than the production builds, which are also available. This aids in debugging during development since the code isn't minified and munged and whatnot.

> **Note**   For performance, it would usually be better to move the two React imports to the bottom of the document, as well as the code in start( ), and not call it onLoad. That's page optimization 101. I did it this way because I think it's slightly easier to grasp what's happening in a more deterministic fashion, and in this example, the page will load fast enough that the difference won't matter much anyway.

If you reload the page at this point, nothing will happen, because we're not using React yet. React will just happily sit there in the background not bugging us! So, now, let's introduce some React action, as shown in Listing 3-2.

Listing 3-2.   Our first usage of React!

```
<!DOCTYPE html>
<html>
  <head>
    <meta charset="UTF-8" />
    <title>Intro To React</title>
    <script crossorigin src="https://unpkg.com/react@18.2.0/umd/react.
    development.js"></script>
    <script crossorigin src="https://unpkg.com/react-dom@18.2.0/umd/react-
    dom.development.js"></script>
    <script>

      function start() {
        const topMostComponent =
          React.createElement("div", { },
            React.createElement("h1", { }, "Bookmarks"),
            React.createElement("ul", { },
              React.createElement("li", { },
                React.createElement("h2", { }, "Etherient"),
                React.createElement("a", { href : "https://www.etherient.
                com" }, "The home page of Etherient")
              ),
```

```
            React.createElement("li", { },
              React.createElement("h2", { }, "Frank's Home"),
              React.createElement("a", { href: "https://www.zammetti.com"
              }, "The web home page of Frank Zammetti")
            )
          )
        );
      const root = ReactDOM.createRoot(document.getElementById(
      "mainContainer"));
      root.render(topMostComponent);
    }

  </script>
  </head>
  <body onLoad="start();">
    <div id="mainContainer"></div>
  </body>
</html>
```

Warning   You might encounter a problem with the loading of the two React files from CDN related to CORS (Cross-Origin Resource Sharing). I ran into it with Firefox, but it won't happen for every user or in every browser. If you do find that the example doesn't work though, and you see errors in your developer tools console talking about CORS, the easy solution is to download the two files from the URLs shown here, save them to the same directory as the example file, then change the two <script> tags in the example to reference the local copies rather than from CDN. You'll also likely need to remove the crossorigin attribute to make it finally work. Keep this warning in mind as you look at the code throughout this book since I can't know for sure who will hit this problem and who won't (I ran into it, but my technical reviewer apparently didn't, e.g., it seems to depend on various factors local to each machine, so I'm just throwing this out there as a general warning in case it comes up, but hopefully it won't for you!).

This will result in the screen shown in Figure 3-2. It's nothing complex, but it gets the point across pretty well.

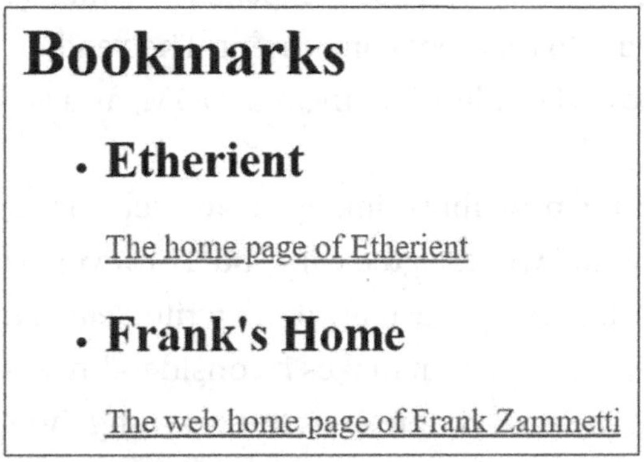

Bookmarks

- **Etherient**

  The home page of Etherient

- **Frank's Home**

  The web home page of Frank Zammetti

Figure 3-2. *Our first React app gets its close-up!*

Okay, so what's going on here?! To start, we have a function `start()` called when the page loads. This function uses what is probably one of the most important things React offers, the `React.createElement()` method. The method signature for it is

```
React.createElement(type, {props}, ...children);
```

This method will construct a new React element, which is the smallest building block of the visual interface of a React app. These are plain old JavaScript objects and thus are cheap and fast to create, as compared to DOM nodes. React will take care of updating the DOM to match all the elements that are a part of that virtual DOM (creating real DOM nodes from the elements and inserting them as appropriate essentially).

It should be noted that, typically, you'll be working with React components. Components are composed of elements; that's the difference. The type you specify here can be a tag name, as shown here, or it can be a React component type, or a React fragment, which allows you to create multiple nested elements at once.

In this `start()` function, `React.createElement()` is used to build up a tree of elements, all of which are children of the top-level `div` element that the variable `topMostComponent` holds a reference to. Each call to `React.createElement()` after that first one is creating a child of the element above it in the tree. Then, when that tree is built up, this code executes:

```
const root = ReactDOM.createRoot(document.getElementById("main
Container"));
root.render(topMostComponent);
```

What that's doing is creating a root component and inserting it into the mainContainer div. This is the uber-component that is the parent to all other React components on the page. Then, the topMostComponent – which is actually a tree of components – is rendered into that root component. The render() method takes that built-up virtual DOM tree and renders it to the real DOM, and voila, we have stuff on the screen!

Now, at this point, you're probably thinking "wow, React is verbose and looks annoying to write," and, well, I would agree with you! However, what you're going to find in the next chapter is that people usually don't write React apps like this. Instead, they use something called JSX, and that makes it considerably easier to write React apps with. We'll get into that in the next chapter, but the key thing though is that when you write a React app with JSX, under the covers, it will produce code similar to this, so I think it makes a lot of sense to understand how React is doing things in the end. Plus, there may be a reason specifically you want to write your apps this way, one of which is when you want to add some React components to an existing app. In such a case, you're likely not going to rewrite the whole thing in JSX. You'll more likely just want to insert some components somewhere onto your existing page. With code like this, you can do precisely that.

But I glossed over a few things here. One of which, props, I'm going to get into more in the next section, but you can start to get a sense of what they're about in the line:

```
React.createElement("a",
  { href : "https://www.etherient.com" },
  "The home page of Etherient"
)
```

It doesn't take much to figure out that props are how you pass data into an element (or component, as it happens). But there's a bit more to it than that, so let's come back to that in the next section.

One thing that you should realize here is that we really haven't dealt with components at all, and, hey, that's the title of this section! I've also said that components are really the foundation of React, so let's remedy having not seen them yet by rewriting the code a bit, as shown in Listing 3-3.

Listing 3-3. Finally, some of those components he's been on about!

```
<!DOCTYPE html>
<html>
  <head>
    <meta charset="UTF-8" />
    <title>Intro To React</title>
    <script crossorigin src="https://unpkg.com/react@18.2.0/umd/react.
    development.js"></script>
    <script crossorigin src="https://unpkg.com/react-dom@18.2.0/umd/react-
    dom.development.js"></script>
    <script>

      function start() {

        class Bookmark extends React.Component {
          render() {
            return (
              React.createElement("li", { },
                React.createElement("h2", { }, this.props.title),
                React.createElement("a", { href : this.props.href }, this.
                props.description)
              )
            );
          }
        }

        const topMostComponent =
          React.createElement("div", { },
            React.createElement("h1", { }, "Bookmarks"),
            React.createElement("ul", { },
              React.createElement(
                Bookmark, { title : "Etherient", href : "https://
                www.etherient.com", description : "The home page of
                Etherient" }
              ),
```

```
            React.createElement(
                Bookmark, { title : "Frank's Site", href : "https://
                www.zammetti.com", description : "The web home of Frank
                W. Zammetti" }
            )
          )
        );
      const root = ReactDOM.createRoot(document.getElementById(
      "mainContainer"));
      root.render(topMostComponent);
    }

    </script>
  </head>
  <body onLoad="start();">
    <div id="mainContainer"></div>
  </body>
</html>
```

The Bookmark class is how we define a proper React component, which is why it extends the React.Component class. React components have several characteristics that you'll see throughout this book, but perhaps the most important is a render() method. Without that, it won't be much of a component! The render() method, which is the only thing your component is *required* to contain, is responsible for returning one of several things:

- Another React component

- A React element

- An array of either of those

- A fragment

- A portal (a more advanced topic that won't be covered in this book)

- A string or a number (these are rendered as plain text nodes in the DOM)

- A boolean or null (results in *nothing* being rendered)

Of these, the first two are almost always going to be what you return. You would think that arrays or fragments would be common too, but it's more common to return a single component or element that itself has children, which accomplishes much the same goal.

You can also now see the other side of props, meaning how you use them within a component. The `this.props` member will be present on any component thanks to React, and React populates it for you when you use the component using whatever you pass as the second argument to `React.createElement()`, and you can use the data in props as appropriate inside the component. Here, it's just rendering the three props (`title`, `href`, and `description`) as part of the elements returned.

Speaking of using a component, you can see that being done in the `topMostComponent` definition. This time, we call `React.createElement()` but now we pass it the name of the React component as the first argument, React instantiates that component for us and passes the props to it, and whatever that component's `render()` method returns effectively is inserted at that point in the tree.

Hopefully, you can start to see some of the benefits of this componentized approach. Now, you can avoid having a bunch of redundant `React.createElement()` calls and instead encapsulate it inside a component and reuse the component wherever you need a Bookmark to appear. There are no real rules about how you break the interface down; I could have created a custom component to encapsulate the `<h1>` elements and maybe called it a `BookmarkGroup` component. Whatever makes sense to you is the answer.

Note   In later chapters, we're going to talk about something called *functional components*. At the risk of stealing my own thunder, that's another way to write React components, and it's kind of considered the more "modern" way to do it and is generally preferred by most developers. When we get there, you'll see that some of what I said here is no longer true or at least comes in a different form. But, this form of *class-based component*, as it's known, is still alive and well, you can still write them with the very latest version of React (as of the time of this writing at least), and in fact there are some cases where you may want to or even *need* to, even if you find functional components are more to your liking generally. But, like I said, we'll get there eventually, so don't sweat it yet!

Components Need Info: Props

As you saw in the previous section, props, which is short for properties, is how information is passed into components. For the simple HTML elements created earlier, that can be the attributes of those elements that you're familiar with: href for a link or the text inside an <h2> element (the text isn't *technically* an attribute of the <h2> tag itself, it's actually a text node nested inside the <h2>, but at least in practice it's the same thing). For custom components, you get to define whatever props it needs. For the Bookmark component, that's title, href, and description.

What's important to realize about props is three things. First, they are always passed down from a parent component to a child. In the case of the topmost component, you can consider React itself to be the "parent component" conceptually. In any case, the source of the information is always the parent component. Now, where the data that is the value of a prop comes from in the parent can be many things. It could be literal text as you see in the example code we're dealing with here. It could be the value of a variable inside the parent component. It could be a value that comes from some other object that the parent retrieves. But, from the perspective of the child component, the value comes from the parent always.

Second, props are only given to the child component when it's being created. This is a crucial point because it ties in with the third thing, which is that props are immutable. This will strike you as odd at first because, I mean, how could that be?! What if we wanted to change the description of one of our Bookmark components in response to the user editing it somehow? Clearly, that's gonna be a problem if props can't be altered.

But it's true: once set, props cannot be changed.

The way it works is that any time a change must occur to a component, React will re-render part of the DOM tree. Remember all that stuff about virtual DOM and how React does diffs to determine what to redraw? Well, the level above that is that some data in your code needs to change that React recognizes for it to know it has to do any of that work. We're going to look at something called state next, but where that matters in terms of props is that when state changes, whatever that is, React will determine what components need to be re-rendered as a result.

Not just re-rendered in fact, but destroyed and recreated from scratch! That means that the component will need to be passed its props from the parent again. If the state impacts those props – because remember I said the values of props could come from many places, and state is one of them – then the new values will be passed to the component when it is recreated. In that way, the `description` of a `Bookmark` could "change" because we will, in fact, wind up with a whole new `Bookmark` component with a new `description` value.

So, yes, props can't be changed once they are passed to the child and the component is created with them, but nothing says the component can't be destroyed and recreated with all-new prop values, and that's precisely what happens under the covers. It's almost like cheating, if you think about it!

Components (Sometimes) Need Memory: State

Effectively, there are two types of data that serve to control components in some way. You've already seen one: props. Now let's look at the other: state.

Props, you know now, are read-only and do not change during the lifetime of a component. If props need to change, then the component will be destroyed and recreated. If you think there must be a more efficient way to deal with data that you know will change, then you'd be correct, and that way is state. Changes to state do not cause React to destroy and recreate a component, at least not directly. Instead, it will change just the tiniest portion of the virtual DOM tree that the change demands, and then the minimum real DOM changes will result. Of course, sometimes that might still mean destroying an entire component, or even an entire component tree, but it all depends on whether the change in state reflects in a change to a component's props.

Let's see a concrete example. Building on the previous code, let's make some changes to our Bookmark class. It will now be like Listing 3-4.

Listing 3-4. The altered Bookmark class (and, by extension, React component)

```html
<!DOCTYPE html>
<html>
  <head>
    <meta charset="UTF-8" />
    <title>Intro To React</title>
    <script crossorigin src="https://unpkg.com/react@18.2.0/umd/react.
    development.js"></script>
    <script crossorigin src="https://unpkg.com/react-dom@18.2.0/umd/react-
    dom.development.js"></script>
    <script>
```

```
function start() {

  class Bookmark extends React.Component {

    constructor(props) {
      super(props);
      console.log("Bookmark component created");
      this.title = this.props.title;
    }

    render() {
      return (
        React.createElement("li", { },
          React.createElement("h2", { }, this.title),
          React.createElement("a", { href : this.props.href }, this.
          props.description),
          React.createElement("button", {
            onClick : () => {
              this.title = this.title + "-CHANGED";
              this.setState({});
            }
          }, "Click me")
        )
      );
    }

  } /* End Bookmark. */

  const topMostComponent =
    React.createElement("div", { },
      React.createElement("h1", { }, "Bookmarks"),
      React.createElement("ul", { },
        React.createElement(
          Bookmark, { title : "Etherient", href : "https://
          www.etherient.com", description : "The home page of
          Etherient" }
        ),
```

```
    React.createElement(
      Bookmark, { title : "Frank's Site", href : "https://
      www.zammetti.com", description : "The web home of Frank
      W. Zammetti" }
    )
  )
);
const root = ReactDOM.createRoot(document.getElementById(
"mainContainer"));
root.render(topMostComponent);

} /* End start(). */

    </script>
  </head>
  <body onLoad="start();">
    <div id="mainContainer"></div>
  </body>
</html>
```

The first thing to note is the constructor that I've added. There are two reasons to have a constructor (it is otherwise optional). The first is so that when you try this code out (you *are* following along and trying the code out, right?!), you will see that when state changes, the constructor does not fire after the two initial times (one per Bookmark in the tree), proving that state changes don't result in component recreation. Note that in a constructor for a React.Component instance, you must call the superclass's constructor and pass it the props that will be passed into the constructor. You'll get some nasty JavaScript errors in your dev tools console if you fail to do this (ask me how I know!).

The second reason is the line where title is set as a member variable, and its initial value is taken from the props that are passed in. This variable becomes the state of this Bookmark component. There are no rules with how you store the state inside your component. Many people choose to have a single state variable that is an object that contains all the state for the component, and I frankly tend to do that too. But it can simply be "naked" class members like this too. Whatever makes sense to you, React will accommodate.

Now, down in the call to `React.createElement()` that creates the `<h2>` element, note the change there: rather than getting the value from `this.props` like before, it now comes from `this.title`. That's key, as you're about to see!

A new child element has been added at the end, this one a `<button>` HTML element. Now, the first interesting thing is that the second argument to `React.createElement()`, which you'll recall is the props to pass to the component, can include functions! At the end of the day, this argument is just an object, and what's in it can be virtually anything, so long as it has meaning to your component (or will just be ignored by it, that's a valid possibility too). Here, because we're creating a button and because buttons typically do something when clicked, an `onClick` event handler function is passed in. React knows how to create a `<button>` HTML element, and it knows how to attach that function, so we get a button that does something when clicked, just as we need. The "something" it does when clicked is to change the `title` property of the class.

Now, if that's all it did, then nothing would happen, at least nothing evident on the screen. Yes, the value of the variable would change, but React wouldn't know that anything had happened. You see, React isn't monitoring your state and proactively re-rendering the screen as appropriate. No, you have to inform it that state has changed, and that's precisely what the `setState()` method is for. This method is provided by the base `React.Component` class that our `Bookmark` custom component class extends. It informs React that this component, and its children, may need to be re-rendered (React will make the final determination).

The argument passed to `setState()` is one of two things: either a function or an object. If it's a function, then it's what is called an *updater function*. This function receives two arguments: the current state of the object and its props. This function must then return an object that will be the new state of the component. It's important to understand that this function must *not* mutate the state object passed in! Instead, it must create a new object and return it. If you change the incoming state object, then nothing will appear to happen (unless you return that same object, but that's a code smell and can sometimes lead to some real nastiness, so don't do that).

Alternatively, and what I've done in the example, is pass `setState()` an object, an empty object in this case. What this does causes React to perform a shallow merge of the object with the component's current state. In this case, since I've already altered the state variable, that means that the resulting object has the new value, so what's returned is a valid new state object.

Note   In general, it's probably better to always use an updater function. While it involves a little more code and work on your part, it tends to be safer. For a simple example like this, it hardly matters, but as a rule, I'd suggest always doing it that way. And, plus, it's definitely more of a functional approach, which is a popular paradigm these days, so if nothing else, you'll be hangin' with the cool kids this way! And, once we actually discuss functional component later in this book, you'll see that you pretty much don't have a choice – but then, React will actually help you out! But again, don't worry about this yet, just wetting your appetite a little bit.

A crucial thing to understand about setState() is that it is more of a request than a demand. What I mean is that React will enqueue setState() calls, and the work it results in, and may batch many requests to optimize DOM updates. So, you aren't so much telling React to update the component right *now*; you're asking it to do so at some point in the future. Of course, we're not talking about hours or even minutes or seconds later, but the change won't necessarily be immediate. It is asynchronous in other words, and as a result, you can also pass a second argument to setState(), a callback function. This function will be called after the update has occurred. This callback mechanism isn't relevant in such a simple example, but you may find times where you do need it, when you need to trigger some action but only after the screen has been updated.

In the world of React, there's quite a lot more to state than this (if you've ever heard the term Redux, then that's one such thing: it's another way of dealing with state more globally, but it's a topic I won't be covering in this book). But, at an elementary and fundamental level, this is what state is all about, and you absolutely can use what you've learned in this section alone to deal with state in your React apps.

Note   One other point of terminology: as you've seen, not all components have state. These are, quite obviously, termed *stateless* components. Any component that has state is, equally as obviously, called a *stateful* component.

Making Them Look Good: Style

The final thing I want to touch on is styling in a React app.

Now, at the end of the day, when building an app with React we're still talking about HTML, JavaScript, and CSS. Components will always render down into some combination of those. So, we can do things very directly if we wish. For example, if we want to make the color of our Bookmark titles red, we could add this to the page:

```
<style>
  h2 {
    color : red;
  }
</style>
```

That'll get the job done. Of course, we could put this in a separate .css file and import it into the document, just like always with CSS.

Another alternative is to explicitly name a CSS class to use in the component's code. So, let's alter that style definition a little bit:

```
<style>
  .bookmarkTitle {
    color : red;
  }
</style>
```

Now, in our Bookmark code, the call to React.createElement() that creates the <h2> for the title specifically, let's use that style:

```
React.createElement("h2", { className : "bookmarkTitle" }, this.title)
```

Since class is a reserved word in JavaScript, React makes us use className instead. But that will result in the style being applied all the same.

You could also define the style inline with the element, like this:

```
React.createElement("h2", { style : { color : "red" } }, this.title)
```

The style prop must be an object mapping CSS attributes to values. This approach is an important one because it leads to a concept termed CSS-in-JS. If you notice, you're effectively defining your CSS in JavaScript here. Further, there's absolutely no reason you

couldn't take that object that defines the styles for the <h2> element out of the
React.createElement() call and define it independently:

```
const bookmarkTitle = { color : "red" }
```

Then you just do

```
React.createElement("h2", { style : this.bookmarkTitle }, this.title)
```

You could put all your style objects for your entire application like those in separate
styles.js file, and now you've started down the path of skipping CSS, in a sense, and
doing it all in JavaScript. Oh, to be sure, you're still dealing with CSS obviously, but in an
arguably more flexible way.

However, components are meant to be self-contained entities, remember? Given
that, shouldn't that include their style too? But, then, isn't it better code structure to keep
the styles at least somewhat separate from the layout code? Most people think so. All that
taken together, you might wind up with something that looks like Listing 3-5.

Listing 3-5. The Bookmark component, now with 100% more style

```
<!DOCTYPE html>
<html>
  <head>
    <meta charset="UTF-8" />
    <title>Intro To React</title>
    <script crossorigin src="https://unpkg.com/react@18.2.0/umd/react.
    development.js"></script>
    <script crossorigin src="https://unpkg.com/react-dom@18.2.0/umd/
    react-dom.development.js"></script>
    <script>

      function start() {

        class Bookmark extends React.Component {
          constructor(props) {
            super(props);
            console.log("Bookmark component created");
          }
```

```
        title = this.props.title;
        titleStyle = { color : "red" }
        render() {
          return (
            React.createElement("li", { },
              React.createElement("h2", { style : this.titleStyle },
              this.title),
              React.createElement("a", { href : this.props.href }, this.
              props.description),
              React.createElement("button", {
                onClick : () => {
                  this.title = this.title + "-CHANGED";
                  this.setState({});
                }
              }, "Click me")
            )
          );
        }
      }

      const topMostComponent =
        React.createElement("div", { },
          React.createElement("h1", { }, "Bookmarks"),
          React.createElement("ul", { },
            React.createElement(
              Bookmark, { title : "Etherient", href : "https://
              www.etherient.com", description : "The home page of
              Etherient" }
            ),
            React.createElement(
              Bookmark, { title : "Frank's Site", href : "https://
              www.zammetti.com", description : "The web home of Frank
              W. Zammetti" }
            )
          )
        );
```

```
    const root = ReactDOM.createRoot(document.getElementById("main
    Container"));
    root.render(topMostComponent);

  }

  </script>
</head>
<body onLoad="start();">
  <div id="mainContainer"></div>
</body>
</html>
```

Now, the Bookmark component's style is defined within the Bookmark class, achieving encapsulation, but then within the class the style information is abstracted from the code that produces the layout in the render() method. This is arguably a cleaner way to write component code.

Whichever approach you choose, whatever meets your needs, the bottom line is that React offers several approaches to styling your components and thus your user interface.

In the End, Why React?

All of that is fine and dandy, but it doesn't answer a fundamental question: Why would anyone want to use React?

I think, at least in my mind, a few critical points in React's favor are the following:

- **Simplicity** – As you've seen, React amounts to four fundamental pillars: components, props, state, and style. There isn't much to it as a basic level. It doesn't take much to get started with it, as you saw, and it doesn't have a lot of complicated baggage like some other frameworks do (the counterargument, of course, is that all that complexity provides additional power, and ultimately that's the judgment call you have to make as a developer).

- **Easy to integrate into existing projects by not being overly opinionated** – You can add React to an existing project little by little if you want, and this is in large part thanks to the fact that React doesn't impose a rigid application architecture on you like other options do.

Like with the simplicity argument, there is a negative to this: it's more possible to screw things up with React than with something like, say, Angular, precisely *because* of that lack of opinionated mindset.

- **A bit of luck!** – React began growing in popularity right around the time something else was happening: Google's Angular framework, another popular front-end development tool, jumped from version 1 to version 2. This was a significant event for Angular users because the version change was not backward compatible and, frankly, caused a lot of headaches for a lot of people. Many of those people began looking for a more straightforward option that didn't seem as likely to repeat that mistake, and React was gaining a foothold right around that time. So, Google and Angular's misstep aided React, if only indirectly.

- **Backing** – Many people have less than positive feelings about Facebook these days, but one thing you can't deny is that they are a large corporation, and when a development tool has sizeable corporate backing, it tends to become a "safe" choice for technologists to suggest on the job. React has had that going for it right from the start.

Summary

In this chapter, you took your first steps into the world of React. You got a brief tour of where it all started, why it came into being, and who's responsible. We talked a bit about what it offers, why that's valuable, and why it's become so popular. Then, you saw some basic React code and got familiar with the four main pillars of React: components, props, state, and style.

In the next chapter, we'll look at a few more advanced React concepts and dive just a little deeper into what React has to offer us as application developers.

CHAPTER 4

A Few More Words: Advanced React

In the last chapter, we began looking at React, the popular JavaScript application framework. There, you were introduced to the basic concepts that every React developer deals with.

In this chapter, we'll delve a little bit deeper, looking at a few more concepts that are important when writing React apps. Perhaps most importantly is JSX, which provides us a better way (in most developers' opinion, I think it's fair to say) to write React apps.

A Better Way to Write React Code: JSX

JSX, which stands for JavaScript XML, is an extension to the JavaScript language that adds XML syntax to the language. In a sense, it allows us to embed XML (or HTML, which at least conceptually is a child of XML) inside JavaScript without having to resort to things like string concatenation, DOM methods or React function calls. At its core, JSX is interested in allowing us to define tree structures with attributes in a more elegant way than all those JavaScript function calls you saw in the last chapter.

If you think back to Chapter 1 and the discussion of components, there might be a light bulb above your head right now! React is *nothing but* trees (of components) with attributes (props)!

However, although it's effectively an extension of JavaScript, it's *not* a part of JavaScript! No, it's a bolted-on thing that requires a preprocessing step, the output of which is pure JavaScript. But I'm jumping ahead a bit. We'll get to that in the next section!

71

© Frank Zammetti 2022
F. Zammetti, *Modern Full-Stack Development*, https://doi.org/10.1007/978-1-4842-8811-5_4

The reason JSX came about – aside from the obvious of developers not liking to code their UIs as a series of function calls as you saw in the last chapter – is because the React team realized that it's kind of pointless to separate rendering logic from UI logic. That's something we've been doing for a long time. For example, you put your markup in an HTML file, but then you (usually) put your UI logic in a JavaScript file. But these things are intrinsically coupled. How events are handled, how the state of your application changes in response to user interactions, how data is prepared for display, all of that is mixed together, so does it really make sense to separate along lines of *technology* like that?

An argument can be made that no, it doesn't make sense, and that's the argument React makes. Instead, the division in React is on boundaries based on *concerns*. That's where components come into play: they are separating the various concerns a UI has (a button is concerned with letting the user trigger an action, a grid is concerned with displaying data, etc.). But each component is an encapsulated whole: it contains the logic that knows how to render itself as well as the logic that knows how to deal with the various events that can affect it.

While you absolutely can do all of this without JSX just by adhering to some architectural principles and being disciplined with your code, JSX provides, arguably, a more elegant way to do so. But, especially since most developers are coming from an HTML/JS/CSS background, JSX provides a more natural way into the world of React by allowing them not to have to think in terms of `React.createElement()` but in something more akin to what they're already familiar with.

Yeah, Okay, So What Does It LOOK LIKE?!

So, what does JSX look like? Well, here's a simple example using a `MaterialButton` component (which we'll assume is a real component and is available to our code, but this could be any component if course):

```
const button = <MaterialButton color="red"
  onClick="alert('clicked');">
  Click Me
</MaterialButton>;
```

Huh? If you've looked at JavaScript at all (which, remember, I'm assuming you have for our purposes here!) that will probably give you cold chills because obviously that wouldn't be valid JavaScript syntax! You can't set markup like that, XML like that, as the value of a variable! Not without putting it in quotes and making it a string anyway.

Earlier, I mentioned a preprocessing step that we have to do with JSX. That step, simply put, is to compile it into standard JavaScript. But, before we even get to that, what do we expect that final JavaScript to look like? Considering that we expect the JavaScript to use React, the answer is that it's going to look something like this:

```
React.createElement(
  MaterialButton,
  { color : "red",
    onClick : function() { alert('clicked'); }
  },
  "Click Me"
)
```

That should look familiar to you at this point!

What's more, if you embed components in JSX...

```
const button = <MaterialButton color="red"
  onClick="alert('clicked');">
  <ButtonLabel text="Click Me" />
</MaterialButton>;
```

you'll get nested calls as you would expect, given what JSX compiles down to:

```
React.createElement(
  MaterialButton,
  { color : "red",
    onClick : function() { alert('clicked'); }
  },
  React.createElement(ButtonLabel, { text : "Click Me" })
)
```

Okay, so that's JSX in simplest terms. But, clearly, if we load that in a browser, it's gonna spit it back at us unceremoniously because it's not valid JavaScript. How do we get valid JavaScript from JSX? To explain that, we have to take a quick detour and talk about something called Babel.

A Slight Detour into Babel Land

When a new version of JavaScript comes out, it takes time for browsers, and the JavaScript engines they use, to catch up. There is a period of time when there may be some cool new features in the language that you can't use without risking some of your customers not being able to run your code (this is of course true for users who are using older browsers). This is true for the JavaScript engine that underpins Node too: you may have to avoid some language features as you write your code until the engine is updated. Sometimes, a particular browser or engine might never implement a feature you want to use, and certainly trying to keep track of which environment your great new code will run in and which it won't becomes a headache in a hurry.

To give a concrete example, consider this bit of JavaScript:

```
const newArray = [ 44, 55, 66].map((num) => n * 2);
```

That code will work in the latest version of Chrome, Firefox, and Opera. But it won't work in Internet Explorer 11 (and – HOORAY! – that browser is no longer with us!). If your work requires that you support that browser, which you may still have to for a while, then you've got a problem if you really want to write your code like that.

That's a problem that has existed for a long time, but JavaScript has been evolving quickly over the last decade or so as its usage has increased dramatically, so the problem has only gotten worse over time. Solutions do exist, though: every new feature in the language can be refactored and written using the earlier language features, often with some compromises, but essentially functioning as the new features do. This approach is often called a *polyfill*.

That's not an ideal solution, though, because it's a lot of work for developers, whether directly (developing and testing the polyfill itself and ensuring it works across all target browsers) or indirectly (waiting for someone else to do it and release it to the world). It also almost always yields worse performance than the same function implemented natively in the JavaScript engine.

This is where Babel comes in. Rather than have to go through that effort, Babel allows you to write your code using the new language features you want. What happens next is you run that code through Babel, and Babel takes care of generating the appropriate polyfill code. Babel is considered a *transpiler*, meaning it transforms and compiles at the same time. That means your workflow is altered: there is now a step you must do before you can actually run your code. Yes, you can still find that you have inferior performance, but the truth is that the people working on Babel are pretty smart, so the delta is likely to be small in most cases, if there's any performance penalty at all.

To use Babel, you first have to install it. Before that, though, let's begin a new project. Choose a directory and `npm init` the project, using all the default options. Once that's done, you can install Babel:

```
npm install --save-dev @babel/core @babel/cli
```

Once that's done, you'll be able to run Babel. To do so, issue the command

```
npx babel
```

The `npx` command is something that is installed by newer versions of NPM. It's an executable, installed alongside the `npm` executable, that is a proxy allowing you to run packages and the CLI tools some packages provide. In the past, you would usually be directed to install Babel globally, which would add the appropriate path entries to your system, allowing you to run it. Now though, the advice usually given is to install Babel local to the project (so that different projects can use different versions of Babel as appropriate). But doing that doesn't give you those same path entries. That's where `npx` comes in: it lets you run those tools without those path entries. Moreover, it can run packages without even installing them! This is handy if you just want to try something out, or if it's a one-off tool that you don't actually want to have installed all the time.

Now, running Babel like this won't do anything yet. That's because, first, you have to tell it what to transpile. So, let's create a file called `test.js` and into it put the code from before:

```
const newArray = [ 44, 55, 66].map((num) => n * 2);
```

Then, execute

```
npx babel test.js
```

What happens? Well, uhh, still nothing, actually! Babel will echo back the code from the file, but nothing is changed, nothing is produced. That's because out of the box, Babel doesn't do anything – it doesn't know how to transform the code. You have to add some plugins to it to give it that knowledge. Plugins are what define the rules for transpiling one language (or version of a language) into another. If you want to see a list of all the plugins available, check out this site: `https://babeljs.io/docs/en/plugins`. For our purposes though, we'll just need one, which we, of course, can install with NPM:

```
npm install --save-dev @babel/plugin-transform-arrow-functions
```

Now, there's still another step, and that's to tell Babel to use that plugin. To do that, we have to create one more file: the `.babelrc` configuration file. Its contents should be

```
{
  "plugins": ["@babel/plugin-transform-arrow-functions"]
}
```

With that in place, Babel now knows to use this plugin when processing our file, which it will do if we execute the `npx babel test.js` command again. The output you'll then see should be

```
const newArray = [44, 55, 66].map(function (num) {
  return n * 2;
});
```

Notice how the arrow function was replaced with standard `function()` syntax? That's Babel doing its thing! The `plugin-transform-arrow-function` is the plugin you use when you know you want to use arrow functions but that a target JavaScript engine you want you code to run on doesn't yet support them (that would be a pretty ancient engine at this point, but still). And, in this case, what it replaces it with should have no impact on performance, so it's a very fair trade indeed!

You'll likely want to write that output to a file rather than the console, and to do so is simple enough:

```
npx babel test.js --out-file test_new.js
```

Sure enough, this is a very simple example, and the code looks fairly similar before and after transpilation occurs. But, for more complex JavaScript, the difference can be rather drastic.

One final thing, do you think it might be inconvenient to have to install a plugin for every single JavaScript feature you want to be able to transpile? The answer is, hopefully, a clear yes! For this reason, Babel provides the notion of *presets*. These effectively are logical groupings of plugins that can be enabled all in one batch. There are several presets, but the two most used are `env` and `react`.

The env preset allows you to do this in your `.babelrc` file:

```
{ "presets": [
    [ "@babel/preset-env", {
      "targets" : {
        "browsers" : [ "last 3 versions", "safari >= 6" ]
      }
    }]
  ]
}
```

That tells Babel, "I want you to produce code that will work in the last three versions of all browsers, and for Safari, support anything from version 6 on up." Babel will take care of installing the appropriate plugins. Also, if you're working in Node and don't care about browsers, you can do

```
{ "presets" : [
    [ "@babel/preset-env", {
      "targets" : { "node" : "7.00" }
    }]
  ]
}
```

That tells Babel to support Node back to version 7.

To make use of this preset, you need to install a single plugin:

```
npm install --save-dev @babel/preset-env
```

Once that's done, and `.babelrc` altered as shown in the preceding text (removing the `@babel/plugin-transform-arrow-functions` plugin), the output will now be

```
"use strict";
var newArray = [44, 55, 66].map(function (num) {
  return n * 2;
});
```

That's the same as before, only now with the `"use strict";` at the top and, critically, not having to explicitly tell it which plugins to use!

Compile JSX

The previous section described the env preset, but what about the react preset I mentioned? That's the key to being able to produce plain old JavaScript from our JSX files. To do that, we have to make some changes. First, we'll need to install the preset:

```
npm install @babel/preset-react --save-dev
```

You will then need to add a new preset in .babelrc to let Babel know how to deal with JSX (and some related React plumbing):

```
{ "presets" : [
    [ "@babel/preset-react" ]
  ]
}
```

Note   You only need the react preset, you don't need the env preset, so if you're following along, then you can remove the env dependency from package.json. However, it does no harm to leave it there, so it's entirely up to you.

Now, rename the test.js file to test.jsx and replace its contents with the JSX from earlier:

```
const button = <MaterialButton color="red"
  onClick="alert('clicked');">
  Click Me
</MaterialButton>;
```

With those tasks complete, you can now run Babel against the test.jsx file, just as you did against the test.js file before, but now the output should be something like this:

```
const button = /*#__PURE__*/React.createElement(MaterialButton, {
  color: "red",
  onClick: "alert('clicked');"
}, "Click Me");
```

Just as expected, we get some plain old JavaScript from the JSX, and what's more, it looks just like the sort of JavaScript we wrote in the previous chapter!

That funky comment you see is a special marker that Babel adds to indicate that the function here is *pure*, meaning that it has no side effects. This is useful for a concept called *tree shaking*, which is the ability of a tool (like Uglify or babel-minify) to go through all your code and remove any "dead" code, that is, code that isn't actually needed. This comes into play when we use something like Webpack, which is a tool you'll be introduced to in later chapters. Those tools can work without such marker comments, but it provides them useful hints that makes them more efficient and perhaps more able to do their job generally. In short, just kind of mentally ignore those comments because they're not meant for you (and, in truth, you'll tend to not look at the output of something like Babel anyway because it rarely does you any good – it's not the code *you* wrote, after all!).

And Now, Put It All Together

Now that we know what JSX is, what it looks like, and how to compile it into valid JavaScript, let's put all the pieces together! Here, we'll take the very simple example from the previous chapter and rewrite it using JSX.

First, let's take the simple project created in the last section and rename `test.jsx` to `main.jsx`. That's our source file that will be compiled into plain JavaScript. But, to do anything with that final product, we'll also need an HTML file. So, create a file named `index.html` and insert the following content into it:

```html
<!DOCTYPE html>
<html>
  <head>
    <meta charset="UTF-8" />
    <title>Intro To React</title>
    <script crossorigin src="https://unpkg.com/react@18.2.0/umd/react.
    development.js"></script>
    <script crossorigin src="https://unpkg.com/react-dom@18.2.0/umd/
    react-dom.development.js"></script>
    <script src="main.js"></script>
  </head>
  <body onLoad="start();">
    <div id="mainContainer"></div>
  </body>
</html>
```

That's basically the same as what you saw in the previous chapter, minus all the React code. Instead, the main.js file, which we don't have yet, is being imported.

So, let's now get that main.js file! First, we need some JSX to compile into it. To do that, replace the contents of main.jsx with this:

```
function start() {
  class Bookmark extends React.Component {
    constructor(props) {
      super(props);
      console.log("Bookmark component created");
    }
    title = this.props.title;
    titleStyle = { color : "red" }
    render() {
      return (
        <li>
          <h2 style={this.titleStyle}>{this.title}</h2>
          <a href={this.props.href}>
            {this.props.description}
          </a>
          <button onClick={() => {
            this.title = this.title + "-CHANGED";
            this.setState({});
          }}>
          Click me
          </button>
        </li>
      );
    }
  }
  ReactDOM.render(
    <div>
      <h1>Bookmarks</h1>
      <ul>
```

```
    <Bookmark title={"Etherient"}
      href={"https://www.etherient.com"}
      description={"The home page of Etherient"}
    />
    <Bookmark title={"Frank's Site"}
      href={"https://www.zammetti.com"}
      description={"The web home of Frank W. Zammetti"}
    />
   </ul>
  </div>,
  document.getElementById("mainContainer")
 );
}
```

All I've done is I've taken the code for the final example in the last chapter, and I've replaced all the React.createElement() calls with their JSX equivalents. I've done this in both the custom Bookmark component's definition and the component tree created in the ReactDOM.render(). Hopefully, you'll agree that looks a lot cleaner and easier to understand.

With that in place, now we can compile our JSX:

```
npx babel main.jsx --out-file main.js
```

Oh, but if you do that right now, you're going to be greeted by an error message *"Support for the experimental syntax 'classProperties' isn't currently enabled."* To deal with that, we need to install another Babel plugin to provide support for that language feature:

```
npm install --save-dev @babel/plugin-proposal-class-properties
```

We also need to tell Babel to use it, so an entry is added to .babelrc:

```
{
  "presets": [ "@babel/preset-react" ],
  "plugins": [ "@babel/plugin-proposal-class-properties" ]
}
```

Once that's done, the compilation should be successful, and we'll have a main.js file ready to be used. The contents of that file should look something like this:

```
function _defineProperty(obj, key, value) { if (key in obj) { Object.
defineProperty(obj, key, { value: value, enumerable: true, configurable:
true, writable: true }); } else { obj[key] = value; } return obj; }

function start() {
  class Bookmark extends React.Component {
    constructor(props) {
      super(props);

      _defineProperty(this, "title", this.props.title);

      _defineProperty(this, "titleStyle", {
        color: "red"
      });

      console.log("Bookmark component created");
    }

    render() {
      return /*#__PURE__*/React.createElement("li", null, /*#__PURE__*/
      React.createElement("h2", {
        style: this.titleStyle
      }, this.title), /*#__PURE__*/React.createElement("a", {
        href: this.props.href
      }, this.props.description), /*#__PURE__*/React.
      createElement("button", {
        onClick: () => {
          this.title = this.title + "-CHANGED";
          this.setState({});
        }
      }, "Click me"));
    }

  }

  ReactDOM.render( /*#__PURE__*/React.createElement("div", null, /*#__
  PURE__*/React.createElement("h1", null, "Bookmarks"), /*#__PURE__*/React.
  createElement("ul", null, /*#__PURE__*/React.createElement(Bookmark, {
```

```
    title: "Etherient",
    href: "https://www.etherient.com",
    description: "The home page of Etherient"
  }), /*#__PURE__*/React.createElement(Bookmark, {
    title: "Frank's Site",
    href: "https://www.zammetti.com",
    description: "The web home of Frank W. Zammetti"
  }))), document.getElementById("mainContainer"));
}
```

Well, that's not exactly what we wrote in the previous chapter, is it?! But it *does* bear some resemblance to it at a high level, and that's what matters because it proves that our JSX was compiled into plain JavaScript that uses React properly. Now, if you load index.html in your browser, you should be greeted with the same screen as this example produced in the previous chapter, complete with button click event handling.

That, in a nutshell, is JSX!

Note   I neglected to mention one thing you started seeing in Chapter 3: those unpkg URLs for the script tags in these HTML files. unpkg.com is a fast, global Content Delivery Network (CDN) for everything on npmjs.org. You can use it to quickly and easily load any file from any package using a URL like this: unpkg.com/:package@:version/:file, which can be very handy, especially early in development when you might just want to have a single HTML file and mess around in it.

Whither Props?

JSX lets us pass props into our components just as easily – maybe even easier – as we do with the direct React.createElement() calls. You saw it earlier when the color of the MaterialButton was set. But what about when the value of a prop isn't static like that? That's where prop expressions come into play. Here's an example of passing a prop, in this case, a variable color to the MaterialButton component from earlier:

```
const buttonColor = "red";
const button = <MaterialButton color={buttonColor}
  onClick="alert('clicked');">
  Click Me
</MaterialButton>;
```

Now, the `buttonColor` variable's value will be passed as the value of the `color` prop when the `MaterialButton` component is created.

Any valid JavaScript expression can be contained within the braces, so we could do

```
color={buttonColor + "Alt"}
```

You can also pass string literals using expressions. So, `color="red"` is equivalent to `color={"red"}`. There's no real reason to prefer one over the other except perhaps if you want to use expression notation consistently. React and JSX don't really care either way though.

Note too that props in JSX syntax will default to true if you pass nothing for their value. So, `<MaterialButton enabled />` is equivalent to `<MaterialButton enabled={true} />`.

You can also use the spread operator for a prop value when you want to pass all the properties of an existing object as props to a component. For example:

```
<MaterialButton color={"red"} enabled={true} />
```

You could write this differently using the spread operator:

```
const props = { color : "red", enabled : true };
<MaterialButton {...props} />
```

This can be handy if you have several prop values that need to be dynamic, and you need to "calculate" the values elsewhere in your code before the component is constructed.

Default Props

Recall from earlier, in the last chapter, actually, I said that parent components always pass props down to their children, which then use them however they wish (or not at all – entirely their choice!). This works great in most cases, but what happens if a component doesn't pass a particular prop down to the child? There's nothing that enforces a parent passing *all* props down to its children, so it's something that can happen.

One simple thing you can do is, in the child component, something like this:

```
class Bookmark extends React.Component {
  constructor(props) {
    super(props);
    console.log("Bookmark component created");
  }
  title = this.props.title;
  titleStyle = { color : "red" }
  render() {
    return (
      <li>
        <h2 style={this.titleStyle}>{this.title}</h2>
        <a href={this.props.href}>
          {this.props.description || "Unknown" }
        </a>
        <button onClick={() => {
          this.title = this.title + "-CHANGED";
          this.setState({});
        }}>
        Click me
        </button>
      </li>
    );
  }
}
```

Take a look at the <a> element there. Notice the || in the expression that defines the text of the element? If the parent doesn't pass down a description in the props, then using the or operator like this will result in "Unknown" being the text of the <a>.

While that will work, sprinkling or's all over the place doesn't exactly make for clean code, and React recognizes this. So, instead, you can use the defaultProps property. This is a special property that React makes available on the component class, and it is where you can define default values for props:

```
class Bookmark extends React.Component {
  constructor(props) {
    super(props);
    console.log("Bookmark component created");
  }
  static defaultProps = { description : "Unknown" };
  title = this.props.title;
  titleStyle = { color : "red" }
  render() {
    return (
      <li>
        <h2 style={this.titleStyle}>{this.title}</h2>
        <a href={this.props.href}>{this.props.description}</a>
        <button onClick={() => {
          this.title = this.title + "-CHANGED";
          this.setState({});
        }}>
        Click me
        </button>
      </li>
    );
  }
}
```

Here, we go back to just referencing this.props.description in the <a> definition
like before, but now the defaultProps definition right after the constructor provides the
"Unknown" value when the parent doesn't pass a description down. You can supply
default values for all props or any subset you want to in this way.

It's a handy facility that makes for much cleaner code, so it's usually a good idea to
define defaultProps. Remember that if you don't do so and a prop isn't passed, its value
is going to be undefined. That might be okay in some usages, but not all (e.g., indeed, we
wouldn't want to show "undefined" for the text of that <a> element).

Typing Props

In the next two chapters, and for the remainder of this book, we're going to be writing our code not in JavaScript, as all the examples thus far have been written in, but in TypeScript. Not to jump ahead, but TypeScript adds the notion of data types to the normally typeless JavaScript (well, loosely typed to be really more accurate, but to a large extent, the distinction doesn't matter).

However, even if you wanted to stick with plain old JavaScript, having some notion of data types is usually a Very Good Thing. Imagine if you had a prop on a component that expects a number, which maybe it does some calculations with, and then displays the output. What happens if you mistakenly pass a string instead? Well, React and JavaScript underneath it are going to do their best to work with what you gave them. In some cases, you might get a valid result displayed. In others, though, the type coercion that will happen under the covers might result in a gibberish answer (that's the classic JavaScript interview question of what the difference between 7+7 and 7+"7" is, what they each result in – and if you don't know what each of those will produce, please, go try it now and then go read up on type coercion because it's something you definitely need to know about generally when doing JavaScript development).

To avoid that, React introduces something called `propTypes`. This is like `defaultProps` in that it's another property of a component class, but this time it's one used to tell React what the types of your props are. If you then pass an incorrect type at runtime, React will output a helpful message to the JavaScript console.

To use it, you must do two things. First, add `propTypes` to the component class:

```
function start() {
  class Bookmark extends React.Component {
    constructor(props) {
      super(props);
      console.log("Bookmark component created");
    }
    static propTypes = { description : PropTypes.number };
    title = this.props.title;
    titleStyle = { color : "red" }
    render() {
      return (
        <li>
```

```
        <h2 style={this.titleStyle}>{this.title}</h2>
        <a href={this.props.href}>
          {this.props.description}
        </a>
        <button onClick={() => {
          this.title = this.title + "-CHANGED";
          this.setState({});
        }}>
        Click me
        </button>
      </li>
    );
  }
}
ReactDOM.render(
  <div>
    <h1>Bookmarks</h1>
    <ul>
      <Bookmark title={"Etherient"}
        href={"https://www.etherient.com"}
        description={"The home page of Etherient"}
      />
      <Bookmark title={"Frank's Site"}
        href={"https://www.zammetti.com"}
        description={"The web home of Frank W. Zammetti"}
      />
    </ul>
  </div>,
  document.getElementById("mainContainer")
);
}
```

Here, I'm doing something kind of silly just to prove the point: I'm defining the type of the description prop as a number. That doesn't make much sense in context, but it will demonstrate how this works well enough.

But, if you compile that and try to use it, you'll hit an error because `PropTypes` isn't known, and that value is what tells React what type the prop is. So, we need to import that. All you need to do is add a `<script>` tag to the `index.html` file:

```
<!DOCTYPE html>
<html>
  <head>
    <meta charset="UTF-8" />
    <title>Intro To React</title>
    <script crossorigin src="https://unpkg.com/react@18.2.0/umd/react.
    development.js"></script>
    <script crossorigin src="https://unpkg.com/react-dom@18.2.0/umd/react-
    dom.development.js"></script><script crossorigin src="https://unpkg.
    com/prop-types@15.8.1/prop-types.js"></script>    <script src="main.
    js"></script>
  </head>
  <body onLoad="start();">
    <div id="mainContainer"></div>
  </body>
</html>
```

`PropTypes` is supplied in a separate module, so that's what we need to import. Once both those things are done, and after you compile the JSX file and open the HTML page in your browser, you'll see the following error in the dev tools console:

```
react.development.js:1818 Warning: Failed prop type: Invalid prop
`description` of type `string` supplied to `Bookmark`, expected `number`.
in Bookmark
```

Perfect! React is aware of the type of the description prop and flags it when we pass a string rather than a number. This makes finding some otherwise tricky to ferret out bugs very easy, so it's generally good advice to always supply `propTypes` on your custom components, right alongside `defaultProps`.

There are about two dozen prop types available as of this writing, and you can find a list of them here: https://reactjs.org/docs/typechecking-with-proptypes.html. These types are actually functions and are called validators. As such, it's quite possible for you to add your own just by appending them on to the PropTypes class or, more usually, just passing a function in propTypes:

```
static propTypes = { description : descriptionValidator };
```

The descriptionValidator() function will be passed the collection of props, the name of the prop being validated, and the name of the component. If it then returns null, then React assumes everything is okay; otherwise, the function would return an Error object (another class provided by the PropTypes module) that describes the problem.

Note   One that is worth calling out is PropTypes.element.isRequired. This tells React that your component requires one and only one child component. This is common enough that I wanted to mention it specifically.

Component Lifecycle

The final topic I want to talk about concerning React is the component lifecycle. You've already seen one: the render() method. But, while render() is really the final thing we're trying to get to with a component, it's not the whole picture.

Every single React component goes through a series of distinct stages in a well-defined order, which is illustrated in Figure 4-1.

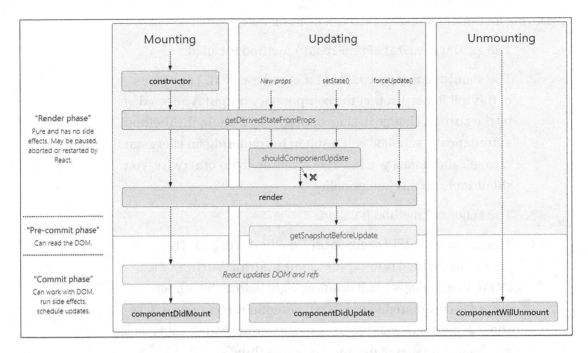

Figure 4-1. *The lifecycle events of a React component*

In sequence, during initial construction, the order will be as follows:

1. The component class's constructor is called. That should be
    pretty obvious: it's a JavaScript class after all, and if they define
    a constructor, then that always gets called first (and if they don't
    specify a constructor, then an automatically added one will be
    called).

2. The `getDerivedStateFromProps()` method is called. This is
    responsible for returning an object to update the state or null
    if there is nothing to update. This is called during the initial
    construction of the component, called "mounting," because it's
    when the component is constructed, of course, but is also when
    it is added, or "mounted," to the virtual DOM, as well as during
    subsequent updates.

3. The `render()` method is called. You already know about this one!

4. The `componentDidMount()` method is called immediately after the
    component is inserted into the virtual DOM. This is where you
    can do initialization that required actual DOM nodes.

91

During an update, the sequence will be as follows:

1. The getDerivedStateFromProps() method is called.

2. The shouldComponentUpdate() method is called. The results
    of this tell React whether the component's output is affected
    by the current change in state or props. By default, the method
    automatically supplied will result in re-rendering on every state
    change, and unless you have good reason to do otherwise, you
    should rely on this functionality.

3. The render() method is called.

4. The getSnapshotBeforeUpdate() method is called. The
    job of this method is to capture some information from the
    DOM, like perhaps scroll position, right before the render
    output is committed to the DOM, potentially changing it. Like
    shouldComponentUpdate(), most of the time, you should just let
    the default version of this method do its thing.

5. Finally, the componentDidUpdate() method is called. Things like
    network requests for data you need to display are often done here.
    But you can ignore this if you don't need it.

You can override any of these or none of them (except for render(), of course, which
you *have* to override) as your needs dictate.

Note   There are a small handful of other available methods, but they are now
considered legacy, and developers are discouraged from using them, so I'm not
describing them here. I wanted to mention this though in case you see code using
them, you will be aware that it's probably valid code, but no longer code you should
follow, and it's also code that, it's a good bet, will be broken by a future React
update when support for those lifecycle events are removed from React entirely.

Summary

In this chapter, you got a look at a few more React concepts, including JSX, the component lifecycle, PropTypes, and default props. Going along with JSX, you got a brief introduction to Babel. This places all the necessary tools for working with React in your toolbox, preparing you for the application code to come.

But there's one more preparatory topic to look at before the application train leaves the station, and that's where we migrate from JavaScript to TypeScript.

CHAPTER 5

Building a Strong Foundation: TypeScript

In the previous four chapters, where we looked at Node and React, in both of those, you saw code written in JavaScript. That makes total sense given that Node uses Google's V8 JavaScript engine to execute code, and React is (most usually at least) used to create browser-based applications, and browsers speak JavaScript (along with HTML and CSS of course).

But there is, at least arguably, a better option, one that overcomes many of the perceived shortcomings of JavaScript and makes for more robust code and easy maintenance of JavaScript-based applications. That option is called TypeScript, and in this chapter and the next, I'll introduce to you the core concepts associated with what has become one of the hottest languages around.

As with Node and React, this chapter and the next are not an exhaustive discussion of the topic. You won't learn every last nook and cranny TypeScript has to offer. But these chapters will build the foundation. Further concepts will be introduced in context in the coming chapters as necessary.

What Is TypeScript?

Somewhere around October of 2010, Microsoft started to realize that JavaScript, while becoming very popular, had several shortcomings that frequently lead to more error-prone code written by developers. In the eyes of some people, both inside and outside of Microsoft, JavaScript wasn't a mature enough language for what was being built with it.

So, the company began an internal project to address what they, and many others, saw as problems with JavaScript. In October of 2010, they made public that project and called it TypeScript.

© Frank Zammetti 2022
F. Zammetti, *Modern Full-Stack Development*, https://doi.org/10.1007/978-1-4842-8811-5_5

TypeScript can be thought of as a wrapper, of sorts, around JavaScript, or an extension to it. A key point to remember is that all valid JavaScript code is *also* valid TypeScript code. TypeScript, however, adds things on top of JavaScript, the key thing being data types, as the name clearly implies. This is a significant benefit because it allows IDEs and other developer tools to provide IntelliSense to the developer, that is, hints about what types are allowed in what situations. With JavaScript and its loosely typed nature, mistakes are easy to make, for example, passing a string where a numeric value is expected. With TypeScript, those sorts of errors are spotted quickly and easily by various tooling, and the key thing to remember is that these problems are caught at compile time, not at runtime as they are with JavaScript – and I dropped a pretty big spoiler there: unlike with JavaScript that just gets executed directly, there *is* a compilation step when dealing with TypeScript.

Over the next seven years, Microsoft evolved the language, adding additional features to make TypeScript more robust. Fast-forward to today and TypeScript (version 4.7.4 at the time of this writing) is one of the most popular languages for building (primarily) web-facing applications.

As I mentioned earlier, one key element that makes TypeScript different from JavaScript, however, is that you can't run TypeScript code in a browser or Node, not natively at least. Neither browsers nor Node understands TypeScript; they only understand JavaScript. So, when working with TypeScript, there is a pre-execution step: you must compile TypeScript. One can imagine a day when, perhaps, browsers and Node will speak TypeScript natively, and no compilation will be necessary, but whether that day comes, it is not this day! So, for now, TypeScript must be compiled, or *transpiled*, as it is frequently termed, into JavaScript for execution.

When TypeScript is compiled to JavaScript, all the TypeScript-y bits are stripped out, leaving just plain old JavaScript. Data types, for example, are purely a development-time construct. Once compilation occurs, they are gone. But, because they were there during development, the compiler will flag type-related errors at that time, rather than having them be discovered at runtime, which is the case with JavaScript generally.

In addition to types, another big advantage of TypeScript is that it supports more modern JavaScript language features but can compile them down to older versions of JavaScript. This means that you can use newer features, such as arrow functions and async/await, even in browsers that don't natively support them, because the compiler produces code that implements them for you in the older JavaScript dialect that the browser understands. In the last chapter, we talked about Babel, and in a real sense, the

TypeScript compiler (which we're going to discuss very soon) does the same thing Babel does in this regard (TypeScript can and does add features to the language as well, even some that will never appear in JavaScript itself).

Jumping into the Deep End

Now that you have a general idea of what TypeScript is, let's get right down to business and see it in action! To do this, we're going to first take advantage of a facility that you'll find on TypeScript's home page at typescriptlang.org called "the playground." You'll find it at typescriptlang.org/play, and on that playground, you can enter arbitrarily the following TypeScript code provided and execute it. It's a great way to experiment with the language and a handy way for me as an author to give you your first look at TypeScript before we need to install any tooling for it!

In Figure 5-1, you can see what it should look like after you enter the example code.

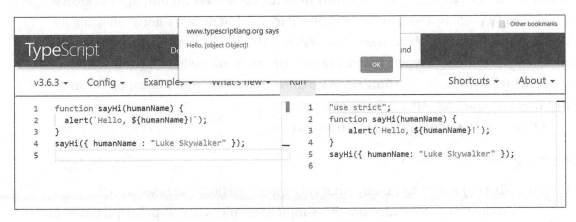

Figure 5-1. *TypeScript in action, on the playground!*

In this figure, I've executed the code, which you can see on the left. Now, there's a couple of things to notice. First, see the red squiggly line underneath the humanName argument? If you hover over that, it will tell you that humanName implicitly has an any type. We'll get to what this means shortly, but for now it's enough to realize that the TypeScript playground is examining your code in real time and is pointing out that you haven't specified a type for the argument (which may or may not be an error, which is why you can execute this code despite that being flagged). The critical point is that it does this before you run the code. That's the point of types and TypeScript itself!

However, perhaps the bigger problem related to types is that you'll notice that the `alert()` message doesn't do what we expect, at least not based on what you'd logically conclude the point of the `sayHi()` function is. It's intended to greet someone by name, but in this case, we're passing an object to it. JavaScript doesn't care of course, there's nothing that tells it that `humanName` really should be a string that contains a person's name, so it just produces an `alert()` message with the object passed in generically, which in this case doesn't give us anything particularly useful and definitely not what we actually want it to produce.

With TypeScript, though, we can fix this! To do so, we add what's called a *type annotation* to the argument by changing the `sayHi()` function's definition to this:

```
function sayHi(humanName: string) {
```

The value after the colon is the type annotation, and this is the secret sauce you'll see time and again in TypeScript code. With that change made, rerunning the example will result in the red squiggly going away from the `humanName` argument – because we're now telling TypeScript what type we expect it to be – but now, we get a red squiggly underneath the entire object passed to `sayHi()`. If you hover over it, you will see the message "Argument of type '{ humanName: string }' is not assignable to parameter of type 'string.'" TypeScript is telling us, in no uncertain terms, that we can't pass an object to a function that expects a string. Cool, right?

Of course, if we change the call to `sayHi()` to

```
sayHi("Luke Skywalker");
```

then the `alert()` shows us exactly what we expect: "Hello, Luke Skywalker!"

A few more things to note about this simple example is that TypeScript, based on the error message from the object, seems to have known that the value of the `humanName` property of the object passed to `sayHi()` was a string even though we didn't explicitly tell it. This implicit typing is called *type inference*, and TypeScript does it any time you declare and initialize a variable in one go (which, obviously, works for object properties like here too). If you declare a variable without initializing it, though, or when a function argument doesn't specify a type, then TypeScript assumes a specialized type: any. This effectively mimics how JavaScript works in that the variable or argument can take a value of any type at any time.

If you're thinking that using TypeScript with nothing but type any references would be kind of silly, then you would be right! As a rule, in TypeScript, you should always declare your types. In fact, even when declaring and initializing in one statement, it's still probably a good idea to declare the type. There may be situations where any makes sense, but you should explicitly decide that if so (and yes, you can declare a variable of argument as being of type any expressly).

Beyond the Playground

Now, the playground is a useful thing to have available, but clearly you aren't going to be using it to develop your real applications. Instead, you'll need to be able to compile and execute TypeScript code on your own machine, and that's where your new best friend, tsc – the TypeScript compiler – comes in!

Installing it is simple, using our friend NPM:

```
npm install typescript
```

As usual, it's your choice whether you want to install it locally or globally (remember that adding the -g argument installs an NPM package globally). Either way, this installs several TypeScript-related things, but the key thing that we care about here is tsc, the compiler, which is your one-stop shop for working with TypeScript code. It can act as a task runner and a bundler and can take the place of Babel, as previously mentioned.

Using it is simplicity itself: all you need to do is execute tsc and tell it what file to compile by doing

```
tsc <filename>
```

Note that you have to use npx to execute it instead:

```
npx tsc <filename>
```

Let's go ahead and take it for a spin! Drop to a command line and navigate to an empty directory. Install TypeScript and then create a new file named index.html with the following contents:

```
<html>
  <head></head>
 <body>
   <script src="app.js"></script>
 </body>
</html>
```

Now, create a file named `app.ts` and in it put the code we just executed on the playground.

Once that's done, compile it using `tsc` with this command (or the npx equivalent):

```
tsc app.ts
```

After that, load up `index.html` in your favorite browser, and you should see the `alert()` message, just like on the playground.

If you look in the directory, you'll see that an `app.js` file was created. That's your compiled code, which is then loaded by `index.html` (notice that we do not load `app.ts` in `index.html` because the browser wouldn't know what to do with it).

Looking at `app.js`, you can see what tsc has produced from your code:

```
function sayHi(humanName) {
    alert("Hello, " + humanName + "!");
}
sayHi("Luke Skywalker");
```

In this simple example, the only real difference is that the type information for `humanName` was stripped off, which confirms what I said earlier: types are only for development time, not runtime.

Configuring TypeScript Compilation

Now that you've seen how to install and use `tsc`, let's talk a little bit more about it and about TypeScript projects.

Usually, your projects will be a bit more complex than just a single file to compile. Typically, you'll have multiple `.ts` files to compile. You could pass all the names on the command line to `tsc`, but that will get burdensome in a hurry. Instead, you can create a file named `tsconfig.json` that will allow you to define your project a little bit and configure how `tsc` works.

You don't need to write this file by hand, though! The `tsc` tool comes with a handy option, `-init`, that will create a basic `tsconfig.json` file for you. Go ahead and, in the same directory as the last section, run

```
tsc -init
```

You'll find a `tsconfig.json` file has been created. The presence of that file effectively makes this directory the root of a TypeScript project as far as `tsc` goes.

One of the first benefits this provides is that now, you can execute tsc without any arguments, and it will dutifully compile any `.ts` files in the current directory, as well as subdirectories. That's already worth the effort, right?

The `tsconfig.json` file isn't required, as you saw earlier, and it has no required elements in it either. However, it does provide a large number of options to configure your project. I won't be going over all of them here, but you can see all available options online at `typescriptlang.org/docs/handbook/tsconfig-json.html`.

I will, however, introduce options as needed throughout the remainder of these chapters, but for the most part, default options will be used. In fact, when you run that `init` comment, only the following options are enabled (with their default value shown in parentheses):

- **target (es2016)** – Specifies the ECMAScript (JavaScript) target version that the generated JavaScript will adhere to: es3, es5, es2015, es2016, es2017, es2018, es2019, or esnext.

- **module (commonjs)** – Specifies the module loader system that will be used (modules and loaders will be discussed in the next chapter): none, commonjs, amd, system, umd, es2015, or esnext.

- **strict (true)** – Enables all strict type-checking options.

- **esModuleInterop (true)** – Enables generation of interoperability code to allow for interoperability between CommonJS and ES modules via the creation of namespace objects for all imports.

- **forceConsistentCasingInFileNames** – TypeScript follows the case sensitivity rules of the file system it's running on. This can be problematic if some developers are working in a case-sensitive file system and others aren't. If a file attempts to import fileManager.ts by specifying ./FileManager.ts, the file will be found in a case-insensitive file system, but not on a case-sensitive file system. When this option is set, TypeScript will issue an error if a program tries to include a file by a casing different from the casing on disk.

- **skipLibCheck** – Skip type checking of declaration files. This can save time during compilation at the expense of type-system accuracy. For example, two libraries could define two copies of the same type in an inconsistent way. Rather than doing a full check of all d.ts files (which are files that define the types of libraries you might use in your own code), TypeScript will type-check the code you specifically refer to in your app's source code. A common case where you might think to use skipLibCheck is when there are two copies of a library's types in your node_modules. In these cases, you should consider using a feature like yarn's resolutions to ensure there is only one copy of that dependency in your tree or investigate how to ensure there is only one copy by understanding the dependency resolution to fix the issue without additional tooling. Another possibility is when you are migrating between TypeScript releases and the changes cause breakages in node_modules and the JS standard libraries which you do not want to deal with during the TypeScript update.

As of this writing, these are the only options that are enabled by default, everything else is commented out (though helpfully *is* actually present, so you don't have to go off looking everything up, most of it is right there for you if you need it). As I mentioned, by default, `tsc` will compile all files in the current directory and subdirectories (if necessary) if a `tsconfig.json` file is present. If you know you need it to skip specific files though, you can add the exclude element and then list the files not to compile. You can also explicitly include things with the files element. These are probably two of the most commonly used additional options, hence why I'm mentioning them here.

The Nitty-Gritty: Types

Now, let's get to the main event in TypeScript and discuss the various types that it supports. As previously mentioned, types are declared with the `:<type>` syntax. This can be in a function declaration to type the arguments:

```
function sayHi(humanName: string) {
```

You can also declare the type a function returns:

```
function concatStrings(str1: string, str2: string): string { }
```

It can also be used in a variable declaration of course:

```
let a: string = "Hello";
```

In all cases, it's just a colon, followed by one of the supported types, which we'll look at now.

String

You've already seen the string type a few times, and it's no different from the normal string in JavaScript:

```
const bestShowEver = "Babylon 5";
```

As mentioned earlier, TypeScript automatically infers the type of bestShowEver as string, which means this will result in a compiler error:

```
bestShowEver = 42;
```

But also, as I said before, it's better to (nearly) always declare the type:

```
const bestShowEver: string = "Babylon 5";
```

Now there are no games to be played: bestShowEver is a string, and that's the end of it!

Number

TypeScript offers a single number type. There are no integer vs. floating-point values in TypeScript; they're all simply numbers. So you can do

```
const a: number = 42;
```

And you can also do

```
const b: number = 3.14;
```

And, of course, you'll get an error if you try to do either of these:

```
a = "42";
b = "3.14";
```

As with JavaScript, TypeScript allows for hexadecimal and octal literals, though the way you specify octal is different than JavaScript:

```
const a: number = 0xf00d;
const b: number = 0o744; // Zero followed by lower-case o
```

Boolean

The TypeScript boolean type is as simple as it gets; it has a value of true or false and nothing else:

```
const isThisTheBestBookEver: boolean = true;
```

Note that even though 0 and 1 are oftentimes interchangeable for boolean values and will be evaluated as boolean values in logic statements in at least some cases, TypeScript does not allow it:

```
const isThisTheBestBookEver: boolean = 1; // Compiler error
```

This extra rigidity helps avoid some tricky bugs, so let's all say a hearty "thank you" to TypeScript for saving us from ourselves!

Any

The any type, which I mentioned earlier, is the type that a variable, argument, or function return will have if you don't specify a type explicitly:

```
let accountBalance;
accountBalance = 15000;
accountBalance = "15000";
```

Either of those assignments will be okay with tsc because TypeScript will infer type any for the variable.

Of course, you can explicitly declare it to be any as well:

```
let food: any = "pizza";
food = 123; // This is now okay
```

Even if you're using the any type (which you should consider carefully if you think you need to, because often you *don't* really want to use it!), it's still probably a good idea to always define it, so that anyone reading your code knows you intended it to be any.

Arrays

TypeScript supports arrays, of course; what good language doesn't? Just like with variables, if you don't specify a type, the type will be inferred from the initialization values:

```
const pets = [ "Belle", "Bubbles" ];
```

If you initialized an empty array, or had no initialization at all, then type any will be inferred, just like with variables.

This pets array becomes an array of strings, so you can't later do

```
pets = [ 42 ];
```

TypeScript will complain about that because the pets array can only hold strings now.

You can also explicitly type an array with just subtly different syntax than for scalar variables:

```
const pets: string[] = [ "Belle", "Bubbles" ];
```

You still use the :<type> syntax, but the array [] notation must be appended after the type.

Now, what if you have an array where you really do want to allow for strings and numbers and perhaps other types? Well, this is a case where that any type may well be exactly what you want to use:

```
const pets: any[] = [ "Belle", 42 ];
```

But, again, consider this carefully! Is that *really* what you want to do, or might it be better to have two separate arrays? Only you can decide; I'm just suggesting that think it through either way.

Tuples

A tuple is just an array with a specific number of elements of specific types. In plain JavaScript, that might look like

```
const authors = [ "Frank", 46 ];
```

But, critically, there is no enforcement of anything in JavaScript. You could shove a number as the first element and even have a third element in the array. In TypeScript though, that's all enforced, and the way it's declared is with slightly different syntax:

```
const authors: [ string, number ] = [ "Frank", 46 ];
```

Here, we're saying that the authors array must have two elements, and the first must be a string, and the second must be a number. As a result, this will not compile:

```
const authors: [ string, number ] = [ 46, "Frank" ];
```

The types of the elements are wrong here (they're reversed). When you then access an element, say authors[1], the correct type will be returned, a string in that case. Since it's a string, you could call substr() on it, for example, but trying to do the same on the element returned by authors[0] would result in an error since a number does not have that method available. Note too that accessing an element outside the set of known indices results in an error, so authors[2] will result in an error.

Enums

While JavaScript offers a string, a boolean, and a number type (despite it being a loosely typed language, the types do still technically exist), enums are something that JavaScript does not natively offer; they are purely a TypeScript construct. Enums serve to make specific sequences of numbers more human-readable and expressive. Take, for example, this plain JavaScript code:

```
const Pizza = 0;
const FriedChicken = 1;
const IceCream = 2;
```

It's nice that we don't need to remember that a value of 1 means fried chicken in our, I guess, horribly unhealthy food truck sales system – we can use the variable FriedChicken anywhere we need it – but it's still kind of ugly that way to a lot of developers. With enums in TypeScript, which you declare with the new enum keyword, you can do it more elegantly:

```
enum Food { Pizza, FriedChicken, IceCream };
let myFavoriteFood: Food.FriedChicken;
alert(myFavoriteFood);
```

That `alert()` call will show one because TypeScript begins assigning numbers to the named elements in the Food enum starting from zero. That's the value Pizza gets. It then increments by one for each subsequent value, so FriedChicken gets assigned one, and IceCream gets assigned two (and so on, if we added more foods).

You can assign specific values if you wish too, either from the first element onward or anywhere in between. For example:

```
enum Food { Pizza, FriedChicken = 500, IceCream };
let myFavoriteFood: Food.FriedChicken;
alert(myFavoriteFood);
```

Now, the value shown will be 500. But Food.Pizza would still have a value of zero since we didn't assign it a specific value.

Now, here's a good mystery for you: without trying it on the playground, what value will IceCream have? Does it have two, maybe, since TypeScript keeps numbering from where it left off? Or does it perhaps restart numbering, so assigns it zero?

No, it gets a value of 501. Anywhere you explicitly define a value, TypeScript will keep numbering subsequent items, by one, from that value on.

Function

TypeScript lets you declare a function type. This is a way of saying that a variable must reference a function with a particular signature. For example:

```
let myMathFunction: (num1: number, num2: number) => string;
```

Now, myMathFunction can only be assigned a value that is a function with two number arguments, and that returns a string. So, this is okay:

```
function add(n1: number, n2: number): string {
  return "" + n1 + n2;
}
myMathFunction = add;
```

But this is not:

```
function multiply(a: number, b: number): number {
  return a * b;
}
myMathFunction = multiply;
```

Even though the type being returned by multiply() seems to be correct – multiplying two numbers will yield a number – the contract that was defined for the myMathFunction variable says any function it references must return a string, whether that makes sense or not. Note that argument names don't matter, only types do.

Object

Earlier, you saw an error message that seemed to indicate that TypeScript was performing type inference on object properties. As it happens, that's precisely what it does:

```
let person = {
  firstName : "John", lastName : "Sheridan", age : 52
};
```

Here, TypeScript infers the type of the object, including its properties, and this is termed an *object type*. That means that from this point on, person may only reference an object with three properties, firstName, lastName, and age, and they must have the types string, string, and number, respectively. Even trying to assign person = { } later will result in an error because TypeScript will see that as the property types not matching.

Similarly, trying to do person = { a :"John", b : "Sheridan", age : 52 } will be an error because, in contrast to function types, with object types the property names *do* matter (it's only logical: object properties can be in any order, so there's no way for TypeScript to reliably determine the types *except* by name).

Of course, you can also be more explicit if you wish:

```
let person: {
  firstName: string, lastName: string, age: number
} = {
  firstName : "John", lastName : "Sheridan", age : 52
};
```

Note that the properties and values within the object definition do *not* have types defined. That would be redundant as they are already defined in the object type definition.

Null, Void, Undefined, and Never

Three other types are, conceptually, related to one another, so I've grouped them together here. Let's start with null:

```
let favoriteCar = "Camaro";
favoriteCar = null;
```

Yes, TypeScript has a null type that is different from other "null-like" types. Interestingly, null is considered subtypes of all other types, which means you can assign them to anything:

```
let myFavoriteNumber: number = null;
let myFavoriteString: string = null;
```

That is okay, as would a null assignment to a variable of any other type.

In a similar vein as null is undefined:

```
let favoriteCar;
```

Here, `favoriteCar` will have a value of `undefined`, which is different than `null` (a comparison of a variable with a value of `null` and another with a value of `undefined` will not evaluate as equal). But, like `null`, `undefined` is taken to be a subtype of every other type, so similarly you can do a literal assignment with it:

```
let favoriteCar = undefined;
```

But what if you do want to ensure a variable is never `null`? In that case, `tsconfig.json` is your friend! Under the `compilerOptions` section, add a key `strictNullChecks` and give it a value of `true`. With that done, the compiler will complain if you assign `null` or `undefined` to any variable except if it is declared as type any.

Note   If you want to have your mind blown, you could do `let myFavoriteNumber: null = null;`. This would mean you can only assign the value null to `myFavoriteNumber`. Similarly, `let myFavoriteString: undefined = undefined;` will only be allowed to have `undefined` assigned to it. It's probably not useful in any way, but it's a curious side effect of these two types. Finally, doing `let favoriteCar = null;` will result in `favoriteCar` having an inferred type of `null`, not any like you might expect, so effectively this variable can only ever be assigned a value of `null`!

The `void` type is conceptually like the opposite of any: it's like having no type at all! The `void` type is typically only seen as the return type of a function, to indicate the function returns no value. While you declare a variable as type `void`, you can only ever assign a value of `null` to it (and then, only if `strictNullChecks` isn't enabled). Note that TypeScript will figure out the return type by default, so most of the time, it isn't necessary to specify `void`, though as long as you know that's correct, then it's probably better to be explicit.

Finally, never represents the type of values that never occur. For instance, never is the return type for a function expression or an arrow function expression that always throws an exception or one that never returns. Variables also acquire the type never when narrowed by any type guards that can never be true. The never type is a subtype of, and assignable to, every type; however, no type is a subtype of, or assignable to, never (except never itself). Even any isn't assignable to never. For example:

```
function error(message: string): never {
  throw new Error(message);
}

function infiniteLoop(): never {
  while (true) {}
}
function fail() {
  return error("Something failed");
}
```

All three of these functions have a return type of never (for that last one, it's inferred). Never doesn't get used all that often, but it's worth being aware of.

Custom Type Aliases

Let's say you want to create an object type to represent a person. You saw that earlier:

```
let person = {
  firstName : "John", lastName : "Sheridan", age : 52
};
```

That's all well and good, but what happens when you need to create two people? In that situation, you're going to write something like this:

```
let person1 = {
  firstName : "John", lastName : "Sheridan", age : 52
};
let person2 = {
  firstName : "Michael", lastName : "Garibaldi", age : 53
};
```

As you can imagine, that's not a great way to do things. As a rule, developers like to avoid duplicate code like that. Instead, TypeScript offers custom type aliases, which lets you provide a custom name for a type. To do so, you use the new type keyword, like so:

```
type PersonType = {
  firstName: string, lastName: string, age: number
};
```

From then on, you can use it like any other type:

```
let person1: PersonType = {
  firstName : "John", lastName : "Sheridan", age : 52
};
let person2: PersonType = {
  firstName : "Michael", lastName : "Garibaldi", age : 53 };
```

You can choose any name you like; it doesn't have to have type in it as it does here. That way, if you want to change the type definition, you can do it in just one place.

You can even alias native types if you want:

```
type MyAwesomeString = string;
let str: MyAwesomeString = "test";
```

There probably isn't a whole lot of reason to do that, but you can (some people use it as a form of documentation in effect, but I personally would counsel against doing so).

Union Types

Sometimes, you'll have a situation where you want a variable to be able to hold one of several different types, or you want an argument to accept one of various kinds, but you don't want to use any. In that case, *union types* are the answer.

Take this code, for example:

```
let myAge: any;
myAge = 46;
myAge = "46";
```

It might be okay that myAge can store a number or a string because maybe the rest of your code can handle either. Maybe you've got some code like this:

```
if (typeof myAge == "string") {
  alert(parseInt(myAge) * 2);
} else if (typeof myVar == "number") {
  alert(myAge * 2);
}
```

But what if you tried to do this?

```
myAge = true;
```

Unfortunately, that will be allowed because myAge is of type any, and being able to assign a boolean to it would be bad since our code doesn't handle that (plus, for a variable that, presumably, stores a person's age, a boolean doesn't make sense).

So, instead, we can use a union type, which is denoted with the pipe character:

```
let myAge: number | string;
myAge = 46;
myAge = "46";
myAge = true;
```

You can read that as saying that myAge can be of type number or type string. Therefore, the first two assignment statements will be okay, but the third, trying to assign a boolean, will result in a compiler error.

TypeScript == ES6 Features for "Free"!

Recall that when you compile a TypeScript file with tsc, it's really doing a transpilation. It's "compiling" from TypeScript to JavaScript. Earlier, I said that tsc does much the same thing as Babel does, and that's true in this regard. The implication of this is that TypeScript supports most ES6 features. It doesn't support all of them, though, so it's good to know which you should avoid. Fortunately, there is a handy chart you can use here: kangax.github.io/compat-table/es6.

Let's not be negative though, let's talk about some of the features you *can* use! Note that the assumption is that you already have some JavaScript knowledge, so I'm not going to cover every last thing in intricate detail, but certainly, these are probably the most important things that you should be aware of.

The let and const Keywords

First, as all the example code I've shown so far do, you can freely use the let and const keywords (let for variables you want to be able to change the value of later, const for those you don't). Yes, you can still use the var keyword too, but it's suggested you don't since both let and const have block scope rather than var's global scope, which helps avoid a lot of insidious bugs.

Block Scope

Speaking of block scope, that's another important one! In JavaScript, variables for a long time could only be declared with `var`. Such variables have function scope (or global scope when declared outside of any function). That means that you can do some "weird" things like this:

```
function test() {
    if (true) {
      var greeting = "hello";
    }
    alert(greeting);
}
test();
```

Most people see it as a bit weird that you can `alert(greeting)` there and have it work despite `greeting` being declared inside the `if` block. Well, with `let`, that problem is solved! That same code, by just changing `var` to `let`, results in greeting only being available inside the block it's declared in, the `if` statement in this case. If you enter that on the TypeScript playground, it will even flag it as an error. This helps avoid some interesting problems that can crop up when using var. The same is true for `const`, but with that you get the addition of not being able to change the variable's value later. As a general rule, you should use `const` whenever possible, or `let` when it's not, and avoid `var` unless you have a specific reason to use it.

Arrow Functions

With all the examples shown so far, I've used the standard function definition format that uses the `function` keyword. If, like the Dude from *The Big Lebowski*, you're into the whole brevity thing though, you can use arrow functions instead:

```
const test = (name) => {
  alert(`Hello, ${name}`);
}
test("Jack");
```

Arrow functions allow you to skip typing the `function` keyword all the time. They can be even shorter if the function returns a value:

```
const addNums = (a, b) => a + b;
alert(addNums(2, 3));
```

Here, we don't need to type the `function` keyword, and we don't even need to type the `return` keyword!

But we're talking about TypeScript, and yet there are no types here; this is just plain JavaScript. Not to worry, you can type things as well with arrow functions:

```
const addNums = (a: number, b: number): number => a + b;
alert(addNums(2, 3));
```

But brevity isn't the only benefit of arrow functions and maybe not even the biggest. That distinction probably goes to how the keyword `this` is handled. In plain JavaScript, what `this` points to can vary depending on how functions are called. With arrow functions, though, lexical scope is used, which means that whatever contains the function is what `this` will point to at execution time. If the function is in global scope, then this will point to the window object (assuming we're executing in a browser). If the function is inside an object, then `this` will point to that object. It's simple and consistent, and TypeScript makes it available to you!

Template Literals

Something worth noting in that last example is another ES6 feature that you can use in TypeScript: template literals. The backtick ` ` ` character denotes a template literal string, and within it you can insert any valid JavaScript (or TypeScript) expression by wrapping it in ${}. Note that I said expression there because while you can insert variables as shown, you can do arbitrarily complex things:

```
alert(`Hello, ${name.toUpperCase().substr(2)}`);
```

Another great thing about template literals is that they can span multiple lines of source code:

```
alert(`Hello,
  your name is
  ${name}
`);
```

Try that with a plain old string, and you'll face syntax errors, but with template literals, it works just fine.

Default Parameters

With TypeScript, you also can use default parameter values. That means that you can do this:

```
const multNums = (a: number, b: number = 10): number => a * b;
alert(multNums(3));
```

Here, we're saying that if the second number isn't supplied when multNums() is called, then it should have the default value 10. Hence, we get 30 in the alert() when this is executed. This is a simple thing that winds up saving you a lot of time and extra code, so it's truly nice to have in TypeScript too.

Spread and Rest (and As an Added Bonus: Optional Arguments)

The spread operator, which is three periods together, allows an iterable item, things like arrays or strings, to be expanded in places where zero or more arguments (in the case of function calls) or elements (for array literals) are expected or an object expression to be expanded in places where zero or more key-value pairs (for object literals) are expected. As an example:

```
const addNums = (a: number, b: number): number => a + b;
const nums: number[] = [ 5, 6 ];
alert(addNums(...nums));
```

The idea here is that we want to "spread" the values in the nums array into the arguments passed to addNums. This is in contrast to writing something like

```
alert(addNums(nums[0], nums[1]));
```

However, if you try that code, you'll find that there is an error on the ...nums spread argument passed to addNums() that says "Expected 2 arguments, but got 0 or more." The issue here is that because there's a variable number of possible arguments, TypeScript can't make a proper determination about what to do. Fortunately, there are at least two ways to fix this. First, you could do this:

```
const addNums = (a?: number, b?: number): number => a + b;
const nums: number[] = [ 5, 6 ];
alert(addNums(...nums));
```

See those question marks after the arguments of the addNums() function? Those are how you indicate optional arguments in TypeScript. Doing that tells TypeScript that the argument may or may not be present. In this case, we're saying that both can be optional. Now, that doesn't make much sense from the perspective of what the function does, but it does result in TypeScript not flagging this as an error. Note that when using optional arguments, they must always come last, meaning you can't do (a?: number, b: number) because a required argument can't come after an optional one.

However, note that if you pass in three or more values in the nums array, only the first two are added. The function works the same as it did before; the optional arguments only serve to get around the syntax error situation.

The other way you could fix this is by the use of the rest operator, which is simply the spread operator in a different place:

```
const addNums = (...a: number[]): number =>
  a.reduce((acc, val) => acc + val);
const nums: number[] = [ 5, 6 ];
alert(addNums(...nums));
```

Any argument prefixed with the ... operator means that zero or more arguments can be in that place. The result is that you'll get an array inside the function, named as the argument is named, that contains all passed in values in that place. As with optional arguments, rest arguments must come last. With this approach, given we have an array, we can use the reduce() method to add up all the numbers passed in. In contrast to the optional argument approach, this solution results in *all* the numbers being added, no matter how many are passed in, so it is functionally different, and, therefore, which way you go depends on what you're trying to do.

Destructuring

TypeScript supports two forms of destructuring: object and array. And while knowing that is great, knowing what destructuring is would be even better, no?

Consider the following object:

```
const person = {
  firstName : "Billy", lastName : "Joel", age : 70
};
```

Now, if you want to grab the values out of that object, you might do

```
const firstName = person.firstName;
const lastName = person.lastName;
const age = person.age;
```

That'll work, but it's an awful lot of typing! With destructuring, you can get at that data more concisely:

```
const { firstName, lastName, age } = person;
```

Now, you'll have three separate variables named firstName, lastName, and age, and their values will be taken from the person object, because TypeScript (really JavaScript) knows, by virtue of you using the curly braces around the variables, the names of the properties in the object you want to pull out and does so for you. Sweet!

Arrays can be destructured in the same way:

```
const vals = [ "Billy", "Joel", 70 ];
const [ firstName, lastName, age ] = vals;
alert(firstName);
alert(lastName);
alert(age);
```

Here, of course, it's based on order: TypeScript is essentially just doing firstName=vals[0] and lastName=vals[1] and age=vals[2] for you under the covers.

And, as a bonus, for your next job interview, if you get asked the question of how to swap the value of two variables without using a third, here's an answer using array destructuring in TypeScript:

```
let x = 1;
let y = 2;
[ x, y ] = [ y, x ];
alert(x); // 2
alert(y); // 1
```

Here, the array being destructured is created on the fly on the right-hand side of the equals, and then it's just array destructuring as described in the preceding text. "You're welcome" in advance for when you ace that interview and make a ton of money at your new job!

Classes

The final topic I want to cover in this chapter is classes. JavaScript, at least of the ECMAScript 5 and higher variety, supports classes, but TypeScript alters the syntax a bit and adds a fair bit of – wait for it – *class*! It really *classes* the place up is what I'm saying! (I know, I know, terrible dad joke!)

Properties

First, when it comes to properties, rather than having to declare them in a constructor, you can do them a little more elegantly. Instead of this

```
class Planet {
  constructor() {
    this.name = null;
    this.mass = null;
  }
}
```

you can instead do this:

```
class Planet {
  name: string;
  mass: number;
}
```

It may not be a huge difference, but it makes JavaScript look a lot more like other object-oriented languages syntactically.

As you would expect, you can declare your types for the properties like anywhere else in TypeScript as you see there, but now, you don't need to embed them in a constructor. You, of course, still can have a constructor, and that looks the same as in plain JavaScript, but your property declarations are external to the constructor now, if you supply one at all.

Naturally, if you want to set property values at construction time, then you can still do that in the constructor:

```
class Planet {
  name: string;
  mass: number;
  constructor(inName: string, inMass: number) {
    this.name = inName;
    this.mass = inMass;
  }
}
```

Member Visibility

TypeScript adds the notion of member visibility to classes. With plain JavaScript classes, all members are public, that is, available to all other code (there are some tricks you can play to simulate private members so that they are only available to the code of the class itself, but it's not something offered by the language intrinsically). As with plain JavaScript, TypeScript's default visibility is public, but now you can have both private and protected members:

```
class Planet {
  private name: string = "none";
  protected mass: number;
  constructor(inName: string, inMass: number) {
    this.name = inName;
    this.mass = inMass;
  }
```

```
public printName() {
  alert(this.name);
}
}
```

Here, the name property will only be accessible by code within this class. The mass property will be accessible by code within this class as well as by code in any class that extends this one. Putting public before the printName() method is optional since that's the default, but you definitely can do so if you want to be explicit. Note too that, as I've done for name, you can assign a value as part of the declaration if you wish.

Inheritance

When I described protected, I said that it allows the member to be accessible to code within the class and to code in classes that extend it. That provides for inheritance, which is another capability that TypeScript adds (or, more precisely, augments). Let's create a specific planet:

```
class Jupiter extends Planet {
  private colorBands: boolean = true;
  constructor() {
    super("Jupiter", 1234);
  }
}
```

Now we can do

```
let j: Jupiter = new Jupiter();
```

Now we've got an object of type Jupiter, which extends from the Planet class. A few things of note here. First, members can be added to the subclass, as with the colorBands property. Second, calling j.printName() works as expected, because printName() has public visibility. But, if you try to do alert(j.name), then you'll find that you get an error from TypeScript saying that "Property 'name' is private and only accessible within class 'Planet.'" The same is true if you try to alert(j.mass).

However, understand that while j.printName() will print Jupiter's name, if you try to put a method in the Jupiter class itself that accesses name, that won't work. Private members are not inherited, so while the code of the Planet class knows about name and can work with it, the code in the Jupiter class does not and so can't do anything with it (you could, of course, call methods in the base class from the child class to work with it though).

Another thing of note is that if a subclass has a constructor, as Jupiter does, then it must call the superclass's constructor via the super() reference.

An interesting point to understand is that you can override anything in the superclass in the child class, as you can in any good object-oriented language. You must be aware, though, that for properties, those defined in the body of the child class will override any value passed into the constructor. So, if you add protected mass: number = 5555; to the Jupiter class, then the value of its mass property will be 5555 no matter what you pass into the constructor.

With TypeScript, you can override members in the parent class as in most other object-oriented languages, and that works as you'd expect. However, TypeScript doesn't support method overloading in the way most people expect. For example, this won't work in the Planet class:

```
public calcSuperMass(): number {
  return this.mass * 2;
}
public calcSuperMass(): string {
  return "" + this.mass * 2;
}
```

The compiler will complain that you have a duplicate function implementation even though the return types are different. Even a different argument list isn't enough:

```
public calcSuperMass(): number {
  return this.mass * 2;
}
public calcSuperMass(a: number): string {
  return "" + this.mass * a;
}
```

That still won't be allowed for the same reason. Now, all hope is not lost, though: you can, in effect, achieve overloading by using optional parameters or default parameters. So, you could do either of the following:

```
public calcSuperMass(massMultiple?: number): number {
  if (massMultiple) {
    return this.mass * massMultiple;
  }
  return this.mass * 2;
}
// Or:
public calcSuperMass(massMultiple: number = 2): number {
  return this.mass * massMultiple;
}
```

In the first approach, since `massMultiple` is marked optional, you can effectively have `calcSuperMass()` work whether you pass in an argument or not, at the cost of the branching inside the function. In the second approach, you can skip that logic because now a has a default value even if you don't pass it.

I would suggest the second is the better way, but either will achieve the goal. Now, if you instead want to overload the type of an argument, you could use a union type:

```
public calcSuperMass(a: number | string): number {
  if (typeof a === "number") {
    return this.mass * a;
  } else {
    return this.mass * parseInt(a);
  }
}
```

That, too, will work. However, it's probably worse than either of the other two since you are in a sense (kinda/sorta/maybe) going around the type system. But, while it probably doesn't make much sense in this instance, you certainly could have situations where you do want a single function to handle multiple types, in which case this approach gives you a way to do overloading like you want.

Getters and Setters

It is generally considered an excellent pattern to make data members in classes private and then, when necessary, provide outside access to them via getter methods (or accessor methods). Similarly, allowing private members to be set through setter (or mutator) methods is also typically considered good form. Especially for setters, this enables you to have some code that checks incoming values to ensure they are valid in whatever way makes sense for your application.

Because this is so common a pattern, TypeScript offers syntax specifically for these types of methods:

```
class Planet {
  private _name: string = "No name set";
  get name() {
    return `This planet's name is '${this._name}'.`;
  }
  set name(inName: string) {
    if (inName === "Pluto") {
      this._name = "Not a planet";
    } else {
      this._name = inName;
    }
  }
}
let p: Planet = new Planet();
alert(p.name); // 'No name set'.
p.name = "Pluto";
alert(p.name); // 'Not a planet' (sorry, little guy!)
p.name = "Venus";
alert(p.name); // 'Venus'
```

The get and set keywords prefixing a method indicate a getter and a setter method, respectively. What this does for you is it allows you to access the member by the name of the method. In other words, p.name is the same as executing p.name() would be, but you can't call p.name() because TypeScript will tell you that "This expression is not callable. Type 'String' has no call signatures." which is just a fancy way of saying that getters and setters aren't methods in the usual sense, but they *do* execute when you access or set the property that matches the method's name. Note too the use of the _name identifier for the actual property name. TypeScript doesn't require the underscore – you can use any name you wish – but the key point is that the getter and setter method names cannot be the same as that of the private property they access, and prefixing with an underscore is a popular choice to ensure they aren't the same but are still related in some logical way.

Also, worth noting is that you can make read-only properties by only supplying a getter. Another way to achieve this is by prefixing the property with the readonly keyword:

```
class Planet {
  readonly name: string = "No name set";
}
let p: Planet = new Planet();
alert(p.name); // Okay
p.name = "Neptune"; // Error
```

Remember, name will be public by default, which means you normally can do p.name = "Neptune". But, with readonly before it like that, tsc will give an error on that line. This is a good choice if you have properties that you do want accessible, but you know can never be changed by outside code since it will save you from having to provide even a getter. As with much of newer JavaScript and TypeScript, saving a little typing appears to be the primary goal sometimes!

Static Members

TypeScript classes also provide for static members, both properties and methods:

```
class Planet {
  static theBorgLiveHere: boolean = true;
}
alert(Planet.theBorgLiveHere); // true
```

Notice that, in contrast to all the properties and methods you've seen so far that are tied to instances of a class and are thus called *instance members*, we can access the value of theBorgLiveHere without an instance of Planet being created first. That's the very definition of static, and it's just that easy with TypeScript!

Abstract Classes

The final topic related to classes to discuss is abstract classes. An abstract class is simply one that cannot itself be instantiated. It is always meant to be a base class that others extend from. They serve a similar function as interfaces, a topic we'll look at in the next chapter, but the primary difference is that an abstract class can provide some amount of implementation for methods while an interface cannot.

So, by way of example:

```
abstract class BasePlanet {
  name: string;
  radius: number;
  constructor(inName: string, inRadius: number) {
    this.name = inName;
    this.radius = inRadius;
  }
  abstract collapseToBlackHole(inMoreMass: number): void;
  calcDiameter() {
    return this.radius * 2;
  }
}
```

Given this class, with the `abstract` keyword before the `class` keyword indicating this is an abstract class, we can never have an instance of `BasePlanet`. Instead, we can only have, perhaps, `Earth` instances:

```
class Earth extends BasePlanet {
  collapseToBlackHole(inAdditionalMass: number) {
    // Perform physics-breaking 2001-like monolith magic here
  }
}
```

The other thing to note is that while `BasePlanet` implements `calcDiameter()` – because calculating the diameter of a planet from its radius is the same for all planets (well, basically the same; this is a book about programming after all, not astrophysics, so we can ignore some intricacies I think!) – it does not implement `collapseToBlackHole()`. The declaration of that method in `BasePlanet` is declared `abstract`, just like that class, which is a thing you can totally do! And besides, it has no function body, so it wouldn't do much even if that were syntactically allowed. That means that an extending class *must* implement it, as the Earth class does (and, again, since Stephen Hawking is not here to correct us – rest in peace, good sir – we'll ignore the fact that collapsing any body to a black hole essentially comes down to enough mass in a small enough diameter, so you probably wouldn't need each child class to implement that method either). This is an excellent way to "push" the common functionality into a base class while still ensuring that an extending class implements those things that it really must implement to be a valid instance of the base class in a logical sense.

Summary

In this chapter, you got your first look at TypeScript. You got some historical perspective and then saw some of the biggest things it adds to JavaScript, including types (obviously!), ES6 features like arrow functions, template literals, and classes. You learned how to compile TypeScript to JavaScript and a little about how to configure that compilation.

In the next chapter, we'll look at more of what TypeScript brings to the table, including concepts like namespaces, modules, interfaces, decorators, and a bit about debugging. Once through this chapter and the next, you'll have the foundational knowledge about TypeScript on which we can begin to build some projects, along with Node, React, and a few other tools. But let's not put the cart before the horse. Jump over to the next chapter to continue on with TypeScript!

CHAPTER 6

A Few More Words: Advanced TypeScript

In the last chapter, we started looking at TypeScript as a replacement for JavaScript in our projects (though, of course, you now know that it's not actually replacing JavaScript at all, it's just enhancing it significantly). Now it's time to turn the dial up to eleven and explore some other aspects of TypeScript.

The title of this chapter includes the word "advanced" in it, though whether the things in this chapter are especially advanced or not as people typically mean the word is up for debate. It's probably more accurate to say this chapter is just covering some additional TypeScript topics which aren't necessarily more advanced than the others from the previous chapter. I'll also include some extra things that are specific to TypeScript and which aren't found (directly, at least) in JavaScript.

Please note that all the code in this chapter is meant to be executed in the playground. You certainly *can* compile it with `tsc`, but to run it, you'll need an HTML file to load it. The playground is doing all that for you, so for quick, small things like are in this chapter, it's easier just to use the playground.

Interfaces

Interfaces offer a way to define "contracts" within your code or for code that must interface with your code to follow. While types by themselves do this to some degree, interfaces take the concept to a much greater extent and provide much more power to you as a developer.

© Frank Zammetti 2022
F. Zammetti, *Modern Full-Stack Development*, https://doi.org/10.1007/978-1-4842-8811-5_6

Argument/Object Interfaces

To begin our discussion of interfaces in TypeScript, let's first look at a simple TypeScript example:

```
function greet(person: any) {
  alert(`Hello, ${person.firstName}`);
}
const person = { firstName : "Frank" };
greet(person);
```

That, of course, will alert "Hello, Frank" at runtime. But if person didn't have a firstName property, then you would instead see "Hello, undefined". That's not even a TypeScript thing, that's just basic JavaScript.

Situations like these are where interfaces come in: that act as a contract that your code must adhere to in order to avoid such situations. Let's modify that example by creating an interface:

```
function greet(person: { firstName: string }) {
  alert(`Hello, ${person.firstName}`);
}
const person = { name : "Frank" };
greet(person);
```

The interface is defined directly inline in the argument list of the greet() function. Rather than naming a type for the person argument, we instead provide an object, and within that object, we list the properties and their types that the object must have. With that in place, the call to greet() will result in a compiler error since the object passed to greet() here doesn't have the firstName property, it has a name property, which is wrong according to the contract defined by the interface. That proves that TypeScript is performing type checking against the defined interface.

Now, it should be evident that defining the interface "inline" like that probably isn't the best way to do things. If we had another function that we wanted to require the same contract, we'd need to duplicate the interface in two places. TypeScript, as I'm sure you can guess, gives us a way to define the interface separate from its usage:

```
interface IPerson {
  firstName: string;
};
```

130

The name of the interface can be anything you wish, but I like to put a capital I in front of it like here so that I can at a glance differentiate it as an interface from, say, a class name.

Now, we can use that interface in the same way as when it was defined inline:

```
interface IPerson {
  firstName: string;
};
function greet(person: IPerson) {
  alert(`Hello, ${person.firstName}`);
}
function greetLouder(person: IPerson) {
  alert(`HELLO, ${person.firstName}!!!!`);
}
const person = { firstName : "Frank", hairColor : "Black" };
greet(person);
greetLouder(person);
```

Here, take note that the object you pass to greet() can have *other* properties not named in the interface. That's fine. It simply *must* have those defined by the interface, though, or the contract isn't met.

Somewhat curiously, if you pass an object literal, in that case you can *only* specify properties that are in the interface. Otherwise, you'll get a compiler error. In other words, while the previous code works, this will not:

```
interface IPerson {
  firstName: string;
};
function greet(person: IPerson) {
  alert(`Hello, ${person.firstName}`);
}
function greetLouder(person: IPerson) {
  alert(`HELLO, ${person.firstName}!!!!`);
}
greet({ firstName : "Frank", hairColor : "Black" });
```

You can either define the object separately without using an interface at all, as in the first example, or you could define a second interface and use that one instead, or you can use optional parameters to avoid the problem, which is usually the best choice. If you add a ? after the property's name in the interface, then that means it's optional, and now it will work:

```
interface IPerson {
  firstName: string;
  hairColor?: string;
};
function greet(person: IPerson) {
  alert(`Hello, ${person.firstName}`);
}
greet({ firstName : "Frank" }); // Okay now
```

Methods in Interfaces

Interfaces aren't just about object properties though; you can define methods in interfaces as well:

```
interface IPerson {
  firstName: string;
  getGreeting(lastName: string): string;
};
const person = {
  firstName : "Frank",
  getGreeting(lastName: string) {
    return `Hello, ${this.firstName} ${lastName}`;
  }
};
function greet(person: IPerson) {
  alert(person.getGreeting("Zammetti"));
}
greet(person);
```

The result is that when defining an object that will be passed to a function that demands an interface, the methods listed in the interface must be implemented in the object, same as the properties, as getGreeting() is implemented in this one.

Interfaces and Classes

In most object-oriented languages that provide classes and interfaces, classes can implement interfaces to ensure they provide a given contract, and TypeScript is no different:

```
interface IPerson {
  firstName: string;
  greet(): void;
};
class Person implements IPerson {
  firstName: string;
  constructor(inFirstName: string) {
    this.firstName = inFirstName;
  }
  greet() {
    alert(`Hello, ${this.firstName}`);
  }
}
const p = new Person("Frank");
p.greet();
```

You can, of course, add other properties and methods to the class as you wish, but as with interfaces for function arguments, you must implement what the interface declares at a minimum with any class that implements it.

Note that classes can implement more than one interface at a time. You simply name them all in a comma-separated list after the implements keyword. And, naturally, you must fulfill the contracts defined by *all* of them.

Extending Interfaces

As with classes, interfaces can extend other interfaces so that you can build them up as needed:

```
interface IPerson {
  firstName: string;
}
interface INinja extends IPerson {
  numberOfSwords: number;
}
let ninja = {} as INinja;
ninja.firstName = "Ryuki";
ninja.numberOfSwords = 2;
```

Here, you can see how the INinja interface extends the IPerson interface. Something else you can see is the use of the as keyword. This tells the TypeScript type checker to treat an object as being of a given type. An empty object, as ninja starts out as, isn't an INinja automatically as far as TypeScript knows. It's just a plain old object, after all! But, when you say as INinja, that's telling TypeScript exactly what type you want that object to be treated as for the purposes of type checking at compilation time. That means that any rules and conditions the ninja object must meet according to the interface named will be checked. Some of them get checked anyway, as you saw in some of the previous examples, but this is a more explicit way to ensure they happen as you expect. It's a good idea to explicitly type using as in cases like this where the type isn't implicit anyway, such as when instantiating a class.

Note   Interfaces do not get compiled to JavaScript in any way, shape, or form. They are entirely a TypeScript construct used at compile time. If you look at any of the code produced by these examples (which, remember, you can always see on the right-hand side of the TypeScript playground in real time), you'll see that all the interface information is stripped away entirely.

Namespaces and Modules

Namespaces and modules are two concepts that help you to organize your TypeScript code by partitioning them in some logical fashion. We'll start with the simpler of the two (in my estimation at least), namespaces.

Namespaces

A namespace is, simply put, a JavaScript object that contains other code. It provides a wrapper, of sorts, for that code, thus keeping it out of global scope (avoiding global scope pollution in JavaScript is always crucial to avoiding unforeseen consequences, and since TypeScript compiles down to JavaScript, the rule applies in TypeScript just as much).

A namespace is easy to create:

```
namespace MyFirstNamespace {
  export let homeworld = "Jakku";
  export function sayName() { alert("Rey"); };
}
```

The `namespace` keyword, unsurprisingly, denotes a namespace definition, which you then give a name (`MyFirstNamespace`) and then open and close the block as you would any other code block, with braces. Inside the block, anything you define is only accessible within that namespace unless you `export` it. As you can see, you can `export` variables and functions, both of which you can then access as follows:

```
namespace MyFirstNamespace {
  export let homeworld = "Jakku";
  export function sayName() { alert("Rey"); };
}
alert(MyFirstNamespace.homeworld);
MyFirstNamespace.sayName();
```

You can also `export` classes and interfaces from a namespace:

```
namespace MyFirstNamespace {
  export class Jedi { }
  export interface RebelScum { }
}
```

135

To get a handle on this, it can be informative to look at the JavaScript code produced from the previous TypeScript code:

```
"use strict";
var MyFirstNamespace;
(function (MyFirstNamespace) {
    MyFirstNamespace.homeworld = "Jakku";
    function sayName() { alert("Rey"); }
    MyFirstNamespace.sayName = sayName;
    ;
})(MyFirstNamespace || (MyFirstNamespace = {}));
alert(MyFirstNamespace.homeworld);
MyFirstNamespace.sayName();
```

As you can see, TypeScript uses the IIFE (Immediately Invoked Function Expression) pattern to keep the namespace's contents separate from everything else on the page when the code finally executes, thereby keeping global scope nice and clean (aside from the namespace object itself, obviously).

Because what's inside the namespace is partitioned off from everything outside, it means that you could have a homeworld variable elsewhere, and they will not conflict:

```
namespace MyFirstNamespace {
  export let homeworld = "Jakku";
}
const homeworld = "Coruscant";
alert(MyFirstNamespace.homeworld); // Jakku
alert(homeworld); // Coruscant
```

You don't need to worry about naming conflicts when you use namespaces properly, which is indeed a nice problem to avoid in a large codebase!

While namespaces can help organize your code within a single file, they become a bit more useful when you realize that you can break them up into multiple files:

```
// app.ts
SomeNS.someFunc1();
SomeNS.someFunc2();
// file1.ts
namespace SomeNS { export someFunc1() { } }
```

```
// file2.ts
namespace SomeNS { export someFund2() { } }
```

But, to make this work, you must import both of the resultant .js files (file1.js and file2.js) in the HTML file that you execute to run your app (and, of course, you also need to import app.js). Just because they're used in app.ts (and ultimately app.js) doesn't mean that they are automatically available for use like that. Instead of having to import multiple .js files in the HTML document, you can instead have tsc bundle them for you:

```
tsc --outFile main.js file1.ts file2.ts app.ts
```

This will result in a single main.js file being produced that includes the (compiled) contents of file1.ts, file2.ts, and app.ts.

Note   When bundling like this, you must be aware that order can matter. The files are concatenated in the order you provide, so if the result of that concatenation is that some code references other code that isn't in proper source order in the final output file (meaning the referencing code is referencing code defined after it), then you can wind up with a runtime error. Here, if you had app.ts before file1.ts and file2.ts, then code found in app.ts might throw a runtime error when it tries to use something defined in either of those files since they will appear *after* the app.ts contents in the final main.js file.

Even better than having to bundle or import separate .js files and worry about their order is to use a TypeScript-specific syntax for important namespaces, the /// symbol. To use it, in the app.ts file, you would write

```
/// <reference path="file1.ts" />
/// <reference path="file2.ts" />
```

TypeScript, at compile time, will take care of bundling those files together. In this case, you only name the output file, not all the files that go into it, and TypeScript will take care of the rest, including that things are in the correct order.

Once you have the code bundled or properly imported, something else you can do is save yourself some typing by aliasing things in a namespace:

```
import h = MyFirstNamespace.homeworld;
```

This way, you can just do `alert(h)` to see "Jakku." You can dig into nested namespaces if you need to (meaning alias as many levels down in nested namespaces as you wish) or alias the entire namespace itself if you want a shorter/simpler/more logical name.

Oops, I mentioned nested namespace there, didn't I? That's the final thing about namespaces I want to mention: they can indeed be nested! Take a look:

```
namespace SomeNS {
  export namespace InnerNS {
    export someFunc() { }
  }
}
SomeNS.InnerNS.someFunc();
```

Referencing `someFunc()` requires that we dig down through the nested namespace hierarchy, which is what I was talking about before with aliases. If you wanted, you could do

```
import sf = SomeNS.InnerNS.someFunc;
sf();
```

That's much more concise – though whether it's actually better is only a call you can make!

With namespaces, nested or otherwise, how you organize and group your code is entirely up to you, whatever makes the most sense, that's the big takeaway.

If it strikes you that namespaces are a lot like classes and interfaces, then I'd say that's a reasonable observation. They aren't the same, of course – you don't instantiate namespaces as you do classes, and you don't implement namespaces as you do interfaces, to name two differences – but they do serve a similar partitioning function. But namespaces are more lightweight and are purely about code organization, whereas classes are about *things* and interfaces are about *contracts*, so as with anything, choose the tool appropriate to the task at hand.

Modules

Modules are another way of organizing your code, a more powerful way, in fact, than namespaces in many ways.

A module is defined as any TypeScript source file that contains one or more `import` or `export` statements at the top level (meaning not inside a function). Any source file that doesn't meet that requirement is considered an ordinary script source file, and its contents will be made available in global scope like always.

Modules represent their own scope, which is another way of saying that anything inside the module is not visible to anything outside the module unless explicitly exported (and subsequently imported elsewhere), nor can any code inside the module touch anything outside of itself unless explicitly imported. That's similar to a namespace, but remember that a namespace always results in at least the namespace object itself existing in global scope; that's the big difference.

At the code level, you can export anything you like from a module (assume this is in a file named `Modules`):

```
// Variable
export let captain = "Picard";
// Interface
export interface CaptainChecker {
  isGreat(inName: string): boolean;
}
// Function
export function addFirst(inLast: string): string {
  return "Jean Luc " + inLast;
}
// Class
export class Ship {
  const name = "Enterprise";
}
// Type alias
export type cap = captain;
```

To then make use of this, in another source file, you would import the things you need from the module:

```
Import { addFirst } from "./MyModule"
```

After that, you can execute it like any other function:

```
addFirst("Riker"); // Wrong last name, but not the point!
```

Alternatively, you could write your module like so:

```
function addFirst(inLast: string): string {
  return "Jean Luc " + inLast;
}
export addFirst;
```

It's really just a matter of style choice whether you want to separate the export from the definition of what you're exporting. But, with the latter approach, you can do something else:

```
export { addFirst as myAddFirstFunc }
```

Now, addFirst will not be available for import, myAddFirstFunc will be instead. In this fashion, you can have a different name internal to the module as what is externally exposed. Again, it's a matter of style and little else.

If you want to import an entire module, there is a handy shortcut for that:

```
import * as TheModule from "./MyModule"
```

Modules can also have a single default export. You simply use the keyword default after the export keyword for the item you want to make the default export:

```
export default let captain = "Picard";
```

What that does for you is that now your import can be this:

```
import cap from "./MyModule"
```

It's just a bit simpler of a statement; that's all.

One nice thing about modules is that you never have to worry about ordering, meaning what order the various JavaScript files get loaded in. Modules are declarative, meaning everything is based on imports and exports. The reason this can work is that modules require a loader. You see, browsers don't know how to deal with modules on their own. Instead, a loader, which is just some JavaScript that knows how to load modules, takes care of it.

There are several competing module formats and loader mechanisms that have evolved over the years. Some offer slightly different syntax for importing and exporting. Perhaps the best-known module loader, and most used, is called SystemJS. To use it, you must install it first:

```
npm install --save systemjs
```

Then, in the HTML file that loads your app, instead of loading, say, `app.js` directly, you instead load the module loader:

```
<script src="./node_modules/systemjs/dist/system.js"></script>
```

Naturally, you can move that file to another location if you wish; there's no need to leave it in node_modules. But either way, after that, you add some new code to the page:

```
SystemJS.config({ baseURL : "/",
  packages : { "/" : { defaultExtension : "js" } }
});
SystemJS.import("app.js");
```

This configures the module loader, providing it the base URL from which modules are resolved, and allows you to specify which modules are to be loaded (here, it's just saying load whichever are present in the directory). After that, you tell the loader to load your starting file, `app.js`, and it takes care of the rest! Any imports in `app.js`, as well as any exports in any modules, will now be handled by the loader. All the imports and exports that you wrote in your original TypeScript source files will be compiled down to JavaScript that knows how to interact with the module loader, which will then take care of loading everything and ensuring everything is in the right order as necessary.

Decorators

Decorators are an interesting addition to JavaScript that is still in the proposal stage at the time of this writing, but which TypeScript offers as an experimental feature. In order to use them, you have to add the `experimentalDecorators:true` option to your `tsconfig.json` file (or, optionally, you can pass the `--experimentalDecorators` switch to `tsc`, which you can, in fact, do for most options in `tsconfig.json` if you would prefer not to have the config file at all but still use these sorts of options).

Decorators are essentially metadata that you can add to the definition of a number of code elements. If you've ever seen annotations in other languages, like Java, then you are already familiar with the basic concept. Decorators are expressed in the form @<name>, where name must evaluate to a function at runtime. This function will be passed information about the element decorated.

For example, say we want to provide some logging in the constructor function of a class. Let's further say that for whatever reason, we don't want to modify the code within the class (maybe we didn't write it ourselves and don't want to mess around with code provided by someone else). For this, you can use a class decorator. You can do that as follows:

```
function logConstructor(inConstructor: Function) {
  console.log(inConstructor);
}
@logConstructor
class Spaceship {
  constructor() { console.log("constructor"); }
}
const s = new Spaceship();
```

Here, we have a function, `logConstructor()`, that we decorate the `Spaceship` class with. The class just has a simple constructor in it. If you run this in the playground and look in the console of your browser's dev tools, you should see something like this:

```
VM68:9 class Spaceship {
    constructor() { console.log("constructor"); }
}
VM68:12 constructor
```

When the class is instantiated, the function is called. A class decorator like this is always passed just the constructor, but remember that it's the *runtime* constructor, which is why we get the entire `Spaceship` function and not the constructor defined at the source level. In this example, that constructor is logged. Then, the actual constructor of the class that is defined in it executes, which is where the second log output comes from. This decorator mechanism provides us an opportunity to modify the class definition if we want, even potentially returning an entirely new class definition (though, as you might imagine, you can really muck things up by doing that if you aren't careful).

Note   You may see different VM values here, or you might not see any at all, or it might be on the right-hand side. Any of these are okay. The VM notation is something Chrome dev tools (and some other browsers' dev tools as well) does when it can't identify the source of some JavaScript. VM stands for virtual machine and refers to the JavaScript virtual machine, which of course is ultimately the source of the code. This frequently happens when using the JavaScript eval( ) function, and given what the TypeScript playground does, it's not hard to imagine that probably comes into play at some point to make it all work, so seeing those VM strings somewhere isn't surprising. They're also irrelevant for what we're doing here, but it's good to know what it's all about so as to avoid any potential confusion about why what you may see when you run the code isn't 100% identical to what's printed here.

The other types of decorators are the following:

- **Method** – Placed just before a method declaration, the decorator function will be passed either the constructor for a static class or the prototype of the class for an instance member, the name of the decorated method, and a descriptor for the method.

- **Accessor** – Placed just before an accessor declaration, the decorator function will be passed either the constructor for a static class or the prototype of the class for an instance member, the name of the decorated accessor, and a descriptor for the accessor.

- **Property** – Placed just before a property declaration, the decorator function will be passed either the constructor for a static class or the prototype of the class for an instance property and the name of the decorated property.

- **Parameter** – Placed just before the name of the parameter in a function argument list, the decorator function will be passed either the constructor for a static class or the prototype of the class for an instance member, the name of the decorated parameter, and the ordinal index of the parameter in the function's argument list.

Decorator Factories

Sometimes, you'll want to be able to pass information to a decorator in order to vary what the decorator does. To achieve that, you can create a decorator *factory*. In simplest terms, this is a function that returns a function. The function returned is the actual decorator function, and the function that returns it is the decorator factory.

That may seem a bit confusing, so let's see it in code:

```
function logConstructorFactory(inEnabled: boolean) {
  if (inEnabled) {
    return function(inConstructor: Function) {
      console.log(inConstructor);
    }
  } else {
    return function() { };
  }
}
@logConstructorFactory(true)
class Spaceship {
  constructor() { console.log("Spaceship constructor"); }
}
@logConstructorFactory(false)
class Spacestation {
  constructor() { console.log("Spacestation constructor"); }
}
const s = new Spaceship();
const t = new Spacestation();
```

The `logConstructorFactory()` function is the factory. It returns a function, but what function it returns depends on the `inEnabled` argument passed in. This will give us the ability to enable or disable logging: when `true`, we get the function that contains the `console.log()` call; when `false`, we get an empty function so that no logging will occur in the latter case.

Then, the decorator attached to the `Spaceship` and `Spacestation` classes now passes a boolean value to it, enabling logging for the `Spaceship` class and disabling it for `Spacestation`. When executed, in the console you'll see

```
VM73:11 class Spaceship {
    constructor() { console.log("Spaceship constructor"); }
}
VM73:16 Spaceship constructor
VM73:22 Spacestation constructor
```

As expected, the constructor of the Spaceship class is logged, but the constructor of Spacestation is not.

As with plain old decorators, you can use decorator factories for all five types of decorators, not just class decorators.

Third-Party Libraries

TypeScript, all by itself, is pretty great, but modern software is virtually never built with a language alone. Almost certainly, you'll want to bring in third-party libraries to help you along, and you most definitely can do that with TypeScript.

First, to state the obvious, you can use any of the JavaScript libraries you already know and love. Once your TypeScript is compiled down to JavaScript, it neither knows nor cares what other JavaScript code you use.

But you can also bring in third-party TypeScript libraries, and that's really what this section is talking about. Most frequently, you'll use NPM to import them into your project, the same as any other module you use from NPM.

Let's say, for example, that you want to use the popular Lodash library in your code. First, you'll need to install Lodash like any other NPM module:

```
npm install --save lodash
```

But now, there's an additional step – you must also import another related library:

```
npm install --save-dev @types/lodash
```

This extra library is called a type declaration file, or a type binding file sometimes, and it's what tells TypeScript (tsc, more specifically) all about the types that Lodash uses and provides. With that done, you can now use Lodash in your TypeScript code:

```
import * as _ from "lodash";
_.padStart("TypeScript + Lodash = COOL!", 10, "*");
```

It's that easy! What's better is that because of that type declaration file, tsc (and your TypeScript dev tool of choice) knows about Lodash in terms of TypeScript so that it can provide all the same warnings, errors, and IntelliSense, just like it does with your own code.

In NPM, most libraries that provide TypeScript bindings have a secondary library prefixed with @types, so you should look for those when choosing a library. Not all libraries offer them, of course, but that may well factor into your decisions about what libraries you use and which you don't.

Caution   One caveat to be aware of: if you use a library like this, you will almost certainly want to add an exclusion in `tsconfig.json` to skip the `node_modules` directory. If you don't do this, `tsc` will try to recompile any `.ts` file in it.

Debugging TypeScript Apps

Since TypeScript compiles down to JavaScript, you, of course, could debug the JavaScript directly with all the same tooling you use at other times, be that browser dev tools or a full IDE of some sort. But that isn't ideal because you aren't debugging the code you wrote, and that's rarely something you want to do. Besides, the output JavaScript can look very different than the input TypeScript, so it might be challenging to do even if you wanted to.

Given that TypeScript isn't something that executes directly, that would seem to preclude the ability to use a debugger to step through the code or do any of the other things a debugger allows you to do. Sure, you can always revert to good ole `console.log()` debugging, and sometimes that's even easier than a full debugger, but most developers prefer having proper, purpose-made tooling, a debugger being one.

Fortunately, there is a solution available to allow you to use most of the same debugging tools as you do regular JavaScript, and it's pretty simple: source maps.

Source Maps

A source map is an additional file that is generated by tsc when you append the --sourceMap option to it:

```
tsc --sourceMap app.ts
```

With that option, you'll find that alongside the app.js file that is produced, there will also now be an app.js.map file. This file provides debugging tools with... wait for it... a *map* (bet you didn't see that coming!) that correlates the original TypeScript source to the generated JavaScript source.

It really is just that simple!

Wanna see what such a file looks like? Here you go:

```
{
  "version": 3,
  "file": "app.js",
  "sourceRoot": "",
  "sources": [ "app.ts" ],
  "names": [ ],
  "mappings": "AAAA,SAAS,KAAK,CAAC,SAAiB;IAC9B,KAAK,CAAC,YAAU,SAAS,MAAG,
  CAAC,CAAC;AAChC,CAAC;AACD,KAAK,CAAC,gBAAgB,CAAC,CAAC"
}
```

Note that if you look at a real file, it's all on one line, but I've expanded it here to make it a bit easier to comprehend. Now, to be clear, you really aren't meant to look at this file yourself. The truth is it doesn't make much sense to me either when you get to the mappings property (though the rest is pretty obvious I'd say)! I'm sure I could go look up how this file works, but in the end, it doesn't matter. The tools know what to do with it, which is what matters.

Now, let's go back in time to Chapter 5 and the example code there. Remember that, as shown in Figure 6-1?

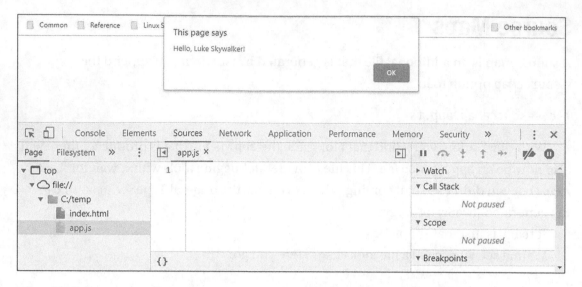

Figure 6-1. *It's a simple example, but it gets the job done – again!*

To refresh your memory, here's the code behind that wondrous display:

```
function sayHi(humanName) {
    alert("Hello, " + humanName + "!");
}
sayHi("Luke Skywalker");
//# sourceMappingURL=app.js.map
```

Hey, wait a minute. That's not the same as in Chapter 5! Indeed, that last line wasn't there. That's the line that tells your tooling that a source map file exists, and it's something else the `--source Map` option does. With that in place, the magic happens, as you can see in Figure 6-2.

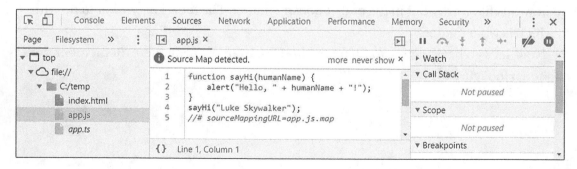

Figure 6-2. *The magic of the source map line*

As you can see, Chrome dev tools sees that line, and as a result, it can even tell you that a source map has been detected. If you look over on the left, you'll see something else: there is now an `app.ts` file listed! Even though Chrome doesn't speak TypeScript natively, that file is now available, and clicking it reveals what you see in Figure 6-3, which shouldn't be at all surprising.

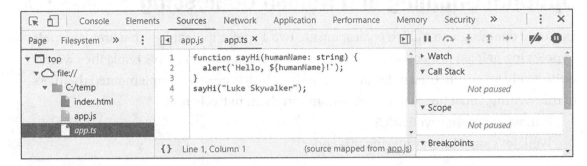

Figure 6-3. *Hey, look, we have our original code!*

Yep, we have our existing code now! Note, however, that for this to work, the app. ts file must be available. So, on a real website, you would need to deploy this file to your server as well as the final `.js` file. Therefore, this isn't something you generally will want to do on a production server. Source maps are a development tool, not a production support tool.

With access to the original source code, we can now use all the debugger goodness Chrome dev tools offers, including breakpoints, as you can see in Figure 6-4.

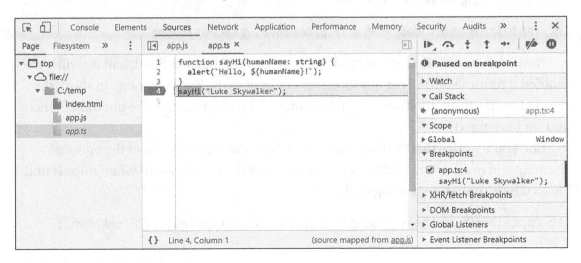

Figure 6-4. *Using Chrome dev tools to debug TypeScript*

Execution has paused on the `alert()` line, and we can inspect variables, step into the code, and do all the other things that a proper debugger allows.

Pretty cool, right?

Optional Chaining and Nullish Coalescing

Optional chaining and nullish coalescing are two TypeScript features that aren't actually TypeScript, at least not anymore. When I wrote the first edition of this book, they weren't quite ready for prime time in JavaScript itself yet, but TypeScript implemented them. As of this writing, most JavaScript engines support them natively now.

But, what are they, you ask?!

Well, let's start by considering this code:

```
let captainOfPrometheis = ships.prometheus.getCaption()
```

What happens if the ships object is null? That's going to cause an error, right? You can't access properties of a null object, can you? In the past, you would have had to do something like this:

```
let captainOfPrometheus = "unknown";
If (ships !== null) { captainOfPrometheis = ships.prometheus.getCaption()
}
```

Now, though, there's a better way:

```
let captainOfPrometheus = ships?.prometheus.getCaption();
```

Now, if ships is null, then `captainOfPrometheus` will be undefined, and we will have avoided a runtime error. That question mark in there is optional chaining. In short, the chain of property/method access will be broken if the object before the question mark is null (or undefined).

But, you'll notice that the code isn't equivalent: the version without the optional chaining will make `captainOfPrometheus` have a value of "unknown" when ships is null. That's where nullish coalescing comes in:

```
let captainOfPrometheus = ships?.prometheus.getCaption() ?? "unknown";
```

You can think of what follows the ?? operator as a "fallback." Its value will be used if the part before it is null or undefined. And yes, you can call a method instead if you wish; it doesn't have to be a literal value as it is here.

As I said, these features aren't specific to TypeScript, though TypeScript – and the TypeScript team – helped push them into JavaScript. And, given how useful they are, I felt they were worthy of mention here.

Summary

In this chapter, you learned about a few more TypeScript concepts, things that might be considered "advanced" (though that adjective is up for debate). Things like interfaces, namespaces, modules, decorators, third-party library usage, and debugging with source maps were discussed. Between this chapter and the previous one, you now have a solid foundation of TypeScript knowledge.

In the next chapter, we'll look at one more tool that we'll need in order to start building apps: Webpack.

CHAPTER 7

Tying It Up in a Bow: Webpack

In the good old days of web development, things were simple. You created a directory, maybe some subdirectories if you were a bit more organized, and into it, you poured all your resources: a stylesheet or two here, a sprinkling of images, some HTML files, and a heaping helping of JavaScript files. Then, a single HTML file served as your entry point, and it would go out and load, by way of tag references in the <head>, all your JavaScript files, as well as your CSS files and images.

Now, at a fundamental level, that's precisely still how things work technically, but over time the picture has gotten... messier. Developers will frequently make use of a large number of smaller, more focused libraries and toolkits. What we build is orders of magnitude more complex with far more moving parts, things you need to include.

Of course, people have realized that this isn't efficient. Each networked request is a new connection to the server, and many of those requests must occur serially, so nothing happens until the resources are loaded (and processed in some way). And worse, what if a script file is loaded at the start that isn't needed until the user performs some specific action? What if they *never* perform that action? You've just wasted a bunch of time and bandwidth and maybe slowed the whole site down for something that you didn't wind up even needing!

And that's before we even talk about how you have to self-organize the code, think of things like ensuring scripts are loaded in the proper order and that everything that one script depends on is both included and loaded before it's used, that code that references other code can find one another at runtime.

And all *that* is before we talk about newer JavaScript tricks like modules and the problem of cross-browser development and the desire to use more modern coding techniques while still supporting older browsers (to a point at least).

© Frank Zammetti 2022
F. Zammetti, *Modern Full-Stack Development*, https://doi.org/10.1007/978-1-4842-8811-5_7

As this evolution has occurred, before long, developers were looking for a way out of this mess, and that's when the notion of bundles was born. In this chapter, we'll talk about one specific bundler: Webpack.

What's a Bundle, and How Do I Make One?

In simplest terms, a bundle is a conglomeration of various resources that a web page needs to function. The obvious component of a bundle is JavaScript, but in some cases it also includes CSS and even images, encoded for use in data URLs (if you aren't familiar with the concept, that's where an image, or other files, is Base64-encoded and included as a string as the source, most commonly, of an `<img>` tag using the `data:` prefix). A bundle most frequently is a single file, though no rule says it must be (well, I would argue that a bundle is *always* a single file, and if you have multiple files, then you, in fact, have *multiple* bundles – but either way, the basic concept is the same). The benefit of a bundle is that it is, usually, just a single request across the network, plus the fact that when creating a bundle, you can layer on other optimizations like code minification and compression and such.

How does one create a bundle? Well, at the most fundamental level, you could do it manually by merely concatenating all your JavaScript files together into one. Do that, and you've got yourself a bundle! But, in that case, it's a bundle of only JavaScript, no other resources like CSS or images, and perhaps more importantly is that when you do that, you have to take on responsibility for ensuring everything is in the right order and that there are no conflicts. IIFEs, or Immediately Invoked Function Expressions, are a way to solve these problems. If each thing you concatenate is inside an IIFE, then there are no worries (well, mostly at least) about scope collisions. Plus, that way, the order no longer matters. The problem with this solution though is that any time a single file changes, you have to rebundle everything, manually concatenate all those files again.

Plus, it becomes difficult to determine if things are being included that are no longer necessary (the term tree shaking refers to determining when an included dependency is not actually being used, and that's more difficult in this approach than what Webpack does, as you'll see). Aside from that, there is also sometimes code that shouldn't be in the bundle for other reasons, maybe because it's only for development, or because it's only needed in specific versions of the page. Then, you'll probably need to create some sort of simple tooling (maybe just some shell scripts) to exclude things that aren't necessary for a given build (and consider if you use a library like, say, React: what if there are parts of the library you don't use? It would be nice if you could leave those out and make the bundle smaller, thereby improving load performance, wouldn't it?).

Further, when thinking of JavaScript, wouldn't it be nice if you could use modules to organize your code and know it would work across all browsers? That's not the case today: not all browser versions support them and those that do have some variances to deal with. This is true whether you start from plain JavaScript or TypeScript, but with TypeScript it's more complicated because you have the compile step to worry about as well (and, to be sure, the TypeScript compiler is doing most of that backward-compatibility work for you). If you could organize your code with modules and not have to worry about compiling your TypeScript yourself, you'd have the best of all possible worlds, right?

For all these reasons, a good tool that can do bundling intelligently is a must, and that's where Webpack comes in.

What's Webpack All About?

Webpack isn't the only bundler out there, but it has quickly become the de facto standard and is, by probably most web developers, considered the best. Although it used to have a reputation for not being exceptionally easy to work with, that has changed with later versions. It's now quite easy to get started!

Webpack can do a lot more than merely bundling code, though. For example, it can transpile TypeScript and even knows how to work with React and its .jsx/.tsx files. So, in the end, Webpack can be more than a bundler; it can be a right and proper and full-featured build tool for your web applications. Most of this is optional and can be added on as you need it, so at the start, Webpack is rather simple, but it is highly extensible so can meet your needs every step of the way.

There are just a few core concepts that you must have at least a basic grasp of to use Webpack with your applications.

Dependency Graph

Start with a basic web page. You have an HTML file, one or more JavaScript files, probably a stylesheet or two, and maybe some images. If you start with the HTML page, it's easy to understand that it depends on those JavaScript, stylesheet, and image files.

Sure, a browser can render that HTML without those things, but it may not look anything like you expect without those additional resources (images won't show up, maybe the page will be entirely blank if it depends on some JavaScript rendering content on load, etc.).

When you tell Webpack to bundle your application, it looks at all the files it finds in your project directory (or that you explicitly name – we'll see how to configure Webpack shortly). It examines them from the point of view of a single starting point, the HTML page usually, and determines which files depend on which others. It builds what's called a *dependency graph* from that analysis, and with that, it can determine what needs to be included, what can be dropped, what order things need to be in, and so on. Without the dependency graph, nothing Webpack does would be possible, so while you won't be dealing with it directly in any way, it's essential to understand that's how Webpack is doing its work on your behalf.

With it, though, Webpack can intelligently create bundles for you that have the minimum amount of code required to make your website or web app work like it should while ensuring that it loads as efficiently as possible in the process.

Entry

When Webpack builds the dependency graph, it's constructing a tree structure under the covers, and any tree structure must begin from a single point, or node, or in the case of Webpack and web applications: a module. By default, Webpack will assume the entry point is called `./src/index.js`, relative to the directory it's run in. But you, of course, can name a different starting entry point, and we'll see how to do that soon. Regardless, from that starting point, the dependency graph is built as Webpack examines the entry point and then recursively examines each file that it in any way depends on or is referenced by it (or by anything it references, recursively, as far as it needs to go).

Output

In the previous section, take note of the location of the default entry point I mentioned: a `src` directory (short for source, obviously). That's the typical model that Webpack follows: a `src` directory where all your unbundled source code lives. But where does Webpack put your bundled code? The answer, by default, is a directory named `dist` (short for distribution). Further, by default, the name of the bundle that will be created is main.js (*most* of the time, you'll get a *single* bundle, and in fact for our discussions here, we're going to assume that's *all* you *ever* get because multiple output bundles are a bit more advanced of a topic and nothing we need to be concerned with for the purpose of this book). All of this can be altered, of course, to ensure you get the output you want exactly where you want it, but we're just considering the default case right now and the basic concepts.

Loaders

Once you know where your code starts, how Webpack will produce a dependency graph from analyzing it, and where it will put the resultant bundle, it's time to look at the concept of loaders, which are components that transform dependencies in some way. Out of the box, Webpack only understands one thing: JavaScript (well, it also understands JSON files, but given that JSON is essentially a subset of JavaScript, it's still really just one thing). To understand anything else, you need to specify a loader for Webpack to work with it. But, whether you use only the default JavaScript loader or add more, the job of a loader is simple: to process some type of file and convert them into valid modules that can be added to the dependency graph and ultimately to be bundled and consumed by your application later.

A loader has two critical attributes associated with it: a *test* property and a *use* property. The test property enables Webpack to determine which files it should transform. The use property specifies what loader to use for it. When put together, a rule is formed that Webpack will follow that basically says: "Hey, Webpack, when you encounter a reference to a file whose path matches the test property, go ahead and process that file with the loader specified by the use property, pretty please?"

As an example, say that you want to include images in your final bundle, and you want those images to be Base64-encoded in JavaScript. Webpack can't do this by default, so you'll need to add a loader, in this case, one called url-loader. To jump ahead a bit, Webpack has a config file, just like TypeScript and NPM do. In it, you would add a rule:

```
module : {
  rules : [
    { test : /\.(jpg|png)$/, use : { loader : "url-loader" } }
  ]
}
```

Now, any time Webpack encounters a file in your `src` directory with an extension of .jpg or .png, because their names will match the regex specified in the `test` property, it will use the url-loader loader to encode it and add it to the bundle.

Don't get hung up on those details, we'll get into it all shortly, but that should give you a good idea how loaders are used. And remember if all you have are JavaScript files, then this isn't necessary because Webpack knows how to handle those automatically (I'll introduce a small handful in upcoming chapters, but for the most part, if you encounter a file type you think you need a loader for, you can see those that Webpack comes with at `https://webpack.js.org/loaders/`, which also provides a like to some common third-party loaders).

Plugins

Plugins are another mechanism available to you in Webpack. Conceptually, they are similar to loaders, but they serve a fundamentally different purpose, and that purpose is virtually anything!

Need to optimize your bundle? Plugin! Need to insert some environment variables into your bundle? Plugin! Need to add I18n resources to your bundle? Plugin! Want to add some sort of copyright notice to the top of each generated bundle? Plugin!

I think you get the point!

Like loaders, plugins require an entry in the Webpack configuration file that I briefly mentioned earlier and that we'll get into more soon. Webpack ships with a good number of plugins, including the following:

- **BannerPlugin** – Adds a banner to the top of each generated chunk

- **CommonsChunkPlugin** – Extracts common modules shared between chunks

- **CompressionWebpackPlugin** – Prepares compressed versions of assets to serve them with Content-Encoding

- **ContextReplacementPlugin** – Overrides inferred context of a require expression

- **CopyWebpackPlugin** – Copies individual files or entire directories to the build directory

- **DefinePlugin** – Allows global constants configured at compile time

- **DllPlugin** – Splits bundles in order to drastically improve build time

- **EnvironmentPlugin** – Shorthand for using the DefinePlugin on process.env keys

- **EslintWebpackPlugin** – An ESLint plugin for webpack for performing static analysis on your source code

- **EvalSourceMapDevToolPlugin** – Enables a more fine-grained control of eval source maps

- **HotModuleReplacementPlugin** – Enables Hot Module Replacement (HMR)

- **HtmlWebpackPlugin** – Creates HTML files to serve your bundles

- **IgnorePlugin** – Excludes certain modules from bundles

- **LimitChunkCountPlugin** – Sets min/max limits for chunking

- **MinChunkSizePlugin** – Keeps chunk size above the specified limit

- **MiniCssExtractPlugin** – Creates a CSS file per JS file

- **NoEmitOnErrorsPlugin** – Skips emit phase on compilation errors

- **NormalModuleReplacementPlugin** – Replaces resource(s) that matches a regex

- **NpmInstallWebpackPlugin** – Auto-installs missing dependencies during development

- **ProgressPlugin** – Reports compilation progress

- **ProvidePlugin** – Uses modules without having to use import/require

- **SourceMapDevToolPlugin** – Enables fine-grained control of source maps

- **TerserPlugin** – Enables control of the version of Terser (for source code minification)

You can also add all sorts of third-party plugins, but that's a much larger conversation that you may never need to have if the built-in ones are sufficient, but at least now you know what to Google for if it comes up.

Modes

Whenever Webpack performs a build, it can be done in one of several modes: development, production, or none. Which mode is used determines which of the built-in plugins are used, if any, and controls what options are passed to them to do their work. In simplest terms, the mode determines what optimizations Webpack does to your bundles.

When the mode is none, as you might guess, it does no optimizations at all.

When the mode is development, the `NamedChunksPlugin` and `NamedModulesPlugin` are enabled. Also, the option `process.env.NODE_ENV` on the `DefinePlugin` is set to a value of `development` (as the name implies, this is associated with using Webpack for Node code, which you absolutely do if you want; Webpack isn't necessarily just about client-side code!).

When the mode is production, the `process.env.NODE_ENV` on `DefinePlugin` is again set, but now the plugins `FlagDependencyUsagePlugin`, `FlagIncludedChunksPlugin`, `ModuleConcatenationPlugin`, `NoEmitOnErrorsPlugin`, `OccurrenceOrderPlugin`, `SideEffectsFlagPlugin`, and `TerserPlugin` are all enabled. The result is a much more optimized bundle, as you would expect to have for a production release.

The mode of a Webpack build can be set in its configuration file, or it can be passed in as a command-line argument, so you have flexibility in that.

Browser Compatibility

In short, Webpack, by default, supports all ES5-compliant browsers (Internet Explorer 8 and lower are not supported). Webpack requires the `Promise` object to implement `import()` statements and `require.ensure()` statements. You can still support older browsers if you wish, but to do so requires loading a polyfill before using those sorts of statements. There is a section in the Webpack documentation that discusses this at webpack.org, but it's a topic I won't be covering here, I just wanted to make you aware of it.

Getting Started with Webpack

Okay, enough with the theory, let's get down to brass tacks and see Webpack in action! To get started, create an empty directory somewhere and initialize a new NPM project:

```
npm init -y
```

Note   This is the first_example for this chapter in the source code for this book, if you're not following along (which I would frankly suggest you do rather than just go directly to the existing source code so that you get a feel for doing all this yourself).

Next, you'll need to install Webpack itself. Let's install it locally to this project so that we can manage the dependency within the project:

```
npm install --save-dev webpack
```

Next, create a src directory, and in it, create a file named index.js. For the contents of that file, write

```
let a = 2;
let b = 5;
let c = a * b;
alert(c);
```

Okay, while that code is clearly nothing special and really doesn't benefit from Webpack, we can still bundle it with Webpack just fine, and at this point, we're ready to do just that! Because Webpack isn't installed globally, we know that we can't just execute it straightaway (if it was installed globally, you could simply execute webpack at a command prompt right now). So, to execute it, we'll have to use npx, as discussed in Chapter 4:

```
npx webpack
```

When you do this, Webpack will request that you install the webpack-cli module, and you should say yes to allow it since you won't get much further than this if you don't! This is what will allow you to execute Webpack commands. You'll only need to do this the first time you execute Webpack for a given project.

Note   You should see a warning about the mode option not being set when you execute this command. That's okay! Webpack will default to production mode if you don't set the mode in the configuration file or pass it on the command line as previously discussed, and this is fine for our purposes here.

When this completes, you should find that you now have a `dist` directory, and within it should be a `main.js` file. Recall from earlier that by default, Webpack looks for `src/index.js` as the entry point and creates `dist/main.js`, and that's precisely what we see here, entirely without telling Webpack anything at all about our project.

Typically, you won't care too much about what's in the output file. In general, you'll rarely look at the final bundle, and you'll even less commonly debug it directly. You effectively must trust that Webpack is doing the right thing for you and that though it may look vastly different, the code it produces does what your original code was intended to do. Yes, you might, at times, find that a bug in Webpack (or a loader or plugin) is an issue, but just like with a language compiler, you must have a level of trust in the tooling.

Getting More Complex

So far, we haven't done any Webpack configuration at all, and instead we have just relied on its default behavior. In a project of any real complexity, that's likely not going to be enough. So, let's get into configuring Webpack. To do so, we'll need a configuration file:

Note   This is the second_example for this chapter in the source code for this book.

```
npx webpack init
```

The result of this is an interactive process similar to that shown in Figure 7-1. In the end, we get a file named `webpack.config.js`. But we actually get a lot more than that!

```
C:\temp\test>npx webpack init
npm WARN config global `--global`, `--local` are deprecated. Use `--location=global` instead.
CLI for webpack must be installed.
  webpack-cli (https://github.com/webpack/webpack-cli)

We will use "npm" to install the CLI via "npm install -D webpack-cli".
Do you want to install 'webpack-cli' (yes/no): y
Installing 'webpack-cli' (running 'npm install -D webpack-cli')...
npm WARN config global `--global`, `--local` are deprecated. Use `--location=global` instead.

added 40 packages, and audited 118 packages in 1s

15 packages are looking for funding
  run `npm fund` for details

found 0 vulnerabilities
[webpack-cli] for using this command you need to install: @webpack-cli/generators package.
[webpack-cli] Would you like to install '@webpack-cli/generators' package? (That will run 'npm install -D @webpack-cli/generators') (Y/n) y
npm WARN config global `--global`, `--local` are deprecated. Use `--location=global` instead.
npm WARN deprecated source-map-url@0.4.1: See https://github.com/lydell/source-map-url#deprecated
npm WARN deprecated source-map-resolve@0.5.3: See https://github.com/lydell/source-map-resolve#deprecated
npm WARN deprecated urix@0.1.0: Please see https://github.com/lydell/urix#deprecated
npm WARN deprecated resolve-url@0.2.1: https://github.com/lydell/resolve-url#deprecated

added 601 packages, and audited 719 packages in 20s

65 packages are looking for funding
  run `npm fund` for details

11 vulnerabilities (3 moderate, 3 high, 5 critical)

To address all issues, run:
  npm audit fix

Run `npm audit` for details.
? Which of the following JS solutions do you want to use? ES6
? Do you want to use webpack-dev-server? Yes
? Do you want to simplify the creation of HTML files for your bundle? Yes
? Do you want to add PWA support? No
? Which of the following CSS solutions do you want to use? CSS only
? Will you be using PostCSS in your project? No
? Do you want to extract CSS for every file? No
? Do you like to install prettier to format generated configuration? No
? Pick a package manager: npm
[webpack-cli]          Initialising project...
conflict  package.json
? Overwrite package.json? overwrite
    force package.json
  create src\index.js
  create README.md
  create index.html
  create webpack.config.js
  create .babelrc
npm WARN config global `--global`, `--local` are deprecated. Use `--location=global` instead.
npm WARN config cache-min This option has been deprecated in favor of `--prefer-offline`.

added 335 packages, and audited 1054 packages in 9s

99 packages are looking for funding
  run `npm fund` for details

11 vulnerabilities (3 moderate, 3 high, 5 critical)

To address all issues (including breaking changes), run:
  npm audit fix --force

Run `npm audit` for details.
[webpack-cli] ⚠ Generated configuration may not be properly formatted as prettier is not installed.
[webpack-cli] Project has been initialised with webpack!

C:\temp\test>
```

Figure 7-1. *The Webpack initialization process*

As you can see, there are a series of questions you're asked, and the answers depend entirely to your project's needs. What form of JavaScript (or TypeScript) will it use? What form of CSS? Do you need PWA (Progressive Web App) support? Would you like to use Prettier to format your code? All of these, and more, could be separate topics all on their own, but I'm not trying to give you all the details here. We're just getting a feel for what Webpack will ask when you initialize a project like this. The Webpack docs will provide the details to you of each of these options.

Finally, it asks if it's okay to overwrite a few files, and the answer is yes in all cases. Typically, you likely wouldn't have created the index.js file first, so there would be no need to overwrite that, but in this case, there is. Also, if you had Webpack installed globally, then you wouldn't need to do the npm init step first either; you could go directly to doing

```
webpack init
```

Since that also creates an NPM package.json file, it's all you really need to do, but it only works if Webpack is installed globally. Since in this case it's not, we had to install it first, hence why we did npm init first and why Webpack now is asking to overwrite package.json.

After that, an npm install is automatically executed to install all the dependencies that Webpack added to package.json, all the things it needs to do its work.

And, then, it does that work! It processes our source file and generates a bundle from it. But it does a lot more than that! Remember when we ran Webpack without a configuration file? We got the output file as we expected, but we had no way to use it. At that point, we would have created an HTML file to load the main.js file so we could see our alert(10) as we expect. When you initialize a Webpack project like this, though, Webpack, in effect, does that step for us behind the scenes.

Note   If you try to do this yourself and find that you get an error about a missing index.html file, simply create an empty file in the root of the project (alongside the package.json file) and that should resolve the issue.

What's more: it provides a web server for it to run on! All you need to do, as seen in Figure 7-1, is execute

```
npm run start
```

That will start up a small web server and even launches the page in your default web browser! Once it does, open your web developer tools, and you should see a message in the console "Hello World from your main file!"

But, oops, we do not see the alert(10) as we should. That's because we allowed Webpack to overwrite the index.js file we originally wrote with a "starter" file, so to speak, and as a result now we have an index.js with the following content:

```
console.log("Hello World from your main file!");
```

To get back to where we want to be, let's now open that index.js file and copy into it the example code from earlier. Do that, save the file, and watch what happens: like magic, after a few seconds, the page automatically refreshes in the browser, and you see the alert(10) message as we expect! What happened is that Webpack continues to monitor the source files, and when it sees them change, it does a build automatically. It then, also automatically, deploys the updated code to the web server, and thanks to the code on the page it created for us, it refreshes the page for us.

At this point, I encourage you to also look at the code in your browser (using View Source) to see the HTML file. Then, also be sure to look at the JavaScript file that it references. I think you'll be rather surprised what's in there! It's far beyond even the already kind of verbose code we saw in the earlier example. But all of it is what allows Webpack to perform all this magic for us. Again, you've got to trust your tools for things like this; there's little choice (I know that I would not want to debug the code I see there!).

Configuration

When you executed the webpack init command, a file named webpack.config.js was created. Let's look now at that file (minus the comments, for brevity):

```
const path = require('path');
const HtmlWebpackPlugin = require('html-webpack-plugin');
const isProduction = process.env.NODE_ENV == 'production';
const stylesHandler = 'style-loader';

const config = {
    entry: './src/index.js',
    output: {
        path: path.resolve(__dirname, 'dist'),
    },
    devServer: {
        open: true,
```

```
            host: 'localhost',
        },
        plugins: [
            new HtmlWebpackPlugin({
                template: 'index.html',
            }),
        ],
        module: {
            rules: [
                {
                    test: /\.(js|jsx)$/i,
                    loader: 'babel-loader',
                },
                {
                    test: /\.css$/i,
                    use: [stylesHandler,'css-loader'],
                },
                {
                    test: /\.(eot|svg|ttf|woff|woff2|png|jpg|gif)$/i,
                    type: 'asset',
                },
            ],
        },
    };

module.exports = () => {
    if (isProduction) {
        config.mode = 'production';
    } else {
        config.mode = 'development';
    }
    return config;
};
```

This is actually code that will eventually be executed by Node on behalf of Webpack, so it begins with an import to provide the node `path` module. The `html-webpack-plugin` module is then imported, which is the Webpack plugin responsible for the creation of that HTML file that loads the finished bundle and allows us to do real-time edits.

After that comes a flag that tells Webpack whether this is to be a production build or not. Finally, a loader is named for handling CSS, which is used later (realize that this is just a JavaScript file, so you have the full language at your disposal here). After that comes the `config` object, the contents of which are targeted to Webpack itself, to configure its operation. The `entry` point is named, so if you wanted to change the source file that is the top of the dependency graph tree, you could do it right there by simply providing the filename and relative path to it.

Next comes some configuration of the `output`, including where it goes (the `dist` directory) and the name of the final bundle file.

The `devServer` property is what is responsible for enabling the built-in web server function, as well as monitoring for source file changes.

Then comes the `plugins` property, which is an array of plugin objects. As you can see, the `html-webpack-plugin` is instantiated (an instance of the `HtmlWebpackPlugin` class, as defined in the associated source file) and added to the array. But before that comes another plugin: `webpack.ProgressPlugin`. As you probably have surmised, this is responsible for showing progress updates on the screen during build operations.

After that comes the `module` property. This allows you to tell Webpack how to build your bundle. The goal here is to provide a set of rules. Each rule has a `test`, which is a regex that matches one or more files. For each rule that matches, the `loader`(s) specified will be used to transform the files, and you can provide options for each loader. Here, we can see that Webpack has added Babel to the mix and specified that any `.js` or `.jsx` file should be handled by it. The configuration for the Babel loader should look somewhat familiar: you can see the `presets` being used as we saw in previous chapters. A loader for handling CSS files is added too, using the configured name from earlier. Finally, a loader for handling all sorts of image assets is added.

Note   Don't get nervous if you run through this and get a different configuration file. The contents depend on the options you select. This file was produced from the options you see in Figure 7-1.

Finally, the `modules.exports` variable is defined to set the configuration mode, which tells Webpack whether this is a production build or not, which impacts what optimizations are performed.

Quite honestly, even this configuration is more than you might need for many projects. But that's the beautiful thing about Webpack: it is highly configurable, so when a need arises, a quick trip to the documentation is all that's likely to be required to find just the right configuration you need.

Using Modules

So far, the examples we've looked at have been straightforward JavaScript examples. What happens though when we want to use more advanced concepts like modules? As you're aware from previous chapters, modules aren't universally supported across all browsers. Not only that but there are several competing module formats available, and they aren't usually interoperable.

This is where Webpack really starts to earn its keep.

Note   This is the third_example for this chapter in the source code for this book.

To see it in action, let's take the second example and modify it. First, replace `index.js` with the following:

```
import getA from "./module1";
import getB from "./module2";
alert(getA() * getB());
```

Next, create a file in the `src` directory named `module1.js` and in it put this:

```
export default function getA() { return 20; }
```

Finally, create a file named `module2.js`, again in the src directory, and in it put

```
export default function getB() { return 30; }
```

Now, as you do this, if you happened to have executed `npm run start` and didn't stop it, you should see that Webpack is dutifully rebuilding as you go. Probably, you will have seen some build failures along the way if you did things in the order I said here, and that's fine. If you edit index.js first, Webpack will try to build it, but won't be able to find module1.js and module2.js yet. Hence, you'll get a build error. That's fine and completely expected.

Ultimately though, once you've made the change to index.js and added the other two files, you should get a successful build (or, if Webpack wasn't monitoring, just execute npm run start again). Either way, you should get the page launched in your browser, and you should see an alert() message showing 600, proving that both modules were bundled together with the entry point, and everything works as we expect it to.

That demonstrates how modules can be used and how Webpack will resolve them correctly and bundle them. It also shows that this will now work across browsers, even on those that don't know about modules. This is arguably the real power of Webpack because now you can organize your code well using modules and know that it's going to work across all browsers (or Node, if this isn't code that you'll be running in a browser).

Wither TypeScript?

As a final topic, let's talk about how we could use TypeScript instead of plain old JavaScript. We'll take the third example from before and change the three source files to TypeScript.

Note   This is the fourth_example for this chapter in the source code for this book.

To start, we need to add TypeScript itself to the project, and we also need to introduce a new loader for Webpack to know how to work with TypeScript, the ts-loader. Begin by installing both:

```
npm install --save-dev typescript ts-loader
```

Next, we need to initialize a TypeScript project, and you know how to do that already, but remember, with TypeScript installed in the project, we'll need to use npx:

```
npx tsc -init
```

That gives us the tsconfig.json file that Webpack needs, and its default form should work for this example.

Tip

If we had initialized the Webpack project with TypeScript support from the beginning, then this would have been done for us already, but since we're building on the previous project, we can't do that (well, we could reinitialize the project as we did earlier, but as you now know, that would overwrite a bunch of files, and this time we want to avoid that to show the progression of adding additional capabilities to the project on the fly).

After that, we must tell Webpack to use the ts-loader. To do that, go into the webpack.config.js file and add the following rule to the modules object:

```
{
  test: /\.ts?$/,
  use: 'ts-loader',
  exclude: /node_modules/,
}
```

Then, change the value of the entry property to ./src/index.ts (.js to .ts). Finally, add the following element to the config object:

```
-resolve : {
  extensions : [ ".ts", ".tsx", ".js" ]
},-
```

Now, Webpack is ready to deal with .ts files and knows to ignore the node_modules directory (otherwise, it would try to compile any .ts files it finds there too). Getting some .ts files to work with is the next step! Go into the src directory and change the three files there from .js extensions to .ts extensions. Since, as you'll recall, all valid JavaScript is all valid TypeScript, that should be all we have to do.

With all that done, if you still have Webpack monitoring for changes, then you should have a clean build, and the page should have refreshed and shown the proper alert() message. If not, do npm run start again and make sure everything works as expected.

That's all it takes to use TypeScript instead of JavaScript! Now you can use all the goodness you learned about in the previous two chapters in TypeScript land to make your projects that much more robust!

And, with that, you now know all the basics about Webpack that you need to build most applications. To be sure, there's much more to Webpack, and indeed you could read an entire book on it and all the options it provides, and I would definitely encourage you to at some point! It's a potent tool that will serve you well if you learn more about it. But this (plus some other things we'll see in later chapters) covers the bases that *any* project of virtually *any* complexity will use, and that's the point: building a foundation.

Summary

In this chapter, we looked at Webpack. You learned what it is, the basic concepts underlying it, how to install it, how to create a basic project with it, and how to configure it, at least at a basic level.

And, with that, we now have all the tools we need to start building our project! When you're ready, jump on into the next chapter so we can start having some fun!

CHAPTER 8

Delivering the Goods: MailBag, the Server

Alright! The stage is set, the players at the ready, and the houselights dimmed… It's time to draw the curtains and start the show!

In this chapter, and the next three, it's time to take all you've learned in the preceding chapters and put it to use building some real apps! And after that, we'll build another using some of what you learned to this point, but adding in a few other things to make it more interesting! For each, we'll build a server component with Node (or Django, in the case of the third app) and a client component with React, but that's about where the similarities end. These will be quite different apps from one another, and each will use a host of supporting technologies to do its thing. We'll use different techniques, approaches, and architectures so that you'll gain as wide a field of view as possible of what modern full-stack application development looks like in the real world.

What Are We Building?

The first application will be dubbed MailBag. This is a generic term for a particular type of bag typically used for collecting, carrying, categorizing, and classifying different types of postal material. If you've ever seen your friendly neighborhood spiderma… err, mailman (or really mailperson, to be more inclusive, but that doesn't work as well with the joke here, so just go with me on this!)… carrying a bag with mail around, that's a mailbag. If you've ever seen an old John Wayne western with a guy riding a horse carrying a bag with mail, that too is a… wait for it… MAILBAG!

In our case, though, there are no horses involved and no postal materials. No, instead, what we're concerned with is digital mail, electronic mail, or email! Squish the two words together to form MailBag, and what we have is an email application or, as it's more commonly known, a webmail system. That's what we're building!

173

F. Zammetti, *Modern Full-Stack Development*, https://doi.org/10.1007/978-1-4842-8811-5_8

Basic Requirements

Any time you build an application, it helps to have a list of requirements. So, let's make such a list for MailBag. Understand that we're not out to exactly copy Gmail or Outlook Mail or any of the other well-known webmail systems out there. No, we're going to build just a small subset of what those offer, but we'll cover what are probably the most essential elements, and we'll choose them such that they allow us to build a good, useful, and, most critical for you the reader, educational application while not being overwhelming in its scope:

- MailBag will be in two parts: a server, which will act as a proxy and will be what communicates with a mail server somewhere, and the client, which will talk to our server to do its work.

- The MailBag server will communicate with an email server whose details will be stored in a text file on the MailBag server (so this is a single-user system), and it will communicate with that email server via the popular IMAP protocol for retrieving mail (sorry POP3 users!) and SMTP for sending messages.

- The MailBag server will provide an API to the client that allows it to get a list of mailboxes for the account, a list of messages for a selected mailbox, and pertinent message details for display by the client. It will allow the user to delete and send messages. Finally, the server will provide for storage of contacts and the associated add and delete functions for maintaining them.

- This chapter is all about the server, so details about the client will come in the next chapter. However, in high-level terms, it helps to have a picture in your mind. I'm sure you've seen a webmail application like Gmail before, and MailBag will be no different fundamentally. The client will be a web-based application that can be viewed in any web browser. It will provide the user a list of mailboxes in their account, the ability to see a list of messages within a selected mailbox, and the ability to choose and view a message, as well as delete it. It will also, of course, allow the user to compose and send a new message to an entered email address. We'll also give them a list of contacts that they can add people to (and remove from) and initiate an email too quickly.

For now, that's all we need to know. It's helpful sometimes, when doing full-stack development, to use this sort of "tunnel vision" approach: we at this point aren't concerned with the client beyond the broad strokes here. Instead, you begin by thinking primarily about just the API your client needs first, and *then* you worry about building the client itself later. When the two are combined, you get the complete MailBag application. But that's all much easier to do when you aren't overwhelming yourself by trying to look at the whole thing as one big entity. As I said, a little tunnel vision can be a good thing, so we'll break this into two parts and attack each separately.

Setting Up the Project

To get started with MailBag, we'll create a directory that will be the root of our project. Since there are two components to this, a client and a server, we'll then create a `client` directory and a `server` directory, and within each of those, we'll create a `src` directory and a `dist` directory. Each of the `client` and `server` directories constitutes a separate project that we can work with individually, and each has a set of source files, obviously, and a directory where the compiled files will go (`dist`, short for distribution). The `src` directory is where our source files will be found, and `dist` is where the compiled (read: executable) files will go after compilation.

Once that's done, navigate to the `server` directory from a command line. Since we're building a Node project, and since most Node projects are NPM projects, the first step is to initialize an NPM project:

```
npm init
```

Just accept all the default values, perhaps just providing a name like "server" or even "MailBag server," whatever you like, it's not critical.

Now, since we know we want to write out code in TypeScript, let's go ahead and install TypeScript itself as a dev dependency:

```
npm install –save-dev typescript@4.7.4
```

Typically, when starting a project, you wouldn't specify versions like this because in all probability, you want to use the latest version available at that time. However, to ensure the code from the book works and isn't broken by something in a later version, I'm specifying versions in all the code for these projects.

At this point, you can ensure TypeScript is now available by executing `tsc` from a command prompt.

D'oh! It doesn't work!

That's right, you must use `npx` to execute it when installed local to the project directory:

```
npx tsc
```

That should work now, displaying basic usage information.

Next, let's initialize this as a TypeScript project too:

```
npx tsc -init
```

After that, you should have not only the `package.json` file but also the `package-lock.json` and `tsconfig.json` files.

Now, we have to make a few tweaks to the tsconfig.json file, specifically the following:

- Uncomment the `"outDir"` element and set its value to `"./dist"`. We want all our compiled files to go into a dist subdirectory.

- After the `"compilerOptions"` element, add `"include": [ "src/**/*" ]`. So, the file should have this form when you're done:

  ```
  {
    "compilerOptions": {
      ...lots of compiler options...
    },
    "include": [ "src/**/*" ]
  }
  ```

  This will ensure that `tsc` only tries to compile files in the `src` directory.

- Although not necessary, also uncomment the `"sourceMap"` option and ensure it's set to `true`, to make debugging easier.

And, at its most basic level, that's the entire development environment!

Source File Rundown

Now that the basic project structure is set up, let's talk about the relatively small handful of source files, again found in the /server/src directory, that will constitute the server codebase. We'll look at each file in turn, but for a quick summary, they will be as follows:

- main.ts – This will be the main entry point and is where we'll define the functions that will constitute the API the server presents to the client (much more on this in the next section!).

- ServerInfo.ts – This will be a configuration file that provides details about the IMAP and SMTP server(s) the server will connect to and where that information will be stored.

- IMAP.ts – Code that talks to an IMAP server to list mailboxes and messages and to retrieve messages. There will be a Worker class within this. That is what the rest of our application code will use, along with some interfaces we'll need.

- SMTP.ts – Code that talks to an SMTP server to send messages. Like IMAP, this will have a Worker class.

- contacts.ts – Code dealing with contacts (listing, adding, and deleting them). Once again, a Worker class will be present, along with an interface to describe a contact object.

In addition to those, we'll have that configuration file I mentioned for IMAP and SMTP server information stored in the /server directory named serverInfo.json. We'll get into that soon.

That, aside from the NPM/Node and TypeScript config files, is all there is to the server codebase. It's not much, but it gets the job done.

Adding Node Modules

The next step is to add the modules and library dependencies we're going to use. There are only five of them, but they're key to the whole thing! We're going to go over each in some detail later, but for now, let's get them added:

```
npm install --save emailjs-imap-client@3.1.0
npm install -save express@4.18.1
npm install --save mailparser@3.5.0
npm install -save nedb@1.8.0
npm install -save nodemailer@6.7.7
```

Just to give you a preview, emailjs-imap-client will provide all the IMAP functionality we need; express will allow us to build our API quickly and easily; mailparser will be needed to gain access to the actual content of a message; nedb will provide us some data storage capabilities; and nodemailer will provide the message-sending SMTP capabilities.

Adding Types

Adding dependencies is all well and good, but since we're using TypeScript and not plain old JavaScript, we want TypeScript bindings for them, too, assuming they are available.

That begs the question: how do you tell if there are TypeScript bindings for a given library? Well, you can certainly just randomly try to install them:

```
npm install --save-dev @types/express@4.17.13
```

Almost always, @types/XXX, where XXX is the name of the library, will work. But not always. There must be a better way to tell, right? Indeed, there is definitelytyped.org. This is a website that, among other things, provides a simple search interface, as you can see in Figure 8-1.

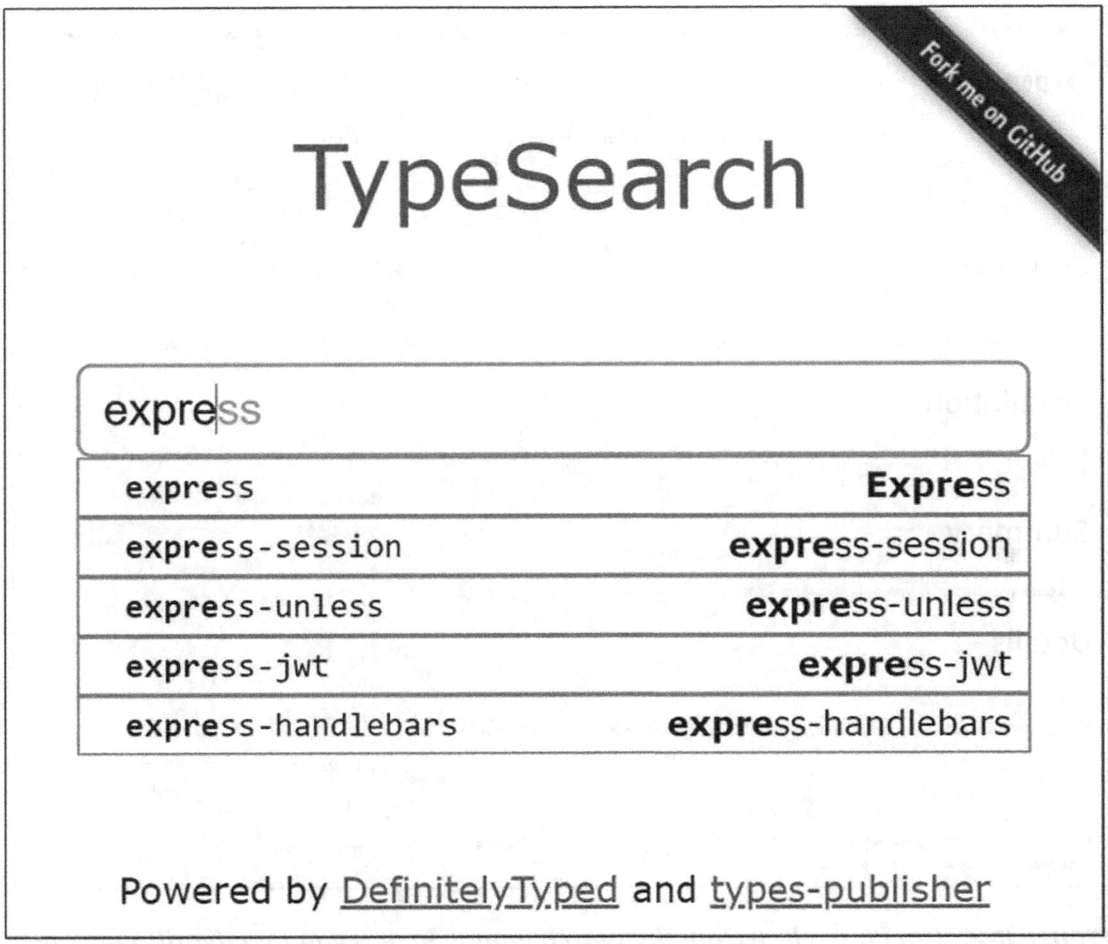

Figure 8-1. *The definitelytyped.org search engine*

As you can see, there are several possible matches, so you can then click one to see if it's what you need. The first one is almost certainly what we're looking for, so clicking it reveals Figure 8-2.

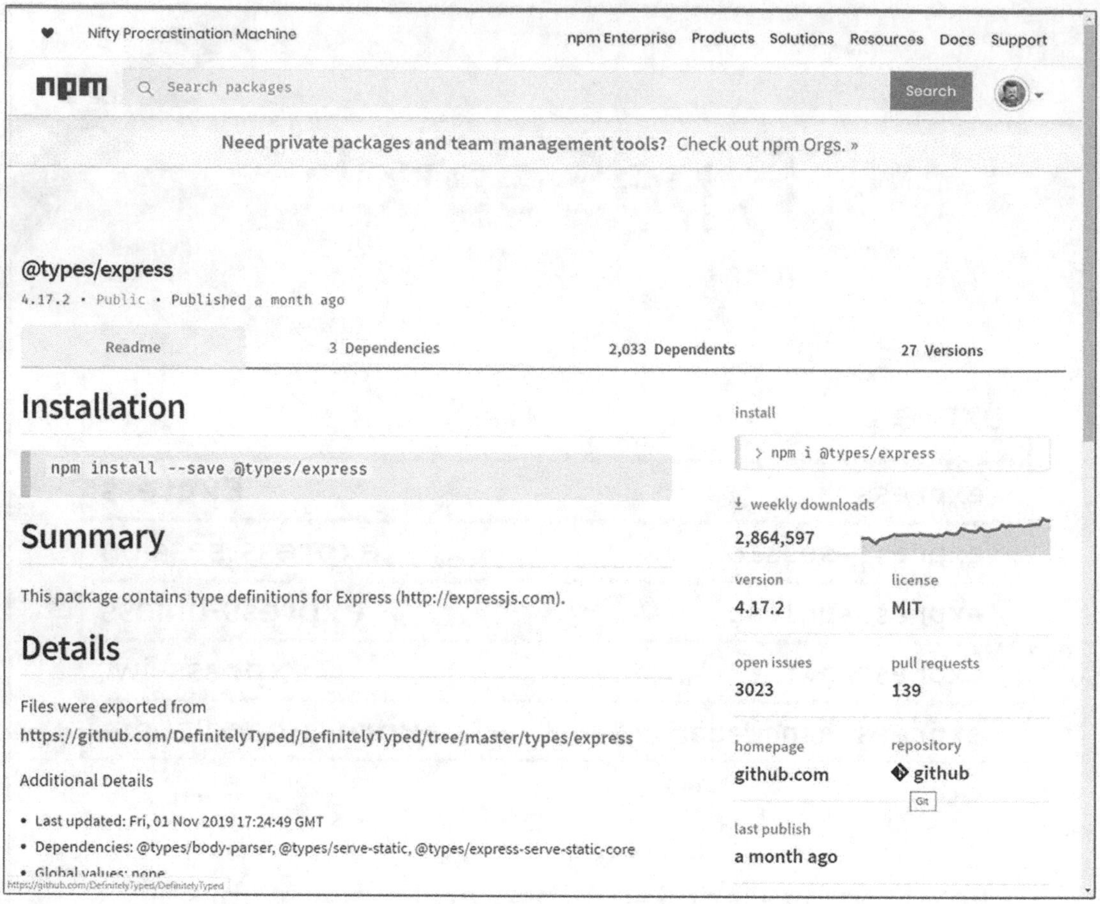

Figure 8-2. *Clicking a link from the search engine brings you to a detail page on npmjs.com*

Ah, that's the right one!

I'll save you the time hunting down the others and tell you that the commands you need to execute, in addition to the Express one previously shown, are

```
npm install --save-dev @types/mailparser@3.4.0
npm install --save-dev @types/nedb@1.8.12
npm install –save-dev @types/node@18.6.0
npm install –save-dev @types/nodemailer@6.4.4
```

Remember that the type bindings are only relevant at development time, not runtime, hence, why --save-dev is used. Also note that at the time of this writing, there was no binding available for emailjs-imap-client. This will cause us some minor trouble later, as you'll see, but nothing too significant. Finally, note that Node itself has TypeScript bindings, and we'll, of course, want those for sure!

A More Convenient Development Environment

At this point, you can compile the source code (err, assuming there *was* source code in the src directory that is!) with tsc. But then, of course, you'd need to start up the server to do anything with it. Assuming main.ts was our main entry point (hint: it is!), then after compiling we'd find a main.js file in dist, so we could start it up easy enough, assuming we were in the server directory:

```
node ./dist/main.js
```

But that's not all that convenient: we need to manually compile when we change a source file and then manually start the server (and manually shut it down first if it's already running). There's gotta be an easier way, right? Yes, there is!

In our package.json file, there's a scripts section. Here, we can provide NPM commands that we'll be able to use on the command line, associated with what they do. In simplest terms, you define a command and then tell NPM what the command line would be if you were doing it manually.

Let's say we want to have a command that will compile all our source code and then start up the server. That's easy enough:

```
scripts: { "compile" : "npx tsc && node ./dist/main.js" }
```

Note that you might have to adjust it for your particular operating system, but ultimately, the value of the "compile" key is what you would manually do: execute npx tsc, followed by executing node ./dist/main.js to recompile the source files and start up the server.

This alone, though, would be problematic if the server was already running. You would need to shut it down yourself first, still manually. And, plus, we again must manually execute this command (which you can do with npm run compile), which is only slightly better.

To solve this problem, we'll add one more development dependency:

```
npm install --save-dev nodemon@2.0.19
```

Nodemon is a handy module that can monitor your JavaScript source files for changes and automatically restart the app when any are detected. Now, we can do

```
node ./node_modules/nodemon/bin/nodemon.js ./dist/main.js
```

After that, any time `main.js` changes, nodemon will see that and restart it. That for sure is better, but we can do even better! Let's add a second script, so that the `scripts` element in `package.json` is now this:

```
"scripts": {
  "compile": "npx tsc && node ./dist/main.js",
  "dev": "node ./node_modules/nodemon/bin/nodemon.js -e ts --exec \"npm run
  compile\""
}
```

What we've done is added a `dev` command that used nodemon. But, in contrast to before, we now add an argument to nodemon, the `-e` option. By default, nodemon watched for changes in `.js`, `.mjs`, `.coffee`, `.litcoffee`, and `.json` files. With `-e` though, we can tell it to watch other types of tiles, `.ts` files in this case. The `--exec` option is used to tell nodemon what to do when those files change, so now any time nodemon sees changes to our TypeScript source files, it will execute the `compile` command.

With that all in place, if we execute `npm run dev`, nodemon will begin monitoring our source TypeScript files. When any change, it will compile them and then start up the resultant `main.js` file. Now, we've got ourselves a nice little workflow: we can happily peck away at our source files, and then compile and restart will be automatic, making our work quicker and our life easier!

Note   If compiler errors occur, nodemon will still try to start up the app because it doesn't know not to. That obviously isn't going to go well, so you need to keep an eye on your console when you make changes to ensure they're valid and running when you expect them to be.

The Starting Point: main.ts

Okay, now that we have our development environment and our project directories all set up, we can finally start to hack some code together, starting with the `main.ts` file.

That is, we *would* be able to, if we didn't have a few short detours to make along the way first! There are a few concepts we need to discuss before getting to the code, but it won't take long, I promise! Once that's done, we can get to the `main.ts` file, which is where our application begins.

A Quick Detour: Time to Take a REST

REpresentational State Transfer (REST) is a set of principles that, when combined, describe how common standards, HTTP usually, can be used to define a remote system interface in a client-server system. Although REST can work over other protocols, in practice it is rarely used with anything but HTTP. REST is a programming and operating system–neutral architecture. It really is just a set of best practices, or patterns, and it's not even all that rigid! But what it allows you to do is to create a web-based API in a de facto, standard way. In fact, the World Wide Web is an implementation of the REST architectural style, whether you know it or not!

The underlying concept is that of resources. In the REST world, a resource is an abstract concept that coherently and meaningfully can be represented in a form that can be transmitted over HTTP. A bank account, a user record, a product description, and a student list for a class described in JSON, XML, or even plain text document form are all valid examples of resources. This document form represents the state of a thing, whether it's the current state (when a client retrieves the resources from a server) or an updated state (a new version of a resource a client sends to a server). The client initiates a "state transition" by requesting a representation of a resource from a server or sending a new representation to the server. When this design is used, the API presented to clients is said to be RESTful.

Perhaps the primary benefit of REST is its simplicity and reduction of overhead. Rather than complex XML messages that must be created and parsed on both sides of the conversation, simpler data formats, most notably JSON, are typically used. These formats are generally easier to create and consume, though at the cost of less rigidity, which is sometimes a problem in terms of validation.

Three components go into the idea of REST. One is the matter of URLs and how you use them to address a given resource or collection of resources. The other is HTTP methods and their meaning. The third is the data format representation of an addressed resource against which you are acting. Let's look at each of these concerns individually.

URLs for Fun and Profit

Simply put, a URL allows you to identify a thing, or set of things, with which you want to interact. In the REST world, a URL identifies a resource or a collection of resources. Of course, you know all about URLs, because you use them every day in your browser. You also know about resources, even if you don't realize that you do, because a web page itself is a type of resource.

With REST, your URLs will nearly always refer to nouns. For example, let's say your website is `www.mysite.com`. Given that, in the REST world, the URL `www.mysite.com/users` might refer to the collection of users available on your website. The `/users` portion is the resource in which you're interested. If you were using such a RESTful API, you would expect to get back a list of users and some data about them (putting aside the question of data format for the moment).

What if, instead, you want to retrieve information about a specific user with the username `bill_gates`? The URL, in that case, might be as follows:

`www.mysite.com/users/bill_gates`

Note that, unlike the more typical URLs you see associated with web pages, you aren't using query string parameters.

`www.mysite.com?user=bill_gates`

Instead of something like that, the parts of the URL path itself serve the same purpose. The critical thing to note here is that we don't deal with verbs in the URL. In other words, you don't write this:

`www.mysite.com/users/add`

The word `add` is a verb, which makes this a non-RESTful URL. Only nouns go into the URL because nouns describe things or states of things. The verbs, the action to perform on the specified resource, are determined by the HTTP method.

Note   Although I've shown it here, when you see a RESTful API described, you will usually see it shown without the domain name: just /users, /users/ bill_gates, or /users/add, for example. The domain name is still necessary, of course, to ensure that the reference to the specific resource is unique across the entire Internet.

Giving Methods Meaning

HTTP methods are the set of values valid in an HTTP method header attribute. When you launch www.google.com in your browser, for example, you are making an HTTP GET request, where GET is the method. If you were to sniff the traffic, as I've done in Figure 8-3, you could see the requests and the GET method associated with them (the initial request is for www.google.com, then the subsequent requests are for the resources that page then loads).

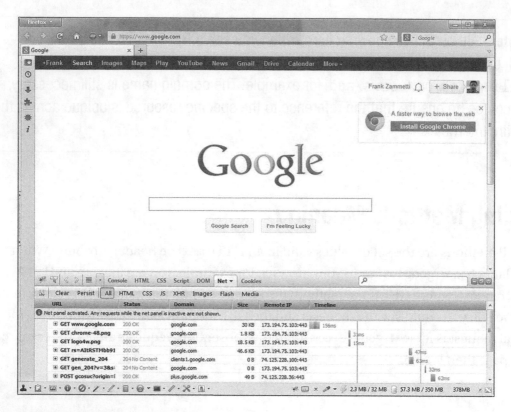

Figure 8-3. *Sniffing some HTTP traffic*

With a RESTful interface, the most common HTTP methods, namely, GET, POST, PUT, and DELETE, are given specific meanings:

- **GET** – Retrieve a resource (or resources). GET is the only method considered "safe," meaning it doesn't result in a data change on the server.

- **POST** – Create a new resource (unsafe).

- **PUT** – Update an existing resource (unsafe).

- **DELETE** – Delete an existing resource (unsafe).

Now, if you go out on the Web and look up REST, you may see some different meanings for these methods, typically for POST and PUT. Sometimes, you'll see it stated that PUT is for both create and updates of a single resource, while POST is for multiple updates. Sometimes, you'll also see it said that you should use POST for both. Another school of thought is that POST should be for things that don't precisely fit the REST model, like a user login request. Any of these approaches are valid because they still adhere to the underlying REST principle of URLs addressing resources, HTTP methods describing actions, and a representation of the current state of an object being transitioned to or from. There is flexibility in the interpretation of REST; that's the point.

Data Format Smackdown

The third part of the REST trifecta is that of state and representing that state. When we talk about state, we mean either the current state of a given resource or the future state of it. When you make a GET request, you are requesting the current state of the resource. When you POST, PUT, or DELETE the resource, the client is saying what the future state of the resource should be after the operation completes.

When you perform a GET or DELETE, all the information required to complete the operation is specified as part of the URL and HTTP header. The method is in the header, and the resource is in the URL, whether it refers to a collection of resources (perhaps /users) or a single resource (maybe /users/bill_gates). When you perform a PUT or POST, there will usually be more information to be transmitted. For a user, that might be the username and password. In those cases, the data is transmitted in the body of the HTTP request. Similarly, when you GET a resource, the transmitted state is also in the body.

What form will the data you transmit to the server, or the data the server returns to you, take? The short answer is it can be in any format that can be sent via HTTP, and it will still be valid REST. However, JSON is by far the most common state representation format. The reason for this is most likely that producing and consuming JSON in JavaScript in a browser is trivial, and this is what most RESTful APIs are accessed from. JSON is inherently a simple data format that, even if you had to write code to produce it by hand, is extremely easy to do (usually no more complicated than calling `JSON.stringify(x)` for object x and, similarly, `JSON.parse(x)` where x is some JSON, to get an actual object). It's simpler than XML, and it doesn't require a unique XML-based language, such as SOAP (Simple Object Access Protocol, the format used for classic non-RESTful web services).

The downside to JSON is that it isn't very rigid about data types and structure. While there have been attempts to produce something along the lines of XML schemas for JSON, the idea being that you can validate a JSON document against its schema, they haven't met with much success. In part, this is because JSON is hugely flexible, and that flexibility plus its simplicity is desirable.

Whether you use JSON or not, any HTTP request, whether going to or coming from the server, should specify the Content-Type header so that the receiver of the state representation knows how to handle it. Sometimes, this handling will be automatic, and it will happen without you specifically coding for it because of the library you used to make your remote calls.

There is a debate about what the response for the various HTTP methods should be for methods other than GET (which is self-evident). When you DELETE a resource, what should be returned? Some say that the resource deleted should be returned, while others say that some sort of simple indicator that the operation was successful should be displayed. Similarly, when you POST a new resource, do you get back the unique resource identifier that you would use to GET the resource? Alternatively, is a copy of the resource you sent in echoed back? Perhaps just a simple "OK" identifier would suffice? You'll see the choices that I made for this project soon, but it's ultimately a question you'll need to answer for yourself because, as with the meaning of the HTTP methods, there is no "one-size-fits-all" answer.

A Bonus Pillar: Response Status Codes

Although I said there were three main pillars of REST, in a sense, there's a fourth: what type of HTTP status code your API gives back for various operations.

Setting an appropriate response code on the server for your clients can be a crucial component to making the interaction as smooth as possible. Once again, you can come up with some different meanings and still be doing valid REST. There is somewhat less debate, however, on what the meanings of various response codes should be and how they should be used, if you're going to use them at all. Sometimes, you'll encounter services that give back an HTTP 200 for anything that's not an outright error. That's perfectly acceptable, but it perhaps isn't the most useful approach.

The following list summarizes probably the most common meaning for the various HTTP status responses:

- **200 – OK**: This response code indicates a successful operation. Usually, this would be used when you DELETE a resource or PUT changes to a resource.

- **201 – CREATED**: This response code is frequently used for POST creation of a new resource.

- **400 – BAD REQUEST**: This response code is usually used to indicate that the data format sent when PUT updating or POST creating a resource was invalid or malformed in some way (500 is frequently used instead of 400).

- **401 – UNAUTHORIZED**: This response code is used to indicate that you need to authenticate before performing the requested operation.

- **405 – METHOD NOT ALLOWED**: This response code is used when the requested HTTP method isn't supported (e.g., perhaps in a read-only interface, you wouldn't support POST or PUT, and 500 is frequently used instead of this).

- **500 – INTERNAL SERVER ERROR**: This response code is generally used when some sort of error occurs that is not covered by the previous scenarios.

In general, the response codes fall into fairly well-defined ranges: codes 100–199 are considered "informational" responses, things the client may want to know but which aren't critical to the API's functionality; 200–299 represent successful responses (while 200 is most common, there are others that are useful, such as 201 Created and 202 Accepted – it's just a question of how detailed you want your API to be for your clients); 300–399 represent redirect conditions of some sort, which may or may not need to be handled by a client; 400–499 are for client errors, 400 Bad Request if they passed in invalid request parameters, for example, or 401 Not Authorized if you have security set up and the client isn't allowed to make the request; and 500–599 represent various types of server errors, whether a generic 500 Internal Server Error or perhaps 501 Not Implemented if an HTTP method was requested that your services don't support. You can dig into the many codes online and determine if you want to use more specific codes in various situations – there are many to choose from!

Now you know the core concepts behind REST. Now, let's talk a bit about how you might write the code of a RESTful API on the server using a popular Node library: Express.

Note   For the sake of simplicity, MailBag will forego using codes as shown in the preceding text and just return 200s in all non-error cases. There's nothing inherently wrong with doing that, and some people actually prefer that approach and argue that it's better for reasons of simplicity. Most things about REST, in the real world at least, tend to be more like guidelines than hard-and-fast rules you must follow, and this is one such example of that.

Another Quick Detour: Express, for Fun and Profit

Express (`https://expressjs.com`), which is perhaps the most popular Node module around, is a minimal (though highly extensible) framework for creating web applications that offers developers a set of robust features that eliminates a lot of boilerplate-type code from your application code. Express offers a broad set of APIs, utility methods, and what it calls middleware to provide many of the everyday things modern web applications need. Being a minimal, thin framework means that Express delivers excellent performance on top of everything else.

Express is especially useful for, but is in no way specific to, writing RESTful API code. If you look back to Chapter 2, where you saw the basic for a web server in node, you'll notice that there's no mention of HTTP methods there. In fact, every request of any type will be handled by the one callback function supplied. That means if you want to implement a RESTful service, that callback will need to interrogate the request object, determine the HTTP method, and then branch accordingly. That's not especially difficult to do, but it's code you have to write yourself, which can get messy. Then, since REST is based on URL structure, you'll need to write code to parse the URL to figure out what resource to deal with. Again, it's not rocket science, but it's work you must do yourself.

Using Express avoids all of that. Instead, you write code like this:

```
const app = express();
app.get("/cars/:vin", function(inRequest, inResponse) {
  // Return a car object with the specific VIN number
});
app.listen(8080);
```

Here, you create an Express application instance, which is the basis of everything you do with Express. Then, you tell the app that for a GET request to a URL in the form `/cars/:vin`, execute the given function. The `:vin` part of the URL tells Express that after `/cars` in the URL will come a value that you want to have presented in the collection of parameters that Express parses out of the URL, and you want to name it `vin` (which you can then access in the function by doing `inRequest.params.vin`). In case you are unaware, VIN is short for "Vehicle Identification Number," and it's a unique number that identifies every car manufactured. So, assuming you have a database of VIN numbers, a GET request to this URL can return an object representing the car associated with the VIN number specified. Finally, you just have to start up the Express app by telling it what port to listen on. That's it! No parsing the URL yourself, no handling different request methods, not even creating a server yourself. Express takes care of all those details for you!

You can, of course, specify handlers for all the other HTTP methods, and you can do whatever you like in the function, return whatever you want, set the status code as you see fit, and so on.

As with everything we've talked about so far, there's quite a bit more that Express can do, and you'll see some of it in the server code here, but we'll just be scratching the surface. Express is a potent tool in the Node toolbox for sure!

Back to the Code!

Okay, so finally, here we are, looking at the code in `main.ts`! It begins boringly enough:

Note   For all the source code listings in this chapter and the next five, all comments have been removed from the code, and the code may have been condensed and reformatted a bit to save some space on the printed page. The actual executable code is the same in the book as in the source code bundle, though.

```
import path from "path";
import express,
  { Express, NextFunction, Request, Response } from "express";
import { serverInfo } from "./ServerInfo";
```

```
import * as IMAP from "./IMAP";
import * as SMTP from "./SMTP";
import * as Contacts from "./Contacts";
import { IContact } from "./Contacts";
```

We have several things to import, and we'll get to what each of them is as each is encountered in the code. Note, though, that the first two imports are for a core Node module (path) and Express and some Express-related things. The remaining four are application imports, code that we'll be writing.

The first real code after the imports is this:

```
const app: Express = express();
```

That creates our Express app, as discussed in the previous section. Now, it's time to add some middleware to Express, that is, some additional bits of functionality that we need our Express app to use:

```
app.use(express.json());
```

This middleware takes care of parsing incoming request bodies that contain JSON, as many of ours will. Our application code will, thanks to this middleware, receive a JavaScript object resulting from the incoming data, saving us the hassle of parsing it ourselves.

Next, we have to think about what this server has to do. First, of course, it will need to provide RESTful endpoints that our client application can call on to do its work. But it has to do something else: it needs to serve our client code to a browser that requests it. When we discussed Express earlier, I mentioned that while it's great for writing REST APIs, that's not *all* it's good for. It can also act as a basic web server (which makes sense given you know Node itself can do that on its own!), and enabling that is very simple:

```
app.use("/",
  express.static(path.join(__dirname, "../../client/dist"))
);
```

The static middleware is another built-in middleware that Express provides for serving static resources. All you need to do is tell it where those resources are, and any requests that come in that map to those requests will be served. We haven't built those resources yet – that's what the next chapter is all about – but given the directory structure we created, you know they must be in the client directory, and further you can assume that they're in a dist directory, just like the server is. We need a proper full path to this directory, though, which is where that path module comes into play, and specifically its join() method. Here, we use a built-in variable that node supplies, __dirname, which is the name of the directory the current script is in, and combine that with a relative path pointing to the client/dist directory. The path.join() method will take care of disambiguating all of that, and we'll wind up with a fully qualified path, complete with proper separators for the current operating system, that is passed to express.static(), and that's all it takes to make Express act as a web server for our soon-to-be-built client code.

Next, we need to play one little trick to make our REST functions later work:

```
app.use(function(inRequest: Request, inResponse: Response,
inNext: NextFunction) {
  inResponse.header("Access-Control-Allow-Origin", "*");
  inResponse.header("Access-Control-Allow-Methods",
    "GET,POST,DELETE,OPTIONS"
  );
  inResponse.header("Access-Control-Allow-Headers",
    "Origin,X-Requested-With,Content-Type,Accept"
  );
  inNext();
});
```

The problem is that if you try to execute any of the REST endpoints that we'll be adding next, you'll run into a CORS (Cross-Origin Resource Sharing) limitation, depending on how you make the call. For example, if you want to just load the client later directly from the file system, without it being served from the server (which is precisely how I was doing development most of the time!), then you will run smack into a CORS limitation and not be able to do so. CORS is a security mechanism built into web browsers that ensures that only certain domains can call your REST services. If you were on the job and writing a REST service, you may only want your clients to be able to call it, not anyone in the world. CORS protects you from that by forcing you to specify the domains that you'll accept calls from. This can also come into play if you want to call a REST service from a web page you loaded from your file system, which is a common thing to do during development. It can also come into play if you want to make requests using a tool for testing REST services, something we'll talk about later in this chapter. In many of these cases, CORS will, by default, result in your calls being rejected, which is good for security but awful for development!

CORS depends on several headers, provided by the server to clients, that all begin with Access-Control-Allow. The browser will interrogate the server before making a request to get these headers, and the values determine what the browser will or won't be allowed to do.

To begin, rather than having to specify specific domains to allow (since I don't know them!), CORS has a catch-all setting that will enable you to make calls from anywhere. The way it works is that the server must return a header Access-Control-Allow-Origin that lists the domains that can call it. If the value of that header is an asterisk, then the browser will allow the call regardless of where it's launched from. This, as it happens, is precisely what we want! So, adding this little bit of custom middleware ensures that all requests to our Express server will be allowed.

But that's not all there is to it! We also have to determine what HTTP methods we'll allow. Without doing so, CORS will again stop our requests even though we allow them from any domain. That's where the second line comes into play. The Access-Control-Allow-Methods header is where we list what HTTP methods we'll accept from clients.

Finally, we need to also tell CORS what additional headers we're going to accept, and this is done with the Access-Control-Allow-Headers header. Specifically, for MailBag, the Content-Type header is sent by the client to indicate that content is JSON (for the operation where we're sending an email or adding a contact, as you'll see later). But I added a few other headers that are typically needed as well. The point is you can determine what is needed for your services and configure these headers as appropriate for your use case.

Writing custom middleware, which is what this bit of code is doing, is a simple matter of supplying a function to the app.use() method. When you do something like express.json() from earlier, it is, in fact, passing a function to app.use(). In this case, though, we must supply our own. This function must have a specific structure; it is passed the incoming request, the generated response, and a reference to the next function.

You see, when Express handles a request, all the middleware that was registered with the app via the app.use() calls forms a chain. Each is executed in turn. So, it makes sense that each link in the chain must execute the next to keep the chain going (or it might also abort the request, if that's necessary). That's why after setting the header on the request object, our custom middleware function calls inNext(). That continues the chain, so the request can continue to be processed as required.

REST Endpoint: List Mailboxes

With those preliminaries out of the way, we can begin to add the various endpoints our service must provide to our client, beginning with a function to get a list of mailboxes:

```
app.get("/mailboxes",
  async (inRequest: Request, inResponse: Response) => {
    try {
      const imapWorker: IMAP.Worker = new IMAP.Worker(serverInfo);
      const mailboxes: IMAP.IMailbox[] = await imapWorker.listMailboxes();
      inResponse.json(mailboxes);
    } catch (inError) {
      inResponse.send("error");
    }
  }
);
```

Remember that REST tells us that retrieving a resource should usually use the GET method, so app.get() is used to register this path. The resource we're getting is a list of mailboxes, so /mailboxes is a logical choice for the path.

All the app.XXX() calls (where XXX is an HTTP method) require a callback function to execute when a matching request is received, and they all receive the incoming request and the response object used to produce the response to the caller. Here, because we're going to make some asynchronous calls using the await keyword, we have to throw an async keyword before the function.

Now, what the function does is simple: it instantiates an IMAP.Worker object – something we'll be looking at later – and then calls its listMailboxes() method, capturing the array of IMAP.IMailbox objects it returns. Even without seeing that code, hopefully, it's pretty obvious what's going on at a conceptual level. It then passes that array to the json() method of the passed in response object, which marshals that array into JSON and returns it to the caller. Should any exceptions be thrown along the way, we'll instead send a plain text "error" response back using the inResponse.send() method. The client will need to react appropriately to that, but that's a story for the next chapter!

This basic pattern you will see repeated in all the remaining endpoint handler methods, with minimal variation. In a sense, our Express app is just acting as a proxy to the IMAP (and also SMTP and Contacts) object, which are responsible for the real functionality. That's a pretty common pattern to implement since it nicely segregates duties. It also means that we can test our IMAP, SMTP, and contact-handling code individually without Express having to be in the mix. Nothing says that you *have* to organize your code this way, but it's a logical way to do so and has a lot of benefits.

REST Endpoint: List Messages

Now that we have a handler for getting a list of mailboxes, let's create one for getting a list of messages in a specific mailbox:

```
app.get("/mailboxes/:mailbox",
  async (inRequest: Request, inResponse: Response) => {
    try {
      const imapWorker: IMAP.Worker = new IMAP.Worker(serverInfo);
      const messages: IMAP.IMessage[] = await imapWorker.listMessages({
        mailbox : inRequest.params.mailbox
      });
      inResponse.json(messages);
    } catch (inError) {
      inResponse.send("error");
    }
  }
);
```

Yep, as I said, that's the same basic pattern, with just a few logical differences: we call `IMAP.Worker.listMessages()` this time, and, of course, we get an array of `IMAP.IMessage` objects this time. Finally, we need to be able to specify the name of the mailbox to get messages for, and as you can see, we have `:mailbox` on the end of the path (anything beginning with a semicolon in the path is taken to be such a replacement token). This is a cue to Express that there will be some dynamic value after `/mailboxes/` in the path, and we want that value presented to our code as a request parameter, which we can access with `inRequest.params.mailbox`.

REST Endpoint: Get a Message

Next, we need a function to get the body contents of a specific message in a specific mailbox because the function to get the list of messages will only get metadata about each message, not the actual message itself:

```
app.get("/messages/:mailbox/:id",
  async (inRequest: Request, inResponse: Response) => {
    try {
      const imapWorker: IMAP.Worker = new IMAP.Worker(serverInfo);
      const messageBody: string | undefined = await imapWorker.
      getMessageBody({
        mailbox : inRequest.params.mailbox,
        id : parseInt(inRequest.params.id, 10)
      });
      inResponse.send(messageBody);
    } catch (inError) {
      inResponse.send("error");
    }
  }
);
```

Once again, the same basic pattern, which just a few minor differences. This time, we need two tokens in the path: the name of the mailbox and the ID of the message to retrieve. After that, we call a different method (getMessageBody()) this time, and now we get a simple string back, which is the content of the message. Also, note that because request parameters are always string, but the getMessageBody() function requires an integer for the ID, that's why parseInt() is needed. Finally, the retrieved message body is returned as plain text via a call to inResponse.send() (the client will be responsible for dealing with the case where this might be an HTML-based message). Also note that the return value from the getMessageBody() call can be undefined potentially, if the message can't be found on the server (it shouldn't really happen, but it's not impossible). So, to be good TypeScript citizens, we need the string | undefined type annotation, which is called a union type. This simply means that the return value can be a string or undefined, and that keeps the TypeScript compiler happy!

REST Endpoint: Delete a Message

Next, the client will need the ability to delete a message:

```
app.delete("/messages/:mailbox/:id",
  async (inRequest: Request, inResponse: Response) => {
    try {
      const imapWorker: IMAP.Worker = new IMAP.Worker(serverInfo);
      await imapWorker.deleteMessage({
        mailbox : inRequest.params.mailbox,
        id : parseInt(inRequest.params.id, 10)
      });
      inResponse.send("ok");
    } catch (inError) {
      inResponse.send("error");
    }
  }
);
```

This looks almost identical to the endpoint for getting a message in that it requires the same path to allow the client to identify a message uniquely. Beyond that, it's a simple call to `imapWorker.deleteMessage()`, passing it the mailbox and integerized message ID, so to speak, and we're good to go. Also, take note that now we're using the HTTP DELETE method, to be good REST citizens, so the `app.delete()` method is used to register this endpoint.

REST Endpoint: Send a Message

Now, it's time to implement the endpoint for sending a message:

```
app.post("/messages",
  async (inRequest: Request, inResponse: Response) => {
    try {
      const smtpWorker: SMTP.Worker = new SMTP.Worker(serverInfo);
      await smtpWorker.sendMessage(inRequest.body);
      inResponse.send("ok");
    } catch (inError) {
```

```
      inResponse.send("error");
    }
  }
);
```

Once again, very simple: the HTTP POST method is used to send a message, so `app.post()` is used to register the handler function. In that function, the incoming request body will contain all the information we need to send a message, including target email address, subject, and message text, and the express.json middleware will have nicely parsed that into an object for us to pass along to `smtpWorker.sendMessage()`. Since the IMAP protocol is responsible for retrieving mailboxes and messages while the SMTP protocol is used to send them, it makes sense to have a separate module for each. But, as you'll see later, each of them presents a `Worker` class that contains the methods we call. We return a simple "ok" string here; nothing more is needed.

REST Endpoint: List Contacts

With all mailbox and message functionality built, we now need to turn our attention to the endpoints needed to deal with contacts. There are three of them, beginning with a function to list contacts:

```
app.get("/contacts",
  async (inRequest: Request, inResponse: Response) => {
    try {
      const contactsWorker: Contacts.Worker = new Contacts.Worker();
      const contacts: IContact[] = await contactsWorker.listContacts();
      inResponse.json(contacts);
    } catch (inError) {
      inResponse.send("error");
    }
  }
);
```

Well, this is getting a little repetitive, isn't it?! Yes, indeed, it's the same pattern that you are by now very familiar with, just dealing with contacts now, and the `Contacts` module and its `Worker` class. And now, we're dealing with `IContact` objects (what that is, it's coming up, I promise!), but other than that, there's nothing new here.

REST Endpoint: Add Contact

Similarly, adding a contact is just like sending a message in that it's another HTTP POST function handler:

```
app.post("/contacts",
  async (inRequest: Request, inResponse: Response) => {
    try {
      const contactsWorker: Contacts.Worker = new Contacts.Worker();
      const contact: IContact = await contactsWorker.
      addContact(inRequest.body);
      inResponse.json(contact);
    } catch (inError) {
      inResponse.send("error");
    }
  }
);
```

The contactsWorker.addContact() method will do all the real work, given the object produced by the express.json middleware from the request body content, and here we're actually returning the added contact that is returned by contactsWorker. addContact(). This is necessary because, as you'll see later, this object will contain a unique identifier added during the save process, and the client will need to display that new contact in the list and will need to know that ID in case the user decides to delete the contact. We could certainly not do this and have the client call the GET contacts endpoint again to get the entire contacts list, which would now include the added contact, but that's kind of wasteful of resources. Returning the added object allows the client to do what it needs to without that additional request, and this is also a pervasive pattern to follow with REST services.

REST Endpoint: Delete Contact

We have just one endpoint left to implement, and that's the one for deleting a contact. As you can probably guess, it looks extremely similar to the endpoint for deleting a message:

```
app.delete("/contacts/:id",
  async (inRequest: Request, inResponse: Response) => {
```

```
  try {
    const contactsWorker: Contacts.Worker = new Contacts.Worker();
    await contactsWorker.deleteContact(inRequest.params.id);
    inResponse.send("ok");
  } catch (inError) {
    inResponse.send("error");
  }
 }
);
```

The path is different, of course, and this time it includes the ID of the contact to delete, and naturally we're using the Contacts module and its Worker class and its deleteContact() method, but beyond that it's just more of the same. A little boring perhaps, but there's something to be said for logical self-consistency too!

Now that the RESTful API is defined and Express is ready to handle those requests, let's get into the details of those Worker classes to see the actual work done. But, before we can do that, we have one other source file we need to look at for the rest to make sense.

Gotta Know What We're Talking to: ServerInfo.ts

The Worker classes for IMAP and SMTP, it should be apparent, will need to know about the server(s) they are talking to. Without an IMAP server and an SMTP server somewhere, the code won't be able to receive or send an email. That's where the ServerInfo.ts file comes into play:

```
const path = require("path");
const fs = require("fs");
```

First, we begin by importing the Node path module again, as well as the fs module, which is the File System module. Note that when importing Node modules, you don't typically type the variables that reference them.

We need these modules in order to read the stored information about the servers. This information will be stored in a file named serverInfo.json in the /server directory. The contents of that file will be

```
{
  "smtp" : {
    "host" : "mail.mydomain.com", "port" : 999,
    "auth" : { "user" : "user@domain.com", "pass" : "xxx" } },
  "imap" : {
    "host" : "mail.mydomain.com", "port" : 999,
    "auth" : { "user" : "user@domain.com", "pass" : "xxx" } }
}
```

You'll need to create this file and supply the applicable information before MailBag will work. I'm gonna go out on a limb here and assume that file is self-explanatory.

Now, we'll define an interface that mimics that file:

```
export interface IServerInfo {
  smtp : {
    host: string, port: number,
    auth: { user: string, pass: string }
  },
  imap : {
    host: string, port: number,
    auth: { user: string, pass: string }
  }
}
```

And we'll declare a variable typed to that interface:

```
export let serverInfo: IServerInfo;
```

Now, the goal is to read the serverInfo.json file in and create an object that adheres to the IServerInfo interface and that the serverInfo variable points to. That's a trivial exercise with Node:

```
const rawInfo: string =
  fs.readFileSync(path.join(__dirname, "../serverInfo.json"));
serverInfo = JSON.parse(rawInfo);
```

The file is read in as a plain string with the fs.readFileSync() function, again using path.join() to get a fully qualified path to the file. Finally, we parse the string into an object and assign it to serverInfo. That's it! After that, we have an object in memory that contains the information needed to connect to the server! Yes, that means that MailBag is a single-user webmail application, and it means you can't change the server information through the UI itself (well, you'll have to trust me about that until the next chapter I suppose, but it's true), which we can consider a feature, not a bug! However, you may want to keep an eye out for the "Suggested Exercises" section later. Hint! Hint!

Time to Send the Mail: smtp.ts

Alright, with the basic API built in Express, let's start to look at the code behind one of the two Worker classes, the SMTP.Worker, for sending emails. This class, which is found in the SMTP.ts source file, makes use of a Node module to do the grunt work, and that's the first thing we need to look at in order to make sense of the application code:

```
import Mail from "nodemailer/lib/mailer";
import * as nodemailer from "nodemailer";
import { SendMailOptions, SentMessageInfo } from "nodemailer";
const nodemailer = require("nodemailer");
```

Of course, we begin with some imports, as most modules do. The first three are related to the nodemailer module, which we're going to take a quick detour and look at next, so let's skip those for now. In addition to those, we have the IServerInfo from the ServerInfo.ts file that we looked at earlier to contain the information needed to connect to the SMTP server.

After that, we begin to define the Worker class:

```
export class Worker {
  private static serverInfo: IServerInfo;
  constructor(inServerInfo: IServerInfo) {
    Worker.serverInfo = inServerInfo;
  }
}
```

When instantiated, the server information must be sent in, and it is then stored in the static serverInfo member. Making this member static is superfluous frankly because this class is instantiated with each usage, so there's no real point in it being static. I just did it this way as a reminder that in TypeScript, classes *can* have static members (and there's no *harm* to it being static in this case).

The sendMessage() method of this class is where the real action is, but before we can look at that, we have a quick detour (or two, as it happens) to take.

A Quick Detour: Nodemailer

The nodemailer module (https://nodemailer.com/about) is a Node module for Node applications to allow "easy as cake" email sending (not my words, that's what the author says about it – though I *do* agree with the sentiment!). This module is nice because it's just a single module and has no dependencies, which is frankly kind of rare in the Node world.

Using it is simple: you create a "transport," which is an object that knows how to talk a particular protocol to send mail with, most usual SMTP, providing the transport whatever information is needed to connect, and then you call the sendMail() method on the transport, passing it the details of the message to send. That, really, is all there is to it! In fact, it's so simple that I'm not going to show a bit of sample code here and will instead just show you the real code used in MailBag and have that effectively be the example!

Another Quick Detour: Generics

But first, before we go into the code, I have to touch on a TypeScript topic that until now hasn't been necessary: generics.

Generics, in simplest terms, is a way to write code that can work on multiple types. It's not a concept specific to TypeScript, but it comes up often in TypeScript. The classic example to demonstrate generics is this:

```
function echoMe(inArg: string): string { return inArg; }
```

It's a simple function that does nothing but returns the argument passed in. Since the argument and the return type are the same, this is a very limited function: it will only work for the string type. What if we wanted to do the same for the number type, for example? Well, there are two choices. One is this:

```
function echoMe(inArg: any): any { return inArg; }
```

Typing the argument and return as any (or specifying to type and allowing TypeScript to infer any) will work, but it gives up a lot of the core benefits of TypeScript in terms of type safety and IDE auto-completion and all that good stuff. Another option is to change echoMe() to echoString() and then add a second function:

```
function echoNumber(inArg: number): number { return inArg; }
```

That, of course, will work too, but now we can't just call echoMe() for a string or number, which would be the ideal answer, wouldn't it?

Well, that's where generics come in! With generics, you can do this:

```
function echoMe<T>(inArg: T): T { return inArg; }
```

The trick is to add <T> after the function name. This is referred to as a type variable (sometimes called type parameters or generic parameters, but they all mean the same thing, and I personally prefer type variable). The letter T is simply a placeholder – you could use any valid identifier there. But T is most typical, so I'm going with it! With this in place, we can specify T anywhere else, like in the argument list as the type of inArg and as the return. TypeScript will now allow any type to be passed in but can still provide warning and errors about type issues where appropriate (and possible). You can then call this as you normally would:

```
alert(echoMe("hello"));
```

However, you get more benefit if you now write it like this:

```
alert(echoMe<string>("hello"));
```

That way, TypeScript will enforce the argument being a string. When it's just a static string like that, you don't gain anything, but imagine something like this:

```
// a is some array passed into your function
for (let i = 0; i < a.length; i++) {
  echoMe<string>(a[i]);
}
```

Now, TypeScript will complain if the array isn't typed as string, but you can still use echoMe() for numbers or any other type the same way.

Note that you do not have to use the same type for the return. For example:

```
function echoMe<T>(inArg: T): string {
  return "-" + inArg + "-";
}
alert(echoMe<number>(42));
```

Here, the type of inArg will be number, but we're returning a string.

Generics aren't just for function arguments and return types, though. We can apply them to interfaces too:

```
interface Args<K, L>{ arg1: K, arg2: L }
function logTypes<T, U>(inArg1: T, inArg2: U): Args<T, U> {
  console.log(typeof(inArg1), typeof(inArg2));
  let args: Args<T, U> = {
    arg1: inArg1, arg2: inArg2
  };
  return args;
}
console.log(logTypes<string, number>("frank", 42));
```

The Args interface is defined, and generics are used for the two properties it contains. Yes, you read that right: generics, plural! You can, in fact, declare as many type variables as you wish and use them however you wish. Here, I want each of the two arguments to have different types potentially, so I declare two type variables. And, to prove that T is nothing special, I used K and L as identifiers. No problem! I could even have written

```
interface Args <arg1Type, arg2Type>{
  arg1: arg1Type, arg2: arg2Type
}
```

But that would strike me as a bit superfluous, but it does make the point: you really can use any valid identifier you want; it doesn't need to be a single letter even.

Next, the logTypes() function is declared, and it too has two type variables. I also specify that the return type must adhere to the Args interface contract, and generics are again used here to ensure any types will be allowed. Inside the function, it's just outputting the types of the two incoming variables to the console and then returning an object of type Args with the passed in arguments assigned to its properties. When executing, in the console you will see a line that says "string number," proving that the types were correctly applied when logTypes() is called and throughout logTypes() and in Args as appropriate. Remember that appending <string, number> when calling logTypes() is optional because TypeScript will infer the types if you don't, but I'd suggest it's good form to do so anyway.

While that's not all you can do with generics in TypeScript, those are the basics, and everything else is just variations on a theme, so I think this is good enough for the basics. Remember that it doesn't always make sense to use generics, but sometimes it very much does, and sometimes you may find that you have to. We'll see one such case soon.

Back to the Code!

Okay, now we can have a look at the sendMessage() method, which is the only other thing in the Worker class.

Worker.sendMessage( )

The sendMessage() method takes in an object that must adhere to the SendMailOptions interface, defined by nodemailer. The inOptions object can contain fields like the from address, the to address, carbon copy addresses (cc), blind carbon copy addresses (bcc), the subject of the message, and the text of the message (text). MailBag, being a simple client, will only support from, to, subject, and text:

```
public sendMessage(inOptions: SendMailOptions):
Promise<string> {
  return new Promise((inResolve, inReject) => {
    const transport: Mail = nodemailer.createTransport(Worker.
    serverInfo.smtp);
    transport.sendMail(inOptions,
      (inError: Error | null, inInfo: SentMessageInfo) => {
        if (inError) {
          inReject(inError);
        } else {
          inResolve("");
```

```
        }
      }
    );
  });
}
```

An issue arises here in that nodemailer doesn't natively provide an async/await-compatible API. It instead uses the callback approach. But, if you go back to the code of main.ts, you'll see that async/await is used everywhere when calling the Worker classes. How can that be?

Any time you have a callback-based API, you can wrap a call to it in a Promise. You then return the Promise from the function that makes the call, and that caller can then use async/await to call it. Then, in the function, you simply have the callback passed to the underlying function reject or resolve as appropriate.

So, here, all the calls to nodemailer are wrapped up in the created Promise object. Inside it, the nodemailer.createTransport() method is first called, passing it the server information. That gets us a connection to the SMTP server. Then, the transport.sendmail() method is called, passing it inOptions, which contains the message details passed in from the client. A callback function is the second argument to transport.sendMail(), and that callback is passed an Error object and information about the sent message. Note that the error object can be null, which to TypeScript is a different type. To avoid a compilation error, we have to use a union again, as you saw earlier, which is what Error | null is. This tells TypeScript that the inError can be one of two types: either Error or null (we also could have inError as any; that would accomplish the goal too, but is less TypeScript-y, so to speak!). Finally, inside the callback, if there is an error object, then something went wrong, and the Promise must reject. Otherwise, it was successful and is resolved.

One final subtle issue comes up here, and it's where that detour into generics earlier comes in! Notice the return type here is Promise<string>. The Promise part makes sense: any function that is to be called with async/await must return a Promise. But why do we have a generic <string> there? Well, TypeScript is smart enough to look at what is ultimately being returned, whether as a result of a resolve or reject, from the function. If the caller specifies a type for the variable that gets the eventual outcome of the Promise, as is good form in TypeScript and as such is done in main.ts, then that type must match, or TypeScript will complain. So, with Promise<string>, we're essentially saying to TypeScript: "this function returns a Promise, but it promises to return a string eventually, so make sure the variable that the returned value goes into is that type." The generic variable declaration is how we express that promised final type to TypeScript.

Time to Get the Mail (and Other Stuff): imap.ts

Having seen how to send messages, now it's time to see how to receive them – as well as listing mailboxes and messages in them! This functionality is housed in the IMAP.ts source file.

Before we look at the actual code, though, we have another one of those detours I appear to be so fond of, this time to discuss two Node modules, this time for dealing with the IMAP protocol and for parsing the body of receive emails.

A Quick Detour: emailjs-imap-client and mailparser

The emailjs-imap-client module (https://github.com/emailjs/emailjs-imap-client) is the one responsible for interacting with the IMAP server on behalf of MailBag. It describes itself as a "low-level IMAP client for all your IMAP needs." Short, but sweet!

Using it is rather simple. First, you create a client:

```
const client = new ImapClient(host[,port][,options]);
```

The port and options are optional, only the host is required. Once that's done, you initiate a connection:

```
client.connect().then(() => { /* Do what you want */ });
```

In a nutshell, that's all there is to using it. Of course, getting real work done requires more code. For example, to get a list of mailboxes and log them to the console:

```
client.listMailboxes().then((mailboxes) => {
  console.log(mailboxes);
});
```

For many operations, you need to select a mailbox first. That's easy to do:

```
client.selectMailbox(<mailbox_name>).then(mailbox) {
  // Do your work
});
```

You get the idea, I'm sure. Pretty much everything you can do with emailjs-imap-client is done in this same way. However, you can also use an async/await approach, as you'll see in the MailBag code itself.

209

In addition to this module, we'll also be using the mailparser module (`https://nodemailer.com/extras/mailparser`). The reason is that when we retrieve a message, its structure is relatively complex, and it can be tricky to consume. For example, what if the body contains embedded images? How do you deal with them? How do you get all the header information into an easy-to-use form, things like from, to, and bcc addresses? If you wrote the code to handle such a message yourself, you would quickly find its complexity ballooning. Better to let a suitable module do the job, and that's precisely what mailparser does.

In simplest form, you can use the `simpleParser` that mailparser provides:

```
const simpleParser = require("mailparser").simpleParser;
simpleParser(source[,options], (err, parsed) => {});
```

The `source` argument is the only one required, and it will, of course, be the message that, in our case, emailjs-imap-client, retrieves for us. What you'll get back is a `ParsedMail` object. This object contains several properties, including `subject`, `from`, `to`, `date`, and `text` (the body of the message in plain text).

As with emailjs-imap-client, the API is set up for async/await calls, and that's how the MailBag code will use mailparser as well.

Back to the Code!

Okay, now to actual `IMAP.ts` code! As always, we begin with some imports:

```
const ImapClient = require("emailjs-imap-client");
import { ParsedMail } from "mailparser";
import { simpleParser } from "mailparser";
import { IServerInfo } from "./ServerInfo";
```

Those should be self-explanatory at this point. We know we need the two modules discussed in the last section, and they won't work without server information, so let's move on to the first interface defined:

```
export interface ICallOptions {
  mailbox: string,
  id?: number
}
```

There are four functions that we need to build here: one to list mailboxes, one to list messages within a mailbox, one to retrieve a message, and one to delete a message. Of those, the last three require the caller to specify the name of the mailbox and the ID of the message. Well, to be more precise, all of them require the mailbox name, but only retrieving and deleting a message require the ID. Therefore, the id property is defined as optional so that we can use it in all cases.

Next, we need an interface for a message itself:

```
export interface IMessage {
  id: string, date: string,
  from: string,
  subject: string, body?: string
}
```

This will be used when listing messages in a mailbox as well as when retrieving an individual message. The difference is that when listing messages, the body of the message will not be returned. We'll have a separate function for the client to call for that. We'll do this to save bandwidth: no sense returning the entire body if we don't know if we need it, which is the case when listing messages. Until the user clicks a message, the body, which is the bulk of a message obviously (in most cases at least), isn't needed. That's why body is optional.

Next, we need an interface for a mailbox:

```
export interface IMailbox { name: string, path: string }
```

That's pretty simple! The name is obviously what will be shown on the screen, and the path is how code will identify a mailbox for operations like listing mailboxes and retrieving a message. The name and path need not match; hence, we need to separate fields for them.

Next, we have a single line of code that will execute when the module loads:

```
process.env.NODE_TLS_REJECT_UNAUTHORIZED = "0";
```

This is (most likely) necessary to make the calls to the IMAP server work. The issue is that, by default, Node will attempt to validate the certificate presented by the server when connecting over TLS (Transport Layer Security – if by any chance you're unfamiliar with TLS, here's a great reference: https://tls.ulfheim.net). This setting tells Node to skip that step. To be clear, this makes a TLS connection insecure, since you can't be sure you're talking to the legitimate server, which is the point of validating the certificate. But there can be a fair bit of work that goes into getting that validation to work, so this setting allows us to skip that. To be clear, if you intend to use MailBag in production, then you *will* want to change this! But, as a learning exercise, one that will be connecting to an IMAP server you provide and so know to be good, it's sufficient, I think. Also note that if you aren't connecting to the server over TLS in the first place, then naturally this is all irrelevant.

Now we come to the `Worker` class. Just like the `SMTP.ts` file, and just like the `contacts.ts` file you'll see later, the `Worker` class here is what the code in `main.ts` interacts with:

```
export class Worker {
  private static serverInfo: IServerInfo;
  constructor(inServerInfo: IServerInfo) {
    Worker.serverInfo = inServerInfo;
  }
```

As with `SMTP.Worker`, the `serverInfo` field is defined static, not because it must be, but just as a reminder that it can be in TypeScript. And, also like `SMTP.Worker`, the server information is passed in to the constructor and stored.

Now, the first real method we come to is `connectToServer()`. This is to avoid redundancy: all the other methods will make use of this when connecting to the IMAP server. It is responsible for creating the emailjs-imap-client object and connecting it to the server:

```
private async connectToServer(): Promise<any> {
  const client: any = new ImapClient.default(
    Worker.serverInfo.imap.host,
    Worker.serverInfo.imap.port,
    { auth : Worker.serverInfo.imap.auth }
  );
  client.logLevel = client.LOG_LEVEL_NONE;
  client.onerror = (inError: Error) => {
    console.log(
      "IMAP.Worker.listMailboxes(): Connection error",
      inError
    );
```

```
  };
  await client.connect();
  return client;
}
```

The client is created, passing in the host and port from serverInfo. We also need to pass in a username and password. That's done in the third argument, which you'll recall from earlier is an optional options argument. One of the attributes it can contain is auth, which must be an object containing a user (username) field and pass (password) field.

I then set the logLevel property on the client to the LOG_LEVEL_NONE constant (also from the client). I did this to keep the output when running quiet because without that, you get a fair bit of logging about what's going on. It's helpful if you need it, but most of the time it's just a lot of noise that we don't need.

After that, an error handler is set up on the client. This will be used when the client. connect() method is called if a connection to the server can't be established. In this case, I didn't get fancy: the error is logged, but that's it. No retrying or anything like that. We'll just let the server blow up in such a case because there really isn't much we *could* do anyway. Finally, the connection is established, and the client returned to the caller.

Worker.listMailboxes( )

The first of the four primary methods is up next, and it's the one for listing mailboxes:

```
public async listMailboxes(): Promise<IMailbox[]> {
  const client: any = await this.connectToServer();
  const mailboxes: any = await client.listMailboxes();
  await client.close();
  const finalMailboxes: IMailbox[] = [];
  const iterateChildren: Function =
    (inArray: any[]): void => {
    inArray.forEach((inValue: any) => {
      finalMailboxes.push({
        name : inValue.name, path : inValue.path
      });
      iterateChildren(inValue.children);
    });
```

```
};
iterateChildren(mailboxes.children);
return finalMailboxes;
}
```

First, we get a client using that `connectToServer()` method from before. Then, it's a simple call to `client.listMailboxes()` to get the list. We then call `client.close()` since the connection isn't needed any longer (and note that there are conditions under which the client actually cannot be reused, so to avoid problems and to keep things simple, I just assumed that it was *always* true; hence, the connection is closed and a new client constructed with each method call).

Now, there's one complication here: the list of mailboxes you get is hierarchical. For example, what you get might be this:

```
{ "root": true,
  "children": [
    {
      "name": "INBOX", "delimiter": "/", "path": "INBOX",
      "children": [],
      "flags": ["\\HasNoChildren"],
      "listed": true, "subscribed": true
    },
    {
      "name": "[Gmail]", "delimiter": "/", "path": "[Gmail]",
      "flags": ["\\Noselect","\\HasChildren"],
      "listed": true, "subscribed": true,
      "children": [
        {
          "name": "All Mail", "delimiter": "/",
          "path": "[Gmail]/All Mail",
          "children": [],
          "flags": ["\\HasNoChildren","\\All"],
          "listed": true, "specialUse": "\\All",
          "specialUseFlag": "\\All", "subscribed": true
        }
      ]
```

```
    }
  ]
}
```

That's a problem because on the client, I want to present a flat list of mailboxes. In addition to that problem, the client will only care about name and path, none of the other attributes supplied here. So, we have some work to do!

The iterateChildren() function is called recursively to deal with the hierarchy. For each mailbox encountered, regardless of level in the hierarchy, it will be added to finalMailboxes. But what's added is a new object that contains just the name and path. The children property is then passed to iterateChildren() to continue through the hierarchy.

In the end, finalMailboxes will be a one-dimensional array of objects, each containing name, and path, exactly like the client will want. Perfect!

Worker.listMessages( )

For listing messages in a named mailbox, the listMessages() method is provided:

```
public async listMessages(inCallOptions: ICallOptions):
Promise<IMessage[]> {
  const client: any = await this.connectToServer();
  const mailbox: any = await client.selectMailbox(inCallOptions.mailbox);
  if (mailbox.exists === 0) {
    await client.close();
    return [ ];
  }
  const messages: any[] = await client.listMessages(
    inCallOptions.mailbox, "1:*", [ "uid", "envelope" ]
  );
  await client.close();
  const finalMessages: IMessage[] - [];
  messages.forEach((inValue: any) => {
    finalMessages.push({
      id : inValue.uid, date: inValue.envelope.date,
      from: inValue.envelope.from[0].address,
```

```
    subject: inValue.envelope.subject
  });
});
return finalMessages;
}
```

In this case, after instantiating and configuring the client, we need to select a mailbox to operate against. The `inCallOptions` object will contain the name of the mailbox in its `mailbox` field, so we pass that to `client.selectMailbox()`, and we get back a mailbox object. Note that there doesn't appear to be a type for this though; hence, `any` is used (this is also true for the client). Next, we need to find out how many messages there are. It's a little weird to me, but the value of the `exists` property of the mailbox object tells us this. If there are no messages, then an empty array is returned.

If there *are* messages, however, we need to retrieve them. To do so requires a call to the `client.listMessages()` method. This method takes in the name of the mailbox, what messages to retrieve, and what properties we want. The second argument is a query that determines what messages we'll get. Here, I've specified that we want messages beginning with the first one and all messages after it (asterisk, as is typical, means all or any value). If you wanted to implement a paging mechanism, you could maybe get the first ten with `"1:10"`, but then the code becomes a lot more complicated pretty quickly (the next ten would be `"11:20"`, and so on, and you'd need to pass that information from the client and keep track of it, and so on). For each message, I want just the unique ID of the message and the metadata about it, called the *envelope*. Critically, we *do not* want the body at this point.

For each message returned, an object is constructed, pulling the information the client will need out of the object returned by `client.listMessages()`: the unique message `id`, the `date` it was sent, where it's `from` (just the email address, which is in the `address` property of the object returned), and the `subject`. The `finalMessages` array containing those objects is ultimately returned, and our work here is done!

Worker.getMessageBody( )

Since `listMessages()` doesn't return message bodies, we need a function to get that, and that's where `getMessageBody()` comes in:

```
public async getMessageBody(inCallOptions: ICallOptions):
```

```
Promise<string | undefined > {
  const client: any = await this.connectToServer();
  const messages: any[] = await client.listMessages(
    inCallOptions.mailbox, inCallOptions.id,
    [ "body[]" ], { byUid : true }
  );
  const parsed: ParsedMail = await simpleParser(messages[0]["body[]"]);
  await client.close();
  return parsed.text;
}
```

There's no special function in emailjs-imap-client to get bodies, you simply use the listMessages() method, but this time specifying that we want the body. More precisely, because the body can be in multiple parts, it's actually an array that we request. Note here that we are specifying a specific message ID in the call, and to do that we have to pass the fourth argument, { byUid : true }, to tell the method that we're listing messages based on a specific ID. Unlike listMessages(), where we were dealing with a range of messages based on their ordinal number, here it's a unique ID for a specific message; hence, that option is required.

Once we have the message, we can then pass it along to the simpleParser() constructor, which parses the message into a ParsedMail object. After closing the connection, we just return the text property of that object, which is the plain text body content, all necessary concatenation of multiple body parts dealt with for us. Note that the client already has any metadata needed for this message; hence, it's only the body content we care about here.

Worker.deleteMessage( )

Finally, we come to the final method this Worker class must provide, the one for deleting a message:

```
public async deleteMessage(inCallOptions: ICallOptions):
Promise<any> {
  const client: any = await this.connectToServer();
  await client.deleteMessages(
    inCallOptions.mailbox, inCallOptions.id, { byUid : true }
```

```
  );
  await client.close();
}
```

This method is similar to getMessageBody() in terms of the call to the client; this time, it's the deleteMessages() method. We again pass it the mailbox name and the unique ID of the message to delete, and we again must tell it that we are, in fact, passing it a unique ID. But, unlike getMessageBody(), we're basically done at that point, save for closing the connection, of course.

Reach Out and Touch Someone: contacts.ts

Now that you've seen how to send and receive mail, let's go in a different direction and look at what goes into the contacts functionality in the contacts.ts file. This will take us until some side topics, and that requires two quick detours!

A Quick Detour: NoSQL

For this app, we need to store data, namely, our contacts. There are, of course, many ways to do this. You could write them out to plain text files. You could store them in cookies in the browser or perhaps the LocalStorage mechanism in the browser. You could store them in a good ole database on a server. In fact, that last one is what we're going to do: a database that lives on the server. That way, our contacts are there when we need them regardless of where we access MailBag from.

Most people think of an RDBMS (Relational DataBase Management System) like Oracle, SQL Server, MySQL, or PostgreSQL when you say the word database. In such a database, you have tables, each with rows of data records and each table having columns of data attributes. If you want to get the list of customers in a table, as an example, the magic of the Structured Query Language (SQL) allows us to write a query like so:

```
select * from test.customers
```

This will get you a list of all users in the table and all the data attributes defined in the table for each.

Now, that's straightforward and highly useful and, I bet, nothing new to you. This is the bread and butter of databases.

The problem, as some see it at least, is that each row in that table has a rigid structure. Each row, which logically represents a customer, has, perhaps, a unique ID, a first name, a last name, a credit card number (don't get any ideas; they're bogus!), and a number of purchases. That's all there is, and every customer you stuff into that table must adhere to that structure. If you need to add attributes later, say, a middle name, you can add a column to the table, but now all of the existing items will have blank or null values in that field (assuming you allow empty or null values) unless you do some extra work. That could be a problem if the code that uses this database doesn't account for it. While adding a column is usually a benign enough change, sometimes what's required is a more complex change than that, and you can easily break things, especially where the relationship between rows is concerned (and remember it's a *relational* database; after all, relationships matter!).

SQL and the RDBMSs it works with are very powerful constructs, and they are appropriate for all sorts of use cases.

Underlying the power of an RDBMS is the concept of ACID, an acronym for Atomicity, Consistency, Isolation, and Durability. ACID describes the ability of the RDBMS to ensure that the data is always in a consistent state at the end of every operation. This is accomplished by many hard rules that you must follow, which results in nothing that might violate ACID being allowed.

While ACID is likely what you want in a banking application, for example, there are some situations where it isn't, arguably, optimal. Sometimes, you don't care about relationships (much), and you don't want to have a rigid structure to your data, and data integrity might not be the highest consideration even.

That's where the NoSQL concept comes into play.

In contrast to ACID, the BASE model underpins NoSQL: Basic Availability, Soft state, and Eventual consistency. This term leads you into a lot of computer science theory, such as the CAP theorem and horizontal vs. vertical scaling, but for developers, it boils down to the idea that the persistent data store loosens the rules!

For a start, you no longer must define a rigid database schema up front. There are no tables at all to define, so you don't have to specify what attributes a customer has, for example, by creating columns in a table for each. That usually means getting started with NoSQL is faster than with an RDBMS.

Instead of tables and rows, you have *collections* of *documents*, each document identified by a key value. What goes in those documents can be virtually anything, and the structure of the document doesn't need to be rigidly defined. In fact, you can have documents with very different structures in a collection at a single time.

You could literally store an image, such as a GIF file, as a document in a collection, or even an executable file if you wanted to. It's simply mapped to a unique key, and that key, among other mechanisms, can be used to retrieve it. You can also store a chunk of textual data in common formats like XML, JSON, or CSV.

The bottom line, though, is that whatever you happen to be storing, it's always mapped to a unique key value. That is, pardon the pun again, the *key* idea! Because of this, there are no SQL queries to write. You look documents up by specific key values or iterate over a collection of documents looking for those that match some criteria you define.

At first, it may seem like there's no way to query a NoSQL database, but that's not the case. It is still, in fact, possible to query a NoSQL database if what you're storing is structured in some way. If you're storing JSON documents, for example, you might have a customer document like so:

```
{ FirstName : "Jack", LastName : "Miller", CreditCardNumber : 123456789,
NumberOfPurchases : 6 }
```

Some key value will identify that, but it's also possible to find only the document with a `LastName` of `Miller` without knowing any of the keys. You don't give up those sorts of capabilities by going to NoSQL; it's just that you no longer have to write SQL queries. Now, instead, and depending on which NoSQL implementation you use, you might write code more like this to find a customer with `FirstName` "Jack":

```
var c = Customers.find({ FirstName : "Jack" });
```

Without getting into the specifics of the code (because for this discussion it doesn't really matter), `Customers` is a collection of documents, and `find()` looks for any that have attributes matching the specified criteria. You'll get back an array of, in this case, JavaScript objects.

At this point in time, JSON is clearly the most used data storage format when working with NoSQL, and for a good reason, NoSQL plays very well with JavaScript, so JSON is a natural choice. JSON is what we're going to be storing for MailBag.

Now that you have the basic idea behind NoSQL down, let's look at the library that allows us to implement it in MailBag: NeDB.

Another Quick Detour: NeDB

NeDB (https://github.com/louischatriot/nedb) by Louis Chatriot is a Node library that presents to our code a simple NoSQL database API. There are TypeScript bindings available for it, so we can use all the TypeScript goodness we want with it too.

You've undoubtedly heard of the popular NoSQL database MongoDB. It is almost certainly the most well-known NoSQL database. I thought about using it for this project, but I decided against it because MongoDB is a separate server that you run and make calls to from your code. I went with NeDB because it is just a library, so it's fully embedded in the server side of MailBag, no additional server to set up and connect to.

But here's the good news: NeDB seeks to mimic a useful subset of MongoDB's API, meaning that most of what you're about to learn will translate easily to MongoDB if you ever want or need to use it.

Under the covers, NeDB stores its data in plain text files that you can open in a text editor if you want, which is helpful in case you ever need to recover anything. It has most of the critical features of MongoDB, certainly everything you'll need: creating documents, updating them, finding them, and deleting them and allowing you to do so across different collections of documents.

To give you a quick flavor of working with NeDB, here's a simple example:

```
const db = new nedb({
  filename : "people.db", autoload : true
});
db.insert({ firstName : "Billy", lastName : "Joel" },
  function (inError, inDocument) {
    if (inError) {
      console.log(`Error: ${inError}`);
    } else {
      db.findOne({ firstName : "Billy" },
        function (inError, inDocument) {
          if (inError) {
            console.log(`Error: ${inError}`);
          } else {
            console.log(inDocument);
          }
        }
```

```
      );
    }
  }
);
```

You create an instance of a database by providing NeDB with the filename of that database and also telling NeDB to load it at that point automatically (or you can manually open it later if you want to). Then, you can call the insert() method, passing it an object to insert, and a callback function. The callback function can do whatever makes sense. In this case, I just retrieve the document that was just inserted using a query and log it to the console (NeDB will add an _id property to the object, so if I wanted to I could have done db.findOne({ _id : inDocument._id}) instead, to retrieve it by its unique key). Remember that NeDB is almost always asynchronous, so you'll need to deal with callbacks (or build a Promise-based wrapper around it if you prefer). The findOne() method does exactly that: finds a specific single document based on some query, here based on the firstName attribute. Of course, if there's a chance there is more than one document with a firstName of Billy, then chances are you want to use the find() method instead, which returns an array of matching documents.

For this server, you won't need too much more NeDB than this, but know that it provides a very rich API, so if you need a simple database module that doesn't have any outside dependencies (as in no additional server to run) and want to use the NoSQL approach, then NeDB is, in my opinion, one of the best choices available in the world of Node development.

Back to the Code!

Okay, let's kick things off, as we always do, with some imports:

```
import * as path from "path";
const Datastore = require("nedb");
```

That's not much, is it? We need NeDB, naturally, and we need path, as you know from the previous section, to get a path to the data file.

Now, let's define an interface to describe a contact:

```
export interface IContact {
  _id?: number, name: string, email: string
}
```

We're going to use this for all use cases, meaning when we add or delete a contact, as well as when listing contacts. In the case of adding a contact, the _id field won't be populated initially, meaning the client won't supply it. Instead, NeDB will be populating that for us, so we have to mark it as optional here; otherwise, our add operation wouldn't meet the contract of the interface as a result of not having an _id field.

With that ready to go, we can start to define the Worker class:

```
export class Worker {
  private db: Nedb;
  constructor() {
    this.db = new Datastore({
      filename : path.join(__dirname, "contacts.db"),
      autoload : true
    });
  }
```

Upon construction, a NeDB Datastore object is created, and a path to the contacts.db file is given. We tell NeDB to load it automatically, and NeDB will create the file for us if it doesn't already exist. This is all we need to prepare for the remainder of the methods this class must provide.

Worker.listContacts( )

First up is providing a list of contacts, which is what the aptly named listContacts() method does:

```
public listContacts(): Promise<IContact[]> {
  return new Promise((inResolve, inReject) => {
    this.db.find({ },
      (inError: Error, inDocs: IContact[]) => {
        if (inError) {
          inReject(inError);
        } else {
          inResolve(inDocs);
        }
      }
```

```
    );
  });
}
```

As with nodemailer, NeDB doesn't provide an async/await-based API, so we have to do the same sort of trick with wrapping it in Promises as we did with nodemailer in order to be able to write our code with async/await. Inside the Promise, it's a simple matter of calling the find() method on the DataStore referenced by this.db and passing no search criteria as the first argument (well, technically an *empty* search criteria object, to be pedantic). That returns us all the records in the contacts.db file, which is our contacts collection, in NoSQL parlance. Since we know that the objects that will be returned will match the IContact interface's structure, we can type the inDocs argument as such, even though technically NeDB doesn't know about our type. It doesn't have to, though: this is all TypeScript territory. Then, just like with nodemailer, we either reject the Promise, passing the error to the caller, or else we return the array of documents, which are our contact objects. Notice the use of generics for the return type: here, we're promising to resolve with an array of IContact objects, which TypeScript is happy to see!

That's all there is to it!

Worker.addContact( )

Next up is addContact(), called to add a new contact to the collection:

```
public addContact(inContact: IContact): Promise<IContact> {
  return new Promise((inResolve, inReject) => {
    this.db.insert(inContact,
      (inError: Error | null, inNewDoc: IContact) => {
        if (inError) {
          inReject(inError);
        } else {
          inResolve(inNewDoc);
        }
      }
    );
  });
}
```

It's even simpler than `listMessages()`, but follows the same basic structure. The `insert()` method this time is what we need, passing the contact to add as the first argument. This method passes the added object to the callback, which will now include an `_id` field, so we return that object to the caller, and eventually the client, so that it can add it to the screen as appropriate (all of which you'll see in the next chapter).

Worker.deleteContact( )

Finally, we need to implement a `deleteContact()` method for removing a contact:

```
public deleteContact(inID: string): Promise<string> {
  return new Promise((inResolve, inReject) => {
    this.db.remove({ _id : inID }, { },
      (inError: Error | null, inNumRemoved: number) => {
        if (inError) {
          inReject(inError);
        } else {
          inResolve("");
        }
      }
    );
  });
}
```

Here, the `remove()` method is used, and for the first time, we need to provide a query. This method receives just the ID of the contact to delete, and we need a match on the `_id` field, hence the query object seen here. This method takes a second argument, an options argument, that provides some additional flexibility (at the time of this writing, the only option was whether to remove multiple documents if more than one matches the selection criteria – when using the `_id` field though, that would never be the case, so an empty options object is sufficient here). In this case, the callback is passed the number of documents removed. Given the way the code is structured and how the client will be written, there's really no situation where anything but a value of 1 would be passed, so I saw no real purpose in returning anything at all when resolving the Promise. As long as it's not rejected, we treat it as a successful removal.

And, with this final method, we've now explored all the code of the MailBag server!

Testing It All

Let's talk a bit about testing. We've built the server side of MailBag, but how do you go about testing it? Obviously, you could write some code, maybe in main.ts, to call the various Worker methods to see if everything works, but that doesn't test the whole thing: How do we know the client-facing API is working right?

To do this sort of holistic testing, without having the client written yet, is a good idea because then we know the server is working correctly and any problems we face while writing the client are likely client-specific issues.

Perhaps the simplest way to do such testing is with the well-known command-line program curl (`https://curl.haxx.se/`). If you're on a *nix system, then you likely have it already. If you're on Windows, like me, then you'll need to download it separately. Fortunately, there's no installation: just explode the archive, and you're ready to use curl.

As a first example, how do we test the function to get mailboxes with curl? That's very easy:

```
curl localhost/mailboxes
```

That presumes the server is running on the same machine, of course, but that's a reasonable expectation at development time. By default, curl will make a GET request to the URL you specify. Assuming the server is running, you should see a response, displayed directly in the console, something like what you see in Figure 8-4 (obviously, what you actually see will depend on the server you connect to and what mailboxes the account has).

```
C:\>curl localhost/mailboxes
[{"name":"INBOX","path":"INBOX"},{"name":"Storage","path":"INBOX.Storage"},{"name":"S
ent Messages","path":"INBOX.Sent Messages"},{"name":"Deleted Messages","path":"INBOX.
Deleted Messages"},{"name":"Archive","path":"INBOX.Archive"},{"name":"spam","path":"I
NBOX.spam"},{"name":"Trash","path":"INBOX.Trash"},{"name":"Drafts","path":"INBOX.Draf
ts"},{"name":"Sent","path":"INBOX.Sent"},{"name":"Junk","path":"INBOX.Junk"}]
C:\>_
```

Figure 8-4. *A simple API test with curl*

We can similarly get a list of messages in a mailbox with

```
curl localhost/mailboxes/INBOX
```

Figure 8-5 is the type of response you can expect to see.

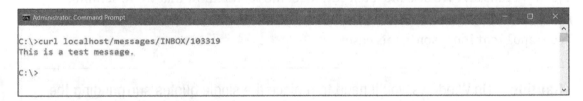

```
Administrator: Command Prompt                                    —    □    ×
C:\>curl localhost/mailboxes/INBOX
[{"id":103319,"date":"Sat, 30 Nov 2019 15:32:05 -0500","from":{"address":"fzammetti@gmail.com","name":"Fran
k Zammetti"},"subject":"test"}]
C:\>
```

Figure 8-5. *A listing of messages in my inbox*

Then, we can get the body of the message easily:

```
curl localhost/messages/INBOX/103319
```

Figure 8-6 is something like you would see if you had this message on your server and in your inbox.

```
Administrator: Command Prompt                                    —    □    ×
C:\>curl localhost/messages/INBOX/103319
This is a test message.

C:\>
```

Figure 8-6. *The boring contents of a boring email!*

To delete that message, we must use the DELETE method of course, and curl supports that as well:

```
curl -X DELETE localhost/messages/INBOX/103319
```

Figure 8-7 shows the result, followed by listing the inbox messages again to show that it's now empty of that message.

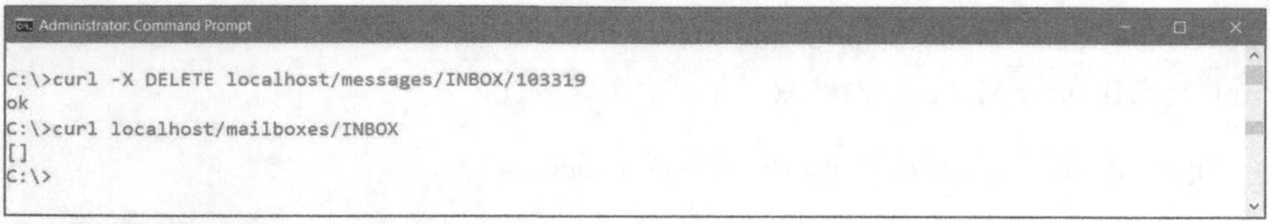

```
Administrator: Command Prompt                                    —    □    ×
C:\>curl -X DELETE localhost/messages/INBOX/103319
ok
C:\>curl localhost/mailboxes/INBOX
[]
C:\>
```

Figure 8-7. *Message gone, inbox empty!*

What about sending messages, you ask? That's easy, too, but it requires a little more curl work:

```
curl -d '{ "to" : "fzammetti@gmail.com", "from" : "fzammetti@etherient.
com", "subject" : "This is a test", "message" : "If you see this then it
worked!" }' -H "Content-Type:application/json" -X POST localhost/messages
```

Since sending a message requires sending data in the body, we must define that data, and that's where the -d (for "data") switch comes into play. We can supply the JSON directly after it. Optionally, you can store the JSON in a file and specify -d <json_filename>. We also must tell curl to let the server know that we're sending JSON, and that's what -H is for. This allows us to set arbitrary request headers, Content-Type:application/json in this case.

Caution   On Windows, you'll need to replace the single quotes surrounding the JSON with double quotes and then escape each of the quotes inside. Otherwise, this won't work.

I'm going to skip the functions for contacts here since it's just more of the same, and I'm pretty sure you get the idea by this point.

Suggested Exercises

It's always good, I think, to take existing code and try and extend and change it a bit. It's an excellent way to get some practice without having to think through everything yourself. With that in mind, here are a few ideas of things you might attempt on your own to sharpen your skills:

- Add an `updateContact()` function using the PUT method to be able to change an existing contact. You'll need to accept the potentially new name and email address, plus the existing `_id`, and then write the NeDB code to update it.

- Set HTTP response codes according to the discussion in the section on REST rather than using 200 for everything. This will give you some experience working with Express and some practice using Postman, Insomnia, or curl to test your changes.

- Write some curl commands to test the contact functions. Then, do the same with Postman to make sure you got these concepts.

Summary

In this chapter, you learned quite a lot! You learned about writing a RESTful API with Node and Express. You learned about finding TypeScript bindings for the Node modules you might want to use, and you learned about several modules, including `emailjs-imap-client` and `nodemail`. You got a look at the NoSQL concept and the NeDB module for storing data using it. In the process, you got a look at some new TypeScript goodness in generics and generally got to see a lot of TypeScript in action.

Now that we have a server built and an API ready, we can begin to build the client portion with React, which is what the next chapter is all about!

CHAPTER 9

Delivering the Goods: MailBag, the Client

With the server side of MailBag ready to go, it's time now to move on to the client side of things! Here, we'll get back to playing with our good friend React, along with some supporting libraries, and we'll hook it all up to the server that was built in the previous chapter. In the end, we'll have ourselves a fully functional webmail application that you could use for real if you wanted to!

What Are We Building?

Unlike the server part of MailBag, the client part is something we can easily take a look at because it is, by its nature, a visual thing. That makes describing what we're going to build easy for an author like me! So let's begin with Figure 9-1, which shows MailBag as it would appear after initial launch (well, in a general sense, what you would actually see would depend on the mail account you hook it up to, but this is linked to my account, so it gives you a general idea at least).

© Frank Zammetti 2022
F. Zammetti, *Modern Full-Stack Development*, https://doi.org/10.1007/978-1-4842-8811-5_9

Figure 9-1. *Our first look at MailBag's client*

I make no representation that this app can compete with the likes of Gmail or Outlook, but it gets the primary job of a webmail application done. Up top, you see that you can create a new message, and you can create a new contact. A list of existing contacts is over on the right, and on the left is the list of mailboxes that the IMAP server used returns. In the center, at the top, is a list of messages in the currently selected mailbox. For example, if I click the INBOX button on the left, I see some messages in Figure 9-2.

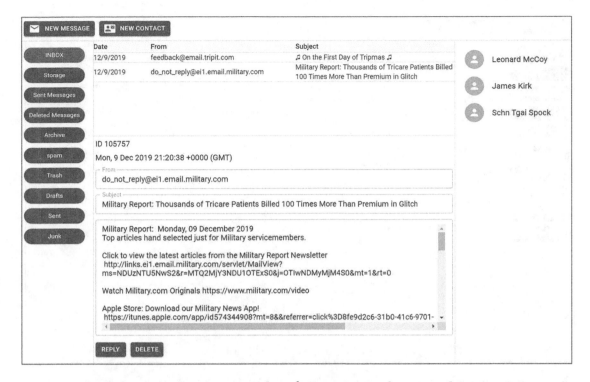

Figure 9-2. A few messages in my inbox (I get A LOT of spam – this was a good day!)

In this screenshot, I've also gone ahead and clicked one of the messages, which shows its details at the bottom. As you can see, I can reply to the message, or I can delete it (and none of the fields above the buttons are editable). When you click the NEW MESSAGE button in the toolbar, you see the same basic screen except that the ID and the date are hidden, the From field becomes a To field, and there is just a single Send button (and everything is editable, naturally).

When you click a contact on the right or when you click the NEW CONTACT button, you wind up at essentially the same place, which is shown in Figure 9-3.

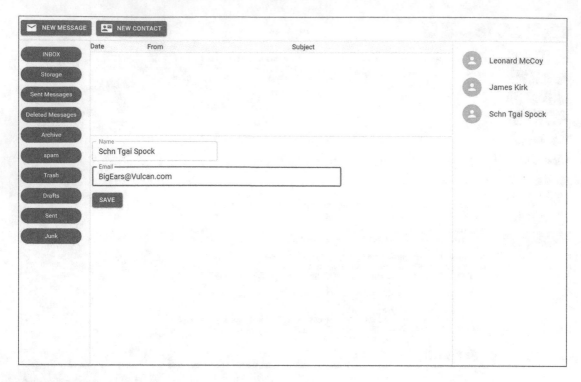

Figure 9-3. *Adding a contact*

Similar to the view of a message, clicking an existing contact shows a screen that is essentially the same except that in that case, the SAVE button becomes a DELETE button (and the fields are read-only).

Note   Although this section is just meant as a walk-through, you of course can (and maybe even should) fire up MailBag now and take a look at it in action. Assuming you've already gone through Chapter 8 and downloaded the source code bundle and installed dependencies, you can fire up the MailBag server, and the client is then available at `http://localhost` automatically.

Basic Requirements

Now that you know what the app looks like, let's catalog the basic functionality it must provide. As I said, we're not challenging Google's webmail supremacy, so the list isn't all that extensive (and, given what you saw in the last chapter, you effectively already know what the list must contain):

- The server must be consulted for a list of mailboxes under a single configured IMAP account once at startup.

- The user can select a mailbox from the list, which will double as a refresh action. The messages will be displayed in a tabular form and will show the date received, subject, and sender.

- Clicking a message shows it below the list, including subject, sender, ID on the server, date received, and, of course, the message itself, as plain text.

- The user must be able to delete the message being viewed.

- The user can begin a new message in reply to the message being viewed. The subject will automatically have "Re:" prepended to it, and the original message will be shown below a bit of marker text.

- A list of contacts will be stored on the server. The user can select a contact from a list and can delete the contact or begin a message to them. They can also, of course, add a new contact.

- Like mailboxes, the server will be consulted once at startup for the list of contacts.

In addition to the requirements, since this is an interface, we need to discuss the overall structure of it, if for no other reason than to provide a common vocabulary to use going forward. The screenshots make it fairly obvious, but the overall structure, or layout, of the interface is described in Figure 9-4.

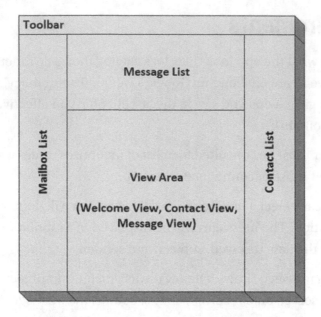

Figure 9-4. *The overall layout of the client in block form*

As you can see, in block form, it mimics the arrangement shown in the screenshots. However, how we achieve that layout is the critical piece of the puzzle, and that's something we're going to talk about a bit later on, after a necessary detour. But, before we get to that, we have to set up the project, so let's do that now!

Setting Up the Project

Setting up the client project is very similar to setting up the client. Create a client directory under the project root directory alongside the server directory. Then, create a src directory in it.

Typically, I would detail the initialization steps to take at this point, but I think you've seen those steps enough between the server code and previous examples, so let's save some time, and, instead, I'll just show you what the package.json file should be after doing a basic npm init and then installing all the necessary dependencies:

```
{
  "name": "mailbag",
  "version": "1.1.0",
  "description": "MailBag",
```

```
  "main": "main.tsx",
  "scripts": {
    "build": "webpack --mode production"
  },
  "author": "Frank W. Zammetti",
  "license": "ISC",
  "devDependencies": {
    "@babel/plugin-syntax-dynamic-import": "7.8.3",
    "@mui/types": "7.1.4",
    "@types/react": "18.0.15",
    "@types/react-dom": "18.0.6",
    "css-loader": "6.7.1",
    "html-loader": "4.1.0",
    "html-webpack-plugin": "5.5.0",
    "style-loader": "3.3.1",
    "ts-loader": "9.3.1",
    "typescript": "4.7.4",
    "webpack": "5.73.0",
    "webpack-cli": "4.10.0",
    "webpack-dev-server": "4.9.3"
  },
  "dependencies": {
    "@emotion/react": "11.9.3",
    "@emotion/styled": "11.9.3",
    "@mui/icons-material": "5.8.4",
    "@mui/material": "5.9.1",
    "axios": "0.27.2",
    "normalize.css": "8.0.1",
    "react": "18.2.0",
    "react-dom": "18.2.0"
  }
}
```

If you download the source archive for this book, that's what you'll find, and you can just do an `npm install` at this point to get everything installed. Otherwise, just overwrite this file with this content (and this is true of the remaining configuration files we're about to discuss).

As you can see, TypeScript is installed, and then too is Webpack. Also, several Webpack loaders and plugins are installed (and some of those result in some additional dependencies being automatically added by NPM).

Note   I also added a script that can be used to execute a build, so now `npm run build` is all we need to do to kick off the build. Also **note** that Axios didn't have type bindings at the time of this writing and normalize.css isn't a library of code, it's a stylesheet, so typing doesn't factor into it.

We'll get back to Webpack in just a moment, but this effectively takes care of the development dependencies. But what about runtime dependencies? Well, I've also installed those as well, and they are as follows:

- **React** – Of course!

- **normalize.css** – A CSS reset to ensure we start with a consistent client-side environment across browsers as far as styles go

- **Axios** – A library for server communications (more on this later)

- **MUI** – A library providing UI widgets to build our UI with based on Google's Material guidelines (more on this later too)

Now, when TypeScript was installed, we got a default `tsconfig.json` file, and that needs to be modified a bit also. Again, I'll just show you what the final file should look like (remember that you will have other content commented out since the `tsc -init` will produce it, but this is the content that should be enabled with the appropriate values):

```
{
  "compilerOptions" : {
    "esModuleInterop" : true,
    "sourceMap" : true,
    "noImplicitAny" : false,
    "module" : "commonjs",
```

```
    "target" : "es6",
    "lib" : [ "es2015", "es2017", "dom" ],
    "removeComments" : true,
    "jsx" : "react",
    "allowJs" : true,
    "baseUrl" : "./",
    "paths" : { "components/*" : [ "src/components/*" ] }
  }
}
```

So far, these are the same basic steps that were done when building the server. But, unlike the server, there are some additional installation and configuration steps we must do because the client will be using Webpack. It will have been installed at this point, but we must initialize this project with Webpack too:

```
npx webpack init
```

That creates a default webpack.config.js file. As an aside, you also should go ahead and delete the .yo-rc.json file that's created since it won't be needed (you can keep the README.md file if you want though). For our purposes here, the answers you give during this step won't matter because we're just going to overwrite the file with the following:

```
const HtmlWebPackPlugin = require("html-webpack-plugin");
module.exports = {
  entry : "./src/code/main.tsx",
  resolve : { extensions : [ ".ts", ".tsx", ".js" ] },
  module : {
    rules : [
      { test : /\.html$/, use : { loader : "html-loader" } },
      { test : /\.css$/,
        use : [ "style-loader", "css-loader"] },
      { test : /\.tsx?$/, use: 'ts-loader', exclude : /node_modules/ }
    ]
  },
  plugins : [
    new HtmlWebPackPlugin({ template : "./src/index.html",
      filename : "./index.html" })
  ],
```

239

```
  performance : { hints : false },
  watch : true, devtool : "source-map"
};
```

You can see the rules defined for handling HTML, CSS, and TSX files, using the loaders installed before.

The `HtmlWebPackPlugin` has a particular purpose. We tell Webpack what HTML file in our source code to start with via the `entry` attribute, and it then modifies it as needed (including adding a proper module loader) so that our app can be launched after Webpack has transformed it. This plug is responsible for that.

The `performance` attribute is necessary because, by default, Webpack will produce a warning or error, depending on various factors, if the final bundle is over 250Kb. Setting `performance : { hints : false }` disables this behavior.

Setting `watch:true` serves much the same purpose as the script entries in the server did: Webpack will watch our source files and automatically rebuild the client if any files change. That gives us that nice, fast turnaround for changes we so liked when working with the server code, but we get it "for free" with Webpack just by adding this attribute!

Finally, `devtool` set to `"source-map"` ensures that a source map is created for the final bundle, allowing us to do some debugging when necessary.

Source File Rundown

Of course, you know we're dealing with files in the `client` directory and, more precisely, in the `src` directory. Like the server code, the client code is laid out the same fundamental way. Critically, the final "executable" client code winds up in the `dist` directory (which would have been created when the Webpack initialization step was done, but you can, of course, add it manually if you skipped that step). But let's talk about the files that make up this application in the `src` directory (and the subdirectories in it):

- `src/index.html` – The main entry point of the application.

- `src/css/main.css` – A regular old CSS file with some shared styles.

- `src/code/main.ts` – The main *code* entry point. This is where React will begin to build our UI from.

- `src/code/Contacts.ts` – Like the server, this is the file that contains a Worker class for dealing with contacts (this is what talks to the server side of MailBag for contacts).

- `src/code/IMAP.ts` – Like `Contacts.ts`, this contains a Worker for performing all the IMAP functions, in conjunction with the server.

- `src/code/SMTP.ts` – Just like `IMAP.ts`, but for the SMTP (send) functionality.

- `src/code/config.ts` – A simple configuration file that will contain information about the server component and your email address.

- `src/code/state.ts` – This is where most of the action of the app actually is, but we'll get to that in due time!

- `src/code/components/BaseLayout.tsx` – A React component that houses all others.

- `src/code/components/Toolbar.tsx` – A React component that is the toolbar.

- `src/code/components/MailboxList.tsx` – A React component that is the list of mailboxes on the left.

- `src/code/components/ContactList.tsx` – A React component that is the list of contacts on the right.

- `src/code/components/MessageList.tsx` – A React component that is a list of messages in a selected mailbox.

- `src/code/components/WelcomeView.tsx` – A React component that serves as just a simple splash screen when the app starts up or when certain operations occur.

- `src/code/components/ContactView.tsx` – A React component that is the presentation of the contact view when a contact is selected or a new one is being created.

- `src/code/components/MessageView.tsx` – A React component that is the presentation of a message or when a message is being composed.

As always, we'll be examining each of these in turn, but I think that gives you a good rundown of what code we'll be looking at. It seems like a lot of files, but really, most of them are very small.

The Starting Point: index.html

This is where it all begins – the entry point to the application:

```
<!DOCTYPE html>
<html lang="en">
  <head>
    <meta charset="utf-8">
    <title>MailBag</title>
  </head>
  <body>
    <div id="mainContainer" style="width: 100vw;height:100vh;"></div>
  </body>
</html>
```

Well, that's kind of anticlimactic, isn't it? Remember earlier when I said that Webpack will transform this file as appropriate to make the app work? Because of that, there's not much for us to do here, so it's a nice, simple HTML document with no real content. It's a little weird that we don't even import any JavaScript because, obviously, that must happen at some point, or else MailBag isn't going to do much! But that's what Webpack takes care of for us, so we don't even have to think about *that* much. But, what we do have to provide is somewhere for React to render our content, and that's where that div you see comes into play. The styling just ensures that the div fills the entire browser window, and that's all we'll need for React to do its thing later.

The Starting Point, Redux: main.tsx

Okay, now it's time to get to some real code! The first file to look at is main.tsx, which is the main entry point code-wise. This is where React will start to execute our application from. Given the .tsx extension, we know that this is a JSX file that is written in TypeScript. And it begins simply enough:

Note   For the remainder of this chapter, to save some trees, I've removed all imports except where they are something unique, as is the case here.

```
import "normalize.css";
import "../css/main.css";
```

It may seem a bit odd to see CSS files imported into a code file like this, but it's okay because JSX and the TypeScript compiler (and Webpack) know how to deal with that on our behalf. That's also why index.html doesn't have them imported, as you'd normally do.

Now, as far as what those files are, `normalize.css` is a CSS reset, meaning that it normalizes initial style conditions on a page across browsers. It takes care of ensuring every browser has the same padding around a given HTML element, for example, or that the margins on the document itself are consistent across browsers. All of that stuff can be different from browser to browser, so using a reset helps ensure that the styles our app uses, which are in the `main.css` file, are applied on a stable, consistent foundation. You don't use any styles in `normalize.css` yourself directly; they're strictly something that gets applied automatically before your app's styles do (which is why `normalize.css` must be imported first, by the way).

With the imports out of the way, it's time for some code:

```
const baseComponent: Root = createRoot(document.getElementById("main
Container")!);
baseComponent.render(<BaseLayout />);
```

That kicks off the React portion of the proceedings, rendering the `BaseLayout` component, which we'll be looking at soon, into the `mainContainer` div in the document (the `index.html file`). With that, we have an app on the screen!

Before we get there, though, there's a fair number of other stops this train must make, starting with application state.

A Quick Detour: State'ing the Obvious

Every React application – well, any nontrivial application anyway – is going to need some sort of state, as was discussed in Chapters 3 and 4. Exactly how you maintain this state is a topic of much debate in the React community. I mentioned Redux in Chapter 3. Redux is a way to have a centralized state object that all the components in the application share. It's a popular approach, but it's just one of many. And you don't need to look outside of React itself if you don't want to because React offers the notion of state by default, and that's what I did with MailBag. The trick, though, is that to have components sharing that state, you have to push it up the component tree as far as needed.

In other words, recall that React always constructs a component tree. Any tree has a single element at the top with children beneath it, and those children can have children, and so on. So, where you place your state object becomes a question, and you answer it by determining which components in the tree need access to it. You simply find the highest component in the tree that is a parent to all that need it, and that's where you put your state.

In MailBag, you're going to find that we have a single component, BaseLayout, that is a parent to all the rest. This is the most logical place to place state then.

However, what *is* state in MailBag, exactly? Well, state in React is nothing but a JavaScript object. You could define it directly within the BaseLayout.tsx code file, but I wanted to have it be separate, just to organize the code a little cleaner. That's what the state.ts file is all about. It defines an object that BaseLayout will include, and it's where all state for the application will live, along with the methods needed to mutate state.

But it's not *quite* as simple as defining an object. We have to play some games in order to make this work, which is why this file's code begins in not quite the way you might expect:

```
let stateSingleton: any = null;
export function createState(inParentComponent: React.Component): any {
```

Rather than just exporting a literal object, we have a function. This function takes in a reference to the component that contains it, BaseLayout, in our case, for reasons that will become apparent shortly. Then, this function simply returns an object, our state object:

```
if (stateSingleton === null) {
  stateSingleton = {
    pleaseWaitVisible : false,
```

The trick here is we need to ensure that there is only ever one instance of our state object floating around, and as it happens, that rule can be broken by React itself re-rendering the base component at various times as the user uses the app. To avoid that, a version of the famous singleton pattern is used, even to the point of naming the variable stateSingleton! The way it works is simple. When the module loads – which will only ever happen once, we're guaranteed of that much – we see if stateSingleton is null or not. If it is, at that point, we'll define the state object. If it's not though, as you'll see at the end of this code, the object is returned. In this way, we can be assured that the state object is only ever built once, which is what we need to ensure.

Our state consists of a series of properties in the object, starting with `pleaseWaitVisible`. This is a flag that will tell our code whether a "please wait" popup, which we'll show every time we call the server, is visible or not. More on this later!

We also need to maintain a list of contacts that the user has created, and that's where the contacts array property comes in:

```
contacts : [ ],
```

Similarly, a list of mailboxes is needed:

```
mailboxes : [ ],
```

And, assuming a mailbox has been selected, we need the list of messages within it:

```
messages : [ ],
```

When the user clicks a mailbox or clicks the NEW MESSAGE or NEW CONTACT button or clicks a contact in the list, what they see in the middle of the screen changes. This we refer to as the "view," and what view is current must be known for React to render the correct content:

```
currentView : "welcome",
```

It starts out with the `"welcome"` view and then changes to one of `"welcome"`, `"message"` (when viewing a message), `"compose"` (when creating a message), `"contact"` (when viewing a contact), and `"contactAdd"` (when adding a contact). How this changes the view is something you'll see later.

Earlier, I mentioned the array of messages in the currently selected mailbox, but how do we know what the current mailbox is? As it happens, we have a property for that:

```
currentMailbox : null,
```

Then, we must think about what state is necessary when either viewing or creating a message. For that, we have a series of properties:

```
messageID : null,
messageDate : null,
messageFrom : null,
```

```
messageTo : null,
messageSubject : null,
messageBody : null,
```

I'd imagine those are all obvious. Note that messageID would only ever be populated when viewing an existing message, and it's the ID of the message on the server.

Similarly, when viewing or creating a contact, we'll need some state too:

```
contactID : null,
contactName : null,
contactEmail : null,
```

The state object also contains a collection of methods that the remainder of the application code calls on to mutate state in various ways. These are termed "state mutator methods," and I'm going to introduce each of those methods as they are first encountered.

So, to wrap this up in a bow, what will happen is that this createState() function will be called at some point inside BaseLayout, and the state object will be returned. That object will then be a member of BaseLayout, and we're good to go.

There's one other catch though: there is some code that will also need this state object that isn't itself a React component. You'll see that later, but that presents a problem because everything so far is predicated on this being used inside a component. To deal with that problem, we have to provide one other function:

```
export function getState(): any {

  return stateSingleton;

} /* End getState(). */
```

Now, even code that isn't inside of a React component has a way to get a reference to that singleton state object, and since that code can't execute before the call to createState() can due to the overall flow of the code, this function just needs to return it, not check for null.

Back to the Code!

Now that you have an idea of what state is in play, we can get back to the code in main.
tsx (after the imports, I mean):

```
const intervalFunction = function(): void {
  if (getState() === null) {
    setTimeout(intervalFunction, 100);
  } else {
    startupFunction();
  }
}
intervalFunction();
```

We have a problem right away because the first thing the app needs to do is to get
a list of the user's mailboxes from the server. But, in order to do that, we need the state
object to exist. That's a problem because that object won't be created until React renders
the BaseLayout component. Unfortunately, that's nondeterministic, meaning that we
can't just start executing code to call the server right now because React may not have
done its thing in time. So, what we'll do is this timeout until we get a state object. Once
we do, we know we have a state object, so it's safe to continue. And, what we continue to
is executing the startupFunction() function:

```
const startupFunction = function(): void {
  getState().showHidePleaseWait(true);
  async function getMailboxes(): Promise<any> {
    const imapWorker: IMAP.Worker = new IMAP.Worker();
    const mailboxes: IMAP.IMailbox[] = await imapWorker.listMailboxes();
    mailboxes.forEach((inMailbox) => {
      getState().addMailboxToList(inMailbox);
    });
  }
  getMailboxes().then(function(): void {
    // Now go fetch the user's contacts.
    async function getContacts() {
      const contactsWorker: Contacts.Worker = new Contacts.Worker();
```

```
      const contacts: Contacts.IContact[] = await contactsWorker.
      listContacts();
      contacts.forEach((inContact) => {
        getState().addContactToList(inContact);
      });
    }
    getContacts().then(() => getState().showHidePleaseWait(false));
  });
};
```

Once the UI is built, the next task that must be accomplished is to call the server and get a list of mailboxes available for the account and a list of contacts the user has created. Any time we call the server, we're going to display a "please wait" popup, so the user knows something is happening. This will also serve the purpose of blocking the UI for a moment so that the user can't go and do something that causes problems while the server works. The showHidePleaseWait() method of the state object, the first of the state mutator methods we've encountered, does this for us:

```
showHidePleaseWait : function(inVisible: boolean): void {
  this.setState(() => ({ pleaseWaitVisible : inVisible }));
}.bind(inParentComponent)
```

You must remember that with React, you don't directly tell components to do things. Instead, you mutate state in some way, using the setState() method on the component that holds the state, which causes React to repaint the pertinent parts of the UI as needed. In this case, to show the please wait popup, all we need to do is update the pleaseWaitVisible state attribute, setting it to true. React will then redraw the UI, and what will happen, something you'll see later, is that the popup element will now be set to visible. This will make sense when we look at the MainLayout.tsx file, but just keep in mind for now that pleaseWaitVisible is set to true when we want the please wait popup to be shown and false when we want it hidden and that React will see that change in state and redraw the screen as needed. That's the key thing right now.

The little problem I alluded to earlier is that since we are limited to calling the setState() method on the component that contains the state object, any code that tries to call it must execute within the context of that component. When we define a separate object for state as I did in order to break it out into its own source file, the this reference in the methods inside state won't be what we need. In other words, any method inside the state object won't have access to setState() because its execution context, at least in some instances, won't be the BaseLayout component.

That's where the bind() statements come in, and you'll see these on every function in the state object. When the state object is constructed via the call to createState(), a reference to the BaseLayout instance was passed in. That's what we bind all the mutator functions to. That way, they will always have access to setState() as we need. Note that if any of them needs to touch the state object itself, which they obviously would need to in at least some cases, they can do so by accessing this.state, since components always expose their state via that property.

With the please wait popup showing, we can now call the server:

```
async function getMailboxes() {
  const imapWorker: IMAP.Worker = new IMAP.Worker();
  const mailboxes: IMAP.IMailbox[] = await imapWorker.listMailboxes();
  mailboxes.forEach((inMailbox) => {

    getState().addMailboxToList(inMailbox);
  });
}
```

We know that getting a list of mailboxes is an IMAP operation from our look at the server code, and since the IMAP Worker class on the client seeks to mimic that API that is exposed by the server to the IMAP Worker class there, it makes sense that we'd be calling IMAP.Worker.listMailboxes() here too. And the code looks almost identical to the endpoint handler function code on the server as a result. We'll look at the client-side IMAP close a bit later, but I think you'll find it rather trivial. The bottom line, though, is that we get back an array of mailboxes, and we then iterate them and call the addMailboxToList() method on the state object (which we can do because we created that getState() function specifically for code like this that isn't executing within the context of a React component). That will update the mailboxes array in state, causing React to render the screen to show the mailboxes on the left.

And the addMailboxToList() method is the next state mutator we've hit:

```
addMailboxToList : function(inMailbox: IMAP.IMailbox): void {
  this.setState(prevState => ({ mailboxes : [ ...prevState.mailboxes,
inMailbox ] }));
}.bind(inParentComponent)
```

First, you have always to remember that when you call setState(), you should never pass references to objects in state. That may sound weird, but it's easy to understand when dealing with arrays, as we are here. Your first inclination would be to directly push inMailbox into state.mailboxes and then try to call this.setState({this.state.mailboxes}). Everyone tries that at first because it seems reasonable! However, it won't work because what you pass into setState() replaces what's in state at the time, and trying to do that with what's already there... well, let's just say React won't like you very much!

Instead, we use the spread operator to effectively create a new object, but one based on the old value in state, which is passed in as prevState to the anonymous function passed to setState(). Now, everything works as expected. Note that you only have to do this sort of copying/updating/setting when dealing with objects and collections.

If you're paying attention so far, you will have noticed that we haven't actually called the server to get the list of mailboxes yet, we've only defined a function to do so. That's because the function that calls imapWorker.listMailboxes() must be marked async since we're await'ing the response. getMailboxes() is marked async, so now we need to call it:

```
getMailboxes().then(function() {
  async function getContacts() {
    const contactsWorker: Contacts.Worker = new Contacts.Worker();
    const contacts: Contacts.IContact[] = await contactsWorker.
    listContacts();
    contacts.forEach((inContact) => {

        getState().addContactToList(inContact);
    });
  }
  getContacts().then(() =>
    getState().showHidePleaseWait(false));
});
```

We don't want to get the list of contacts until the list of mailboxes is done so that we know that all server calls are done before the please wait popup is hidden, so we use the then() syntax to chain them. Inside the then() callback, another function is defined, getContacts() this time, for the same reason: async/await usage. Once defined, we can call getContacts() and again use the then() syntax so that we can call showHidePleaseWait(), passing false this time, to cause React to hide the please wait popup.

The addContactToList() state mutator method is used in there, and it's virtually identical to addMailboxToList():

```
addContactToList : function(inContact: Contacts.IContact): void {

  this.setState(prevState => ({ contacts : [ ...prevState.contacts,
  inContact ] }));
}.bind(inParentComponent)
```

This works the same basic way as addMailboxToList() did, so there's no surprises there.

A Bit of Configuration: config.ts

For the client app to talk to the server, it, of course, has to know its address. The config.ts file meets that need:

```
export const config: {
  serverAddress: string, userEmail: string } =
{ serverAddress : "http://localhost", userEmail : name@domain.com };
```

It's quite simple: it's just a literal object with a serverAddress property that gives the address of the MailBag server. During development, this is likely to be localhost. Also, note that it must contain the protocol prefix. This object also contains the userEmail that provides your email address. I'm gonna guess that's not your email address, so go ahead and update it as appropriate! This file will be imported into the Worker classes as needed.

Hey, speaking of Worker classes, that's exactly what's up next!

A Worker for All Seasons

Just like the server side of MailBag, we have three "Worker" classes on the client side: Contacts.ts, IMAP.ts, and SMTP.ts. These are the interfaces between the client application itself and the MailBag server, and they break down functionally in the same way as their server counterparts. Before we look at the React code itself that defines our UI and makes it functional, let's take a look at these Worker classes so that when you see them being used, you'll know what they're doing.

But how, exactly, does the code in these workers talk to the server? For that, we must take a quick detour!

A Quick Detour: AJAX

AJAX is a technique that came to life, so to speak, at the hands of one Jesse James Garrett in an essay he wrote in February 2005. There, he coined the term AJAX, which stands for Asynchronous JavaScript and XML. The interesting thing about AJAX, though, is that it doesn't have to be asynchronous (but virtually always is), doesn't have to involve JavaScript (but virtually always does), and doesn't need to use XML at all (but probably doesn't 99+% of the time).

AJAX is, at its core, an exceedingly simple and, by no stretch of the imagination, original concept: it is not necessary to refresh the entire contents of a web page for each user interaction, or each "event," if you will. When the user clicks a button, it is no longer necessary to ask the server to render an entirely new page, as is the case with the "classic" Web. Instead, you can define regions on the page to be updated and have much more fine-grained control over user event handling as a result. No longer are you limited to simply submitting a form to a server for processing or navigating to an entirely new page when a link is clicked.

The interesting thing about AJAX is that it is in no way, shape, or form new, and it actually wasn't even when Mr. Garrett coined the term. A decade ago, when AJAX was still somewhat new, I liked to say that you could always tell who has done AJAX before and who hadn't because those who had are mad that it was a big deal and they didn't get credit for "inventing" it themselves!

Nowadays, the term AJAX isn't used as much as before. People tend to talk about "out-of-band requests" or simply "asynchronous requests" or, indeed, simply "server requests" because it's pretty much the de facto way of communicating with a server on the Web when you aren't refreshing the entire page.

At its core, AJAX works because of something invented originally by Microsoft: the XMLHttpRequest object. This is a JavaScript object that allows you to write code like this:

```
let req;
let which;
function retrieveURL(url) {
  if (window.XMLHttpRequest) {
    req = new XMLHttpRequest();
    req.onreadystatechange = processStateChange;
    try {
      req.open("GET", url, true);
    } catch (e) {
      alert(e);
    }
    req.send(null);
  } else if (window.ActiveXObject) {
    req = new ActiveXObject("Microsoft.XMLHTTP");
    if (req) {
      req.onreadystatechange = processStateChange;
      req.open("GET", url, true);
      req.send();
    }
  }
}
function processStateChange() {
  if (req.readyState == 4) {
    if (req.status == 200) {
      document.getElementById("urlContent").innerHTML = req.responseText;
    } else {
      alert("Problem: " + req.statusText);
    }
  }
}
```

Even if this is your first time seeing such code, I bet you can understand it without much trouble. In short, you create an XMLHttpRequest object (branching based on whether the object exists or not, because for a while, not all browsers exposed the object in the same way). You then hook a callback function up to it that will be called whenever the state of the object changes (e.g., when it connects to the server or when the response comes back – the object has an entire lifecycle you can hook into). You give it the URL to connect to, optionally tell it about any data you're sending (in this case, there is none), and, finally, send the request. The callback function will be called, multiple times, in fact, based on the lifecycle events provided. We only care about the readyState 4, which is what occurs when a response comes back. Then, assuming we got an HTTP 200 back, we take the responseText, which is what the server sent, and insert it into a DOM node, presumably a <div>, or do whatever else we want with it. That's it, that's all there is to it.

Nowadays, you wouldn't even write that most likely, and, instead, you'd use the newer Fetch API. Although not quite ubiquitous across all browsers, it's not supported by the majority, so now you can write code like this:

```
const response = await fetch(url);
```

Yep, that's *much* better, isn't it?

However, aside from the browser having to support this API, it also must support async/await, as you can see. If you want to reach the widest audience possible, but you don't want to write all the XMLHttpRequest code as in the preceding text, you'll probably want to use a capable library that abstracts all of this away from you (and, most likely, provides many other benefits). For MailBag, that's exactly what we're going to do!

Getting Some Help: Axios

Rather than doing "naked" AJAX, we'll instead use a popular library for it: Axios (https://github.com/axios/axios). In simplest terms, Axios is a Promise-based HTTP client that works in browser-based code as well as Node-based code equally well. It uses XMLHttpRequest under the covers in a browser and uses the Node http library when used in a Node-based app. Being Promise-based means that you can use async/await with it (or the more "classical" Promise approach), which makes for a very nice API.

Axios offers some more advanced capabilities, including the ability to hook into the request and response cycle to make modifications broadly (think cross-cutting concerns in Aspect-Oriented Programming, or AOP, for things like logging and security). Or, it offers the ability to transform request and response data in various ways automatically and the ability to cancel requests, if necessary.

Using Axios also means security because it includes protection against client-side XSRF, or Cross-Site Request Forgery. This is a trick nefarious sorts can use to transmit requests to the server, masquerading as you, a legitimate user. That's bad news, obviously, and Axios can keep your application safe from it without doing anything special on your part.

Axios has broad browser support and is as easy to use as

```
const response = await axios.get("your_server_url");
```

Or if you don't want to use async/await (what's wrong with you?!):

```
axois.get("your_server_url").then(function(response) {
  // Do something with the response.
});
```

Do you need to POST some data to the server? No problem:

```
axios.post("your_server_url",
  { firstName : "Burt", lastName : "Reynolds" }
);
```

Axios will automatically serialize that object into JSON for transmission to the server (naturally, you can pass an object reference there, it doesn't need to be an object literal like that). It will also automatically deserialize a JSON response so that you have a nice JavaScript object to play with.

You can use any other HTTP method there too: DELETE, HEAD, OPTIONS, PUT, PATCH, whatever you need, it's all there for you.

You can optionally pass a configuration object to any of the request methods after the URL (or even in place of the URL if the object itself contains the URL), which allows you to modify the requests in many ways. The options available are numerous, so I won't go through them all, but a few of particular interest are the following:

- **transformRequest** – You provide a function here, and this will allow you to modify the request data before it's sent to the server. You can do the same for the response using the transformResponse config to alter the response before it's passed to the then/catch handler.

- **params** – You can provide a list of URL parameters to append to the URL with this.

- **timeout** – By default, Axios waits forever for a response (well, at least until the browser itself times out). With this option, you can specify how long to wait.

- **proxy** – Does your network require you to go through a proxy? If so, you can specify that information with this property.

- **onDownloadProgress** – This is a function to be called periodically while a response is downloading, allowing you the ability to show a progress bar or spinner or similar UI element (you can do this with onUploadProgress in the opposite direction too).

Axios is a very robust but extremely simple-to-use library that, for me, is the obvious choice for our server communication needs in MailBag.

Mirroring the Server Part 1: Contacts.ts

The first Worker class we're going to talk about is in the `Contacts.ts` file, which, of course, means we're dealing with the Contacts Worker class. But, even before the Worker class, we find that we have an interface present:

```
export interface IContact {
  _id?: number, name: string, email: string
}
```

If you look back at the Contacts.ts file on the server side, you'll find this same interface. That should make sense to you: after all, we're passing objects back and forth that need to have the same structure on both sides of the conversation!

After that, the Worker class begins:

```
export class Worker {
```

Nothing special there, and again identical to the server. Within the Worker, we find a series of methods, beginning with `listContacts()`.

Listing Contacts

When we want a list of contacts to display on the screen, we need to ask the server for that. We know that, via the Express-based RESTful interface, we ultimately need the `Worker.listContacts()` method in the `Contacts.ts` file on the server to be executed, so we mimic that interface design with `listContacts()` in the client-side Worker class:

```
public async listContacts(): Promise<IContact[]> {
  const response: AxiosResponse =
    await axios.get(`${config.serverAddress}/contacts`);
  return response.data;
}
```

Here, you can see Axios used, as we discussed in the previous section. The `serverAddress` from the config object is used to construct the appropriate path, and this is of course a get request, so that's the Axios method executed. Then, the response is returned, and we're done. Very simple, right? But it serves the important purpose architecturally of abstracting away the MailBag client application from the server. Think of it this way: if you wanted to change the server to use an XML-based message exchange, and you didn't want to use Axios, you'd only need to change the code in this class (and the server, obviously), but the rest of the MailBag client app would be none the wiser. That's good architectural flexibility.

Note   I'm going to go through the rest of these methods, as well as those in the IMAP and SMTP Worker classes, pretty quickly, because they follow the same pattern, which is to mimic the server. No need to linger, I think! But you should still take the time to examine the code and make sure you do understand what's happening, simple though it generally is, for each method presented.

Adding a Contact

To add a contact, the aptly named `addContact()` method is called, accepting an object adhering to the `IContact` interface:

```
public async addContact(inContact: IContact):
  Promise<IContact> {
  const response: AxiosResponse = await axios.post(
    `${config.serverAddress}/contacts`, inContact
  );
  return response.data;
}
```

Once more, it's a simple Axios call, this time a post(), passing inContact as the second argument. Axios takes care of serializing that to JSON and sending it in the request body for us. We get back the same object but now with the _id field added, so that is returned so the caller can add it to the list of contacts for display (we'll get into all of that later).

Deleting a Contact

Deleting a contact is the final bit of functionality this Worker must provide:

```
public async deleteContact(inID): Promise<void> {
  await axios.delete(
    `${config.serverAddress}/contacts/${inID}`);
}
```

Well, that's pretty simple, isn't it? Here, you can see the contact's ID added to the URL, as per our REST interface server design.

Mirroring the Server Part 2: IMAP.ts

The second Worker to look at is in the IMAP.ts files. Just like with contacts, we begin with an interface:

```
export interface IMailbox { name: string, path: string }
```

And also, just like with contacts, this mimics the interface of the same name found in the server version of IMAP.ts. Similarly, we have the same IMessage interface as on the server too:

```
export interface IMessage {
  id: string, date: string, from: string,subject: string,
  body?: string
}
```

After that, the Worker class begins, and we have some methods to look at.

Listing Mailboxes

Listing mailboxes is just like listing contacts in terms of the call to the server, and we find a similar listMailboxes() method for it:

```
public async listMailboxes(): Promise<IMailbox[]> {
  const response: AxiosResponse =
    await axios.get(`${config.serverAddress}/mailboxes`);
  return response.data;
}
```

Yep, just a slightly different URL to call and different interfaces, but otherwise, the same as listing contacts.

Listing Messages

Listing messages in a mailbox is just trivial thanks to the listMessages() method:

```
public async listMessages(inMailbox: string):
  Promise<IMessage[]> {
  const response: AxiosResponse = await axios.get(
    `${config.serverAddress}/mailboxes/${inMailbox}`
  );
  return response.data;
}
```

Here, we just need the path of the mailbox to get messages for, which we get from the inMailbox argument. Then, it's just an Axios get() call again.

Getting the Body of a Message

Remember that the server, when sending a list of messages, does not send the message bodies. We only get the body of a selected message when needed, and that's where getMessageBody() factors in:

```
public async getMessageBody(inID: string, inMailbox: String):
  Promise<string> {
  const response: AxiosResponse = await axios.get(
    `${config.serverAddress}/messages/${inMailbox}/${inID}`
  );
  return response.data;
}
```

We need the ID of the message and the path to the mailbox it's in, but other than that, it's not substantially different from getting a list of mailboxes.

Deleting a Message

The final method in this Worker is for deleting messages, the deleteMessage() method:

```
public async deleteMessage(inID: string, inMailbox: String):
  Promise<void> {
  await axios.delete(
    `${config.serverAddress}/messages/${inMailbox}/${inID}`
  );
}
```

By this point, I'm betting you're pretty comfortable with these Worker methods and how they interact with the server. There's nothing that says I had to mimic the basic layout of the server code on the client. I could have had a drastically different structure to these methods here. So long as they eventually call the server as expected, that's all that matters. But hopefully, you'll agree that mirroring them like this helps keep it all straight in your mind.

Mirroring the Server Part 3: SMTP.ts

The final worker, the one for the SMTP operation of sending a message, is, of course, found in the SMTP.ts file. In this file, there are no interfaces to deal with, and just a single method, so the entire file is this:

```
import axios from "axios";
import { config } from "./config";
export class Worker {
  public async sendMessage(
    inTo: string, inFrom: string, inSubject: string,
    inMessage: string
  ): Promise<void> {
    await axios.post(`${config.serverAddress}/messages`, {
      to : inTo, from : inFrom, subject : inSubject,
      text : inMessage
    });
  }
}
```

I'm going to go out on a limb here and say you probably don't even need this explained at this point! So, with that assumption, let's now move on to the true React code that makes use of the Workers we just looked at.

A Cavalcade of Components

To build a web app usually requires a user interface, and a user interface usually requires widgets, or components. Sometimes, you use the basic ones that HTML itself provides, and it's enough. Sometimes, you build your own using those primitives as building blocks. And, sometimes, you find a good library that suits your needs.

For MailBag, we'll be doing the latter, and the choice I landed on to provide out components is MUI.

A Quick Detour: MUI

Around 2014, Google realized that most of the web app products were going in different directions in terms of look, feel, and function. Android, too, was a completely different beast visually, and in fact, Android is where the eventual solution began. They determined that this wasn't a sustainable direction to go and they needed to come up with something to unify their products.

As a result, the Material design language was created (`https://material.io`). Although it's not terribly important for our work here, I think a very brief description of Material design itself is in order.

Material design is a set of design principles that are informed by how people interact with real objects in the physical world. Primarily influenced by print media, Material design begins with concepts like sheets of paper and their digital equivalents. When you read a book, you turn pages, and that motion is encapsulated in Material design, just as the underlying pattern of the sheet of paper itself is.

Material design is concerned with how layers of content can slide over each other, for example, and those slides, those animations, are key elements. Everything is intended to be reactive to touch (remember that this all started with Android, at least in its initial implementation, so touch was automatically a key part of Material design).

As I said, knowing this doesn't make a *huge* difference in our work here, but a little context never hurt anybody!

Now, what *does* matter is the MUI library itself (`https://mui.com`). Simply put, this is a library of React components built on top of Google's Material design language. Being a React library means you simply add it to your project with NPM like any other library, import the appropriate parts of it, and use it in your code. For example, if you want to put a button on the screen:

```
import React from "react";
import Button from "@mui/material/Button";
const App = () => (
  <Button variant="contained" color="primary">
    Hello World
  </Button>
);
```

Now, I'm glossing over something important here, but we're going to get to it soon (in the section on functional components), but focus on what matters here: React was imported naturally, and too was the Button component from MUI. Then, it's simply a matter of dropping a `<Button>` tag into the code, and we have ourselves a MUI button.

The MUI library offers a wealth of components with which to build a user interface. It has all the usual suspects like buttons, checkboxes, radio buttons, drop-down lists, grids, lists, progress bars, alert dialogs, menus, and a lot more. The website referenced in the preceding text does a great job of presenting it all. You'll find a list of components with numerous simple examples for each and then links for the API of each that details the properties and options available.

It really is an easy-to-use library that also makes your apps look and function great with minimal effort on your part. You'll only see a small portion of what it has to offer in MailBag, so I highly encourage you to spend some time on the MUI website exploring all it has to offer. I think you'll be very impressed, and it will, I bet, quickly become your favorite collection of widgets for building UIs with React.

Another Quick Detour: CSS Grid

One of the first questions you must answer when developing a web app is how you're going to lay out your components. There are lots of methods, each with their own pluses and minuses. But, given that we're trying to use relatively modern techniques in this book, we're going to go with the newest darling on the street: CSS Grid.

Virtually any web page layout can be described in terms of a grid (in fact, I'm not sure there's any that *can't* be). It's all just columns and rows in the end, whether there's only one of each (read: just a single block of content) or whether there are nested grids inside nested grids. All of it just rows and columns.

Let's start with some simple markup (Listing 9-1).

Listing 9-1. CSS Grid example markup

```
<html>
  <head>
    <title></title>
  </head>
```

```
<body>
  <div class="container">
    <div style="background-color:#ff0000;">A</div>
    <div style="background-color:#00ff00;">B</div>
    <div style="background-color:#0000ff;">C</div>
    <div style="background-color:#ff00ff;">D</div>
    <div style="background-color:#ffff00;">E</div>
    <div style="background-color:#00ffff;">F</div>
  </div>
</body>
</html>
```

When loaded in your browser, you'll simply see six rows of content, stacked one right on top of the other, as shown in Figure 9-5.

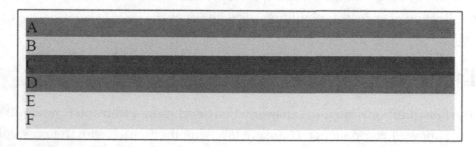

Figure 9-5. *You can't see the colors on the printed page, but trust me, they're there!*

To introduce CSS Grid to the mix, in order to create a more interesting layout, we start with a container element, which we have here. Then, on this element, you define the grid, that is, the rows and columns contained within the grid. The container element already has a class attribute, so we just need to define that style rule:

```
.container {
  display : grid;
  grid-template-columns : 150px 50px 100px;
  grid-template-rows : 100px 100px;
}
```

Now, if you reload the page, you'll see two rows of items with three columns in each, as shown in Figure 9-6. The six <div> elements get dropped into each of the areas defined by the intersection of the rows and columns.

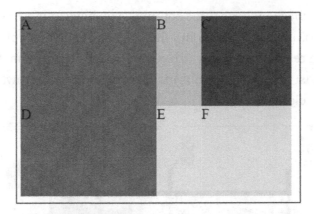

Figure 9-6. *Our beautiful, beautiful grid!*

What's even better is when you start to add some styling to one or more `<div>`'s to tell them where in the grid they should live. For example, let's add some style to element E:

```
<div style="background-color:#ffff00;grid-column:1/4;grid-row:1/1;">E</div>
```

Now, reload the page, and you'll find that the first `<div>` shown, E, extends across the entire grid, as seen in Figure 9-7. The meaning of the `grid-column` and `grid-row` attributes is that it tells the grid what columns and rows the element should cover, but it does so using the grid lines, not the boxes that make up the grid.

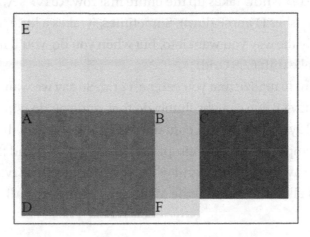

Figure 9-7. *A more interesting grid (well, I think so at least!)*

In other words, when you have three columns, you have four grid lines: the two between the three columns, of course, and the one before the first column and after the last one. So, here we're saying that this <div> should stretch from that first grid line to the fourth one, the last one, which results in it covering the entire row. Figure 9-8 should, expect, make this all clear.

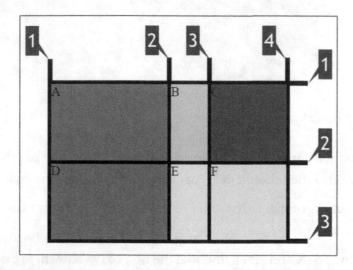

Figure 9-8. *The numbers across the top are the column lines; the ones down the side are the row lines*

Also, because <div> E now takes up the entire first row, <div>'s A, B, and C use the second row, which pushes D and F down. Sometimes, it takes a little tweaking to get your grid to work precisely the way you want it to, but when you do, you'll find that laying out pages is a piece of cake with CSS Grid.

It's also important to realize that you can nest grid. So say we want to have some grid layout within <div> B, we can absolutely do that, and you do it in exactly the same way: apply the display:grid style to a container <div> (along with the grid-template-columns and grid-template-rows as appropriate) inside <div> B and then define the grid in exactly the same way, but now that grid will be constrained to <div> B. And it's exactly this nesting that will allow us to lay out the MailBag UI as shown earlier, as you'll see in action shortly.

Yet Another Quick Detour: main.css

In the source code for this app, you'll find the `main.css` file in the src/css directory. This is an ordinary CSS stylesheet, absolutely nothing special about it. Usually, I would go through it here, but I think it will make much more sense to look at the relatively small handful of CSS rules it contains in context as we go through the various components.

So, that's precisely what I'm going to do! And, given that, we can move on to the code of `BaseLayout.tsx`.

BaseLayout.tsx

Earlier, I mentioned that a single React component will be the parent to all the others, as is always the case, and now it's time to look at it, `BaseLayout`, as found in `BaseLayout.tsx`:

```
class BaseLayout extends Component {
```

First, we start by creating a class that extends React's `Component` class. Next, we have to get the state into the component, as discussed earlier:

```
State: any = createState(this);
```

Hopefully, you're having a "Eureka!" moment right about now. This is where `createState()` is called, and a reference to the `BaseLayout` instance itself is passed in so that all the state mutator methods can be bound to it.

After that, we come to the one method we know must be present, `render()`:

```
render(): JSX.Element {
  return (
    <div className="appContainer">
```

Remember that we're going to be doing the layout of the UI via CSS Grid, so that means that whatever element is at the very top of the page must be our container element, and so it is: a `<div>` with the `appContainer` class applied. That class, found in `main.css` (as they all are), is as follows:

```
.appContainer {
  display : grid;
  grid-template-columns : 150px 1fr 240px;
  grid-template-rows : 50px 1fr;
```

```
  width : 100vw;
  height : 100vh;
}
```

That's just like the example from earlier as far as defining the grid goes, but now you see width and height set using vw and vh units, respectively. The v in those units stands for viewport. So what we're really saying is "make this container element 100% of the width and height of the viewport." In other words, our grid fills the screen, which, of course, is what we want for MailBag (in contrast to the earlier CSS Grid examples where that wasn't the case, the grid used only as much space as was specified in its style definition).

Next, we need to define the please wait popup, and for it, we'll use a Dialog component, supplied by MUI:

```
<Dialog open={ this.state.pleaseWaitVisible } disableEscapeKeyDown={ true }
  transitionDuration={ 0 }
  onClose={( inEvent, inReason) => {
    if (inReason !== "backdropClick") {
      this.state.showHidePleaseWait(false);
    }
  }}
>
  <DialogTitle style={{ textAlign:"center" }}>Please Wait</DialogTitle>
  <DialogContent><DialogContentText>...Contacting server...
  </DialogContentText></DialogContent>
</Dialog>
```

It may seem odd that something like a popup dialog, something that is transient, actually exists at all times and is just hidden and shown, but that's a common thing with React. Here, the open prop gets its value from the pleaseWaitVisible property in state, which you'll recall from earlier I said to keep in mind. When the hideShowPleaseWait() state mutator method is called, that property gets changed, and React notices that. So it will re-render the page, now either hiding or showing this dialog based on the changed prop value.

The disableEscapeKeyDown prop is set to true to prevent them from pressing the ESC key to dismiss it. I also set transitionDuration to 0 so that the animation that it normally does by default doesn't occur, since the call to the server, in some cases, could actually be faster than the transition itself! Indeed, it's expected that, in most cases, this dialog will appear and disappear so fast that the user will just see a flash. But, for times when the network is a bit slower, it's nice to have it there.

The onClose prop defines a function that is executed when the dialog is closed. The trick here is that if the reason the dialog is closed is not because of the area behind the dialog – the backdrop – being clicked, then we need to hide the please wait message. MUI won't know to do this automatically, we have to supply this code. Thankfully, MUI tells us the reason the dialog is being closed, which can occur for several reasons, but the only one we care about here is the backdrop click.

The actual Dialog has as a child a DialogTitle component, and here I set style so that its text is centered (which I just thought looked better), and a DialogContent child, which itself has a DialogContentText child. This is simply the text displayed in the Dialog itself. As an aside, the MUI Dialog component is much more robust and can have buttons you define, or even input elements, virtually anything you can imagine can wind up in a Dialog. It doesn't need to be simple static text as here, but since that's all we need, that's all it is in this case.

With the please wait popup defined, it's finally time to start defining the UI that is always visible, starting with the toolbar:

```
<div className="toolbar">
  <Toolbar state={ this.state } />
</div>
```

Notice the pattern here, which you'll see throughout this component: state is passed down to the Toolbar component (the definition of which we'll see in the next section). Every component that is a child to BaseLayout, save for one (WelcomeView), needs state, and they all get it the same way. That's the other half of what I was talking about earlier in terms of choosing the right component to contain state: just putting the state in a component higher up the component tree doesn't do much unless you pass that state to child components as needed.

Now, as far as the toolbar style rule goes, that's as follows:

```
.toolbar {
  grid-column : 1 / 4;
  grid-row : 1 / 1;
  border-bottom : 1px solid #e0e0e0;
```

```
  padding-top : 8px;
  padding-left : 4px;
}
```

As you can see, we want the toolbar to stretch across the three columns of the grid, just like in the earlier example. I also add some padding to keep the buttons from touching the edges of the screen on the left and top (again, it just looks better to my eyes that way). I also added a border on the bottom to give some separation from the rest of the UI contents (this, too, is a pattern repeated throughout).

Next, we need our list of mailboxes on the left:

```
<div className="mailboxList">
  <MailboxList state={ this.state } />
</div>
```

Hopefully, you're seeing the pattern now! Ignoring for the moment what the MailboxList component is and how it's implemented, the basic idea is the same as for the Toolbar. The mailboxList style rule BaseLayout is

```
.mailboxList {
  grid-column : 1 / 1;
  grid-row : 2 / 2;
  border-right : 1px solid #e0e0e0;
  padding-top : 6px;
  padding-left : 4px;
  overflow : auto;
}
```

That's not much different from the toolbar style rule either, with the exception of overflow set to auto to ensure that the list can scroll if there are more mailboxes than the vertical space allows for.

Next up is the area of the screen below the toolbar and in between the mailbox list on the left and contact list on the right – the center area!

```
<div className="centerArea">
  <div className="messageList">
    <MessageList state={ this.state } />
  </div>
```

This is a situation where we're going to be nesting CSS Grids, so while the outer `<div>` is the content of the second column in the second row of the top-level grid, we also need the contents within this `<div>` to have its own grid structure. The `centerArea` style rule defines that:

```
.centerArea {
  display : grid;
  grid-template-rows : 200px 1fr;
}
```

Here, we only need two rows, we don't need any columns, so it's a simpler definition. The first row in this subgrid, so to speak, is the `MessageList` component, our list of messages in the selected mailbox in other words. So, we need to place it in this subgrid, and the `messageList` style rule does that:

```
.messageList {
  border-bottom : 1px solid #e0e0e0;
  grid-row : 1 / 1;
  overflow : auto;
}
```

Pretty simple, right? Once again, we need this area to scroll, since a message list can be arbitrarily long, so `overflow` is again set to `auto`.

Next up is the second row of this subgrid, and this is what I've termed the "view area." It's where the contact and message views will go, plus the welcome view. Which is showing depends on the state of the app, so we're going to need some logic for React to determine which to render:

```
<div className="centerViews">
  { this.state.currentView === "welcome" && <WelcomeView /> }
  { (this.state.currentView === "message" ||
    this.state.currentView === "compose") &&
    <MessageView state={ this.state } />
  }
  { (this.state.currentView === "contact" ||
    this.state.currentView === "contactAdd") &&
    <ContactView state={ this.state } />
  }
</div>
```

Here is a bit of a trick that is very common in React code: if you want to conditionally render or not render a component, usually based on some value in state, you can use the general syntax:

```
{ <some_variable> === <some_value> && <some_component> }
```

Remember that { } denotes an expression in JSX syntax. Also remember that in JavaScript, && is a short-circuit boolean *and* operation. That means that whatever is on the right of it will only be evaluated if what's on the left is true. Therefore, here, if the boolean outcome on the left is false, then the component won't be rendered because it won't even be evaluated.

So, for the <WelcomeView> component to render, for example, the currentView property in state must equal "welcome". If it doesn't, then React won't render that component. For the MessageView component to render, currentView must be "message" or "compose" (the view does double duty for both of those, as you'll see later). Finally, for ContactView to render, currentView must be "contact" or "contactAdd". In the end, we'll only ever get one of these components rendered as a result, so only one view will ever be shown, and changing currentView in state will allow us to flip between these views. Pretty nifty, right?

What about the centerViews style rule? That's easy:

```
.centerViews {
  grid-row : 2 / 2;
  padding-top : 4px;
  padding-left : 4px;
  padding-right : 4px;
  overflow : auto;
}
```

That places this content in the second row of the subgrid and provides some padding about it to avoid any of its content bunching up on the edges.

Finally, we have only one more component to place, and that's the list of contacts on the right:

```
<div className="contactList">
  <ContactList state={ this.state } />
</div>
```

And, of course, its associated style rule:

```
.contactList {
  grid-column : 3 / 3;
  grid-row : 2 / 2;
  border-left : 1px solid #e0e0e0;
  padding-top : 4px;
  padding-left : 4px;
  overflow : auto;
}
```

Finally, of course, we need to export this component:

```
export default BaseLayout;
```

And with that, our BaseLayout component is done! Now, let's look at the individual components that we just saw used – well, right after one last quick detour, that is!

A Quick Detour: Functional Components

In the previous MUI example, I dropped a little bit of coolness on you out of the blue, something called functional React components. In the past, and with BaseLayout, you've seen components defined this way:

```
class Welcome extends React.Component {
  render() { return <h1>Hello, { this.props.name }</h1>; }
}
```

Sometimes, Component is written React.Component, but it's the same thing, it's just a question of how your imports are done. Either way, what's important to remember, though, is that, fundamentally, a React component is just an object with a render() method at a minimum. And recall that the syntax you see here is JSX. Because of that, you can also define this component in a more concise form:

```
const Welcome = () => ( <h1>Hello, { this.props.name }</h1> );
```

Using functional syntax like this works because JSX is aware of it and can process it. It's clearly not valid JavaScript because if you tried to have HTML embedded in a function like that, it simply wouldn't work. But JSX allows you to do just that.

273

A valid component will be created, and the HTML you see there, the component tree it represents to be more precise, will be returned from an automatically created render() method.

Why would you choose the class-based approach over the functional approach? There are two primary reasons, beyond whether you prefer the brevity of the functional code or not: lifecycle event needs and state needs. If you need access to lifecycle events, then you can't use the functional approach – at least, not without introducing the topics of Hooks, which is something that was added a little later in React, and something I'm not covering in this book because it's a bit of a more advanced topic and not a necessary component of React coding. The same is true of state: if you need your component to have its own state, then you'll need to use the class-based approach (but again, Hooks provides a solution here too).

However, note that with state, it's possible to hoist the state up to a component higher in the component tree and then pass it into the component. So, in a sense, the state limitation is no limitation at all, even before you get into Hooks. You'll be seeing exactly this approach in MailBag because the state object discussed earlier is used in exactly this fashion.

Toolbar.tsx

Now, back to our components, beginning with the Toolbar component, found in the Toolbar.tsx file, which is defined in a functional way just described:

```
const Toolbar = ({ state }): JSX.Element => (
  <div>
    <Button variant="contained" color="primary"
      size="small" style={{ marginRight:10 }}
      onClick={ () => state.showComposeMessage("new") } >
      <NewMessageIcon style={{ marginRight:10 }} />New Message
    </Button>
    <Button variant="contained" color="primary" size="small"
      style={{ marginRight:10 }}
      onClick={ state.showAddContact } >
      <NewContactIcon style={{ marginRight:10 }} />New Contact
    </Button>
```

```
    </div>
  );
export default Toolbar;
```

At a high level, it's a simple component: it just has two `Button` components in it, courtesy of the MUI library. The `Button` component has several options to change how it looks and functions, and here I've used its `variant="contained"` to make it look like a more traditional button rather than the text-only buttons that are common on Android (it has elevation and fill in this form, to be more precise). I also set the `color` to `primary`, which, by default, will give it a blue appearance. The `size="small"` prop makes the buttons smaller than usual, to gain a bit more space in the UI. For the NEW MESSAGE button, I also added a margin on the right so that there would be separation between it and the NEW CONTACT button.

Within each `Button` is an icon, also provided by MUI. The library contains numerous icons, and most have their own components, as `NewMessageIcon` and `NewContactIcon` do. For each, I also again add margin on the right so that the icon has space between it and the text. And, speaking of text, that's the second child of each `Button`, just literally static text.

A button without some sort of click handler code wouldn't be of much use, so both buttons have such a handler hook up to it through the `onClick` prop. In the case of the NEW MESSAGE button, there is an anonymous function defined, and from it, `state.showComposeMessage()` is called. This is necessary because the `"new"` value needs to be passed to it in order to indicate that the `MessageView` component, which we'll look at later, should display in the new message composition mode. When the user clicks a message in the message list, by contrast, the same view is shown, but there will be different fields and buttons, and what is passed to `showComposeMessage()` determines all that.

In fact, here is that method now:

```
showComposeMessage : function(inType: string): void {
  switch (inType) {

    case "new":
      this.setState(() => ({
        currentView : "compose", messageTo : "", messageSubject : "",
        messageBody : "",
        messageFrom : config.userEmail
      }));
    break;
```

```
  case "reply":
    this.setState(() => ({
      currentView : "compose", messageTo : this.state.messageFrom,
      messageSubject : `Re: ${this.state.messageSubject}`,
    }));
  break;

  case "contact":
    this.setState(() => ({
      currentView : "compose", messageTo : this.state.contactEmail,
      messageSubject : "", messageBody : "",
      messageFrom : config.userEmail
    }));
  break;

} }.bind(inParentComponent)
```

As you can see, there are three possibilities. The first, for a value of "new", is when the user wants to compose a brand-new message. In all three cases, the goal is to set currentView in state so that the appropriate view is shown ("compose" in all cases) and to set up any state properties as necessary. For the "new" case, that means clearing out the messageTo, messageSubject, messageBody, and messageFrom fields. The first three will be populated by the user when they enter the values on the compose view (something you'll see a bit later), and messageFrom is set from what's in the config object.

Second, when the user clicks the REPLY button when viewing a message, it's still ultimately the "compose" view we want to go to, but now we prefill the messageTo, messageSubject, and messageBody variables in state.

Third, the "contact" case is when the user clicks the Send Email button when viewing a contact. It's just like the "reply" state except that the messageTo property comes from the contact itself while messageSubject and messageBody are blanked out.

Now, going back to our Toolbar, the second button, NEW CONTACT, doesn't need to do this sort of logic. As a result, there's no need for an anonymous function like for NEW MESSAGE. Instead, we can reference the state.showAddContact() method directly, and that method is

```
showAddContact : function(): void {
  this.setState(() => ({
    currentView : "contactAdd", contactID : null, contactName : "",
    contactEmail : ""
  })); }.bind(inParentComponent)
```

Once again, it's just a case of setting `currentView` appropriately and clearing out any state properties that are involved in user input. In this case, the contact won't have an ID until we save it to the server, so `contactID` is `null`, while `contactName` and `contactEmail` start off as empty strings, which will be reflected initially in the text fields that the user will enter the values in.

Note   For the remainder of these components, I'm just going to show the content of the function, since that's all that's different in them, aside from the obvious of the component's name and export.

MailboxList.tsx

Next, we'll look at the `MailboxList` component from the `MailboxList.tsx` file:

```
const MailboxList = ({ state }): JSX.Element => (
  <List>
    state.mailboxes.map(value => {
      return (
        <Chip label={ `${value.name}` } onClick={ () =>
          state.setCurrentMailbox(value.path)
        }
          style={{ width:128, marginBottom:10 }}
          color={ state.currentMailbox === value.path ?
            "secondary" : "primary" } />
      );
    } ) }
  </List>
);
export default MailboxList;
```

It all begins with a MUI List component. MUI has several components for displaying collections of data in various ways, and List is one of them, and perhaps the most used. Within it, you have one or more child components, one per item in your list.

The list of mailboxes is, of course, in the mailboxes array property of the state object, so we use the map() function on that array to process each item. For each element, a Chip component is returned, which is again a component from MUI. A Chip is a lot like a Button, and in fact, for how it's used here, a Button could have been just as good. Typically, Chips are used to represent things like contacts, but there are no real rules for their use. They look a bit different than buttons, which is why I went with it (that, and just to show you a different component!). But, at the end of the day, each Chip has some label text, which is the name of the mailbox, some styling to set its size and ensure spacing between them, and color. The color prop is interesting because we want the currently selected mailbox to be a different color. The state.currentMailbox stores the path of the currently selected mailbox, so we can do some logic to set the color. If the path of the element of the array being processed is the same as currentMailbox, then the secondary color will be used, which is red. Otherwise, the primary color (blue) will be used. As long as currentMailbox changes when a mailbox Chip is clicked, then we'll get the highlighting of the current mailbox as we want.

And speaking of clicking a Chip, the onClick handler is defined pointing to state. setCurrentMailbox() for that purpose. Again, because we need to pass the path of the clicked mailbox to that method, we need to use an anonymous function to call state. setCurrentMailbox(), the code for which is

---

Note   If you tried to set onClick={ state.setCurrentMailbox } to avoid the anonymous function, then what would be passed to it would be an Event object. While it might be possible to drill down into that object to get at the path of the mailbox, using the anonymous function approach decouples the code a little bit from React or even the browser event model in general and, in my mind, makes what's happening clearer.

```
setCurrentMailbox : function(inPath: String): void {
  this.setState(() => ({ currentView : "welcome", currentMailbox :
  inPath }));
  this.state.getMessages(inPath);
}.bind(inParentComponent)
```

Sure enough, we can see that currentMailbox is indeed set, which highlights it once React sees that state change and re-renders the appropriate part of the component tree. The currentView is also changed to "welcome" because until the user selects a message, there's nothing to show in the view area, and any time that situation arises, I defaulted it to the welcome view.

The other thing that should occur at this point is that the list of messages in the mailbox, if any, should be retrieved. This is accomplished by the getMessages() method:

```
getMessages : async function(inPath: string): Promise<void> {
  this.state.showHidePleaseWait(true);
  const imapWorker: IMAP.Worker = new IMAP.Worker();
  const messages: IMAP.IMessage[] = await imapWorker.listMessages(inPath);
  this.state.showHidePleaseWait(false);
  this.state.clearMessages();
  messages.forEach((inMessage: IMAP.IMessage) => {
    this.state.addMessageToList(inMessage);
  });
}.bind(inParentComponent)
```

Note that this also means that the user can click the current mailbox Chip any time they like to refresh the list. The getMessages() method first shows the please wait dialog, then uses the IMAP.Worker class to call the server for the list of messages. Once returned, the first thing to do is to clear any current list of messages, which is where the clearMessages() method comes in:

```
clearMessages : function(): void {
  this.setState(() => ({ messages : [ ] }));
}.bind(inParentComponent)
```

It's a simple matter of setting a blank array into state for the messages property. Then, for each mailbox object returned, it is added to the list of mailboxes just cleared, via a call to addMessagestoList():

```
addMessageToList : function(inMessage: IMAP.IMessage): void {
  this.setState(prevState => ({ messages : [ ...prevState.messages,
  inMessage ] }));
}.bind(inParentComponent)
```

As you've seen before, the spread operator is used to essentially copy the list of mailboxes into a new object, then a new item is added into it. Finally, the updated array is passed to setState(), and React does its thing to update the list of messages.

ContactList.tsx

While it might seem most logical at this point to jump into the message list and message view code, I want to save those for a little later just because it's where most of the complexity (relatively speaking) is. Instead, I want to hit on the two contact-related pieces of code first, starting with the ContactList component itself, in the ContactList.tsx file, which is the list of contacts on the right-hand side of the screen:

```
const ContactList = ({ state }): JSX.Element => (
  <List>
    {state.contacts.map(value => {
      return (
        <ListItem>
          <ListItemButton
            key={ value } button onClick={ () =>
              state.showContact(value._id,
                value.name, value.email
              )
          }>
          <ListItemAvatar>
            <Avatar><Person /></Avatar>
          </ListItemAvatar>
          <ListItemText primary={ `${value.name}` } />
```

```
          </ListItemButton>
        </ListItem>
    );
  })}
</List>
export default ContactList;
```

As with the mailbox list, we have a `List` component. But, unlike the mailbox list, which just had a series of `Chip` components as children, here, we're going to use some components that are more typically used within a `List`. Here, you have one or more child components of type `ListItem`. In this case, the items come from the array of `contacts` in `state`, so like with mailboxes, `map()` is used to iterate them. For each, a `ListItem` is created. Every `ListItem` contains within it a `ListItemButton` component, so that we have something for the user to take an action upon, clicking it in this case. Each `iListItemButton` must have a unique key, though what the value is isn't something `List` defines – it's up to us. So, in this case, I simply make it the next contact object from the `contacts` array itself. Then, for each, an `onClick` handler prop is attached that calls `state.showContact()`, passing it the unique ID of the contact along with the `name` and `email` properties.

The `showContact()` method is this:

```
showContact : function(inID: string, inName: string, inEmail:
string): void {

this.setState(() => ({
        currentView : "contact", contactID : inID, contactName : inName,
        contactEmail : inEmail
      }));
}.bind(inParentComponent)
```

As you can see, `currentView` is set to `"contact"`, and the three values passed in are set in the corresponding state properties. That way, when the contact view is shown, which we'll be looking at next, the contact's name and email address are showing.

Backing up a bit, the `List` component and its child `ListItem` components don't define what the look of an individual item in the list is. You are free to do whatever you like. So, I use another MUI component, `ListItemAvatar`, which is used to display an avatar, usually a small image of some sort, for each contact. `ListItemAvatar` demands an Avatar child that is the image to display. If we had real avatar images for each contact, we could insert it here (hint: that'd make a good suggested exercise!). But, here, I make each contact have the same image, using the Person icon that MUI supplies. Finally, I want to put the name of the contact next to the image, so for that, we add a ListItemText component. The primary prop is the text to show (there is also a secondary prop you could use to, perhaps, show the email address below the name).

ContactView.tsx

When a contact in the contact list is clicked or the NEW CONTACT button in the toolbar is clicked, the contact view is shown in the view area. This content is provided by the ContactView component in the ContactView.tsx file, and it begins thusly ("thusly"? Who talks like that?!):

```
const ContactView = ({ state }): JSX.Element => (
  <form>
```

Strictly speaking, the form isn't necessary. But remember that render() must always return a single element (and that doesn't change when using the functional component approach – the code here still winds up in a render() method), whether it has children or not. While a <div> would work just as well here, I thought <form>, given its children, made sense.

For its children, we begin with a MUI TextField:

```
<TextField margin="dense" id="contactName" label="Name"
  value={ state.contactName } variant="outlined"
  InputProps={{ style : { color : "#000000" } }}
  disabled={ state.currentView === "contact" }
  style={{ width:260 }}
  onChange={ state.fieldChangeHandler } />
```

As the name implies, the TextField allows users to enter text. Here, we're looking for the contact's name. The margin prop set to dense reduces the space around the field, purely a visual choice in this instance. Similarly, setting variant to outlined results in the field having the border around it, which I felt looked better, rather than being just a single line, which is the default look. The label prop is, of course, the text that tells you what field this is (and which moves above the field from inside it as soon as you start typing, which is a nice Material-ish thing to do). The value comes from state, just like you'd expect, whether it's an empty string in the case of creating a new contact or the contact's name when selecting one from the list. The InputProps prop is used to style the underlying HTML <input> element, which is what provides the base functionality that MUI then builds upon. The problem here is that when a TextField is disabled, which is done by setting the disabled prop (which here is true when state.currentView is "contact" because that's what it will be when the user clicked a contact in the list and so is viewing the contact in a non-editable mode), the text is a gray color. That makes it hard to read. So, by explicitly setting the color to black (#000000), that problem is solved, and it remains readable. I also set an explicit width for the field, one large enough to support the maximum characters allowed.

You may be wondering (a) why I skipped the id prop and (b) how the field knows what the maximum length is, because it's not defined here. The answer is in the onChange handler that's attached:

```
fieldChangeHandler : function(inEvent: any): void {
  if (inEvent.target.id === "contactName" &&
    inEvent.target.value.length > 16) { return; }
  this.setState({ [inEvent.target.id] :
    inEvent.target.value });
}.bind(inParentComponent)
<br />
```

This handler is used on all the editable fields in MailBag, in fact, and you can see where the id prop matters here. If you recall from earlier when discussing the mailbox list, I mentioned that if you don't use an anonymous function in the event handler and instead reference the state mutator method directly, then you'll wind up getting an event object passed in. For that situation, that was problematic, but here it's perfect because the target attribute of the event object is the component triggering the event. That includes the id prop value. So, we can start by checking if this is the contactName field based on the id. If it is, and if the length of the value passed in is greater than 16, which is our maximum name length, then we return immediately. That effectively limits the maximum length of the field. If there's still room, or this isn't the contactName field, then the id again comes into play because we use it to set the appropriate state property. If you look back at the state object, you'll find that the fields associated with editing a contact match the id's used on the TextFields in this code. This is similarly true for the MessageView later. The result is that we have a generic event handler that can be used for all these TextFields, and that will mutate the correct property on the state object.

Note that a <br/> element follows the TextField; otherwise, the two TextFields here would be on the same line. And, speaking of both TextFields, here's the next, this one for entering the email address:

```
<TextField margin="dense" id="contactEmail" label="Email"
  value={ state.contactEmail } variant="outlined"
  InputProps={{ style : { color:"#000000" } }} disabled={
  state.currentView === "contact" } style={{ width:520 }}
  onChange={ state.fieldChangeHandler } />
<br />
```

As you can see, aside from the id and label and the width, it's the same as the name field (there's no maximum length for this field so nothing to consider there – the width is simply arbitrary). So, let's move on to the next thing in this code:

```
{ state.currentView === "contactAdd" &&
  <Button variant="contained" color="primary" size="small"
    style={{ marginTop:10 }} onClick={ state.saveContact }>
    Save
  </Button>
}
```

As in BaseLayout, the conditional render trick is used here because the SAVE button should only be visible when we're adding a contact. Otherwise, this is a MUI button as you've seen before, so let's go explore its click handler, saveContact(), in the state object:

```
saveContact : async function(): Promise<void> {
  const cl = this.state.contacts.slice(0);
  this.state.showHidePleaseWait(true);
  const contactsWorker: Contacts.Worker = new Contacts.Worker();
  const contact: Contacts.IContact = await contactsWorker.addContact({
      name : this.state.contactName,
      email : this.state.contactEmail });
```

```
this.state.showHidePleaseWait(false);
cl.push(contact);
this.setState(() => ({ contacts : cl, contactID : null, contactName : "",
contactEmail : "" }));
}.bind(inParentComponent)
```

We begin, as you've seen a few times before, copying the contacts array. Next, the please wait dialog is shown, and then a call to `Contacts.Worker.addContact()` is made, passing it an object formed from the `contactName` and `contactEmail` fields in state, whose values will have been set when the user typed them in the two `TextFields` from before. When that call comes back, please wait is hidden, the returned contact (which now includes the `_id` field) is pushed into the `contacts` array, and finally `setState()` is called to update the array. I also clear out the properties associated with editing a contact so that the field is clear, in case the user wants to add another contact right away.

After that, we have two more buttons to deal with:

```
{ state.currentView === "contact" &&
  <Button variant="contained" color="primary" size="small"
    style={{ marginTop:10, marginRight:10 }}
    onClick={ state.deleteContact }>
    Delete
  </Button>
}
{ state.currentView === "contact" &&
  <Button variant="contained" color="primary" size="small"
    style={{ marginTop:10 }}
    onClick={ () => state.showComposeMessage("contact") }>
    Send Email
  </Button>
}
```

These two are only shown when a contact has been clicked from the list, and they provide the user the opportunity to delete the contact or send a new email to them. Note that for both, I added some margin on the top to separate them from the email field, and for the DELETE button, I also have some on the right so the buttons themselves don't bunch up. For the DELETE button, the `onClick` handler can point directly at the `deleteContact()` method in the state object because that method will already have access to everything it needs to do the delete (namely, the contactID property in state), but for sending an email, we need to know the source of the action, as you saw earlier, hence why we need to use the anonymous function approach here.

As far as that deleteContact() goes, here it is:

```
deleteContact : async function(): Promise<void> {
  this.state.showHidePleaseWait(true);
  const contactsWorker: Contacts.Worker = new Contacts.Worker();
  await contactsWorker.deleteContact(this.state.contactID);
  this.state.showHidePleaseWait(false);
  const cl = this.state.contacts.filter(
    (inElement) => inElement._id != this.state.contactID
  );
  this.setState(() => ({ contacts : cl, contactID : null, contactName : "",
  contactEmail : "" }));
}.bind(inParentComponent)
```

It's much the same as what you've seen before: show please wait, call the server via the Contacts.Worker.deleteContact() method, and then remove it from the list. To remove it, we must find it first. The filter() method of the contacts array in state allows us to do that. For each element in the array, the function we provide to filter() is executed and is passed the next element. If the _id property of the element isn't state.contactID, then true is returned, which filter() takes to mean we want the element included in the new array that it's constructing. Simply put, all elements in state.contacts will be copied into the new array cl *except* for the contact being deleted. What that new array built, we can pass it to setState(), which results in React re-rendering the list, sans that contact. As with adding a contact, the contact editing–related properties in state are cleared, and we're done.

MessageList.tsx

Next up is the message list, which means the MessageList component in the MessageList.tsx file. Here's pretty much the whole thing:

```
const MessageList = ({ state }): JSX.Element => (
  <Table stickyHeader padding="none">
    <TableHead>
      <TableRow>
        <TableCell style={{ width:120 }}>Date</TableCell>
        <TableCell style={{ width:300 }}>From</TableCell>
        <TableCell>Subject</TableCell>
      </TableRow>
    </TableHead>
    <TableBody>
      { state.messages.map(message => (
        <TableRow key={ message.id }
          onClick={ () => state.showMessage(message) }>
          <TableCell>
            { new Date(message.date).toLocaleDateString() }
          </TableCell>
          <TableCell>{ message.from }</TableCell>
          <TableCell>{ message.subject }</TableCell>
        </TableRow>
      ) ) }
    </TableBody>
  </Table>
export default MessageList;
```

The Table component is another MUI component for displaying data like List that you saw earlier, but this one essentially mimics an HTML table. That's ideal for the message list because it should look like a typical table, or grid as it's sometimes called. We have a header row, which we want to ensure stays "stuck" at the top even if the user scrolls to see more of the list, and that's what the stickyHeader prop set to true does for us. Then we have three columns, one each for Date, From, and Subject. So, inside the Table component goes firstly a TableHead component, which demarks the header. Inside that is a TableRow, since the header row is, in fact, a row like any other despite it being the header. Finally, inside that TableRow goes three TableCell components, one for each column in the table. The first two have specific widths assigned, which will cause the third, the Subject column, to take up the remaining horizontal space.

After the TableHead comes a TableBody, again, just like a plain old HTML table. Inside the TableBody goes a TableRow for each message. We iterate the list of messages found in state.messages with map() like you've seen for mailboxes and contacts. For each of the three data elements to display, we drop a TableCell into the TableRow and render the appropriate properties from the message object into it. That's about all there is to it!

You'll also, no doubt, notice that there is an onClick prop on the TableRow housing the message. When the row is clicked, we need to display in the view area below, which is what the showMessage() state mutator method does:

```
showMessage : async function(inMessage: IMAP.IMessage): Promise<void> {
  this.state.showHidePleaseWait(true);
  const imapWorker: IMAP.Worker = new IMAP.Worker();
  const mb: String = await imapWorker.getMessageBody(
    inMessage.id, this.state.currentMailbox
  );
  this.state.showHidePleaseWait(false);

  this.setState(() => ({
    currentView : "message", messageID : inMessage.id, messageDate :
    inMessage.date, messageFrom : inMessage.from,
    messageTo : "", messageSubject : inMessage.subject, messageBody : mb
  }));}.bind(inParentComponent)
```

Once the please wait popup is shown, the IMAP.Worker.getMessageBody() method is called, passing it the ID of the message and the path of the current mailbox. The server is called, the body returned, and please wait hidden. Finally, the setState() call is made to change the view and populate all the message details, including the body. The result is that the message is displayed, all pertinent details visible to the user in the view area below the message list.

MessageView.tsx

MessageView is perhaps the most complex of all the components, and even it isn't anything that'll hurt your brain! It all begins with a plain old HTML form:

```
<form>
```

As with ContactView, we need a single container for fields here, and a `<form>` again makes sense, though it doesn't need to be a `<form>` element.

Speaking of the fields that follow:

```
{ state.currentView === "message" &&
  <InputBase defaultValue={ `ID ${state.messageID}` }
    margin="dense" disabled={ true } fullWidth={ true }
    className="messageInfoField" />
}
{ state.currentView === "message" && <br /> }
```

First, we need a field to display the ID of the message. Since this isn't something that will ever be editable, a `TextField` isn't needed. And, while it certainly could have just been a plain old `<div>`, I decided to use another MUI component, just to give you a little more exposure to it. The `InputBase` component serves as the basis for many of MUI's form field components and provides a minimal set of style rest and state logic. It's perfect for our purposes because it looks an awful lot like `TextField` from an API standpoint, but is a bit simpler. The `defaultValue` prop is the message ID, prefixed with a static "ID" text to serve as a label of sorts. The `margin` prop is again set to `dense` to reduce space around it, and the field should always be `disabled`, so that prop is set to `true`. The `fullWidth` prop, set to `true`, stretched the field across the entire width of its container, which ensures we always have enough space to display the content. Finally, a little bit of styling is needed, but this time it's done with a `className` prop rather than inlining the styles, and that leads us to the last style rule in our `main.css` file:

```
.messageInfoField {
  color : #000000!important;
}
```

That serves much the same purpose as the styling on the `TextField`s you saw earlier to make the text readable when the field is disabled. Note that appending `!important` was required here to get the color to override the default gray color, not an uncommon thing to have to do with CSS.

After that comes another `InputBase` component, this time for the message's date:

```
{ state.currentView === "message" &&
  <InputBase defaultValue={ state.messageDate } margin="dense"
    disabled={ true } fullWidth={ true }
```

```
    className="messageInfoField" />
}
{ state.currentView === "message" && <br /> }
```

Of course, conditional rendering is used to only show these fields when the value of currentView is "message", that is, when viewing an existing message, as opposed to when this view is shown for composing a message.

One last field remains after that:

```
{ state.currentView === "message" &&
  <TextField margin="dense" variant="outlined"
    fullWidth={ true } label="From"
    value={ state.messageFrom }
    disabled={ true }
    InputProps={{ style : { color : "#000000" } }} />
}
{ state.currentView === "message" && <br /> }
```

The From field is again only shown when viewing an existing message, and like the previous two InputBase fields, this one stretches across the entire container thanks to fullWidth being set to true. Of course, this field is never editable, hence disabled set to true with no logic.

Now we get into some fields that are shown only when composing a message:

```
{ state.currentView === "compose" &&
  <TextField margin="dense" id="messageTo" variant="outlined"
    fullWidth={ true } label="To"
    value={ state.messageTo }
    InputProps={{ style : { color : "#000000" } }}
    onChange={ state.fieldChangeHandler } />
}
```

The To field is obviously needed, and like From, we stretch it across the entire container to allow the user as much room to enter long addresses as possible. You can see our friendly neighborhood state.fieldChangeHandler() method again being used, which means that the id here must match the state property that should get the value of whatever the user enters here, which it does.

Then, we need a subject field:

```
{ state.currentView === "compose" && <br /> }
<TextField margin="dense" id="messageSubject" label="Subject"
  variant="outlined" fullWidth={ true }
  value={ state.messageSubject }
  disabled={ state.currentView === "message" }
  InputProps={{ style : { color : "#000000" } }}
  onChange={ state.fieldChangeHandler } />
<br />
```

There's nothing new there frankly, so let's move on to the field where the user will enter the actual text of the message:

```
<TextField margin="dense" id="messageBody" variant="outlined"
  fullWidth={ true } multiline={ true } rows={ 12 }
  value={ state.messageBody }
  disabled={ state.currentView === "message" }
  InputProps={{ style : { color : "#000000" } }}
  onChange={ state.fieldChangeHandler } />
```

Ah, here we have a few new props! When multiline is set to true, MUI will render an HTML <textarea> under the covers. That implies that we can set rows and cols value, and we can, though only rows is used here because fullWidth is set to true. So, what we wind up with is a <textarea> that fills the entire available horizontal space and allows for 12 rows of text to be input (it will, of course, scroll to accommodate more as necessary, as a <textarea> does by default). Other than that, though, this is the same as the other fields.

After the fields, we must work on the buttons that we need, beginning with the one to send the message being composed:

```
{ state.currentView === "compose" &&
  <Button variant="contained" color="primary" size="small"
    style={{ marginTop:10 }}
    onClick={ state.sendMessage }>
  Send
</Button>
}
```

That's a pretty straightforward Button component, isn't it? Given there's nothing new, let's jump right to that sendMessage() state method referenced in the onClick prop:

```
sendMessage : async function(): Promise<void> {
  this.state.showHidePleaseWait(true);
  const smtpWorker: SMTP.Worker = new SMTP.Worker();
  await smtpWorker.sendMessage(this.state.messageTo,
    this.state.messageFrom, this.state.messageSubject,
    this.state.messageBody
  );
  this.state.showHidePleaseWait(false);

  this.setState(() => ({ currentView : "welcome" }));
}.bind(inParentComponent)
```

Again, this code is very much like other methods you've seen. We show the please wait dialog; call the appropriate Worker method, passing it the properties from state that will have been populated as the user typed values into the fields, thanks to that fieldChangeHandler() method; hide please wait; and finally change the view to the welcome view, since it doesn't make much sense to go somewhere else or even to stay on the compose view at that point.

Next, we have a button that only shows up when the user clicks a message from the message list, namely, the one to reply to the message:

```
{ state.currentView === "message" &&
  <Button variant="contained" color="primary" size="small"
    style={{ marginTop:10, marginRight:10 }}
    onClick={ () => state.showComposeMessage("reply") }>
    Reply
  </Button>
}
```

For all intents and purposes, it's the same as the NEW MESSAGE button in the toolbar, but the one difference is that showComposeMessage() must be called and passed a different value, so it's anonymous function time again! And, of course, this button is only shown when state.currentView is "message", not when it's "compose".

Similarly, the last button to deal with, DELETE, is also only shown when viewing an existing message from the message list:

```
{ state.currentView === "message" &&
  <Button variant="contained" color="primary" size="small"
    style={{ marginTop:10 }}
    onClick={ state.deleteMessage }>
    Delete
  </Button>
}
```

By this point, you should have a very good handle on MUI Buttons, right? I expect so! Therefore, it's time for the final method in state, the deleteMessage() method, hooked to this button via its onClick prop:

```
deleteMessage : async function(): Promise<void> {
  this.state.showHidePleaseWait(true);
  const imapWorker: IMAP.Worker = new IMAP.Worker();
  await imapWorker.deleteMessage(
    this.state.messageID, this.state.currentMailbox
  );
  this.state.showHidePleaseWait(false);
  const cl = this.state.messages.filter(
    (inElement) => inElement.id != this.state.messageID
  );

  this.setState(() => ({ messages : cl, currentView : "welcome" }));
}.bind(inParentComponent)
```

This is very much the same as the deleteContact() method, except that it calls IMAP.Worker.deleteMessage() of course, passing it the message's ID and the path to the current mailbox and then filtering the state.messages array to remove it from the list.

We have just one more component left to examine, and here it comes!

WelcomeView.tsx

I saved perhaps the simplest component for last – `WelcomeView`:

```
<div style={{
  position:"relative", top:"40%", textAlign:"center",
  color:"#ff0000"
}}>
  <h1>Welcome to MailBag!</h1>
</div>
```

Yep, that's literally it! The styling here serves to center the text (well, it's actually a hair closer to the top than the bottom, which I think looks a little better) and then just a big, red `<h1>` element.

And that, my friend, is MailBag, all done and ready to serve your email needs!

Suggested Exercises

As with the server, I've left some things that you could do to enhance the MailBag client app that I think would serve as excellent learning experiences to put what you've learned to the test:

- Did you notice that all emails are treated as plain text, whether they are or not? Wouldn't it be nice to see HTML messages displayed as they're intended to? I think so! See if you can pull that off. As a hint, the server will need to be altered to return HTML instead of plain text (should be a one- or two-line change), and then the client will need to display it (you might try just inserting the content into a `<div>`, or perhaps an `<iframe>`, but either will require you to make additional changes to `MessageView.tsx`).

- Allow the user to upload pictures for their contacts. There are several approaches, but you might consider using a plain old HTML form with a `<file>` element, but then you'll need to consider how to alter the server to accept it. Then, store the image in a temporary location and make the client fetch it to display it. Then figure out how to store it in NeDB when they save it (hint: Base64-encoded is probably a good answer there). Note that this most likely would not be part of the RESTful API of the server, so you'll need to figure out how to make this coexist with the existing service endpoints.

Summary

In this chapter, we completed the MailBag app, building the client side of it. In the process, you learned about things like conditional rendering with React, the MUI component library, a bit about AJAX and the Axios library for doing it, and CSS Grid. The result is a complete application, MailBag, that, while pretty basic, does the job as a webmail client pretty well.

One project down, just one to go! And the next one is going to be something quite a bit different: a game!

CHAPTER 10

Time for Fun: BattleJong, the Server

In my professional capacity as an architect and team lead, I am sometimes asked by junior developers what they can do to improve their skills. Should they watch YouTube videos about various topics in software development? Are there good books they should read? What about side projects?

My advice has always been the same: to get better at anything, software development very much included, you've got actually to do the thing you want to get better at! Nothing beats experience. So yes, side projects are the way to go.

However, not all experience is equal. With programming, there is one thing that I genuinely believe improves developer skills more than any other type of side project, and that's games. Even if you're a business developer like me, games are where it's at.

Why is that? Simply put, games force us to confront many different software development challenges: algorithms, data structures, optimization, smart design, flexible architecture, and so on. That's before you even think about the more obvious things like visual design and graphics. They also, by their nature, are an exciting challenge to face because they are, by their nature, meant to be fun! Shouldn't the process of *making* a game be fun too? Indeed, it is, even when being challenging – and it *will* be challenging, and in ways you can't predict!

So, in this chapter and the next, we're going to take that philosophy to heart and build ourselves a game using React, TypeScript, and Node, as well as a few other things. To be sure, this isn't going to be a AAA game title a la *Halo* or even something as addicting as *Minecraft*. But it will afford you the chance to view what you've learned through a different lens and use some different development muscles, all of which will provide you some new perspectives – along with some new skills – with which to create going forward.

© Frank Zammetti 2022
F. Zammetti, *Modern Full-Stack Development*, https://doi.org/10.1007/978-1-4842-8811-5_10

What Are We Building?

In all probability, you've played Mahjong before, but if not, Figure 10-1 shows you what it looks like.

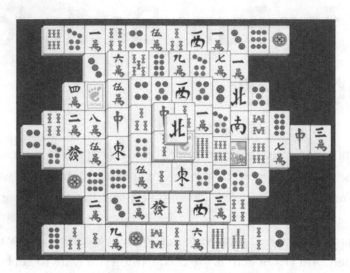

Figure 10-1. *A basic Mahjong Solitaire layout*

To be more accurate, what's depicted there is actually called Mahjong Solitaire. Plain old Mahjong is a little different, though they both are played with tiles depicting various Chinese symbols – perfectly logical given that the game was invented in China during the Qing dynasty (1636–1911). Mahjong is vaguely similar to Poker in that you are trying to create "hands" using tiles you are given at the start plus the tiles on the board, and you play with multiple people, usually four.

Mahjong Solitaire, on the other hand, is, as the name implies, played in solitude by one person. The goal is to find matching tiles and remove them from the board. The trick is that the board is three-dimensional: there are five layers of tiles in that screenshot, and you can only match and remove pairs that are "free," which means that there is no tile above them and none to either the left or right of each. You continue until you either remove all the tiles, which is considered a win, or you have no more legal moves left, which is regarded as a "dead-ended" board.

Now, our little game here, BattleJong, is going to be a bit different. First, we'll do away with the Chinese symbols and go with something... different. We'll get to that in the next chapter! Also, we're going to make this a bit more social: as the word "Battle" in the name implies, you're going to play against another person.

The way it will work is that you'll play simultaneously with someone else. You'll get up to ten points per matched tile pair. However, how long it takes you to find a match will deduct from that number. You'll always get at least one point per match, but you could get anything from one to ten, depending on how long you take each time. In the end, whoever has the highest score wins.

It's not a complicated game mechanic to be sure, and it's not even original, as versions of Mahjong like this were done as far back as the mid-1990s in the DOS days. But, for our purposes here, it's perfect: being not too complicated means it won't be overwhelming, and the need to play against someone introduces the need for some sort of server. And it's not just any server: we need it to be real time, and the server needs to be able to send data to the client at any time. This makes for a challenge and, more importantly, allows me to introduce some new things to the mix.

Basic Requirements

Before we get to the code (which there is surprisingly little of, as you'll see), let's outline the exact requirements, and let's also note whether it's (at least primarily) a client concern, a server concern, or both:

- Each player should see a board similar to (but a bit different from) Figure 10-1 (client).

- They should be able to click a tile, have it highlighted in some way, and then click another (client).

- If they match, the pair should be removed, and the server must be told how many points resulted from the match. The server must then update the other player with that information and keep track of the cumulative score of both (both).

- Logic should be in place to ensure each player can only select "free" tiles (client).

- When a player launches the client, it must contact the server and "register" the user. Once two players are registered, the game will begin automatically (server).

- Whenever a player clears the board, or it is determined that there are no more valid moves left, the server should be told (both).

- Once both players register the board completed, the server will determine who won based on score and inform both players (server).

As you can see, most of the work is really client side, which means it'll be covered in the next chapter. However, the server certainly does have some work to do, so let's get to work building it!

Setting Up the Project

First things first: let's create the project by creating a directory and then executing the NPM commands that, by now, you probably know by heart:

```
npm init
```

Just accept all defaults, as usual, to create an NPM/Node project. Then

```
npm install typescript@4.7.4 --save-dev
npx tsc -init
```

That gets TypeScript all set up. Finally, to ensure we can develop without having to constantly build and restart ourselves, let's add nodemon to the mix:

```
npm install nodemon@2.0.19 --save-dev
```

That gives us the basic setup we need for the server.

Note   You may be wondering why, in the two projects presented in this book, I didn't use Webpack on the server side. Indeed, you *can* do so. However, my feeling is that since server-side code by its nature isn't being shipped down to a browser, there's less need for Webpack there. Bundling up your code efficiently matters less when it's just going to be sitting on a server. I'd rather keep the workflow more uncomplicated and not introduce another tool to the toolchain when working on that code, so I left Webpack out of the server-side mix for those reasons, not because of any technical issues.

Some tsconfig.json Changes

At this point, you would have yourself a default tsconfig.json file for TypeScript configuration. For the most part, the default configuration will suffice, but there are a few changes needed or at least desired. Here is the effective `tsconfig.json` used for this project:

```
{
  "compilerOptions": {
    "target": "es5",
    "module": "commonjs",
    "sourceMap": true,
    "outDir": "./dist",
    "strict": true,
    "noImplicitAny": true,
    "strictNullChecks": true,
    "strictFunctionTypes": true,
    "strictBindCallApply": true,
    "strictPropertyInitialization": true,
    "noImplicitThis": true,
    "alwaysStrict": true,
    "esModuleInterop": true,
    "forceConsistentCasingInFileNames": true
  },
  "include": [ "src/**/*" ]
}
```

Most of this you've seen before in the previous project and examples, but what's new is the setting that is collectively under the heading of "Strict Type-Checking Options," from the "strict" property to the "alwaysStrict" property. These are concerned with helping us write better TypeScript code by tightening the screws of the rules imposed on us a bit:

- **strict** – This enables all strict type-checking options. That means that it will enable noImplicitAny, noImplicitThis, alwaysStrict, strictBindCallApply, strictNullChecks, strictFunctionTypes,

301

and `strictPropertyInitialization`. You can override any of these as you wish though, and explicitly enabling them is redundant, but does no harm.

- **noImplicitAny** – This will cause tsc to raise an error any time it detects that a variable as part of an expression or declaration was of type any implicitly (in other words, if you don't specify a type, even if it's any). This forces you to declare types more consistently.

- **strictNullChecks** – In strict null checking mode, the `null` and `undefined` values are not in the domain of every type and are only assignable to themselves and any (the one exception being that `undefined` is also assignable to `void`).

- **strictFunctionTypes** – With this enabled, function-type parameter positions are checked contravariantly instead of bivariantly (both contravariant and bivariant). This topic can get pretty complicated and would take a lot of space to explain properly here, so I'm going to refer you to some existing documentation to do the job for me: `www.stephanboyer.com/post/132/what-$are-$covariance-$and-$contravariance`.

- **strictBindCallApply** – Simply put, this enables stricter checks when you use the `bind()`, `call()`, and `apply()` functions. Since these can get you into trouble if you aren't careful, having them checked more robustly is a Very Good Thing!

- **strictPropertyInitialization** – This ensures that non-undefined class properties are initialized in the constructor. Note that this option requires that `strictNullChecks` be enabled to take effect.

- **noImplicitThis** – This will cause tsc to raise an error if it encounters "this" expressions with an implied any type.

- **alwaysStrict** – This causes tsc to parse your code in ES6 strict mode and also to include the `"use strict"` directive at the top of output JavaScript files to enable a stricter ES6 adherence policy at runtime.

As a rule, I suggest always enabling these checks. It will lead to writing better TypeScript code in almost all situations. You could run into some cases where you need to disable them for one reason or another, but I'd start with them enabled and only disable if you *really* need to.

Adding Node Modules

Next, we need to add the Node modules that we'll be using. For this project, there's only two:

```
npm install express@4.18.1 --save
npm install ws@8.8.1 --save
```

Express you already know about, and the ws library is what we'll use for client-server communications. But I can't get into that just yet because there's a bit of precursor explanation that has to happen. That'll be coming in short order, but before that, we need to complete the project setup.

Adding Types

Finally, since we're using TypeScript, we like to have types for as much of what we're using as possible. Fortunately, there are types available for everything this project uses:

```
npm install @types/node@18.6.0 --save-dev
npm install @types/express@4.17.13 --save-dev
npm install @types/ws@8.5.3 --save-dev
```

With those installed, we're good to go for the server side of BattleJong.

Source File Rundown

Believe it or not, but for this project, there is only a single source file to deal with, and it's not even all that large (under 150 lines of actual code!).

So let's get right into it!

The Starting Point (the ONLY Point, in Fact!): server.ts

The server.ts file begins, not surprisingly, with a few imports:

```
import path from "path";
```

As you've seen before, the path library that Node itself provides is used to construct directory paths on our server; in this case, it'll be used to get a path to the static resources that make up the client so that they can be loaded via HTTP. And, to make HTTP available, we need Express:

```
import express, { Express } from "express";
```

Finally, we'll need that mysterious ws library that you saw added earlier:

```
import WebSocket from "ws";
```

Ooh, WebSocket, that sounds interesting! You may have even heard the term before, and now "ws" probably starts to make some sense! Let's see what that's all about now, shall we?

A Quick Detour: WebSockets

The World Wide Web was initially conceived as a place where it was the client's responsibility to request information from a server, and indeed that's how most interactions today still occur. Everything is initiated by the client requesting some information or requesting some operation be performed. But that eliminates a host of interesting possibilities or at least makes them more difficult and nonoptimal since you wind up having to use various clever hacks.

For example, if you have a machine that provides stock prices to a client to display in a dashboard, the client must continuously request updated prices from the server. This is what's referred to as the "polling" approach. The downsides, primarily, are that it requires constant new requests from the client to the server (read: lots of network traffic), and the prices will only be as fresh as the polling interval, which you typically don't want to make too frequent for fear of overloading the server. The prices, therefore, aren't truly real time, something that can be very bad if you're an investor.

With the advent of AJAX techniques, developers started to investigate ways to have bidirectional communication, in which the server could *push* new stock prices out to the client. One such method is called "long polling." Sometimes called Comet, long polling is a technique by which the client opens a connection with a server, as usual. But then, the server holds the request open. It never sends the HTTP response completion signal, so the connection persists. Then, when the server has something to transmit to the client, the connection is already established, and the information can be sent immediately to the client. This trick is sometimes referred to as a "hanging-GET" or "pending-POST," depending on the HTTP method used to establish the connection.

This can be tricky to implement for many reasons, but probably the key one is that the connection processing thread is held on the server. Given that it's an HTTP connection and HTTP servers have some limit on the number of such request processing threads they can support, the overhead to keeping them alive for a long time is not at all inconsequential. Before long, your server can be brought to its knees, even without seemingly having all that many clients connected.

The WebSocket protocol was created to allow this sort of persistent connection without all the problems of long polling or other approaches. WebSockets is an Internet Engineering Task Force (IETF) standard that enables bidirectional communication between a client and a server. It does this by a special handshake when a regular HTTP connection is established. To do this, the client sends a request that looks something like this:

```
GET ws://websocket.apress.com/ HTTP/1.1
Origin: http://apress.com
Connection: Upgrade
Host: websocket.apress.com
Upgrade: websocket
```

First, notice the protocol in the GET URL: ws. This indicates a WebSocket connection. Then, notice that Upgrade header value. That's the magic bit. When the server sees this, and assuming it supports WebSockets, it will respond with a reply such as this:

```
HTTP/1.1 101 WebSocket Protocol Handshake
Date: Mon, 21 Dec 2017 03:12:44 EDT
Connection: Upgrade
Upgrade: WebSocket
```

The server "agrees to the upgrade," in WebSockets parlance. Once this handshake completes, the HTTP request is torn down, but the underlying TCP/IP connection it rode in on, so to speak, remains. That's the persistent connection with which the client and server can communicate in real time, without having to reestablish a connection every time. To be clear, there is still overhead the server must maintain, but because TCP/IP requires considerably fewer resources than does HTTP riding on top of it, more persistent connections can be maintained with WebSockets than with any clever HTTP hack.

WebSockets also comes with a JavaScript API, supported by all current browsers, that you can use to establish connections, and both send and receive messages (and messages are what we call data that is transmitted over a WebSocket connection, in either direction). We'll get into that API in the next chapter when we build the client, but for now, we need to think about how WebSockets is used on the server side.

There are several options available to us, but I'm going to use perhaps the simplest and the one that mimics the browser API as closely as possible. That API is contained in a library called, simply enough, ws. You can read about it here: `https://github.com/websockets/ws`. But, to give you the core concepts quickly and easily, here's a complete example of using it:

```
import WebSocket from "ws";
const wsServer = new WebSocket.Server({ port : 8080 });
wsServer.on("connection", (socket: WebSocket) => {
  socket.on("message", inMsg => {
    socket.send(inMsg);
  });
});
```

Simply put, you begin – after importing the library, of course – by constructing a WebSocket server and tell it what port to listen on. Since port 80 is normally for HTTP traffic, I went with 8080, so that it's similar, but different.

The next part is vital: you must define what happens when messages are received from the client (I suppose you don't *have* to do this, but then not much is ever going to happen in your application!). To do this, you have to first listen for the "connection" event, which you do by calling the on() method of the WebSocket.Server instance, as shown. Several events occur (message, close, error, headers, and listening, in addition to connection), but connection is the most important one because it's the first time you have reference to the WebSocket object that will be associated with this client going forward. Each connected client will have its own WebSocket instance, so you need to hook up a "message" event handler function to that WebSocket. It's important to understand that you're hooking it up to each individual WebSocket that's created by a client connecting, not to the WebSocket.Server. This is a common mistake, so be careful!

From that point on, any messages that are sent from the client (however that happens – it doesn't matter right now!) will be handled by this function. In this case, all it does is echo the message back to the client, and here you can see how information is sent from the server to the client: the send() method of the WebSocket instance for that client. Note that any code that has a reference to this WebSocket can send messages to the client, not just code inside the message event handler. For example, as long as you keep a reference to the WebSocket in global scope, you could have some code in a timeout() firing every ten seconds to send a message to the client.

That, basically, is how the ws library is used on the server side, minus one or two other things that we'll get to as we look at the code. WebSockets, in general, isn't a complicated thing from a developer standpoint, and you'll see that's true on the client side as well in the next chapter.

Back to the Code!

Okay, now that we know about WebSockets, we can get to examining the rest of the code in server.ts. Ironically, after the imports, the first thing we encounter is *not* WebSockets related at all:

```
const players: any = { };
```

When a player connects to the server, they will be added to this object. Each property in this object will be a player, and each property will be an object in the form:

```
{ score: number, stillPlaying: boolean }
```

The score is, obviously, the player's current score. The stillPlaying property will be true to start and will remain true until the client signals that the player has either cleared the board, or they have no more valid moves available, at which point it will flip to false. The two objects in this players object are keyed by PID, or Player ID.

This object and its children, in essence, represent the "game state" at any given moment in time, at least as far as the server is concerned.

Serving the Client: The Express Server

Our client app, which we'll build in the next chapter, needs to be served by the server so a player can load it in their browser. To provide this functionality, we'll use the Express library:

```
const app: Express = express();
app.use("/", express.static(path.join(__dirname, "../../client/dist")));
app.listen(80, () => {
  console.log("BattleJong Express server ready");
});
```

That should look familiar to you because it is essentially the same code you saw in the MailBag app. For BattleJong, though, we're not defining a RESTful interface, so all we need is the static middleware to serve the contents of the client/dist directory.

At this point, we have an HTTP server listening on port 80. Next, we need to set up another server, this one for WebSocket connections (yes, you absolutely can create multiple servers from a single Node source file!).

Handling Messages: The WebSocket Server and Overall Game Design

Before we get into the code, let's talk about the overall flow of events in the game from the server's perspective. There is a well-defined sequence of events – and corresponding messages – that occurs during the game from start to finish. Figure 10-2 shows a flowchart of that sequence.

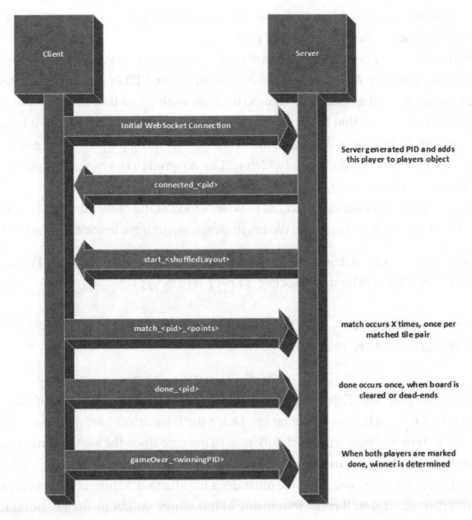

Figure 10-2. *The overall sequence flow of events that makes BattleJong work*

When the client is initially loaded, it connects to the server via WebSockets. Although there is nothing our code *has* to do at that point as far as WebSockets is concerned, the code sends a "connected" message to the client. As part of this message, the PID is sent. All subsequent messages from the client must include this as it's how the server identifies the correct player for various operations.

Once there are two players connected, the server sends the "start" message to both players. This message includes a shuffled layout. We'll get into all of that later. For now, suffice to say it's the arrangement of tiles that the client should display.

From that point on, the client will send one of two messages: "match" or "done." The match message is for when they match a tile pair. The server needs to know the PID and how many points the player got, so those are part of the message. This message can be sent multiple times during the course of gameplay.

Once the player either clears the board or there are no more valid moves left, the "done" message is sent. All the server needs to know is the PID in that case (because it doesn't care whether the board was cleared or dead-ended), so that's all that's sent.

Once the server sees that both players have sent the done message, then it looks at the scores and sends to both players the PID of the winning player. The client will determine what to do based on that (which will be covered in the next chapter, but in short, either a "you won" or a "you lost" message will be shown).

Now that you understand the overall flow, let's look at the code that makes it work, at least on the server side of the fence. We begin by constructing a WebSocket.Server:

```
const wsServer = new WebSocket.Server({ port : 8080 }, function(): void {
  console.log("BattleJong WebSocket server ready");
});
wsServer.on("connection", (socket: WebSocket) => {
  ...Interesting Stuff Here...
});
```

It's even simpler than Express: instantiate WebSocket.Server, courtesy of the ws library, and tell it what port to listen on. That's the bare minimum we need to do. Optionally, you can supply a callback function to execute once the server is ready, and here I use it to display a log message.

Once that's done, the key thing we must do is handle that "connection" event, as previously discussed. You'll recall that inside of it is where you hook up a handler for the "message" event, and that's exactly what the "Interesting stuff here" is (I just felt it would be more intuitive to see this code separate from the code it's contained in):

```
socket.on("message", (inMsg: string) => {
  const msgParts: string[] = inMsg.toString().split("_");
  const message: string = msgParts[0];
  const pid: string = msgParts[1];
  switch (message) {
    ...More Interesting Stuff Here...
  }
});
```

Every message that comes from the client, or that is sent from the server, will be in the form "<message>_<pid>_*" where <message> is the message being received or sent, <pid> is a unique ID associated with each player (more on this shortly), and * is additional data (not needed by all messages).

I'll describe each of the messages in turn next and show the code associated with each.

Message: "match"

Okay, so the game is in motion, and the players are matching tiles. Each tile they do so, the server must be told about it with a message in the form "match_<pid>_<score>". The code that handles this message is the first case of our switch (message) statement:

```
case "match":
  players[pid].score += parseInt(msgParts[2]);
  wsServer.clients.forEach(
    function each(inClient: WebSocket) : void {
      inClient.send(`update_${pid}_${players[pid].score}`);
    }
  );
break;
```

The score that the client sends is added to the player's current score by adding it to the score property of the object corresponding to this player in the players object (remember that this object's properties are keyed by PID). Now, the client that sent this message knows its score, of course, but the other player needs to be told about it. To keep things simple, we're going to broadcast, so to speak, the score to both players and let them act appropriately.

To do so, we must iterate over the connection of connected clients. Note here that this is a property of the WebSocket.Server instance, not the particular client's WebSocket that initiated this message, like most of this code has been using. It makes sense: the WebSocket server itself would be the thing that knows about all connected clients, not an individual client's WebSocket. For each client, the iteration provides us the WebSocket for that client, so we can call send() on each to send a message in the form "update_<pid>_<score>". The client will take that information and update its

311

display accordingly (as you'll see in the next chapter, the score of both players is updated in real time on each player's screen).

Message: "done"

When either a player clears the board or the board has no more valid moves left ("dead-$ended"), the done message is sent, in the form "done_<pid>":

```
case "done":
  players[pid].stillPlaying = false;
  let playersDone: number = 0;
  for (const player in players) {
    if (players.hasOwnProperty(player)) {
      if (!players[player].stillPlaying) {
        playersDone++;
      }
    }
  }
  if (playersDone === 2) {
    let winningPID: string;
    const pids: string[] = Object.keys(players);
    if (players[pids[0]].score > players[pids[1]].score) {
      winningPID = pids[0];
    } else {
      winningPID = pids[1];
    }
    wsServer.clients.forEach(
      function each(inClient: WebSocket) : void {
        inClient.send(`gameOver_${winningPID}`);
      }
    );
  }
break;
```

There's a bit more work here that needs to happen, but not all that much. First, the player that sent this message is marked as done by changing the stillPlaying property of the object associated with it in the `players` collection to `false`. Next, we need to see if both players are done. Since `players` is an object and not an array, we can't just access `players[0]` and `players[1]` to do this check. Instead, we have to iterate the properties of the object. That's where the `for` loop comes in. But we have to be careful to only look at properties defined on the object itself, not any that may come from its prototype, which is why we do `players.hasOwnProperty(player)`. After that, it's a simple matter of incrementing `playersDone` if `stillPlaying` is `false` for each player.

If we finish that loop and `playersDone` is 2, then the game has ended. In this case, it's time to determine a winner! That's easy enough: we get an array of keys in the `players` object and then compare the scores of both, pulling the PID of the winning player out. Finally, the "gameOver_<winningPID>" message is broadcast to both players, and our work here is done!

Note   Eagle-eyed readers will notice that the iteration in the check of `stillPlaying` could have been done the same way as the score comparison was made, thus avoiding the iteration (or vice versa). This is true, and I just did it two different ways to give you some different approaches to consider for accomplishing these things. If I were writing this code "for real," so to speak, I'd have done it with `Object.keys` both times I think, but as they say on the Interwebs: YMMV (Your Mileage May Vary).

Finishing Up the WebSocket Server

At this point, our WebSocket server is set up to handle the two messages the client can send, but there's still a little bit left to be done inside the callback function passed to the `wsServer.on("connection")` statement (remember that what we've been looking at is all contained in that!).

First, we have to generate the PID I've been talking about:

```
const pid: string = `pid${new Date().getTime()}`;
```

Nothing fancy required here; we just use the current time. Next, we need to add an object to the `players` object to represent this player:

```
players[pid] = { score : 0, stillPlaying : true };
```

Now, the server is ready to go. So, the next step is to inform the user of their PID, which is done by sending a "connected_<pid>" message:

```
socket.send(`connected_${pid}`);
```

Finally, if we now have two players ready to go, then we can start the game! To do so, a "start_<layout>" message is sent:

```
if (Object.keys(players).length === 2) {
  const shuffledLayout: number[][][] = shuffle();
  wsServer.clients.forEach(
    function each(inClient: WebSocket) : void {
      inClient.send(
      `start_${JSON.stringify(shuffledLayout)}`
      );
    }
  );
}
```

Naturally, we need to broadcast this message, as you've seen before. But what gets sent to both players is a shuffled layout, meaning the random distribution of tiles on the board. That random layout is produced by a call to the shuffle() function, and that's our next (and last, as it happens) stop on the BattleJong server train!

Of Tiles and Board Layouts

I've mentioned the board layout a few times, but what does that really mean in terms of code? Well, recall earlier that I described a Mahjong Solitaire layout as being multiple levels of stacked tiles. If you want to model that in code, there's probably more than one way, but perhaps the most natural is a multidimensional array. Each primary dimension of the array is one of five layers of tiles, starting with the bottom-most layer. The secondary dimension will then represent each row. The tertiary dimension will then represent a column, or a specific tile, in the row.

In other words, what we're dealing with is simply five grids laid on top of one another. In each position of each layer, there either can be a tile or not. And, in the case of Mahjong, and BattleJong by extension, a tile can be one of 42 types.

But that's jumping ahead just a bit. We don't need to worry about types yet; we just need to worry about which positions have tiles and which don't. For that, we have the layout construct, which is that multidimensional array I described:

```
const layout: number[][][] = [
  [
    [ 0, 1, 1, 1, 1, 1, 1, 1, 1, 1, 1, 1, 1, 1, 0 ],
    [ 0, 0, 0, 1, 1, 1, 1, 1, 1, 1, 1, 1, 0, 0, 0 ],
    [ 0, 0, 1, 1, 1, 1, 1, 1, 1, 1, 1, 1, 1, 0, 0 ],
    [ 0, 1, 1, 1, 1, 1, 1, 1, 1, 1, 1, 1, 1, 1, 0 ],
    [ 1, 1, 1, 1, 1, 1, 1, 1, 1, 1, 1, 1, 1, 1, 1 ],
    [ 0, 1, 1, 1, 1, 1, 1, 1, 1, 1, 1, 1, 1, 1, 0 ],
    [ 0, 0, 1, 1, 1, 1, 1, 1, 1, 1, 1, 1, 1, 0, 0 ],
    [ 0, 0, 0, 1, 1, 1, 1, 1, 1, 1, 1, 1, 0, 0, 0 ],
    [ 0, 1, 1, 1, 1, 1, 1, 1, 1, 1, 1, 1, 1, 1, 0 ],
  ],
  [
    [ 0, 0, 0, 0, 0, 0, 0, 0, 0, 0, 0, 0, 0, 0, 0 ],
    [ 0, 0, 0, 0, 1, 1, 1, 1, 1, 1, 1, 0, 0, 0, 0 ],
    [ 0, 0, 0, 0, 1, 1, 1, 1, 1, 1, 1, 0, 0, 0, 0 ],
    [ 0, 0, 0, 0, 1, 1, 1, 1, 1, 1, 1, 0, 0, 0, 0 ],
    [ 0, 0, 0, 0, 1, 1, 1, 1, 1, 1, 1, 0, 0, 0, 0 ],
    [ 0, 0, 0, 0, 1, 1, 1, 1, 1, 1, 1, 0, 0, 0, 0 ],
    [ 0, 0, 0, 0, 1, 1, 1, 1, 1, 1, 1, 0, 0, 0, 0 ],
    [ 0, 0, 0, 0, 1, 1, 1, 1, 1, 1, 1, 0, 0, 0, 0 ],
    [ 0, 0, 0, 0, 0, 0, 0, 0, 0, 0, 0, 0, 0, 0, 0 ]
  ],
  ... Three more layers' worth of data ...
];
```

To save space, I've only shown the first two layers' worth of data, but there are simply three more arrays of arrays for those layers. Simply stated, where you see a zero, there is no tile. Where you see a one, there is a tile.

As you look at this, if you can sort of mentally strip away the 0s and just try to visualize the pattern of the 1s and you compare it to the Mahjong layout shown at the start of this chapter, you should be able to begin to see how the overall layout is built up from these layers (note that I altered the arrangement from the standard Mahjong layout just a little, purely for aesthetic reasons – I like perfect symmetry!).

That provides us the basic layout of the tiles, but it doesn't tell us which tiles (which 1s) are which type of tile. For that, we need the shuffle() function.

Shuffling the Board

The goal of the shuffle() function is to take that underlying layout array of arrays (of arrays!) and change all the 1s to other values that correspond to tile types. I mentioned earlier that there are 42 tile types, which is the standard number for Mahjong, so I stuck with that. When we get to the client code, you're going to find that there are 42 image files named 101.png, 102.png, 103.png, and so on. Therefore, our goal here is to change each 1 in layout to 101, 102, 103, and so on.

Let's see how that's done:

```
function shuffle(): number[][][] {
  const cl: number[][][] = layout.slice(0);
  let numWildcards: number = 0;
  const numTileTypes: number = 42;
  for (let l: number = 0; l < cl.length; l++) {
    const layer: number[][] = cl[l];
    for (let r: number = 0; r < layer.length; r++) {
      const row: number[] = layer[r];
      for (let c: number = 0; c < row.length; c++) {
        const tileVal: number = row[c];
        if (tileVal === 1) {
          row[c] = (Math.floor(Math.random() * numTileTypes)) + 101;
          if (row[c] === 101 && numWildcards === 3) {
            row[c] = 102;
          } else {
            numWildcards += numWildcards;
          }
        }
      }
    }
  }
```

```
    }
    return cl;
}
```

Before we get into this, I want to point out that this uses the American-style shuffle, which is a purely random shuffle and can lead to an unsolvable arrangement. In our case, that's okay because since both players will be using the same layout, it doesn't so much matter that there's no path to clearing the board, what matters is that they're on an even playing field regardless.

We begin by cloning the `layout` array. We don't want to alter it in case we want to start a new game, so a clone it is. Next, we're going to allow our layout to have up to four wildcard tiles. Wildcard tiles are tiles that can match any other tile type. Some Mahjong variants have wildcards, and some don't. I decided to include them, but they will be random like the tiles, which means not all shuffles will produce a layout with wildcards. But, because I don't want there to be more than four, we're going to need to keep track of how many are randomly selected, if any.

So, the real work is done by iterating over each layer in the layout, then each row in a layer, and, finally, each tile (or column) in the row. Every time we hit a 1, it's time to select a tile randomly! We choose a random number from 0 to 41 (`numTileTypes` is 42, which gives us our upper bounds, non-inclusive, to the random selection) and then add 101 to it to get a value that will correspond to one of our tile images on the client.

Now, if the value chosen is 101, that's going to be the value for a wildcard. In that case, we need to see how many wildcards have already been selected. If we've already filled our quota of wildcards, then the value is bumped to 102 so that it's no longer a wildcard.

Finally, the non-randomized layout is returned and will then be sent to the client as you saw earlier.

At this point, we've got ourselves a BattleJong server in search of a client to make it a complete game!

Suggested Exercises

It's a bit tough to suggest exercises for this chapter because most of what I might recommend would require changes on the client side as well. However, here's a couple to consider:

- Rather than use Express to serve the client, can you write "naked" Node code to do it? You must ensure that it doesn't conflict with the WebSocket server, of course, but it's not really as hard as it may at first seem.

- Can you rework the `shuffle()` function such that it only produces a shuffle that is winnable? You'll have to research how to do this (and there are multiple approaches) and then implement the algorithm.

Summary

In this chapter, we built the not especially complicated server side of the BattleJong equation. In the process, you learned about WebSockets and started to exercise your game programming skills a bit.

In the next chapter, we'll tackle the client side of the game and see how to hook it up to the server to complete the puzzle and have ourselves a fully playable two-$person game.

CHAPTER 11

Time for Fun: BattleJong, the Client

In the last chapter, we began building BattleJong, our little "social" Mahjong game. Now, it's time to dive in and create the client side, which is where most of the game code is found.

Let's begin by talking about what we're building, where you can finally see what this thing is going to look like!

What Are We Building?

In the previous chapter, you saw what a typical Mahjong game looks like. BattleJong will look substantially the same, but because I'm such a huge sci-fi nerd, I'm going to give it a sci-fi bend, as you can see in Figure 11-1.

© Frank Zammetti 2022
F. Zammetti, *Modern Full-Stack Development*, https://doi.org/10.1007/978-1-4842-8811-5_11

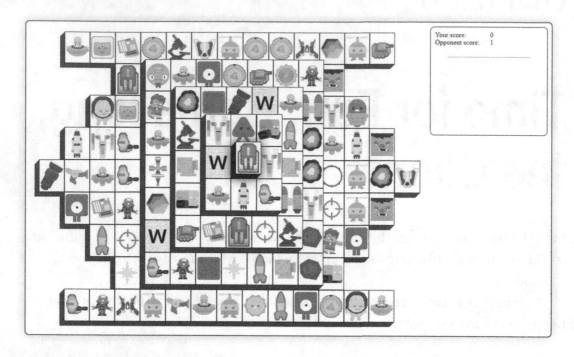

Figure 11-1. *An ancient Chinese game meets the future!*

The layout is very simple here: your playboard on the left and a "control" area in the upper right. In the control area will be shown your current score and your opponent's current score, along with messages below that will change according to what state the game is in. You can see too that I've clicked the topmost tile to show it in its highlighted state.

That, really, is all there is to the client side of BattleJong visually.

Basic Requirements

Given the aforementioned simplicity, the requirements are all straightforward:

- Upon loading the client in the browser via accessing the server's URL, if you're the first player, you'll be in a "waiting" state until another player connects to the server.

- Once the other player connects, or if you were the second player to connect, the game will begin automatically, the board appearing on the left.

- You play according to the basic rules of Mahjong Solitaire, as discussed in the previous chapter, until the board is cleared or dead-ended. Once either happens, you will be in a waiting state again until your opponent also finishes.

- Once both players finish, the winner is shown in the control area.

- Clicking a tile, assuming it's free, highlights it.

There's not much more to it than that!

Setting Up the Project

Setting up this project is simple enough; most of it you've seen and done before:

```
npm init (use all defaults)
npm install --save-dev typescript@4.7.4
npx tsc -init
npm install webpack --save-dev@5.73.0
npm install webpack-cli -save-dev@4.10.0
npm install html-webpack-plugin --save-dev@5.5.0
npm install ts-loader@9.3.1 --save-dev
npm install style-loader@3.3.1 --save-dev
npm install css-loader@6.7.1 --save-dev
npm install html-loader@4.1.0 --save-dev
npm install url-loader@4.1.1 --save-dev
```

Naturally, you can (and probably should, unless you want to do it all from scratch) download the source code bundle for this book and execute npm install to get all the dependencies installed (the initialization steps will have already been done for you).

The one new element here is the url-loader dependency, which is a Webpack loader. Let's talk about that after we talk about the TypeScript config file.

Some tsconfig.json Changes

The effective TypeScript config file for the client side of this project is

```
{
  "compilerOptions": {
    "target": "es5",
    "module": "commonjs",
    "lib": [ "es2015", "es2017", "dom" ],
    "jsx": "react",
    "sourceMap": true,
    "outDir": "./dist",
    "strict": true,
    "noImplicitAny": true,
    "strictNullChecks": true,
    "strictFunctionTypes": true,
    "strictBindCallApply": true,
    "strictPropertyInitialization": true,
    "noImplicitThis": false,
    "alwaysStrict": true,
    "noUnusedParameters": true,
    "noImplicitReturns": true,
    "noFallthroughCasesInSwitch": true,
    "baseUrl": "./",
    "esModuleInterop": true,
    "forceConsistentCasingInFileNames": true
  },
  "paths" : { "components/*" : [ "src/components/*" ] }
}
```

If you compare this to the version for the server, you'll find them to be nearly identical, and most of the differences are related to one being client-side code and one being server-side code.

For example, the lib element here is needed to ensure we have included the library code associated with ES2015, ES2017, and the browser DOM, which, of course, isn't required on the server. The jsx element is needed on the client too given we're building the app with React, but not the server. The baseURL option is necessary for the client in order for dependencies to be resolvable at runtime, and, again, the server doesn't need that. Finally, in this case, we have a paths element to tell Webpack where our React component source files are, but on the server side, we just needed the include element to point it at the src directory.

One thing I skipped there, a difference, is the `noImplicitThis` option. As you can see, `strict` is set to `true`, which means that all the strict checks are enabled (and as I mentioned in the previous chapter, it's redundant, though not an error, to then have each explicitly enabled). However, this option causes lots of compiler errors in `socketComm.ts` and `state.ts` to be reported, and I didn't see a clean way to have it enabled while avoiding the errors. So, this is one of those cases I mentioned in the previous chapter where disabling the option that otherwise is good to enable is needed. This also shows that you definitely can enable and disable individual checks, and the setting overrides the `strict` setting. There's no conflict there, which is nice since it provides you granular control over these checks.

Some webpack.config.js Changes

Now, let's jump back to Webpack and see its config file:

```
const HtmlWebPackPlugin = require("html-webpack-plugin");
module.exports = {
  entry : "./src/code/main.tsx",
  resolve : {
    extensions : [ ".ts", ".tsx", ".js" ]
  },
  module : {
    rules : [
      {
        test: /\.png$/,
        use : { loader : "url-loader",
          options : { limit : 65536, esModule : false, }
        }
      },
      {
        test : /\.html$/,
        use : { loader : "html-loader" }
      },
      {
        test : /\.css$/,
```

```
        use : [ "style-loader", "css-loader"]
      },
      {
        test : /\.tsx?$/,
        loader: 'ts-loader',
        exclude : /node_modules/
      }
    ]
  },
  plugins : [
    new HtmlWebPackPlugin({ template : "./src/index.html", filename :
    "./index.html" })
  ],
  performance : { hints : false },
  watch : true,
  devtool : "source-map"
};
```

Save for one thing, it's the same as what you saw for MailBag, but the one thing is very interesting and that's the url-loader, the dependency you saw imported as part of the project setup.

The question we must answer here is: How do we include images in a project that Webpack will package for us? It turns out there are several answers, but the one I'm using is the url-loader. What this does for us is it encodes any images it finds (note the test for the loader matching .png) in Base64 and then embeds it into the final bundle. This is nice because it overall generally leads to better performance in terms of load time because the browser doesn't need to open new connections to the server to fetch images. They're already there in what was initially downloaded!

The module allows us to set a size limit too. Here, for any image larger than 64k, Webpack will use the file-loader, which is what it uses by default. This would load the images in the usual way a browser usually would.

The esModule config option is essential here because, by default, this loader will generate JS modules that use the ES module syntax. In order to be able to import the images in our code files and treat them like any other code module – which is exactly what we want to do and will be doing later – we need to set this option to true. Otherwise, you will run into compilation problems with TypeScript.

Adding Libraries

As far as libraries go, there are no new ones needed for this project, just React, naturally, and normalize.css:

```
npm install normalize.css@8.0.1 --save
npm install react@18.2.0 --save
npm install react-dom@18.2.0 --save
```

That didn't take long, did it?

Adding Types

As with libraries, there are only a few TypeScript types needed:

```
npm install @types/react@18.0.15 --save-dev
npm install @types/react-dom@18.0.6 --save-dev
```

That gets us all the TypeScript goodness we can have for this project, so now we can dive into what the files are that make up the project.

Source File Rundown

Although not as minimal as the server's single source file, the client doesn't have that many files to consider either:

- **src/index.html** – Our main entry point

- **src/css/main.css** – A single stylesheet

- **src/code/d.ts** – A file we'll get into later for something for TypeScript that you haven't seen yet

- **src/code/main.tsx** – Our main code entry point

- **src/code/socketComm.ts** – Contains the code that communicates with the server via WebSockets

- **src/code/state.ts** – A state object, just like in MailBag (and similarly, most of the interesting code is here)

- **src/code/components/BaseLayout.tsx** – Also as with MailBag, a base React component to sit at the top of our component tree

- **src/code/components/ControlArea.tsx** – A component for the control area in the upper right

- **src/code/components/PlayerBoard.tsx** – The primary component of the app in essence, where the gameboard is

There is also an `img` directory that contains 42 files named `tile101.png`, `tile102.png`, and so on. There are, obviously enough, the 42 tile images that are used on the board.

The Starting Point: index.html

As with MailBag, it all starts with a simple HTML document, `index.html`:

```
<!DOCTYPE html>
<html lang="en">
  <head>
    <meta charset="utf-8">
    <title>BattleJong</title>
  </head>

  <body>
    <div id="mainContainer" style="width: 100vw;height:100vh;"></div>
  </body></html>
```

And, also as with MailBag, there isn't much to see here because React will be constructing the UI, and for that, we need some code, and that leads us to…

The REAL Starting Point: main.tsx

We begin in the main.tsx file, with a few imports:

```
import "normalize.css";
import "../css/main.css";
```

As with MailBag, we want a clean slate as far as styles go, so `normalize.css` is brought in. Then, our application-specific stylesheet, `main.css`, is likewise imported. There aren't many style definitions in that file, but I'll introduce pieces of it as we encounter the style classes throughout the rest of the code.

After that, React is imported:

```
import React from "react";
import { createRoot, Root } from "react-dom/client";
```

Finally, the `BaseLayout` component is as well. This will be the component at the top of the component hierarchy that will contain state for all the child components:

```
import BaseLayout from "./components/BaseLayout";
```

And, once that's all imported, it's time to render us an interface:

```
const baseComponent: Root = createRoot(document.getElementById("mainCont
ainer")!);
baseComponent.render(<BaseLayout />);
```

At this point in app execution, you'd have the basic screen up, though the playboard is initially hidden (unless you are the second player to connect to the server), so it's mostly an empty screen. Still, it's a start!

Now, let's see what that `BaseLayout` component has in store for us.

The Basic Layout: BaseLayout.tsx

The `BaseLayout` component starts with some React imports, as you'd reasonably expect for a React component:

```
import React, { Component } from "react";
```

Then, we have three application imports, one for the `ControlArea` component, one for the `PlayerBoard` component, and one for our state object code:

```
import ControlArea from "./ControlArea";
import PlayerBoard from "./PlayerBoard";
import { createState } from "../state";
```

After that, it's time to build a component. This is how it starts:

```
class BaseLayout extends Component {
  state: any = createState(this);
```

I again use the same pattern as in MailBag, where state is housed in the topmost object, and the state object is constructed via a call to createState(), which is code you'll see later.

Next, we run into the render() method:

```
render(): JSX.Element {
  return (
    <div className="appContainer">
      <div className="playerBoard">
        <PlayerBoard state={ this.state } />
      </div>
      <div className="controlArea">
        <ControlArea state={ this.state } />
      </div>
    </div>
  );
}
```

Note the type of the return from render() is JSX.Element. That's a React type, of course, and because we want to be using TypeScript to its full potential, it's a good idea to specify this type.

Everything is contained with a single <div>, and that <div> has the appContainer style class from main.css applied, which is as follows:

```
.appContainer {
  position : absolute;
  height : 750px;
  left : 50%;
  top : 50%;
  transform : translate(-50%, -50%);
  border : 2px solid #0000ff;
  border-radius : 10px 10px 10px 10px;
  -moz-border-radius : 10px 10px 10px 10px;
  -webkit-border-radius : 10px 10px 10px 10px;
```

```
  display : grid;
  grid-template-columns : 960px 300px;
  -webkit-box-shadow : 0 0 25px 0 rgba(255, 200, 0, 0.75);
  -moz-box-shadow : 0 0 25px 0 rgba(255, 200, 0, 0.75);
  box-shadow : 0 0 25px 0 rgba(255, 200, 0, 0.75);
}
```

The entire element is to be centered both horizontally and vertically, which is where the left and top values come into play. But that only works if position is set to absolute and if the element has a defined height, so those are both done. Then, one final piece of the centering puzzle is needed: the translate transformation. This shifts the topmost <div> halfway left and up, which, all together, gets the centering I want.

I also apply a blue border and round the corners to make it look nice and apply a drop shadow around the whole thing (extending in all four directions) so that it has something of a glowing yellow look to it. Finally, display is set to grid, and two columns are defined, the first for the gameboard and the second for the control area.

Speaking of the gameboard, that's the next element in the hierarchy, the one with the playerBoard style class applied, and that class is

```
.playerBoard {
  grid-column : 1 / 2;
}
```

As you know from the previous project, that puts this <div> into the first column. Then, into this <div> goes a PlayerBoard component, passing it the state object. Obviously, we'll be looking at that shortly.

The second child <div> is the second column and is where the control area goes. It has the following style applied:

```
.controlArea {
  height : 240px;
  margin : 10px;
  padding : 10px;
  grid-column : 2 / 3;
  border : 1px solid #000000;
  border-radius : 10px 10px 10px 10px;
```

```
  -moz-border-radius : 10px 10px 10px 10px;
  -webkit-border-radius : 10px 10px 10px 10px;
}
```

In this case, I don't want the control area to take up the entire column, so I define a height. I also add some margin and padding to keep its contents from bumping up against the border (and to give some separation between the outer border and the control area's border). Of course, I have to tell the grid layout where this element goes in the grid, so that's done. Finally, the control area is given a border with some rounded corners, again just for aesthetics.

The control area houses the aptly named ControlArea component, and why not jump right into that now?

Feedback and Status: ControlArea.tsx

The ControlArea component is the area in the upper right-hand corner where the scores are displayed, as well as messages at various points in the lifecycle of the game. It's not at all complex, but it does introduce a new React concept:

```
const ControlArea = ({ state }: any) => (
  <React.Fragment>
```

What's that React.Fragment about? Well, as you'll recall, the render() method must always return a single component. That component can, of course, have as many children as you like, but, ultimately, it's a single top-level component being returned. But what happens when what you really need to return is a list of components? You're going to have to find some component to be its parent. While that's often easy (and there are frequently many choices, with <div> being very common), wouldn't it be nice if you could return a list of components without adding extra nodes to the DOM? Because remember, that's what's going to happen when you return a component: HTML will be produced and added to the DOM. And sometimes, it won't be so simple: remember that each component you add to the hierarchy has a render() method, and all of them must return a single component.

To illustrate this, imagine you were trying to render a plain old HTML table, and you create a Table component along with a TableHeader component for the header that you nested under your Table component. HTML tables usually have multiple headers for the columns, so the TableHeader component might be something like

```
const TableHeader = () => (
  <th>Column 1</th>
  <th>Column 2</th>
  <th>Column 3</th>
);
```

Hopefully, you see the problem: you'll hit a compiler warning (or error, depending on settings) because you're trying to return multiple items from `render()` (remember that `render()` is implicit when using the functional approach to components like this). If you try to wrap all the `<th>` elements in a `<div>`, that would solve the compiler issue, but it will result in invalid HTML because `<div>` isn't valid at that point in a table. So, that's not a good solution.

That's where `React.Fragment` comes in. It acts as a parent component, but unlike `<div>` (and most other components), it doesn't output any HTML itself. It's strictly a container for children. In this case, I have a list of `<div>` elements, as well as some `<br>` elements that I want to return, and, essentially, it's just a list of such elements, all at the same level in the hierarchy. Using `React.Fragment` here makes a lot of sense.

Scores

Here's the first batch of children that go inside the `React.Fragment`:

```
<div style={{ float:"left", width:"130px" }}>
  Your score:
</div><div>{state.scores.player}</div>
<div style={{ float:"left", width:"130px" }}>
  Opponent score:
</div><div>{state.scores.opponent}</div>
<br />
<hr style={{ width:"75%", textAlign:"center" }} />
<br />
```

The two scores use a total of four elements, two for each label and two for each actual score. The labels are floated left and given a specific width so that the `<div>` elements that follow them, where the scores are, will be lined up nicely. The scores come from state, of course, and specifically the `scores` property. But we'll get to that later.

Game State Messages

While the scores are always present, the messages that can appear below them are not, and they change. So, we're going to use some conditional rendering again as you saw in MailBag, and the first message that may be shown is what you see when you're waiting for an opponent to join:

```
{ state.gameState === "awaitingOpponent" &&
  <div style={{ color:"#ff0000", fontWeight:"bold",
    textAlign:"center" }}>Waiting for opponent to join</div>
}
```

As I'm sure you've surmised, the gameState property of the state object tells us what state the game is in. We can be waiting for an opponent, actually playing, waiting for the game to end because our board has dead-ended or has been cleared, and the game can be over. The first state is when we're waiting for an opponent, so appropriate verbiage is shown, as you can see.

When the board is dead-ended, we again show a suitable message:

```
{ state.gameState === "deadEnd" &&
  <div style={{ color:"#ff0000", fontWeight:"bold",
    textAlign:"center" }}>
    You have no moves left.
    <br /><br />
    Waiting for opponent to finish.
  </div>
}
```

Similarly, when the board has been cleared, we congratulate the player, because that's super cool of them:

```
{ state.gameState === "cleared" &&
  <div style={{ color:"#ff0000", fontWeight:"bold",
    textAlign:"center" }}>
    Congratulations!
    <br /><br />
    You've cleared the board!<br /><br />Waiting for opponent
    to finish.
```

```
    </div>
}
```

Finally, when the game is over, we tell them that, along with who the winner was, as determined by the server:

```
{ state.gameState === "gameOver" &&
  <div style={{ color:"#ff0000", fontWeight:"bold",
    textAlign:"center" }}>
    The game is over.
    <br /><br />
    { state.gameOutcome }
  </div>
}
```

Like I said, this isn't a tough component, not much in it. But the next one is where most of the action is, naturally enough, since it's where the game is played!

Where the Action Is: PlayerBoard.tsx

The PlayerBoard component is what you see on the left-hand side of the screen and is where the player plays the game. It begins with some imports, as always:

```
import React, { CSSProperties, ReactElement } from "react";
```

Oh, but look, we have two new ones. CSSProperties and ReactElement. Keep those in mind, as we'll see them in use soon, and I'll explain what they're all about then.

Before that, though, we have a series of imports, 42 of them to be precise, and that number should ring a bell:

```
import tile101 from "../../img/tile101.png";
import tile102 from "../../img/tile102.png";
...40 more...
```

Yes indeed, one for each image! As you'll recall, Webpack will include our images as Base64-encoded strings in the final bundle and will also wrap them up in a module definition. That's why we can import them here. It may seem weird to import images –

and I'd agree it is! – but essentially, at this point, they *are* code, and we'll be using them as such. But, before we can, we must solve for one small problem, and it's where the d.ts file comes into play.

A Quick Detour: Custom Type Definitions

Any time you see a d.ts file – and you'll see them frequently with TypeScript – it means that the developer has provided TypeScript some additional type information about an API written in JavaScript. This allows TypeScript to do its thing, ensuring that types are correctly used and everything else it provides. This contrasts with the other alternative: rewriting the API in TypeScript. Imagine if you want to use jQuery, but there isn't a TypeScript version available. As long as you have a declaration file for it, you can still use it in TypeScript, complete with all the checking (and IntelliSense inside an IDE) that it provides.

Note   Frequently, you'll see index.d.ts instead of d.ts. Anything *.d.ts is a TypeScript declaration file, the full name is more just programmer-driven convention than any hard-and-fast rule, so some variation is normal.

This all comes into play with the image imports. If you don't have this d.ts file, you'll find that tsc flags each of those imports as an error saying that the module can't be found. You can technically still get them to import using require() notation, but it's something of an eyesore to use import everywhere but require() just for the images, so better to make it work the ideal way I figure. The way to solve this is to declare a module for TypeScript, which is what we find in the d.ts file:

```
declare module "*.png" {
 const value: any;
 export = value;
}
```

Now, TypeScript will know that the image files, any module name ending in .png in fact, are a valid module. The code will compile, and everything will work as expected.

Remember definitelytyped.org? If you go there and pull up a random module in the search engine, when you get to the NPM page for the module, you should see a link somewhere to where the files were exported from. Click that link, and you should see some sort of `*.d.ts` file in the list of files. Doing that, you can view the type information provided for any JavaScript module you want to use.

Back to the Code!

Getting back to the `PlayerBoard` component's code, we begin by functionally constructing the component:

```
const PlayerBoard = ({ state }: any) => {
```

Note here that I need to specify the type of any for the state object because, otherwise, I'll get a compiler warning due to the `noImplicitAny` check being turned on (this wasn't the case in MailBag).

Next, we have some variables that define metadata about the tiles:

```
const tileWidth: number = 72;
const tileHeight: number = 88;
const tileShadowWidth: number = 11;
const tileShadowHeight: number = 11;
```

To lay the tiles out properly on the screen, we need to know their width and height. But we also need to know the width and height of the drop shadow on each because the board will be constructed by overlapping these shadows.

Next, we have two other variables that express metadata:

```
const xAdjust: number = 10;
const yAdjust: number = 36;
```

These are used to push the arrangement of tiles down and right a little bit so that the tiles are centered within the left-hand column and not touching up against the border on the top and left.

After that, we have an array that will contain components, one per tile, when we render them later:

```
const tiles: ReactElement[] = [ ];
```

The problem here is in determining the type (which we must do since the noImplicitAny check won't allow us to either choose a type or explicitly use any, which you usually should try and avoid wherever possible for maximum TypeScript goodness). As you'll see soon, we're going to be rendering an <img> element for each tile. We're going to populate this tiles array with those elements. So, what's the appropriate type?

The ReactElement class is the answer.

Instances of this class are virtual DOM elements that represent an instance of a DOM element (like an <img>), a React component, or a fragment. A ReactElement describes what you literally see on the screen, whereas a component is a level above that: a single component can be composed of numerous ReactElement instances even.

You can roughly think of ReactElement as a base class in an object-oriented language in the sense that you can usually have a generic reference to a more specific object through a variable typed as the base class. For example, in Java, a variable of type Object can reference any other type of object because Object is the base class of all other classes in Java. ReactElement isn't precisely the same because it's not an object-oriented relationship, but you can effectively treat it like it is, which is exactly why the type of the tiles array can be ReactElement (an array of them, to be more precise), and we can later have <img> instances in it, and TypeScript won't complain about the typing.

Finally, we have two more variables:

```
let xOffset: number = 0;
let yOffset: number = 0;
```

These aren't metadata, though; these are used throughout the render process to determine where to place tiles.

The Render Process

The render process is what's next, and it begins thusly:

```
for (let l: number = 0; l < state.layout.length; l++) {
  xOffset = xOffset + tileShadowWidth;
  yOffset = yOffset - tileShadowHeight;
  const layer: number[][] = state.layout[l];
```

The overall flow here is that we're going to iterate over the layers in the layout (which can be found in the state object that we'll look at later, but for now understand that it's simply the layout passed from the server in the same form that you saw in the last chapter). Then, for each layer, we'll iterate the rows in it. Then, for each tile in the row, we'll render it. The xOffset and yOffset will result in the tiles of each layer being shifted right and up a little bit, enough so that the tiles overlap the previously rendered ones, and we get the correct appearance from the board.

Next, after pulling the layer data out of the layout, we iterate the rows in it:

```
for (let r: number = 0; r < layer.length; r++) {
  const row: number[] = layer[r];
  for (let c: number = row.length; c >= 0; c--) {
    let tileVal: number = row[c];
```

For each row, we iterate the tiles in it, and for each we grab its value. With that, we do some logic:

```
if (tileVal > 0) {
  const xLoc: number = ((c * tileWidth) - (c * tileShadowWidth)) + xOffset
  + xAdjust;
  const yLoc: number = ((r * tileHeight) - (r * tileShadowHeight)) + yOffset
  + yAdjust;
```

First, only a value greater than zero is rendered because zero means there is no tile in a given grid slot, and negative one would mean the file has been cleared. So, we need to figure out where to place the tile. Every tile will be positioned absolutely, so we need to figure out the x and y location (left and top in style terms). Since what we're really rendering is a grid, the math is straightforward. For xLoc, it's the column number (variable c) multiplied by the width of the tile, which gives us a horizontal row of tiles. Then, we have to account for the tile shadow since we want them to overlap, so we subtract out the width of the shadow times the column again. Next, we need to account for the 3D look of the grid. To do this, each layer shifts the tiles in it by a little bit up and right. That's where xOffset comes into play. Finally, with the location determined, we need to ensure that the entire grid of tiles is pushed away from the upper-left border, so xAdjust is added.

The vertical location yLoc is calculated in the same way but now using tile and shadow height and the row number as a multiplier.

Now, I said there that each tile would be positioned absolutely, and this is where that CSSProperties import from earlier is used:

```
const style: CSSProperties = {
  position : "absolute",
  left : `${xLoc}px`,
  top : `${yLoc}px`
};
```

The issue being solved here is that when I render the <img> tags, they're all going to have a similar style definition, just being different in the xLoc and yLoc values. So, it makes sense to have that be a common element, a common object, which is what it is here. However, the value of the style attribute, as you'll see soon, can't just be a string or even a plain old JavaScript object. It must be a CSSProperties instance, so that's the type used here and why it had to be imported. But, the type aside, it really is just an object, nothing special otherwise.

Next, we have to account for the possibility that the tile is highlighted because it's selected. This is implemented by applying a style class to it. We know it must be highlighted if its value is greater than 1000, so:

```
let className: string = "";
if (tileVal > 1000) {
  className = "highlightTile";
  tileVal = tileVal - 1000;
}
```

Of course, the values of our tiles are numbered 101–142, so in order to get the right tile displayed, we need to subtract 1000 from tileVal.

Now, as for the highlightTile style class applied, that's as follows:

```
.highlightTile {
  -webkit-filter : drop-shadow(0px 0px 50px #ff0000)
    contrast(150%) saturate(200%);
  filter : drop-shadow(0px 0px 10px #ff0000)
    contrast(150%) saturate(200%);
}
```

I apply a red drop shadow to the element, but with no horizontal or vertical offset and a big blue, which gives the effect of a glowing edge all around it. I also bump the contrast and saturation up so that it stands out a bit more. It's a simple way to implement a highlight but rather effective.

The final piece of the puzzle is actually to render the tiles:

```
const key = l.toString() + r.toString() + c.toString();
switch (tileVal) {
  case 101 : tiles.push(<img key={key} style={style} src={tile101}
    className={className}
    onClick={()=>state.tileClick(l, r, c)} alt="" />); break;
  case 102 : tiles.push(<img key={key} style={style} src={tile102}
    className={className}
    onClick={()=>state.tileClick(l, r, c)} alt="" />); break;
  ...40 more...
}
```

The first line is necessary because remember that any time you have a series of repeating components in React, as in a list, for example, each of them needs to have a unique key associated with it. Here, the unique key is a concatenation of the layer (l), plus the row (r), and finally the columns (c). That ensures each <img> that we're about to render has that unique key to keep React happy.

For each of the 42 tile types, we have a case in a switch. They're all the same save for the value of the src attribute. Here, you can see how the CSSProperties style object is used and how the src points to one of the imported image modules (see, I told you we're using those like code!). Each also gets the className, which is blank for all but the highlighted tile, if any. Finally, each tile gets an onClick handler that calls the tileClick() method in the state object, passing it the layer, row, and column number of the tile. We'll look at that in the section about the state object. Oh, the alt attribute also has to be defined to avoid a compiler warning (or at least an IDE warning in my IDE of choice).

Once all the tiles have been pushed into the tiles array, we can finally return the output of this (implicit) render() method:

```
return (<React.Fragment>{ tiles }</React.Fragment>);
```

Once again, React.Fragment is used to be the one component returned, but now it has a child that is the tiles array. React will dutifully recognize that we want all the elements in the array to be children of the React.Fragment, and we're good to go.

Note   The imports and the switch statement frankly bother me because having 42 of each would usually be seen as redundant coding, and I would agree! However, I see no way to do like you can in Java and do a star import to get all the images imported in one line, nor do I see a way to dynamically name the tile in the <img> tag. The type of src isn't a string, so simple concatenation won't do, and I couldn't see a way to reference it dynamically either (something like, maybe, const s: any = tile[tileVal];). Perhaps you're more clever than I am and can figure something out, and I wouldn't mind hearing about it if you did – you can teach me something! – but sometimes there is no elegant solution (at least no obvious one), so you just gotta do what you gotta do.

Talking to the Server: socketComm.ts

Next, let's look at the socketComm.ts source file, which contains the code that talks to the server via WebSockets. It begins with a single import:

```
import React from "react";
```

As it happens, this import is only needed for TypeScript purposes – if this were plain JavaScript, it wouldn't be needed – and where it's needed is the very next line:

```
export function createSocketComm(
  inParentComponent: React.Component
) {
```

Much like the state object that you saw in MailBag (and like the state object you'll see next in *this* project), a function is necessary to return an object that will be used by the rest of the code due to binding requirements. The argument passed in is a React.Component, so that's why we need the import: to be able to specify the type of this argument (contrast this with the argument to the createState() method in the MailBag state object where it wasn't typed, so this import wasn't needed there).

Next, it's time to connect up to the server:

```
const connection: WebSocket = new WebSocket("ws://localhost:8080");
```

The browser provides the WebSocket object (assuming a relatively newer version: IE11+, Edge 18+, Firefox 11+, Chrome 78+, Safari 13+, Opera 64+), and our app just needs a single instance, pointed to the server and using the ws protocol prefix. You, of course, can change this URL as appropriate, so long as the server is changed accordingly. This line establishes communication with the server, assuming it's listening.

Next, an event listener is hooked up to the WebSocket object to log a message when the connection is opened:

```
connection.onopen = () => {
  console.log("Connection opened to server");
};
```

That's all we need to do in this instance, so there's not much to see. Also, handling errors in some way is a good thing to do, so that event handler is hooked up next:

```
connection.onerror = error => {
  console.log(`WebSocket error: ${error}`)
};
```

Since error recovery can be a whole topic on its own, I went the simple route and just ensured that the error is logged. As relatively simple as this API is, I felt that this was sufficient.

Handling Server-Sent Messages

Now, we get to the heart of things: handling the various messages that can come from the server at various points in the game. For this, we have a single event handler function set up:

```
connection.onmessage = function(inMessage: any) : void {
  console.log(`WS received: ${inMessage.data}`);
  const msgParts: string[] = inMessage.data.split("_");
  const message: string = msgParts[0];
```

First, it should be noted that what you receive in this function is an object. This object, most importantly to us, has a data attribute. This is the string message that was sent from the server.

After logging the message that was received, the message is broken into its constituent part. The first part of the message is a specific message. I know you're shaking your head right now at that sentence – I realize it's confusing! Let me try and clear it up: the client WebSocket receives a message from the server, and the inMessage argument represents that. Let's call this the WebSocket message. But, within that WebSocket message string is a message that pertains to the game itself, something application defined, so that you can call that the game message.

This game message is what this function is concerned with primarily because, next, a switch statement is used:

```
switch (message) {
  case "connected":
    this.state.handleMessage_connected(msgParts[1]);
  break;
  case "start":
    this.state.handleMessage_start(JSON.parse(msgParts[1]));
  break;
  case "update":
    this.state.handleMessage_update(
      msgParts[1], parseInt(msgParts[2])
    );
  break;
  case "gameOver":
    this.state.handleMessage_gameOver(msgParts[1]);
  break;
}
}.bind(inParentComponent);
```

Each of the four game messages that the server can send is forwarded along to an appropriate method in the state object to do the actual work associated with each message, and we'll be looking at those in the next section. With those calls go the information in the WebSocket message string following the game message portion, which is specific to each message. For all but the update message, there's just a single piece of information to send, so it's the second element in the array produced by the call to split() earlier. For update, two pieces of information are sent.

Finally, because we need all of this to execute within the context of the BaseLayout component, this onmessage event handler function is bound to inParentComponent.

Sending Messages to the Server

The final bit of code found in this source file is a simple method for sending messages to the server:

```
(createSocketComm as any).send = function(inMessage: string): void {
  console.log(`WS sending: ${inMessage}`);
  connection.send(inMessage);
};
```

That's really all there is to it! The caller is presumed to have constructed a valid message, and the send() method exposed on the WebSocket instance is all it takes to send it. It couldn't be easier!

At this point, createSocketComm() in socketComm.ts is done, save for one key thing:

```
returncreateSocketComm;
```

That's the final line in this function. That allows the caller to save a reference to the object, which is needed to be able to call the send() method later.

The Main Code: state.ts

Okay, now we come to the final source file that makes up BattleJong, and it's where most of the real work is: state.ts. As with MailBag, this code is concerned with constructing an object that will contain the application state that will be housed in the BaseLayout component and then flow down to any child components that need it. The methods exposed as part of this object are concerned with mutating state in some way, but in this app, that really means it winds up containing a good chunk of the core game logic since that logic will ultimately mutate state, so it's logical for it to be here.

It begins, as most of our modules do, with some imports:

```
import React from "react";
```

```
import { createSocketComm } from "./socketComm";
```

React is obvious – we won't get very far building a React app without importing React itself! – and socketComm, you of course know, is how we talk to the server.

A Few Interfaces for Good Measure

Next up, we find a few interfaces. Note that these are in the TypeScript module that state.ts represents, but it's not in the state object that will ultimately be constructed and used in the rest of the app:

```
interface ISelectedTile { layer: number,
  row: number, column: number, type: number }
interface IScores { player: number, opponent: number }
```

The first, ISelectedTile, is the definition for an object that describes a tile that is currently selected. It contains all the information that is needed to identify a tile (layer, row, and column), and it also contains the type of tile it is, and you'll see why that is needed very soon.

The IScores interface describes an object that stores the current score of the player and the remote opponent.

Both of these are used to avoid duplication of code: without them, we'd need to copy and paste these type definitions in a couple of places in this file's code – unless we wanted to skip typing entirely – neither of which is a great option in general.

The Beginning of the State Object

Now, it's finally time to start building the state object itself. This begins very much like the state object in MailBag did, with a function:

```
export function createState(
  inParentComponent: React.Component
) {
  return {
```

We're returning an object literal, and I usually like to put all my object fields (or properties) first, and that is indeed what we find first:

```
layout : <number[][][]>[ ]
```

The server, you'll recall, sends the layout of the board to each client when the game begins. This is where that layout gets stored. But something new is presenting itself here, and as a result, I think it's time for...

A Quick Detour: TypeScript-Type Assertions

As in many object-oriented languages, typecasting is sometimes necessary. Typecasting, in general terms, is when you assign a value of one type to a variable declared as another. That will sound weird if you've never seen it before, but in terms of object-oriented languages, it makes sense.

Imagine you define a class called Shape. You then define a class called Circle that extends from Shape. Object orientation tells us that all Circle instances are also Shape instances due to that inheritance relationship. Therefore, you can have a variable declared as type Shape that points to an object of type Circle. There's a bit more to casting in some cases, but for our purposes here, this is enough to give you the basic idea.

Casting isn't purely about objects and classes, though. You can also type primitive types. For example, in most languages, a variable of type double can reference an int value because a double can fully contain the value of an int.

In TypeScript, these situations are called type "assertions," but it essentially means the same as casting. It's a purely compile-time mechanism as it has no effect at runtime (it does no special type checking or data restructuring or anything like that), and it's a way for you as the programmer to tell the compiler "look, I know more about this type than you do, so trust me, this is what it is." That is sometimes necessary because as good as tsc is, it can't always determine the type of a reference, and sometimes it's tricky for you to be able to tell it.

Such is the case with this layout property. The first problem is that because this is part of an object literal definition, which means that the colon is already used to separate the property name from its value, there's no way to attach a type. In other words, this won't work:

```
layout: number[][][] : []
```

It will yield a compiler error due to the ambiguous meaning of the two colons. So, from a purely syntactical point of view, we need something else. That's where the angle brackets placed before the value comes in. This says to tsc: "this value is of the specified type, whether you know it or not!" Here, you know that the layout passed from the server is a three-dimensional array of numbers, so we need to express the same type here.

The other problem is that in this case, TypeScript has no way to know what the type of the value is. Without the cast, all it knows is that it's an array, but it doesn't know what the elements of the array are. Yes, we could, in theory, define it as any[ ][ ][ ], but we'd still need the cast syntax due to this being a property in an object literal.

Note that there is a second form of casting in TypeScript: using the as keyword. This line could have been written:

```
layout : [] as number[][][]
```

There's no *technical* difference between the two forms – they mean the same thing – so it's a matter of preference. However, note that in a .tsx file, you *must* use the as keyword because the angle bracket approach can yield syntax errors in JSX when used with TypeScript.

Note   As a general statement, it seems that most TypeScript developers have taken to favoring the as keyword approach. I'm an old Java guy, so my brain automatically goes to angle brackets. The bottom line is that it's up to you, but you may be more in line with most other TypeScript developers by sticking with the as keyword approach.

Back to the Code!

Now, getting back to the code in state.ts, we have more properties to declare on the state object:

```
selectedTiles : <ISelectedTile[]>[ ]
```

This property, which uses the interface defined earlier as its type (again using type casting), is where the selected tiles are stored.

Next, we have a property to hold our scores:

```
scores : <IScores>{ player : 0, opponent : 0 }
```

After that, we have a key property to making everything work, one that tells us what "state" the game is in:

```
gameState : <string>"awaitingOpponent"
```

The game can be in one of five states at a given moment: "awaitingOpponent" (when you are the first player to connect to the server and are waiting for another to connect), "playing" (when the game is being played, obviously!), "deadEnd" (when your board has dead-ended), "cleared" (when you have cleared your board), and "gameOver" (when both players have either cleared or dead-ended the board and a winner has been determined). This gameState value changes as various events occur and is primarily what is used to show the appropriate message in the control area.

The next property is needed when the game has ended:

```
gameOutcome : <string>""
```

This value will be set when the server tells the client which player won.

Speaking of players, each has a unique ID, as you saw in the last chapter, and we need to store that in state:

```
pid : <string>""
```

The next property is our socketComm object:

```
socketComm : <Function>createSocketComm(inParentComponent)
```

Note that the type is Function because that's effectively what gets returned by the call to createSocketComm().

Finally, we need to keep track of how long it takes the player to clear a tile or, more precisely, how long it's been since their last match:

```
timeSinceLastMatch : <number>0
```

Those properties represent all the state (plus the odd socketComm instance, which isn't *state*, per se) needed to make BattleJong work.

Message Handler Methods

After the properties are defined, we find a series of simple methods, the ones called from the socketComm code in response to the messages that can be sent by the server, beginning with the handler function for the connected message:

```
handleMessage_connected : function(inPID: string) : void {
  this.setState({ pid : inPID });
}.bind(inParentComponent),
```

All we need to do when this message is received is store the player ID sent to the client in state, so that one is very easy.

The next handler is for the start message, sent when the second player connects to the server, and the game begins:

```
handleMessage_start: function(inLayout: number[][][]): void {
  this.setState({
    timeSinceLastMatch : new Date().getTime(),
    layout : inLayout,
    gameState : "playing"
  });
}.bind(inParentComponent),
```

We need an initial time so that we can determine how long it takes to match the first tile pair. Of course, we need to store the layout sent from the server too. Finally, the gameState needs to transition to the playing state. The result of this all being set in state is that the board will now appear, with the shuffle done by the server showing the appropriate tiles, as a result of React seeing the change in state and the PlayerBoard component reacting to it.

The next message we need to deal with is update, sent whenever either player clears a tile:

```
handleMessage_update:
  function(inPID: string, inScore: number) : void {
  if (inPID !== this.state.pid) {
    const scores: IScores = { ...this.state.scores };
    scores.opponent = inScore;
    this.setState({ scores : scores });
```

```
  }
}.bind(inParentComponent),
```

This method received the player ID of the player the update is for and the new score for that player. So, we need to see if the message is for the current player or not. If it's not, then the `scores` property is cloned, the opponent's score is updated, and the `scores` object is set back into state, resulting in a screen update. Note that nothing needs to be done if the `update` message was for *this* player because the score will already have been updated, as you'll see the code for soon.

The final message is for when the game ends:

```
handleMessage_gameOver: function(inPID: string) : void {
  if (inPID === this.state.pid) {
    this.setState({ gameState : "gameOver",
      gameOutcome : "**** YOU WON! ****" });
  } else {
    this.setState({ gameState : "gameOver",
      gameOutcome : "Tough luck, you lost :(" });
  }
}.bind(inParentComponent),
```

All we need to do is see if the winning player, as specified by the server, is this player, based on the player ID. If it is, the "you won" message is set in the state object's gameOutcome property; otherwise, the "you lost" message is set. The message will be displayed on the screen once React triggers the update.

The Big Kahuna: tileClick( )

Now we come to what is the longest, probably most complex (though it's still nothing overly complicated!), and certainly key bit of code that makes BattleJong tick, the one that gets called any time you click a tile:

```
tileClick : function(inLayer: number, inRow: number,
  inColumn: number) : void {
```

The tileClick() method is passed the layer, row, and column of the tile that the player clicked. That's all it needs to do its work. But, before it even gets to the real work, there are a few trivial rejections that need to be done:

```
if (this.state.gameState !== "playing") {
  return;
}
```

The board isn't visible until gameState is either "playing" or "gameOver," but in the latter case, we don't want the player to be able to click tiles, so we'll abort early if gameState isn't "playing."

Next, we need to determine if a tile *can* be selected:

```
if (!this.state.canTileBeSelected(inLayer, inRow, inColumn)) {
  return;
}
```

The canTileBeSelected() is a helper function that tells us whether a tile is free, in terms of Mahjong rules. Let's jump over to that function now.

Helper Function: canTileBeSelected( )

This function, in its entirety, is

```
canTileBeSelected : function(inLayer: number, inRow: number, inColumn:
number): boolean {
  return
    (inLayer == 4 ||
      this.state.layout[inLayer + 1][inRow][inColumn] <= 0
    ) &&
    (inColumn === 0 || inColumn === 14 ||
      this.state.layout[inLayer][inRow][inColumn - 1] <= 0 ||
      this.state.layout[inLayer][inRow][inColumn + 1] <= 0
    );
}.bind(inParentComponent),
```

The test here is simple:

- If the tile is in the topmost layer (4) OR there is no tile above it

- AND if the tile is in the first (0) or last (14) column OR there is no tile to either the left or right of it

- THEN it's free, ELSE it's not

At this point, we know that the tile can be selected, so we can start the real work, beginning with cloning the layout (since we're going to alter it):

```
const layout: number[][][] = this.state.layout.slice(0);
```

Next, we need to see what the selected tile is, what its type is:

```
const currentTileValue: number = layout[inLayer][inRow][inColumn];
```

We need to determine that because of this next check:

```
if (currentTileValue <= 0) {
  return;
}
```

This keeps the player from trying to select a blank space.

Following that, we have to grab some other values out of state:

```
const scores: IScores = { ...this.state.scores };
let gameState: string = this.state.gameState;
let timeSinceLastMatch: number = this.state.timeSinceLastMatch;
let selectedTiles: ISelectedTile[] = this.state.selectedTiles.slice(0);
```

We need to clone scores because we might be updating it. Likewise, gameState might be changing (if they clear or dead-end the board), so that's grabbed too. To determine how many points they get, if they match a pair (if this is the second tile being clicked), we will need to know how long it took, so timeSinceLastMatch is needed. Finally, one way or another, the values in selectedTiles will be changing regardless, so that gets cloned now too. Doing all of this now just makes the code later a bit cleaner and removes some redundancy.

With that done, the true logic can begin. First, we need to deal with the case where the tile they clicked was already highlighted. In that case, we want to de-highlight it. When a tile is highlighted, its tile type value gets 1000 added to it, so that's the basic check:

```
if (currentTileValue > 1000) {
  layout[inLayer][inRow][inColumn] = currentTileValue - 1000;
  for (let i: number = 0; i < selectedTiles.length; i++) {
    const selectedTile: ISelectedTile = selectedTiles[i];
    if (selectedTile.layer == inLayer &&
      selectedTile.row == inRow &&
      selectedTile.column == inColumn
    ) {
      selectedTiles.splice(i, 1);
      break;
    }
  }
} else {
  layout[inLayer][inRow][inColumn] = currentTileValue + 1000;
  selectedTiles.push({ layer : inLayer, row : inRow,
    column : inColumn, type : currentTileValue });
}
```

First, we revert the value so that it's back to just its basic tile type value (101–142). Next, we need to remove it from the selectedTiles array. Because this is an array and not a keyed object, we have little choice but to examine all members of the array; find the one that has the layer, row, and column value of the tile that was clicked; and then splice() that element out. There are several ways this code could be written, but I chose to just do a straight iteration over the array elements to find the match, then break out of the loop when found (I chose this route not for any specific reason other than it seemed simplest to me).

The else branch deals with the case where the tile wasn't previously highlighted. In that case, we add 1000 to the tile type value to indicate it's highlighted and then push an object into the selectedTiles array for this tile.

With the highlighting taken care of, we now need to see if there are two tiles selected, in which case we have some more work to do:

```
if (selectedTiles.length === 2) {
  if (selectedTiles[0].type === selectedTiles[1].type ||
    selectedTiles[0].type == 101 ||
    selectedTiles[1].type == 101
  ) {
```

If the type of both tiles matches, or if either of them is a wildcard (101), then that's a matched pair. When that happens, we first must clear the pair by setting their tile type to −1 in the layout:

```
layout[selectedTiles[0].layer][selectedTiles[0].row]
  [selectedTiles[0].column] = -1;
layout[selectedTiles[1].layer][selectedTiles[1].row]
  [selectedTiles[1].column] = -1;
```

Recall that the PlayerBoard component won't render anything in a given position when it sees a tile type of −1.

Next, it's time to calculate how many points they get:

```
let calculatedPoints: number = 10;
const now: number = new Date().getTime();
const timeTaken: number = now - timeSinceLastMatch;
const numHalfSeconds: number = Math.trunc(timeTaken / 500);
calculatedPoints -= numHalfSeconds;
if (calculatedPoints <= 0) {
  calculatedPoints = 1;
}
scores.player += calculatedPoints;
timeSinceLastMatch = now;
```

The way this works is that they start with ten points for a match. From that, we subtract a point for every half a second taken. But we want to be nice here, so they always get a minimum of one point. Finally, the player's score is updated (which is why the logic is what it is in the "update" message handler as you saw earlier), and we record the new time in timeSinceLastMatch so that we start counting from this moment toward their next match.

Next, we have to let the server know what happened via a "match" message:

```
this.state.socketComm.send(
`match_${this.state.pid}_${calculatedPoints}`
);
```

The server needs to know the player ID and how many points they got, so that's the message that is constructed.

With that out of the way, the next task is to see if the board is either cleared or dead-ended. For that, another helper function is employed:

```
const anyMovesLeft: string = this.state.anyMovesLeft(layout);
```

Helper Function: anyMovesLeft( )

The anyMovesLeft() function is somewhat complicated, so let's break it down into bite-sized nuggets:

```
anyMovesLeft : function(inLayout: number[][][]): string {
  let numTiles: number = 0;
  const selectableTiles: number[] = [ ];
  for (let l: number = 0; l < inLayout.length; l++) {
    const layer = inLayout[l];
    for (let r: number = 0; r < layer.length; r++) {
      const row = layer[r];
      for (let c: number = 0; c < row.length; c++) {
        const tileVal: number = row[c];
        if (tileVal > 0) {
          numTiles += 1;
          if (this.state.canTileBeSelected(l, r, c)) {
            if (tileVal === 101) {
              return "yes";
            }
            selectableTiles.push(tileVal);
          }
        }
```

```
      }
    }
  }
```

Remember that it's the cloned `layout` array that we need to examine right now because the `layout` property in state hasn't been updated yet, so that's why it gets passed to `anyMovesLeft()`. Once there, the first task is to get a list of all free tiles. To do this, we need to iterate through the entire layout – and remember it's a three-dimensional array. Thus, we have nested loops here – and for each, call the `canTileBeSelected()` function.

Now, if a tile is determined to be free, and it's a wildcard, then we automatically know that the board has not dead-ended because a wildcard can match any other tile type. And, because we start with an even number of tiles, and they only ever get removed in pairs, that means that there must be at least two tiles left. Therefore, there is at least one move left for sure, and we can short-circuit this function by returning "yes" right then and there.

Otherwise, the tile is pushed into the `selectableTiles` array for further scrutiny. That scrutiny begins with a simple check:

```
if (numTiles === 0) {
  return "cleared";
}
```

Obviously, if there are no tiles at all, then there can be no more moves left! This case means that the player just cleared the board, so we let the caller know with the return value "cleared." By the way, this should make it apparent now why this function can't return a simple boolean true or false: because there are actually three outcomes! There could be a move left, there could be no moves left due to a dead end, or there could be no moves left due to the board being cleared. The caller needs to differentiate those outcomes, so a string is returned instead.

At this point, we know that there are still selectable tiles, and we know that there are no wildcards (i.e., no *selectable* wildcards – there still could be some unselectable ones). Therefore, the next trick is to see if there are any matches.

Your initial thought here might be that you would need to iterate over this array and compare each element to every other element to find at least one match. And certainly, that would work. But there is a more efficient approach:

```
const counts: number[] = [];
for (let i: number = 0; i < selectableTiles.length; i++) {
```

```
  if (counts[selectableTiles[i]] === undefined) {
    counts[selectableTiles[i]] = 1;
  } else {
    counts[selectableTiles[i]]++;
  }
}
```

First, you count how many times each tile type occurs. This uses an associative array, meaning that the tile type becomes the key of an array element. With that done, the check to see if there are any matches left becomes very simple:

```
for (let i: number = 0; i < counts.length; i++) {
  if (counts[i] >= 2) {
    return "yes";
  }
}
```

That's it! If any element of the array has a value greater than or equal to two, then that means there is a match left to be made because, remember, we already checked that these tiles are selectable.

If there are no such values found in the array, then the final possible return value is returned:

```
return "no";
```

So, jumping back to the code in tileClick(), now that we know if there are any moves left, we can act accordingly:

```
switch (anyMovesLeft) {
  case "no":
    gameState = "deadEnd";
    this.state.socketComm.send(`done_${this.state.pid}`);
  break;
  case "cleared":
    scores.player += 100;
    gameState = "cleared";
    this.state.socketComm.send(`match_${this.state.pid}_100`);
```

```
    this.state.socketComm.send(`done_${this.state.pid}`);
  break;
}
```

A return from anyMovesLeft() of "no" indicates a dead-ended board, so gameState is transitioned to that state, and the server is notified that this player is done. A return value of "cleared" indicates the board was cleared, in which case we give them a point bonus, in addition to transitioning gameState and telling the server that they are finished. Note that we must send *two* messages here because the server needs to know about the point bonus too. There's no special message for that, though; we simply tell the server that another match occurred via the "match" message. It doesn't matter that one technically hasn't occurred. The server only needs the number of points to add here, so we can force that message to do double duty.

Now, all that logic was for dealing with a pair of tiles being selected, but what happens if this tile click event was the second tile of an unmatched pair? Well, that's where the else branch of the opening if statement comes in:

```
} else {
  layout[selectedTiles[0].layer][selectedTiles[0].row]
    [selectedTiles[0].column] = layout[selectedTiles[0].layer]
    [selectedTiles[0].row]
      [selectedTiles[0].column] - 1000;
  layout[selectedTiles[1].layer][selectedTiles[1].row]
    [selectedTiles[1].column] = layout[selectedTiles[1].layer]
    [selectedTiles[1].row]
      [selectedTiles[1].column] - 1000;
}
```

In this situation, all we need to do is revert the tile value of the two tiles to their 101–142 range, and we're done.

Regardless of whether we just handled a matched pair or not, both tiles would be either cleared or deselected now, so they need to be removed from selectedTiles:

```
selectedTiles = [ ];
```

Only one thing remains to be done, but it is absolutely key:

```
this.setState({
  gameState : gameState,
```

```
  layout : layout,
  selectedTiles : selectedTiles,
  scores : scores,
  timeSinceLastMatch : timeSinceLastMatch
});
```

None of the code in `tileClick()` to this point will have altered state, but that needs to occur lest nothing changes on the screen! So, a quick call to `setState()` takes care of it. I didn't want to introduce any sort of conditional updates here either; I figured it was easier just to update everything that could have changed, whether it actually did or not.

And with that, our journey through BattleJong is complete!

Suggested Exercises

One great thing about a game is there's never a shortage of things you could do to it to expand it. I'll suggest just a few things, some relatively straightforward, some that would be significantly more challenging (and therefore more useful as a learning experience):

- Introduce the idea of "attack tiles." Choose one of the existing tile types and declare it an "attack" type, just like how the wildcards are handled. When the player matches two of them, they gain an "attack." With it, they can click a button (that you'll add to the control area), and it will send a message to the server that is then sent to their opponent. The result is that the opponent loses 50 points and gets, say, four tile pairs added back. Nasty, but fits in with the "battle" part of BattleJong well! I'd suggest using Material-UI for this, but maybe you should instead find a different UI library for React, just to get some other experience?

- Add the ability for a player to shuffle their board up to five times per game. This is often a part of Mahjong Solitaire's implementations. It allows a player to get through a dead-ended board, at least a few times.

- Provide alternate tilesets and let the player choose the one they like. You'll have to come up with X*42 tile graphics, where X is how many tilesets you want to provide.

Summary

In this chapter, we built the client side of BattleJong, making it a complete game. You learned a little more about Webpack, dealing with images specifically, and you saw the client side of the WebSocket equation. Of course, you got some experience with basic game design as well, but that was inevitable when building a game, wasn't it?!

In the next – and final – chapter, we'll cover one last topic, something that plays a role in modern application development: app deployment using containers and Docker specifically.

CHAPTER 12

Bringing the Dev Ship into Harbor: Docker

With both MailBag and BattleJong built, it's time to touch on another topic that has become very common in modern application development to deal with the problem of application distribution: Docker. In this chapter, you'll learn what Docker is and what containerization generically is, and you'll learn how to "wrap up" both of the applications we built over the last four chapters together with Docker so that it is quick and easy to distribute them to other developers (and possibly even end users).

An Introduction to Containers and Containerization

Before we even talk about containers, let's talk about virtual machines, or VMs.

A VM is essentially an emulation of a real, physical computer. You have your actual computer, which is considered the "host" for a VM, and then on top of that host, you have some sort of hypervisor. This may sound a bit circular, but a hypervisor is an entity that allows VMs to be run on top of it. In other words, it's an abstraction layer between a VM and the physical host machine it's running on. The job of a hypervisor is to distribute the resources of the physical machine – CPU, memory, and so on – between VMs running on it (and the host OS too, of course), and these VMs we call "guests."

Hypervisors come in two flavors: hosted hypervisors and hardware hypervisors. The difference is that hosted hypervisors run on top of the host OS, while hardware hypervisors run underneath the OS. The primary difference is performance: hardware hypervisors provide much better performance than hosted hypervisors.

However, with either type, a crucial consideration is that the virtual machine approach is fundamentally heavyweight. What I mean is there is a lot of overhead involved because, remember, a VM is essentially an emulation of a machine.

361

F. Zammetti, *Modern Full-Stack Development*, https://doi.org/10.1007/978-1-4842-8811-5_12

That's right, it's emulating everything: *including the hardware*. On any given piece of physical hardware, regardless of hypervisor type, there will be a limit to how many VMs you can run on it because of this, and performance will never be *quite* as good as a non-VM situation.

Containers seek to avoid this "weight" issue in favor of something lighter on resources so that a physical machine's resources can be used more efficiently and shared between more running applications, thereby allowing a physical machine to do more.

In contrast to a VM, a container performs operating system–level virtualization. This is achieved by abstracting what's known as "user space," that is, where your applications run. There is no emulation occurring with containers. Instead, they actually *share* kernel space with the host OS. But a container looks like a VM in most other regards in that they represent an isolated user space where your applications can run. In this way, you can have many containers running, all with their own user space but sharing the kernel resources of the host operating system. This is a far more efficient approach than VMs and allows for many more containers to run on a given host system.

A key point about containers is that they allow you to package up not only your application but also its runtime environment. Yes, that means things like a JDK for a Java application and JavaScript libraries for a Node app (not to mention Node itself!), but it also means the underlying operating system environment. When you create a container, you start from a blueprint known as an image. The image almost always begins with an operating system and then has stuff added to it, building up to the final image. So, if you want to package up your Node application, you will also, in a container, package up a version of, say, Linux that it will run on. You can think of an image as a snapshot of an OS file system at a given point in time, but it's not a snapshot of your host OS, it's a snapshot of the result of a series of steps used to build up the image layer by layer.

Containers function as if they were the sole OS on the hardware. Anything running in them is unaware that they are on a shared system, just like a VM, but it's still just a process running on a host system, not a fully emulated computer and OS on top of it, and it's not going through a hypervisor like a VM is.

A container relates to an image in that the image is the blueprint, and a container is an instance of the image. You can think of it like a class-object relationship: classes are essentially the blueprint that is used to build instances of that class that we then call objects.

This yields what is perhaps the most significant benefit of containers: a consistent runtime environment without the overhead of a VM. The host operating system mostly doesn't matter (with some caveats concerning cross-platform containers, vis-à-vis Windows containers on Linux hosts and vice versa). Only what's in the container matters, and only what's in the container will impact the functioning of the app(s) in that container. You can change the host operating system and know that what's in the container will still be the same environment you originally build, and so everything will work as it always has, no fear of breakage due to the host change.

Another benefit of containers is that they start fast, almost instantly in most cases, which makes them easy to scale. If you have an application running in a container and the load on it starts getting too heavy, it's relatively quick and easy (assuming your application code allows for this) to spin up more containers with instances of your app running to share the load.

Container capabilities have been built into Linux for many years, but it only began to gain traction with the introduction of something that made dealing with the technology much easier: Docker.

The Star of the Show: Docker

Using "naked" containers on Linux is... not pleasant. It can be complex to get them working and, even more so, to manage all the images and containers you may spawn from them. It's doable, but it was difficult enough for a long time that containerization didn't get used very much. You must deal with two key features of Linux: control groups, or cgroups, and namespaces. These deal with how processes and their resources can be grouped, isolated, and managed as a unit by the kernel and limits on what a given process can see. If that sounds kind of technical and complicated, well, that's because it is! Even for those well versed in Linux, it can get hairy.

That all changed with the introduction of Docker, which is the product of a company named – not surprisingly – Docker! In simplest terms, Docker is just a set of tools that makes it easy, from a command line, to build images, create containers, and manage it all, including interacting with remote repositories of images. For a while, Docker was a Linux-only technology, but that's changed in recent years, and you can now use Docker on every major operating system.

There are three main components to Docker:

- **Docker daemon** – This is a background process that runs on a host machine that is responsible for various tasks, including the management, building, running, and distribution of containers. This is what interacts with the underlying containerization capabilities, the stuff that is kind of not fun to deal with manually.

- **Docker client** – This is a CLI that you interact with, which makes calls to the daemon on your behalf. This, combined with the daemon, makes the human interface to the underlying containerization capabilities much easier to use.

- **Docker Hub** – A public registry of images maintained by the company Docker. Using Docker Hub is entirely optional, and you even can set up your own if you wish, but it is very commonly used. In either case, it's a repository of images that you can easily pull from to "spin up" containers ("spin up" is a common phrase for when you create a container from an image).

Once you get Docker installed, it's the Docker client, and perhaps Docker Hub, that you'll interact with. So, let's see about getting it installed so we can start playing with all this stuff!

Installing Docker

How you install Docker varies from operating system to operating system, so I couldn't detail the process for every possible variation here. However, I can tell you that on Windows, it's just a regular application installation (assuming you're running Windows 10 – older versions of Windows are a bit more involved to get set up), and on Linux, it's just installing a small handful of packages.

The URL you need to have in mind is this: `https://docs.docker.com/install/`. This is the official Docker installation page. There, you will find instructions for installing Docker for a variety of systems. Please visit there and follow the instructions applicable to your system.

Once you do, the final step will be to test that Docker is running and ready for you to play with. To do that, drop to a command prompt and execute this command:

```
docker info
```

At this point, it doesn't matter what OS you're using, the commands you issue to Docker are the same across all of them. You should see a dump of information, most of which won't mean much to you yet (though you're smart and I'm sure you can figure a lot of it out!). Figure 12-1 is an example of what you might see (the actual data could differ on your system).

```
root@LinuxServer:/home/fzammetti# docker info
Client:
 Debug Mode: false

Server:
 Containers: 0
  Running: 0
  Paused: 0
  Stopped: 0
 Images: 0
 Server Version: 19.03.2
 Storage Driver: overlay2
  Backing Filesystem: extfs
  Supports d_type: true
  Native Overlay Diff: true
 Logging Driver: json-file
 Cgroup Driver: cgroupfs
 Plugins:
  Volume: local
  Network: bridge host ipvlan macvlan null overlay
  Log: awslogs fluentd gcplogs gelf journald json-file local logentries splunk syslog
 Swarm: inactive
 Runtimes: runc
 Default Runtime: runc
 Init Binary: docker-init
 containerd version:
 runc version:
 init version:
 Security Options:
  apparmor
  seccomp
   Profile: default
 Kernel Version: 5.3.0-26-generic
 Operating System: Ubuntu 19.10
 OSType: linux
 Architecture: x86_64
 CPUs: 2
 Total Memory: 3.834GiB
 Name: LinuxServer
 ID: KB4P:Q6T5:EEZK:R6H5:C4W5:4TX4:MYPF:W3BH:UHV5:GUKU:LLPM:2GVH
 Docker Root Dir: /var/lib/docker
 Debug Mode: false
 Username: fzammetti
 Registry: https://index.docker.io/v1/
 Labels:
 Experimental: false
 Insecure Registries:
  127.0.0.0/8
 Live Restore Enabled: false

WARNING: No swap limit support
root@LinuxServer:/home/fzammetti#
```

Figure 12-1. *Output of the docker info command execution*

If you don't see this, then take the time to go over the installation instructions again for your system so that you have a reliable Docker environment before we move on. You'll see different values, of course, but as long as it's a dump of reasonable-looking information and not an error, then all is well.

Your First Container: "Hello, World!" of Course!

Okay, so, Docker is installed and ready to go, what can we do with it? As is customary when talking about seemingly anything in programming, we'll start by spinning up a "Hello, World!" container. As luck would have it, Docker Hub, the central and public image repository run by Docker, has just such an image available! We can pull the image down to our local machine and use it to create a container all with one, simple command:

```
docker run hello-world
```

Go ahead and execute that, and after a couple of seconds, you should see something like Figure 12-2 greet you.

```
root@LinuxServer:/home/fzammetti# docker run hello-world
Unable to find image 'hello-world:latest' locally
latest: Pulling from library/hello-world
1b930d010525: Pull complete
Digest: sha256:d1668a9a1f5b42ed3f46b70b9cb7c88fd8bdc8a2d73509bb0041cf436018fbf5
Status: Downloaded newer image for hello-world:latest

Hello from Docker!
This message shows that your installation appears to be working correctly.

To generate this message, Docker took the following steps:
 1. The Docker client contacted the Docker daemon.
 2. The Docker daemon pulled the "hello-world" image from the Docker Hub.
    (amd64)
 3. The Docker daemon created a new container from that image which runs the
    executable that produces the output you are currently reading.
 4. The Docker daemon streamed that output to the Docker client, which sent it
    to your terminal.

To try something more ambitious, you can run an Ubuntu container with:
 $ docker run -it ubuntu bash

Share images, automate workflows, and more with a free Docker ID:
 https://hub.docker.com/

For more examples and ideas, visit:
 https://docs.docker.com/get-started/

root@LinuxServer:/home/fzammetti# █
```

Figure 12-2. *The Docker hello-world, up and running!*

As I said, this did a couple of things for you automatically, and in fact, part of what it did was to output, well, *precisely what it did*! That's helpful, isn't it?

Now, if you execute that command again, you'll find that it's even faster this time, and that's because the image has already been downloaded from Docker Hub and is stored on your system, so that step can be skipped. Instead, Docker spins up a new container almost instantly.

In short, the docker run command is how you start new containers.

A Quick Rundown of Key Docker Commands

For most Docker work, only a small handful of commands are needed. Anything more would constitute more advanced Docker functionality, and as this is meant as only an introduction, most of that won't be covered. But let's look at the basics now.

Listing Images

How can you tell what images and containers there are available on your system? Well, that's easy:

```
docker images
```

That will list all the images downloaded onto your system. Figure 12-3 shows what it might look like after trying the first example.

```
root@LinuxServer:/home/fzammetti# docker images
REPOSITORY            TAG                   IMAGE ID              CREATED               SIZE
hello-world           latest                fce289e99eb9          12 months ago         1.84kB
root@LinuxServer:/home/fzammetti#
```

Figure 12-3. *A list of images on your system*

Listing Containers

For listing containers, it's just as easy:

```
docker ps
```

Modeled on the Linux ps command, that command shows your containers, but it only shows you *running* containers. After this example container finishes its work, it shuts down immediately. Therefore, you won't see it listed there. However, the container still exists in a sense, and you can see it by adding an option to the previous command:

```
docker ps -a
```

Figure 12-4 shows the result which, if you've been following along, should show two containers in the Exited state.

```
root@LinuxServer:/home/fzammetti# docker ps -a
CONTAINER ID   IMAGE          COMMAND        CREATED          STATUS                    PORTS      NAMES
70bc454eb92a   hello-world    "/hello"       10 seconds ago   Exited (0) 8 seconds ago             awesome_ishizaka
87f4039f7efb   hello-world    "/hello"       4 minutes ago    Exited (0) 4 minutes ago             thirsty_curie
root@LinuxServer:/home/fzammetti#
```

Figure 12-4. *The nonrunning containers on the system*

Starting (and Stopping) Containers

You could start a container again if you want:

```
docker start <container_id_or_name>
```

For this hello-world container, however, nothing will happen when you do this, and the container will exit immediately. It only seems to show that helpful information when initially run.

You can also stop a running container:

```
docker stop <container_id_or_name>
```

As a quick aside, at this point, you may realize that entering the container IDs that Docker generates can get annoying in a hurry (and, plus, you've seen me write `<container_id_or_name>`, implying you can do something other than using the default ID). Fortunately, Docker also generates a name for each container, as you can see in the `ps` output (and it can often be quite entertaining to see what it spits out!). However, it's more user-friendly to give it a name yourself, which you can do with an option:

```
docker run --name MyAwesomeContainer hello-world
```

Now you should see a container with the specified name, which you can then use to interact with it.

You should also be aware that when using the ID, you can enter a partial ID starting from the beginning and entering enough to be unique. For example, you could enter 70b here instead of typing the entire ID and that will work too (just entering 7 should, in theory, work, but as a general rule I suggest always entering three characters at a minimum to be sure). In my opinion, providing a name is the overall better and easier approach so you have less chance of accidentally doing something to the wrong container (in theory, at least!), but my eagle-eyed technical editor reminded me of the ID-shortening approach, and it was a good thing to mention, so remember to tip Herman the technical reviewer on your way out this evening!

Remove Containers and Images

You'll probably want to clean up those containers at some point, and there's a command for that:

```
docker rm <container_id_or_name>
```

If the container is running, Docker won't let you remove it until you stop it.

Likewise, you can remove images:

```
docker rmi <image_id_or_name>
```

As with containers, Docker won't allow you to delete an image that's used by a container, regardless of whether it's running or not, so you'll need to clean up the containers first.

Pulling Images

What if you want to download some images but not immediately start containers based on them? That's easy enough:

```
docker pull hello-world
```

Now, the image will be downloaded if it's not already on your system (if it is, docker will try to update it if the latest version is newer than what's on your system). After that, you can do a `docker run` to spin up containers like before.

You can push images to a repository as well, but we'll get to that later.

Searching for Images

While I think it's much easier to go to Docker Hub through the Web to look for images, which you can do at `https://hub.docker.com/`, you also can search for an image directly from the command line:

```
docker search hello-world
```

This returns a list of many images that include the string "hello-world" in their name.

Attaching to a Container

Sometimes, you'll want to treat containers like VMs and log in to them. To demonstrate that, we'll need a container that will continue running, so let's use Nginx for that:

```
docker run -d -p 8080:80 --name my_nginx nginx
```

The -d option "detaches" the terminal session from the container, which causes it to run in the background (assuming whatever is inside the container doesn't exit immediately). You'll be returned to your command prompt, but the container will continue to run. The -p option is for exposing network ports. Here, we're saying that port 8080 inside the container should be exposed as port 80 on the host machine's network interface.

Once you execute this command, do a docker ps, and you should see a running container for the first time.

Now, with a container running, we can go ahead and attach to it:

```
docker exec -it my_nginx /bin/bash
```

Here, you can see a few things. First, the -i option keeps STDIN open so that it can be interacted with. The -t option allocates a new pseudo-tty terminal session. The / bin/bash at the end is a command that is executed after the container is started. All three combined results in you being "inside" the container. The command prompt you see at that point is the command prompt *inside* the container itself. Go ahead and do some bash-y stuff (e.g., ls), and you should notice that what you see differs from your host operating system (though if you're using Ubuntu, then it's going to look very similar anyway). Execute the exit command and you'll be dropped back to your actual command prompt.

Viewing Container Logs

Finally, without attaching to a container, you can view the logs produced inside of it:

```
docker logs my_nginx
```

Here, "logs" include anything routed to standard out, barring any specific configuration done inside the container.

At this point, you know most of the basics for using Docker. But all of that was based on existing images. What about creating your own? Let's do that now!

Creating Your Own Image

Now, as cool as I hope you find Docker at this point, it would be considerably more useful if we could create images ourselves, wouldn't it? Let's do it and find out!

First, we'll need something to stick in the container. So, let's start by creating a very simple Node app. To begin, create a directory – name it dockernode – and then initialize a new NPM project in it:

```
npm init
```

Just accept all defaults for it. Next, add Express to it:

```
npm install –save express
```

Finally, create a server.js file and put the following code in it:

```
const express = require("express");
const app = express();
app.get("/", (inRequest, inResponse) => {
  inResponse.send("I am running inside a container!");
});
app.listen("8080", "0.0.0.0");
console.log("dockernode ready");
```

You can, at this point, start this little server:

```
node server.js
```

You should be able to access it at http://localhost:8080.

Of course, what it returns, "I am running inside a container!", is a dirty lie at this point! So, let's go ahead and make it true!

To do so, we must add another file to the mix: Dockerfile. Yes, that's literally the name! A Dockerfile is a file that tells Docker how to build an image. In simplest terms, it is basically a list of commands that Docker will execute, as if it were you, the user, inside a container. Virtually any valid bash commands can be put in it, as well as a few Docker-specific ones. Docker will execute the commands in the order they appear in the file, and whatever the state of the container is at the end becomes the final image.

So, here's what we need to put in this `Dockerfile` for this example:

```
FROM node:10
WORKDIR /usr/src/app
COPY package*.json ./
COPY server.js ./
RUN npm install
EXPOSE 8080
CMD [ "node", "server.js" ]
```

The first command, `FROM`, is a Docker-specific command (the only one required, in fact) that tells Docker what the base image is. All images must be based on some existing image. If you want to start "from scratch," the closest you can generally get is to choose an image that is nothing but an operating system. In this case, however, since we're using Node, we can start from an image that, yes, has an operating system, but then also has Node already installed on top of it. Alternatively, we could start with an image like `ubuntu` and then put the commands into the `Dockerfile` that would install Node (`apt-get install nodejs`), and we would wind up with an image that is basically the same as this. But let's be lazy and use what's already there!

Note   Images can have tags attached to them, which you can *roughly* think of as version numbers. Here, we're telling Docker that we want to use the latest image named node that includes Node v10.x. The tags are image specific, so you'll need to consult Docker Hub (or whatever repository you're using) to see what it means for a given image.

The next command, `WORKDIR`, really does two things, potentially. First, it creates the named directory if it doesn't already exist. Then, it does the equivalent of a `cd` to that directory, making it the current working directory for subsequent commands.

Next, two `COPY` commands are used. This is another Docker command that copies content from a source directory on the host to a destination directory in the image's file system. The command is in the form `COPY <src> <dest>`, so here we're saying to copy from the current working directory on the host (which should be the project directory) to the current working directory in the image (which is now the one created by the WORKDIR command) any file named package*.json (which means package.json and package-lock.json) and our server.js file.

After that, we must think as if we're executing these commands ourselves. If someone gave us this Node project, we would next need to install the dependencies listed in package.json. So the Docker RUN command is used, which tells Docker to execute whatever command follows as if we were doing it ourselves at a command prompt (because remember that basically is what a Dockerfile is!). You know all about the npm install at this point, so after this is done, all the necessary code for the application to run is present in the image.

Now, in this case, we need to expose a network port; otherwise, our host system, let alone any other remote systems, won't be able to reach our Node app inside the container. It's a simple matter of telling it which port to expose, which needs to match the one specified in the code, obviously.

Finally, we want to specify a command to execute when the container starts up. There can be only one of these in the file, but we can do virtually anything we want. Here, we need to execute the equivalent of node server.js as we did manually to test the app.

The CMD command allows us to do this. The format this command takes is an array of strings where the first element is an executable, and all the remaining elements are arguments to pass to it.

Once that file is created, it's time to build the image! That just takes a simple command invocation:

```
docker build -t dockernode .
```

Do that, and you should see an execution something like Figure 12-5.

```
root@LinuxServer:/home/fzammetti/dockernode# docker build -t dockernode .
Sending build context to Docker daemon  2.004MB
Step 1/7 : FROM node:10
10: Pulling from library/node
146bd6a88618: Pull complete
9935d0c62ace: Pull complete
db0efb86e806: Pull complete
e705a4c4fd31: Pull complete
c877b722db6f: Pull complete
645c20ec8214: Pull complete
53e9643162ac: Pull complete
6ecbd1f662ed: Pull complete
0355199adbee: Pull complete
Digest: sha256:49f77fd32e8e796f85581a8d2321c2a9f1b084e1f8b9baa02cb28bce49563ad5
Status: Downloaded newer image for node:10
 ---> ea119cebc1c3
Step 2/7 : WORKDIR /usr/src/app
 ---> Running in 01359626288a
Removing intermediate container 01359626288a
 ---> 06b6a708256e
Step 3/7 : COPY package*.json ./
 ---> 99d125606405
Step 4/7 : COPY server.js ./
 ---> e7cfa4efc873
Step 5/7 : RUN npm install
 ---> Running in 2a0cedcf1baf
added 50 packages from 37 contributors and audited 126 packages in 1.918s
found 0 vulnerabilities

Removing intermediate container 2a0cedcf1baf
 ---> 0fa32e4186ef
Step 6/7 : EXPOSE 8080
 ---> Running in 2a759d67f7a6
Removing intermediate container 2a759d67f7a6
 ---> 5bfb4833e21a
Step 7/7 : CMD [ "node", "server.js" ]
 ---> Running in fc88caad3713
Removing intermediate container fc88caad3713
 ---> 2c4257c922b4
Successfully built 2c4257c922b4
Successfully tagged dockernode:latest
root@LinuxServer:/home/fzammetti/dockernode#
```

Figure 12-5. *Building the dockernode example image*

Note   If you're doing this under Windows, what you see may look somewhat different than what is depicted here. But, regardless, it should look at least similar, and you can use your own experience and knowledge gained up to this point to determine if anything is wrong. Generally speaking, errors should be pretty obvious, and everything else should be nothing drastically different from what is shown here.

Now, if you do a docker images, you should see the dockernode image there. If it is, you can spin up a container based on it:

```
docker run --name dockernode -p 8080:8080 -d dockernode
```

At this point, the container should be running (confirm with docker ps), and the app should be reachable from a web browser. Also, if you do

```
docker logs dockernode
```

you should now see the "dockernode ready" string. You could attach to the container if you wanted to now and play around.

Note   Don't get confused here: dockernode is the name (tag) of an image, but it's also the name assigned to a running container (and also the name of the project directory). It's perfectly allowed to have an image tag that matches a container name; however, you may generally not want to do that to avoid any potential confusion.

One final thing I want to mention is that it's a good idea after you build an image – or if you're troubleshooting an image that isn't building right – to check its contents. The quickest and easiest way to do that is

```
docker run -it <image_id_or_name> sh
```

That's another way to get an interactive shell into a running container, but it should generally work with virtually any image, and, most importantly, it will work even if the container shuts down immediately. To be clear, if nothing is running in the container, that won't change. If your app crashes on startup, for example, it will still do so. But, now, you'll be able to browse the file system, including, critically, any log files that may have been written.

Of course, if there's a problem at a lower level, like at the OS level, then this, in fact, may not work. In such instances, another useful command to know is

```
docker image inspect <image_id_or_name>
```

This will provide you detailed information about the image and its history (there is also a literal `docker image history <image_id_or_name>` command that delves into an image's actual build history more).

Deploying to Docker Hub

Now that you've built an image, let's talk about getting it into a repository, Docker Hub, specifically (though this all applies to any repository you might interact with).

First, to put an image into Docker Hub (referred to as pushing), you need an account. So, head on over to hub.docker.com and create an account for yourself. You will be allowed to have one private repository (where a repository refers to an image essentially) with a free account, as well as unlimited public ones. That'll be plenty good enough for what we're doing here.

Once you set up the account, the next step is to create a repository. To do so, assuming you're viewing your account in the Docker Hub website in a web browser right now, you should see a Create Repository button right there near the top. Click that, and then give your repository a name. For the sake of what we're doing, name it `<your_username>/modern-full-stack-development-dockernode` (it's a good idea to namespace any of your repositories with your username unless you're building some sort of official image that many people would be interested in, think things like Nginx, Node, or Ubuntu).

Assuming you have the dockernode image built, it's time to push it to Docker Hub! To do so, you will first need to log the Docker CLI into Docker Hub. That's easy enough:

```
docker login --username <your_username>
```

You will then be prompted for your password. Note that if you've elected to set up two-factor authentication, then it won't be your password you enter but will instead be the authentication key created when you set that up. But, either way, you should see something like Figure 12-6.

```
root@LinuxServer:/home/fzammetti/dockernode# docker login --username fzammetti
Password:
WARNING! Your password will be stored unencrypted in /root/.docker/config.json.
Configure a credential helper to remove this warning. See
https://docs.docker.com/engine/reference/commandline/login/#credentials-store

Login Succeeded
root@LinuxServer:/home/fzammetti/dockernode# █
```

Figure 12-6. *Logging in to Docker Hub from the Docker CLI*

At that point, you're ready to push your image:

```
docker push <your_username>/modern-full-stack-development-dockernode
```

If you refresh your account page on Docker Hub, you should now see some changes. Click the repository, and you should see a "latest" tag has been created. That's it. Your image is now on Docker Hub!

Note   It's possible you'll get a message about not having a tag locally, depending on what OS you're running this on, and various versioning possibilities. If that happens, you'll need to issue the following command before the push command will work to put a tag on the image: docker tag dockernode <your_username>/ modern-full-stack-development-dockernode:latest.

If you want to test it, delete the image on your system (`docker rmi dockernode`) and then pull the image (`docker pull <your_username>/modern-full-stack-development-dockernode`), and you should be able to spin up a container based on that.

You could now make that repository public if you wanted, which would then allow anyone else who wants it to pull your image and use it or perhaps base their own image on it.

Wrapping Up MailBag and BattleJong

Now, you have everything you need to containerize MailBag and BattleJong, which is the ultimate goal we've been working toward (note that I won't be containerizing Fooderator here - but maybe that would be a good exercise for you to try on your own? Hint-hint!).

We'll start with the source code for MailBag, and for the sake of this exercise, *do not* run npm install in either the client or server directories. We want just the "naked" source code here. All you really need to do is add a Dockerfile:

```
FROM node:10
WORKDIR /usr/app/mailbag
COPY client ./client
COPY server ./server
WORKDIR /usr/app/mailbag/client
RUN npm install
RUN npx webpack --mode production
WORKDIR /usr/app/mailbag/server
RUN npm install
RUN npx tsc
EXPOSE 80
CMD [ "node", "./dist/main.js" ]
```

As with dockernode, we'll start with the plain node image. From that, we create a directory in the image for the project. Then, we make it our work directory and copy in both the client and server directories to it. Note that when you copy a directory into an image, you need to specify the target directory explicitly. Just putting a period won't work as it does with files.

After that, since I said not to install the dependencies, we need to get them into the image. Otherwise, this project won't run (in fact, it won't *build*, let alone run, and you should realize that we do indeed have to build it since it's not in its executable form as it stands). So, the npm install is run after switching to the client directory.

But we still have to build the client because it's not in its final form – there's no dist directory yet – so then it's just running Webpack to do the job for us. That produces the dist directory and its contents.

Then, we need to do the same thing for the server, though there we're just compiling with tsc, no Webpack involvement there.

Finally, we expose port 80, since that's what the server listens on, and then start the server by executing the equivalent of node ./dist/main.js.

Now, if you do this, you will hit a problem when Docker gets to the RUN npm webpack –mode production line: it will hang, never completing the image. The reason is straightforward: remember that we configured Webpack to monitor our files and automatically rebuild when they change? Well, that's exactly what it's going to do as the image is being built, so it will never complete. To fix that, you need to go into the webpack.config.js file and set watch to false. After that, the build should be successful, and everything else should work as expected.

For BattleJong, it's almost exactly the same! Aside from the directory names in the Dockerfile needing to be changed, of course, everything else should be the same except for one thing: the final line in the Dockerfile needs to be changed to

```
CMD [ "node", "./dist/server.js" ]
```

The name of the file that is our server is different, but besides that, it's the same.

Note   I have created images for both of these apps on Docker Hub, as well as dockernode, and you can pull them any time you want. They are named fzammetti/modern-full-stack-development-dockernode, fzammetti/modern-full-stack-development-mailbag, and fzammetti/modern-full-stack-development-battlejong. In fact, if you search for fzammetti on Docker Hub, you'll also find images for many of the apps from my previous books.

Suggested Exercises

This is another of those chapters where suggesting exercises specific to its topic is a little tough by its very nature. However, one thing immediately comes to mind, and it's something that would test *all* your skills in one go, not just Docker knowledge:

Create a new app using everything you've learned throughout this book so far, package it with Docker, and push it to Docker Hub for all the world to see!

How about your own game of some sort? Or, maybe a calculator? Perhaps an address book for contacts? What about copying Google Keep for taking notes? You could always write an app to store bookmarks.

Basically, anything that interests you, go for it! It doesn't need to be anything world-changing; it just has to touch on most, if not all, of the topics I've covered in this book. If you can accomplish that, then I've succeeded in my task of teaching you a thing or two!

Summary

In this chapter, you learned about Docker and containerization, learned how to create an image from the applications we built together, and saw how to run them.

Over the remaining two chapters, we'll go off on a different path with some different technologies, but still using a lot of what you've learned along the way so far. When you're ready, let's get to it!

CHAPTER 13

Feed Your Face: Fooderator, the Server

As a married man with a great wife who handles most of this sort of thing, I know how difficult building a menu for the family can be (she's a professional chef, so it's kind of her thing), and then building a shopping list from that, all based on recipes that maybe the kids like some but I hate, or that is healthy for me but the kids don't like it *because* it's healthy, and so on.

So, when I thought about a project to demonstrate the things I wanted to cover next, that struggle came to my mind, and I thought to myself: "Self, this sounds like a match made in heaven!"

So, in this chapter, we're going to build ourselves an app that my wife would love that we'll call Fooderator (because it sounds Silicon Valley-ish to me). Its goal will be to make that challenge a little easier by giving us a place to store our recipes, build a menu from them, and then have a shopping list automatically generated from it. In the process, we'll learn a bunch of new things, including a new React widget library, some new tools to help get our work done, and a whole new server-side tech stack!

Wait, What Are We Building?!

Okay, so I broadly described the app we're building, but let me give you a little more detail.

Fooderator will present the user the ability to create and update three types of data:

- **Recipe** – A recipe holds four pieces of information: a name, a description, a rating (1–5 stars), and how many people the recipe serves. So, a recipe for pizza might look something like this:

  Name=Pizza

F. Zammetti, *Modern Full-Stack Development*, https://doi.org/10.1007/978-1-4842-8811-5_13

Description=Possibly the best food ever
Rating=5
Serves=2

- **Ingredients** – Of course, a recipe without ingredients wouldn't be of much value! So, each recipe will have some number of ingredients, where each ingredient has three pieces of information: a name, an amount, and an amount unit. So, an ingredient might look something like this:

  Name=Cheese
  Amount=5
  Amount Unit=Cups

  Each recipe has some number of ingredients as "children."

- **Menu items** – Once we have recipes, we want to be able to build a menu with them, a menu simply being a list of recipes that we want to make. Think of a menu as a few days' worth of dinners, so a different recipe each day. So, for each day, we have a menu item, which really is just a reference to a recipe.

Each of those data elements is going to literally be a type of data the server (and ultimately the client) will manipulate. So, we'll need an API that lets us create, read, update, and delete (our basic CRUD operations) recipes (which will include ingredients) and an API to create, read, and delete menu items (we're not going to allow updates, just because there's no point, given that they're simply references to recipes). And, finally, we'll need a function we can call that says "hey, take all the recipes on the menu, total up all the ingredients needed, and return that as a shopping list." This way, my wife knows exactly what she has to go buy at the grocery store to be able to make all the items on the menu for the week!

Although this chapter won't deal with the client, I just want to give you a brief idea of what it will do. The user will have three different "views," so to speak: one for recipes, one for a menu, and one for the shopping list. The recipe view will allow them to view a list of recipes, edit them, delete them, or add new ones. The menu view will allow them to add recipes to the menu and remove ones already on it. Finally, the shopping list view will simply show them the ingredient list based on the menu (that one is a read-only view). It is, fundamentally, a pretty simple project. But, it's got enough in it to show quite a lot of new material.

That gives you a basic idea of what the server-side code will need to do and what the client-side code will provide to the user, but there's clearly a lot of details still missing, and I don't expect you to have a full and clear picture of it all yet. But, we're at the 30,000-foot level, as the saying goes, talking very high level about what we're building, that's all, so that's perfectly fine. We're going to talk more later about how this data will be represented in more detail, and how it will be stored, and of course how to build the API to manipulate it all, and the whole next chapter is about the client.

Before we get to any of that though, we need to talk about a few new things that are even more foundational, starting with a whole new language!

Python Slithers In

The two earlier projects used Node and JavaScript/TypeScript exclusively for both client and server sides. In this project, I want to expand your horizons a little bit and introduce a whole new language: Python.

Make no mistake: this chapter is in no way, shape, or form meant to be a complete explanation of Python. Indeed, whole books are written about that; there's no way I could possibly teach you everything in a single chapter. In fact, beyond some brief introductory stuff, I'm primarily going to show you the code and then explain it – including the pertinent Python concepts – as we go. You certainly won't be a Python expert by the time we're done, but I think you'll have at least a foundation that you can build on with other resources if you so choose. And, Python is fundamentally not all that difficult to learn, so I don't think you'll have any trouble understanding things as we go.

Python is one of the most popular languages out there today. In fact, most surveys I've seen show it as #2 behind JavaScript/TypeScript. It's big in the Artificial Intelligence and Machine Learning space, very popular for writing scripts to do all sorts of DevOps-type things, and it's increasingly becoming popular for first-time programming classrooms. That's because it's a pretty simple and fairly expressive language.

If you've never seen it before, what does a simple Python program look like? Well, here's an example (Listing 13-1).

Listing 13-1. A simple but a bit more than "Hello, world!" Python program

```python
import random
import sqlite3
import time

def getRandomID():
    return round((time.time() * 1000) + random.randrange(10, 100000, 1))

conn = sqlite3.connect("C:\\temp\\test.db")
conn.execute("""
    CREATE TABLE IF NOT EXISTS users (
        id INTEGER NOT NULL PRIMARY KEY AUTOINCREMENT,
        name TEXT,
        age INTEGER
    );
""")
sql = "INSERT INTO users (id, name, age) VALUES (?, ?, ?)"
data = [
    (getRandomID(), "Alice", 21),
    (getRandomID(), "Bob", 22),
    (getRandomID(), "Chris", 23)
]
conn.executemany(sql, data)
data = conn.execute("SELECT * FROM users WHERE age <= 22")
for row in data:
    print(row)
```

I'd be willing to bet that you can follow most of that code even if it's your first time seeing Python. But, let's break it down a little bit.

The very first thing to point out is perhaps the one most unusual thing about Python, and that's that indentation matters and there are no block delimiters (curly braces). Jumping ahead a bit, look at the line below the one that begins with def. Don't worry about what it is or does yet, but do note that the second line is indented by four spaces. This is critical! If your indentation is not consistent and correct, a Python program won't work, at least not as you expect. Whitespace matters, in contrast to most other languages! The indentation you see delineates a block of code; it defines a scope in other words. All lines with the same indentation belong to the same block of code, and if there is a block nested within another, then you simply indent the nested block more. How much you indent is generally up to you (though four spaces per block is pretty typical and it's what I've used throughout), but it has to be consistent, and if you get it wrong, you'll be greeted with an `IndentationError` from Python, or your code won't work as expected. Think of what might happen if you have an `if` statement, and a line of code that you *expect* to be executed only when the condition is true *actually* executes *all the time* because you didn't indent it properly, and so it's not actually part of the `if` block of code! This takes some getting used to, since most other languages ignore whitespace, but not Python, for better or worse!

Let's break down the code now. First, we see some import statements. This, like in JavaScript, allows us to import packages (or modules, as they're sometimes referred to) of code to use. This example will be dealing with a database, specifically SQLite (which comes packaged with Python, which is a hint for the future!), and we're also going to need to generate some random numbers seeded by the current time, so the `random` and `time` packages come into play.

After the imports, we have that `def` line, which is Python's way of saying "I want to define a function." Here, it's a function named `getRandomID()`, which we'll call later to create records in a database. It makes use of the `round()` function – which is a globally available function in Python – to round off the result of adding together the current time (the call to the `time()` function of the `time` package, which we imported) times 1000 to got it into a more useful range, to a random number in the range 10–100,000 (counting by 1s) by calling the `random.randrange()` function. It doesn't look all that different from JavaScript fundamentally, does it?

And remember that indentation matters! If that function had more than one line of code, they would all need to be indented four spaces. And then, if there was something like an `if` statement, or a `for` loop, then the code in those blocks would need to be indented four spaces again (or two spaces, or six spaces – how many spaces is up to you, but you must be consistent with it).

After that, our executable code begins. There's no main function in Python, so execution simply begins at the top of the file and works its way down. The first code after the imports and the function definition connects to a database. If you're unfamiliar with it, SQLite is a simple, embedded relational database, so we're going to be working with

SQL here. All you need to do is point it at a file and call the `connect()` function of the `sqlite3` package (which you'll notice is what we imported), and the file will be opened (or created if it didn't exist already). Yes, that single line of code creates a database!

Note that Python deals with strings like virtually every other language: quotation marks denote a string (and three quotation marks as you see here allow you to break a string across multiple lines of code). But, you should also know that Python is considered dynamically typed. Notice that I didn't need to define the type of that conn variable (or, if you look ahead a few lines, the sql variable). Python will do type checking at the time a line of code executes, so if you try to do something like add a number to a string, you'll get a runtime error. And, the type of a variable can change over the lifetime of that variable. In this regard, Python is again very much like JavaScript.

Back to the code, now that we have a database, we need a table. The `create()` function on the `conn` object, which was returned to us from the call to `sqlite3.open()`, is used, and we pass it basic SQL to create a table.

I assume here that you have at least some knowledge of SQL – but, this is actually the only SQL you'll find in this book, so if it's new to you, don't worry, you won't need to know it anymore – but, aside from some of the keywords there that you may not know, I'd bet that SQL is fairly understandable: it's just naming a table (users) with three columns (id, name, and age) and providing their types (a number, text, and another number, respectively).

You can see that Python supports another form of string: the triple-quoted string. This is used to break a string up across multiple lines without having to do string concatenation. It's a pretty clean approach.

Now that we have a table, we want to add records to it. First, we define a variable named `sql` that holds the SQL insert statement to add a record to a table. Again, even if you're new to SQL, it should be self-explanatory, except, perhaps, for those question marks. These are placeholders, and they'll come into play a few lines from now.

Before that though, we need some data to insert, and that's where the next couple of lines come in. The `data` variable references an array, and Python uses the same square bracket notation as most other languages for that. The elements of the array are tuples, used to store multiple values in a single variable, and the parentheses denote that. These elements contain the ID, name, and age of three people.

Now that we have some data, let's insert it into the table! The executemany()
function on the conn object allows us to do that by feeding it the SQL to execute and
the list of data to use. For each element in the data array, the SQL statement we defined
earlier is executed, and the values are inserted in place of the question marks, in the
order they appear in each tuple. So, Python winds up effectively executing three SQL
statements:

```
INSERT INTO users (id, name, age) VALUES (<id>, 'Alice', 21)
INSERT INTO users (id, name, age) VALUES (<id>, 'Bob', 22)
INSERT INTO users (id, name, age) VALUES (<id>, 'Chris', 23)
```

where <id> is a randomly generated ID value.

And, with that, we have data in the table, which we can prove by querying the table,
which is what the next line does, by calling the execute() function on the conn object
and capturing the returned data in the data variable. That data is an iterable collection,
which means we can use a for statement to iterate over it and print() each object
(where print() is another globally available function). This form of for loop doesn't
require any index variable since data is iterable; in other cases, you can construct a more
typical for loop for an index variable.

Note throughout all of this that python variables and functions can be named just
like in JavaScript, so there's nothing funky to consider there.

And believe it or not, you just learned about half of what you'll need to know about
Python for this project! The rest we'll get to later as we write the server-side code.

Uhh, I Can Has Python?!

But, of course, one quite important thing I left out was how, exactly, do you get Python
on your machine? Because I'm sure you want to try that example code, right?

Fortunately, that's easy: visit python.org, which looks something like Figure 13-1 at
the time of this writing.

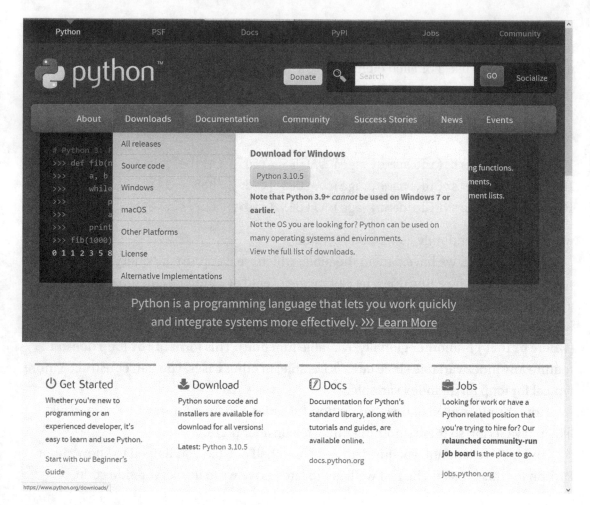

Figure 13-1. *The python.org website*

There, hover over the Download link, and you should see a mega-menu appear that should suggest the right download for your system. Follow the instructions to download and install it. Note that if you're on a Windows system, be sure to check the "Add Python 3.10 to PATH" checkbox, and at the end, click the "Disable path length limit" option. These are necessary to ensure everything works as expected later.

Once complete, go to a command prompt and start the Python interpreter. Depending on the install and your OS, that'll either be done by typing py, python, or python3.10 (or whatever version it is that you downloaded) and pressing Enter (and if none of those work, the website should supply the right instructions, but one of those definitely *should* work). Once you do that, you should find yourself in the Python interpreter or REPL (Read-Eval-Print-Loop) interface. To test it, just do:

```
print("Yes, it worked!")
```

and press Enter. The text should be echoed back to you. You can then exit by typing `quit()` and pressing Enter. Once you're back at a command prompt, enter `pip` and press Enter. You should see some usage information. Don't worry about what that is for now, just ensure that the `pip` command is at least found.

If that all works, you now have Python set up and ready to go for this project. The next thing we need to talk about is how to write a Python-based web app, and for that, we're going to use a popular framework called Django.

Note that at the time of this writing, the latest version of Python available is 3.10.4. A newer version should be okay as long as it's still a 3.10.x version, but if you run into any problems, you can download the exact version from the website as well to be sure it's not a version issue, though you have to drill down into the download options a bit to find it.

Django Unchained

Quentin Tarantino would be so proud of this section title!

When you write server-side code with Node, you have a choice. First, you can write it from the ground up, not pulling in any libraries beyond what Node itself offers. This works reasonably well for small projects, but once they get larger, developers tend to go with the second option of finding a library or framework to build on top of. You saw Express, for example, in earlier projects, though that's only one option (albeit perhaps the most popular).

The situation is much the same with Python. Python provides enough basic plumbing code out of the box that you could write your own server from "first principles," so to speak. But, more times than not, developers tend to want something a little more robust that saves them from all the really basic, boilerplate coding. Django is just that thing.

Django is a web development framework that seeks to help you avoid having to sweat all the small stuff and instead focus on the core logic of your application. It's a fairly opinionated framework, supplying reasonable defaults for most things and reducing the boilerplate code you have to write to, frankly, almost nothing.

How do you get started with Django? Well, that's easy, and the answer is the same for Django as most other Python packages that you might want to add: `pip`. Pip stands for Package Installer for Python, and it serves the same basic purpose as does NPM for Node. Just like with NPM, you can list the packages that have been installed:

```
pip list
```

These are packages that are installed globally. With Python, there is a concept called virtual environments (or venv) that works conceptually a lot like a directory with a package.json file does for Node and NPM in that a project like that can have its own set of dependencies specific to it. However, just to keep things simpler, we're not going to mess with venv for this project, and instead we'll install everything globally, and the first thing we'll install is Django, with the following command:

```
pip install django==4.0.4
```

Pip will go off and do its thing, and you can then list packages again to confirm it's been installed (you'll see some other packages too, which are things Django depends on, so they got installed too).

Note that if an updated version came out and you wanted to upgrade, you could do

```
pip install django --upgrade
```

That will upgrade Django, and any of its dependencies, as needed.

Creating a Django Project

Now that you have both Python and Django installed, let's see what it takes to start a Django project. As with most frameworks today, doing so requires issuing a command or two from a command prompt. Create an empty directory somewhere and navigate to it at a command prompt, then type this command and press Enter:

```
django-admin startproject fooderator
```

You should find that it does, well, nothing, seemingly! But, in fact, a new Django project has been started! A new directory named `fooderator` will have been created. Navigate to it and look at the contents. You should see a file `manage.py` and a directory `fooderator`. That's your new project!

And, it's a fully working project at that point! To start it, type this command and press Enter:

```
python manage.py runserver
```

This is how you will start the server going forward in all cases, and this will show you some startup information, including the URL to launch in your browser. Do so, and you should see what is shown in Figure 13-2.

Figure 13-2. *A default Django web app*

It really is that simple to get a working app up and running! Of course, what you do next is up to you, but it's helpful – necessary, really! – to understand the basic app structure that was created for you first:

- The outer fooderator root directory is a container for your project. Its name doesn't matter to Django, so feel free to rename it as you see fit.

- `manage.py` is a command-line utility that lets you interact with this Django project in several ways, like starting the server, as you saw.

- The inner `fooderator` directory is the actual Python package for your project. Its name is the Python package name you'll need to use to import anything inside it (e.g., `import fooderator.urls`).

- `fooderator/__init__.py` is just an empty file that tells Python that this directory should be considered a Python package. This isn't terribly important for this project, but it's good to know.

- `fooderator/settings.py` has various settings and configuration for this Django project. We won't need to mess with anything here; the defaults will be fine.

- `fooderator/urls.py` is a file that has the URL declarations for this Django project. It is, in effect, a "table of contents" of your Django-powered site.

- `fooderator/asgi.py` is the entry point for ASGI-compatible web servers to serve your project. This has no bearing on Fooderator, but ASGI is the spiritual successor to WSGI, which is…

- `fooderator/wsgi.py` is the entry point for WSGI-compatible web servers to serve your project. WSGI is a Python standard between web servers, frameworks, and applications that allows the server to forward requests to a Python-based application (which is what ASGI is too, just a newer, more robust version of WSGI). As with `asgi.py`, this isn't relevant for our work here.

Just for the sake of the curious, ASGI stands for Asynchronous Server Gateway Interface, while WSGI stands for Web Server Gateway Interface. Not important for this project, but maybe wins you some free beer at a trivia contest some time!

Obviously, there's a lot of details here that I'm skipping over, things like the settings and configuration available. Fortunately, Django has rather good documentation, which you can find here: `www.djangoproject.com`. This documentation will give you all those details, and more, when and if you need them. But, like I said, one of the attractions of Django is that it doesn't require a lot of configuration; its defaults will be good for probably 95% of cases and certainly for this project.

Creating an App

Now that you have an environment – a project, in other words – set up, we need now to add an app to it (two, in fact, in the case of Fooderator). A Django project can consist of one or more apps, typically related in some way. There are no real rules to what apps you have, it's whatever makes the most sense to you. For example, maybe you want to have a website that has some blog posts, plus an administrative interface to create posts. So, you might decide to create two apps for that, one for viewing posts and one for the admin functions. Maybe you also want to give users the ability to view and add comments to posts, so you might choose to create a third app. It's all up to you.

As before, Django comes with command-line tools to create apps, via the `manage.py` script that you used to create the project. It just takes two quick commands to set up the two apps we need:

```
python manage.py startapp client
python manage.py startapp restapi
```

Now, what are the apps, you ask? Fooderator will consist of two parts: an app that serves the client (the HTML, CSS, JS, images, etc. that make up the client side of Fooderator) and an app that is the REST API that the client will call to store and manipulate the data elements I described earlier. The `client` app will use all Django defaults, meaning we won't need to actually write any code at all there. Well, you know, no code other than the client code itself, of course, but that's for the next chapter.

In order for Django to do anything with this app, we need to tell it about the app. This is done in the `settings.py` file in the `fooderator/fooderator` directory (yes, that's right: remember that the directory with the same name as the project directory is where Django project configuration is stored, and in this case, we need to configure the project to be aware of the new app). Specifically, we need to add an element to the `INSTALLED_` `APPS` array:

```
INSTALLED_APPS = [
    'django.contrib.admin',
    'django.contrib.auth',
```

```
    'django.contrib.contenttypes',
    'django.contrib.sessions',
    'django.contrib.messages',
    'django.contrib.staticfiles',
]
```

That's what you'll see by default. All you need to do is add an element to that array:

`'client'`

The other app, the `restapi` app, is added in the same way, and that app is where we'll need to write some actual code (and is what we'll be focusing on for the remainder of this chapter). But, it will wind up being not much code thanks to another package we'll add: DRF.

Because all the apps in a Django project are served from the same domain, that means that our client will be able to call our REST API without running afoul of any CORS restrictions, so we get a nice separation of concerns by breaking it up into two projects without all the hassle CORS can sometimes be.

Taking a REST with DRF

I haven't shown you how yet, but with Django, you can map a URL to a Python function that produces some HTML very easily. Don't worry, you'll see how to do that a little later. But, knowing it's possible at all, you can imagine how you might write a RESTful API with Django.

You might have several functions, and some will execute on POST requests, some on GET requests, and so on. You might read some files to get your data, use basic string manipulation to produce JSON, and then return it. You could certainly do all of this and have a functional REST API in the end.

But, that's a fair bit of code to have to write yourself, even if it's not particularly complex. Because writing a REST API is such a common thing these days, there's a much better way available to us: DRF. DRF stands for Django REST Framework, and it's an add-on package that reduces the amount of code we have to write, in some cases to just one or two lines!

First, we need to install DRF. You know how to do that already:

```
pip install djangorestframework==3.13.1
```

Once you do that, you'll be able to add DRF to an existing app, and in this case, we'll add it to the `restapi` app.

How do you do that, exactly? The same way you added the `client` and `restapi` apps: by updating the `INSTALLED_APPS` array with a new element:

```
'rest_framework'
```

Once that's in place, DRF is ready to be used. But, there's one more thing we need to install that is related to DRF, and that's a package called Core API. This package will be used later to deal with our data (it will be part of a mechanism that automatically translates objects that have data about our recipes, menus, and shopping list items to and from JSON). So, install it next:

```
pip install coreapi==2.3.3
```

and then add it to the `INSTALLED_APPS` array as well:

```
'coreapi'
```

With those packages both installed, we're ready to dig into writing our Fooderator REST API.

Setting Up the API

The first step to doing that is to tell Django about our API. More specifically, we have to describe the URL pattern that Django should route to the `restapi` app. This is done by editing the `fooderator/fooderator.urls.py` file. By default, it looks like this:

```
from django.contrib import admin
from django.urls import path

urlpatterns = [
    path('admin/', admin.site.urls),
]
```

The `path()` function that is imported is used to provide an object of the proper type for inclusion in the `urlpatterns` array. Essentially, it says "this particular URL path is handled by this particular view," where a "view" can mean a collection of other views provided by some other code, as is the case for the `admin/` path. A view, at the code level, is a Python function (or a class, as you'll see later) that produces the output for a particular URL.

You get an admin interface – which is why it was imported – by default for some management functions of your apps, which is what the first import pulls in. You can access it via `http://127.0.0.1:8000/admin`. Before you can do that though, you have to create a "super user" account. To do that, execute this command:

```
python manage.py createsuperuser
```

Follow the prompts to set up the user and password, then restart the server again, and you'll be able to log in. This admin interface isn't of much use to us for our purposes here though, so let's get back to the main task at hand here, which is adding a path for our API. To do that, we need to add an import:

```
from django.urls import include
```

And then, a mapping for the API:

```
path("api/v1/", include("restapi.urls")),
```

What this does is make it so that any request to the Django server that begins with `/api/v1/` (following the domain name) will be mapped to the `restapi` app and, more specifically, the URL patterns it defines, and that's the next thing we're going to add!

Adding Endpoints

With the `/api/v1/` URL pattern going to the restapi app, the next step is to tell that app what specific URL patterns map to what functions in our Python code (which we haven't written yet, of course). The way we do that is in the `urls.py` file in the `fooderator/fooderator/restapi` directory. It can be confusing, I know, but realize that this is a different `urls.py` file than the one we edited in the last section, which was in the `fooderator/fooderator` directory. It's kind of funky, but you get used to it!

But, hey, wait a minute! There is no `urls.py` file in the `fooderator/fooderator/`
`restapi` directory! What gives?! Well, Django didn't know what would be in our app
when it was created, so it didn't create the file for us; we'll need to do that ourselves. It's
pretty simple though:

```
from django.urls import path
from restapi import views
```

As before, we need the `path()` function, but now we also need to import the `views`
object from the `restapi` package. This is something else we haven't written yet, but we
will! In short, the `views` object will contain the functions that will service each of our
endpoints.

After that, we just need to add entries to `urlpatterns`:

```
urlpatterns = [
    path("recipe/", views.RecipeListCreateAPIView.as_view()),
    path("recipe/<int:pk>/", views.RecipeUpdateDeleteAPIView.as_view()),
    path("menuitem/", views.MenuItemListCreateAPIView.as_view()),
    path("menuitem/<int:pk>/", views.MenuItemDeleteAPIView.as_view())
]
```

As you can see, each entry is the return from a call to that `path()` function. As before,
the first argument to each is the URL pattern that Django will match to know which
function to call. Note that these patterns can contain values in angle brackets, as in
`recipe/<int:pk>/`, and what that does is capture part of the URL and pass the data to
the view as a keyword argument. In Python, you can pass arguments to a function in the
form XXX=YYY where XXX is any name you like and YYY is a value. In this way, you can
reference those arguments by name in your code. That may not sound much different
than arguments in general, which you of course also reference by name in the function's
code, but the main difference – and benefit – is that you can pass such arguments in any
order, because it's ultimately the name that matters, not their position in the argument
list. For an endpoint like `/recipe/<int:pk>/` that is used to update or delete a recipe,
we need to pass the ID of the recipe as part of the URL as per REST semantics, so this
pattern results in an integer (`int`, which is one of several converter functions that can be
specified to manipulate the string parsed from the URL into another data type or form)
which is the primary key (`pk`) being parsed out of the URL and passed to the view under
the name pk. The primary key is the unique identifier of a recipe in our database – but
I'm getting ahead of myself, so put that tidbit aside for just a moment!

The second argument to `path()` is the view function or class that will generate the response for that endpoint, which are taken from the `views` object that we'll get to later. For each, we need to call `as_view()` on it to return a function suitable for use by Django.

What we're setting up here are endpoints for the four basic CRUD operations for both recipes and menu items. That means endpoints where we can create, update, delete, and retrieve list of recipes and the same for menu items. You may wonder why there's only two for each model type defined. It's because the URL for listing and creating a recipe is the same; they only differ by the HTTP method. The same goes for menu items. And, likewise for updating and deleting a recipe or menu item, the URL is the same, and only the HTTP method differs. Since here we don't need to concern ourselves with the HTTP method, only the URLs matter; hence, we only need two mappings for each model type. That's also why the view names are what they are: `RecipeListCreateAPIView` conveys that it handles both list and create functions, and `RecipeUpdateDeleteAPIView` conveys that it handles both update and delete functions (we can name them however we wish, of course, but these made sense to me).

Note that we don't need endpoints for ingredients because we'll deal with them as part of recipes, and we also don't need an endpoint here for generating a shopping list because that will be handled in a different way, as you'll see a few sections from now.

With these URL patterns in place, we need to now write the views that will be called for each of these patterns. These functions will work with data though, so before we can really write them, we need to talk about how our data will be stored and accessed by our code.

Creating Models to Model Our Data

One of the wonderful things about Django and DRF is that they make working with data remarkably easy. They use an ORM approach – which stands for Object-Relational Mapping if you've never heard it before – to make it more or less automatic.

Django ships with support for the SQLite database right out of the box. SQLite is a simple but still pretty powerful relational database, so we're dealing with tables and rows of data typically that relate to other rows in other tables. SQLite is a simple file-based database and is embedded in Django, which means you don't need to bother with a separate server.

What's better is that the ORM approach means that you don't even have to deal with creating your database and table structure yourself, nor do you ever have to write SQL (Structured Query Language) yourself! All you need to do is define some classes (which, yes, Python also supports), tell Django about them, and it will handle all the details for you with just a few management commands to execute.

Now, we're talking about ORM here and how you don't need to build the database yourself, but it's still helpful to understand what the schema of the database looks like. Figure 13-3 shows you this.

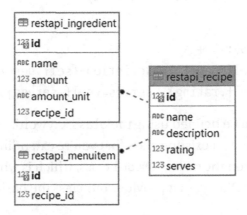

Figure 13-3. *The database schema we eventually want to have*

When Django creates this for us, the table names are prefixed with the app name, so `restapi_recipe`, for example. Note the key relationships here: both ingredients and menu items reference a recipe via the id field. In the case of ingredients, it's a one (recipe) to many (ingredients) relationship. For menu items, one menu item references one recipe, but there of course can be multiple menu items, hence why the diagram shows a one-to-many relationship (or many-to-one, depending on how you look at it).

As mentioned, this structure is a by-product of the code we write, we don't need to create this ourselves, and we begin the process by adding a new file in the `restapi` project named `models.py`. A model is what we call a class that "models" your data. In simpler terms, it's where you define the types of entities your code will work with. In Fooderator, that means Recipes, Ingredients, and MenuItems.

This new file begins with a single import:

```
from django.db import models
```

The models object contains several constants and functions that we'll need to tell Django about the types of data we have in our objects. And, the first such object we'll create – the first class, to be more precise – is a model of our Recipe model:

```python
class Recipe(models.Model):
  name = models.CharField(max_length=100)
   description = models.CharField(max_length=500)
   rating = models.IntegerField(default=1)
   serves = models.IntegerField(default=1)

   def __str__(self):
       return f"Recipe: " + \
           f"name={self.name}, description={self.description},
           rating={self.rating}, serves={self.serves}"
```

In Python, classes can be defined using the class keyword. You give your class a name, and if you like, name an existing class that you're extending. Here, we're creating a new class Recipe based on the models.Model class, which is what we imported earlier and is a class provided by Django that provides our class the basic plumbing for it to be a data model class.

One interesting note about classes in Python: they're also objects! When you define a class like this, you're also creating an instance automatically. Python's notion of classes and object orientation comes from concepts of Smalltalk, so it can be a little weird compared to other OOP languages sometimes. Fortunately, for what we're doing in this project, you can think of them pretty much like any other class-based language you're familiar with; there should be little difference that you need to be aware of – but I wanted to point out that there's much more to it in Python, should you want to go further down that path on your own.

After that, we need to add fields to our class. As described in the "Wait, What Are We Building?!" section, we need four fields: name, description, rating, and serves. We also need to tell Django what type they are, and the allowed types are conveniently attributes on the models object we imported. For each, there is various additional information you can provide, though mostly it's optional, and it varies from type to type. Here, we define maximum lengths on the CharFields – which are just string value fields – and set some default values for the IntegerFields, which obviously whole store numbers. If you look at this and compare it to the database schema from earlier, you should see the relationship.

Given this model class, Django has all the information it needs to be able to create that schema for us automatically (well, just the `restapi_recipe` table at this point, of course).

The `def __str__(self)` line defines a method on the class, in this case a special method that Python uses any time you want a string representation of the class (if you've ever worked in Java, this is the same as the `toString()` method, which also exists in JavaScript – same basic idea in all cases). A class can implement certain operations that are invoked by special syntax (such as arithmetic operations or subscripting and slicing) by defining methods with special names. This is Python's approach to operator overloading, allowing classes to define their own behavior with respect to language operators.

In the case of __str__, Python's default implementation isn't terribly helpful because it doesn't know what you really want to show, so it gives you some internal information that probably isn't what you want or need. So, we define a version that overrides the default and which displays all the information from the instance of the class being displayed (e.g., passing it to the `print()` function). Note here the use of the `f""` string notation. This allows us to insert tokens into the string, as in `{self.name}`. The `self` keyword is always a reference to the instance of the class the method is executed on, so it's easy to access those fields this way.

Now that we have a recipe model, let's do one for ingredients:

```python
class Ingredient(models.Model):
    recipe = models.ForeignKey(Recipe, on_delete=models.CASCADE)
    name = models.CharField(max_length=100)
    amount = models.IntegerField(default=0)
    amount_unit = models.CharField(max_length=50)

    def __str__(self):
        return f"Ingredient: " + \
            f"name={self.name}, amount={self.amount}, amount_unit={self.
            amount_unit}, recipe_id={self.recipe_id}"
```

As you can see, it's pretty much the same as the Recipe class, save for one thing: that `recipe` field. The `ForeignKey` field type is how we define relationships for Django, because otherwise it has no idea how ingredients relate to recipes or even that they do relate to each other at all. By defining this field as `ForeignKey`, and by passing to that function the name of the class it relates to, a many-to-one relationship is established.

Interestingly, note that we aren't defining keys of either of these entities. If you were building the database yourself, there would need to be some key field (or fields) in the recipe table that an ingredient record references to set up that relationship. Here, just telling Django the class an ingredient relates to is enough because it will handle the details of the keys for us (you can see it in the schema: it's the id fields, which you'll note aren't in our models – Django creates them automatically due to the ForeignKey relationships).

In addition, we want to ensure that if a recipe is deleted, the ingredients under it are deleted as well (without us having to do it manually). That's where the on_delete arguments come in. The models.CASCADE value tells Django that we want a deletion of a recipe to "cascade" down to all the ingredient records too.

It's worth noting that Django only supports many-to-one relationships, and that's why you have to define the relationships on the child entities (ingredients), not the parent entities (recipes). That can seem backward at times, but it's just the way it is because relationships in an ORM can be difficult generally, and this is one way to make it a little easier to implement.

In the __str__ method, you'll notice the backslash. This is a line continuation marker in Python and is how we can break long lines of code up across multiple lines.

Finally, we need to add a model for the menu items:

```
class MenuItem(models.Model):
    recipe = models.ForeignKey(Recipe, on_delete=models.CASCADE)

    def __str__(self):
        return f"MenuItem: " + \
            f"recipe_id={self.recipe_id}, recipe={self.recipe}"
```

As with ingredients, menu items relate to recipes, so again we need to establish that relationship, and, again, we want menu items to be deleted when recipes are deleted (it would be a bug if we still had a menu item referencing a recipe that was no longer there). Otherwise, it's the simplest of the three model classes.

Migrations

With those model classes defined, Django actually has all the information it needs to create a database for us! But, we do still have to tell it to do so, and that just takes two commands, starting with this one:

```
manage.py makemigrations
```

Migrations are Django's way of propagating changes you make in your models into the database, and this command creates those migrations. In this case, we don't yet *have* a database at all, so what we're migrating into the database is the initial model structure itself. You can think of that command as preparing the changes that will be made to the database. When executed, Django will work out all the necessary SQL statements and record them (you'll find a `migrations` folder is created at this point in the restapi project – you can ignore it as it's not something you should generally touch, but that's what it's for). To actually implement the changes, you need a second command:

```
manage.py migrate
```

That tells Django to go ahead and actually make the changes. Since at this point, we have no database, one will be created, in the form of a new file, db.sqlite3, in the root of the fooderator project file.

To prove this, I'd like you to download an app called DBeaver Community Edition. This is a great – and free (at least for the community edition) – application for working with all sorts of databases. You can grab it here: `https://dbeaver.io/`. It's a Java-based app, so you'll need to ensure you have Java installed too. Once you install it, or run the portable version that requires no installation (which is my recommendation), you can fire it up, and you should see something like Figure 13-4, though yours will be mostly empty.

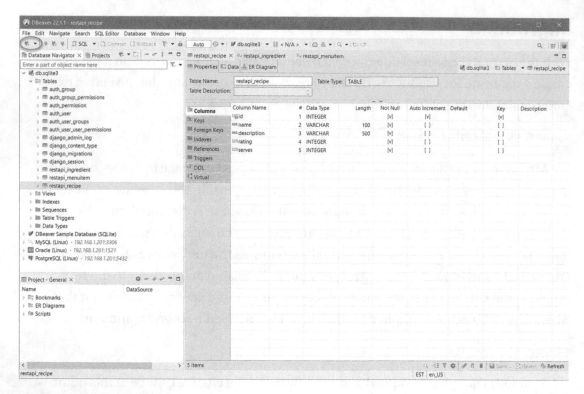

Figure 13-4. *DBeaver*

The first step to making it not empty and looking more like what you see here is to create a connection to the SQLite database. To do that, click the icon you see circled in the toolbar, and look for SQLite, which should be near the top of the list of databases you can connect to. Click it, and then browse to the db.sqlite3 file that was created earlier. You can use the Test Connection button to ensure there are no errors, and if there are not, then save the connection, which should then appear on the left-hand side in the Database Navigator section.

You can then simply expand it, then expand Tables, at which point you should see several tables like you see in Figure 13-4, including the restapi_recipe, restapi_ingredient, and restapi_menuitem tables. You can then click those to see the details on the right about it, browse and edit the data, and even see the ER diagram from earlier there.

DBeaver is an extremely valuable tool to have, especially when working with an ORM like Django has, because it can sometimes be very helpful to see the structure that was created to validate that you coded your models right and also if you want to make changes outside the code to test things.

Any time you amend your model classes, you'll need to make `migrations` again and `migrate` after that again. Django will then make the necessary changes in your database. Note, however, that it's fairly easy to get into a situation where the changes are too large to be done properly, or there could be some conflict with the existing structure, and Django may give you some errors when you try to run those commands. During development, the solution is simple: delete the `db.sqlite3` file, delete the `migrations` directory, and that will allow you to start from scratch. You will obviously lose your data, but it will allow you to get back to a working state at least.

It's great that we now have model classes that we could use in our code and a database where those entities are stored. That's all, of course, necessary to getting the REST API for Fooderator going! However, at this point, it's not enough to be able to build that REST interface quite yet. Something else we need to deal with is something called serializers.

Serializers to Handle Our Models

Serializers allow complex data, like model instances most importantly for us here, to be converted to native Python data types, as well as providing deserialization functions to go the other way. That is, converting parsed data back into complex types. Both of these things are needed for a REST API if you think about it because HTTP, which REST is built on top of, is always string-based. You may POST JSON to a RESTful endpoint, but JSON is itself a string. That string needs to be converted to some native data type that the language your API is written in can work with, and then there has to be a mechanism to convert a native data type back into JSON (or XML, or whatever other format you'll send back to the client via HTTP). That's where serializers enter the picture in the Django world.

To create them, we start by adding another new file to the `restapi` app named `serializers.py` (Django is nothing if not predictable, right??). Then, as with `models.py`, we start with a couple of imports:

```
from rest_framework import serializers
from restapi.models import Ingredient, MenuItem, Recipe
```

First, like with the model classes, we're going to make use of several things provided by Django, and they're all in the serializers object. Next, we need to import the model classes we created before because the serializer classes we're about to write will reference them.

And, the first of those classes – of which there will be three to match our Recipe, Ingredient, and MenuItem model classes – is the IngredientSerializer (the name of the class must be in the form "<model_class_name>Serializer"):

```
class IngredientSerializer(serializers.ModelSerializer):
    class Meta:
        model = Ingredient
        fields = ("id", "name", "amount", "amount_unit")
```

First, you may be wondering why the serializer for an Ingredient model class instance comes before the serializer for a Recipe model class instance in the code, as opposed to the models.py file where we defined the Recipe class first. Usually, the order doesn't matter here, but it *does* matter in this instance because the RecipeSerializer, which we're going to look at now, references the IngredientSerializer, so if they were reversed, we'd get an error.

A serializer class extends the serializers.ModelSerializer class, which, like models, gives our class some basic behaviors as defined by Django and, in effect, "turns it into" a serializer.

The other important part of this is that class Meta: line, and this requires some explanation.

Python supports the notion of *metaprogramming*. There is the notion of a meta class, which is a class that helps instantiate other classes. Part of this notion is the ability to provide information about the class outside of the code (if you've ever seen annotations in Java, then you've seen a form of metaprogramming). In the case of this serializer, we're actually declaring an inner class called Meta on the IngredientSerializer class (yes, Python allows for inner, or nested, classes), which is something of a special case in that Django knows about it and how to use it. And then, below it, we're providing some options to Django so that when it creates one of these serializer instances, it knows how to configure that instance. Here, we're telling it what model object this serializer knows how to serialize and deserialize (Ingredient), and we're telling it what fields to include when performing those operations because you may not always want all fields to be included (more on this shortly!).

Django now has all the information it needs to be able to serialize and deserialize an Ingredient object. Similarly, we do the same for the Recipe model class, but in that case, we have a bit more work to do. Before that though, it begins the same:

```
class RecipeSerializer(serializers.ModelSerializer):
    class Meta:
        model = Recipe
        fields = "__all__"
```

In this case, we do want all the fields to be serialized, and the __all__ value is a handy shortcut to tell Django that. In fact, this is really what you should use by default unless and until you have a specific reason not to.

Next, we need to add a field to the serializer:

```
ingredient_set = IngredientSerializer(many=True)
```

This is a field that will store a collection of Ingredient objects, because of course a recipe wouldn't be of much use if it didn't tell you what ingredients to use! Notice that the field is referencing the IngredientSerializer, which is why it had to be defined first (because remember that Python executes code top-to-bottom). The call to the constructor (which is what this is) specifies that there can be many instances of this object referenced by this field.

This is the reason we couldn't use the __all__ shortcut in the IngredientSerializer. If we did, it would produce errors when we try to POST a recipe to our REST API later.

Next, we have to deal with the fact that the JSON that is POST'd to create a recipe can (and usually will) include an array of ingredients. Django doesn't know how to handle that nested data automatically and especially when there's a relationship involved that we had to write special code to handle in the serializer. So, in order to make this work, we have to write the code that Django and DRF will use when creating a Recipe instance. This code isn't terribly complicated, fortunately:

```
def create(self, validated_data):
    ingredient_validated_data = validated_data.pop("ingredient_set")
    recipe = Recipe.objects.create(**validated_data)
    ingredient_set_serializer = self.fields["ingredient_set"]
    for each in ingredient_validated_data:
        each["recipe"] = recipe
    ingredient_set_serializer.create(ingredient_validated_data)
    return recipe
```

We override the `create()` method, which is passed a reference to the serializer instance and validated data that was sent into the serializer. There is a capability with Django and DRF to validate (and convert) incoming data in various ways, but Fooderator doesn't do anything but the default validations, things like marshaling strings to numerics as needed, so that much is simple.

So, the first step is to get the data for the ingredients. If you think about what will be happening here later, the client will eventually POST JSON to the recipe creation endpoint of our REST API, and that JSON will include an array of ingredients. Django will have parsed that all out and given us the data in the `ingredient_set` field. So, we grab that, since we'll need it. Next, we call the `Recipe.objects.create()` method. This uses the ** notation, which gives you all the keyword arguments (except for those corresponding to formal parameters). This is a shortcut in Python that allows you to pass a variable list of keyword arguments to a function, as seen here.

With that data, Django knows how to create an instance, so we get back a `Recipe` model class instance with the data fields populated. This is the "one" in our one-to-many relationship. Django not only knows how to create the model class instance, but it knows how to create a recipe record in the database. What it doesn't know how to do though is create ingredient records that are related to that recipe record. We have to do that ourselves. To do so, we're first going to need an `IngredientSerializer` instance, and we can do that by referencing the `ingredient_set` field in the `RecipeSerializer` instance (which, remember from earlier, is in fact an `IngredientSerializer` instance).

Next, we iterate over the list of ingredients Django parsed out. Here, you can see what a `for` loop looks like in Python or at least one form of it. Since `ingredient_validated_data` is an iterable list, we can plug it into a `for` loop like this easily. Then, for each recipe in the list, we set the `recipe` field to reference the `Recipe` object created a few lines ago. This satisfies the "many" part of the one-to-many relationship because since Django only supports many-to-one relationships, that means each child object must reference the parent (each "many" must reference each "one"), which it now does (Django knows how to create ingredient records in the database, but it's the relationship on create that it has a problem with).

The last step is to use that `IngredientSerializer` instance we got before and ask it to serialize the list of ingredients. Then, we just have to return the `Recipe` instance, since that's what the `create()` method has to return: an instance of the model class the serializer handles. And with that done, we now have a recipe saved in the database, along with all the ingredients for it (because Django does all that automatically for us behind the scenes thanks to its ORM approach).

In similar fashion, when a recipe is updated, we must update the ingredients as well, for all the same reasons we had to handle it ourselves in create(). However, to keep things simple, the approach I opted to use is to actually delete any existing ingredient records and then re-create them. That's simpler than trying to update each ingredient but is effectively the same result in the end. So, the code in the update() method we must write looks a lot like the create() method, but with a few additional lines of code:

```
def update(self, instance, validated_data):
    instance.name = validated_data["name"]
    instance.description = validated_data["description"]
    instance.rating = validated_data["rating"]
    instance.serves = validated_data["serves"]
    instance.save()
    for ingredient in instance.ingredient_set.all():
        ingredient.delete()
    ingredient_set_serializer = self.fields["ingredient_set"]
    ingredient_validated_data = validated_data.pop("ingredient_set")
    for each in ingredient_validated_data:
        each["recipe"] = instance
    ingredient_set_serializer.create(ingredient_validated_data)
    return instance
```

Since we're overriding what Django would do for us by default, we have to make sure we do the equivalent to that default implementation, and that means setting the four fields to the new values that came in through the validated_data collection. Once that's done, we need to call save() on the instance, which updates the database (in the create() method, we didn't need to do this ourselves because it's done as part of the Recipe.objects.create() call).

Next, we have to delete the ingredient records from the database. To do that, we'll use one of several query functions available to us, instance.ingredient_set.all() in this case, since we of course want to work with all the ingredients. This results in a SQL query being executed, and what we get back is an object called a QuerySet, which is simply the results of a SQL query in an iterable form, which means we can again use a for loop to iterate over it. For each result, we can call the delete() method on it to remove the record from the database.

So, at this point, we have an updated recipe record in the database, but no ingredient records. So, just like before, we need to create those ingredient records, and the code is the same for that as in the create() method because, effectively, we *are* creating new ingredient records at this point. Finally, the instance – a Recipe model class instance – is returned, to fulfill the contract of the update() method, and that's it, we're good to go!

The final serializer is for the menu items on a shopping list:

```
class MenuItemSerializer(serializers.ModelSerializer):
    class Meta:
        model = MenuItem
        fields = "__all__"
```

This is the simplest one because there's no special logic we need to perform, nor are there any fields we need to exclude from serialization, so it's about as bare-bones as you can get, but it'll do the job just fine for us.

Finally: Adding Those Views I Promised!

Now that we have model classes, and serializers that can work with them, it's time to write the code that backs each of our RESTful endpoints. These are called "views," and they are, in the case of Fooderator, relatively simple things that you mapped to URLs in the urls.py file earlier.

First, as is usually the case, there's some imports we need to do:

```
from django.http import HttpResponse
from rest_framework import status
from rest_framework.response import Response
import rest_framework.generics
import json
from restapi.models import Ingredient, MenuItem, Recipe
from restapi.serializers import MenuItemSerializer, RecipeSerializer
```

Since these functions will provide an HTTP response of some kind, we need the HttpResponse object from the django.http package to help with that. And, since we're talking about REST endpoints, HTTP status codes have meaning, and we'll need to use them, which the status object from the rest_framework DRF package gives us. Quite obviously, we're going to have to render a response, so the Response object is needed too. The final import from DRF we need is the `generics` object. This provides functions for telling DRF what type of HTTP requests our views will support, crucial to making a REST API. Then, since we know we'll be returning JSON, we import the `json` package, provided by Python natively, to help us produce that JSON. After that, we'll need our model objects and serializers, of course, so they are all imported.

Recipes

At this point, we're ready to write our first view, the one for listing and creating recipes, which begins like this:

```
class RecipeListCreateAPIView(rest_framework.generics.ListCreateAPIView):
    """This endpoint allows for listing all recipes in the database (GET),
    or creating one (POST)"""
    queryset = Recipe.objects.all()
    serializer_class = RecipeSerializer
```

Err, wait, that's a class, not a function, isn't it!? Indeed, it is! This is considered a "class-based view" (as opposed to a function-based view, which we'll see later), and the benefit is that since classes can extend other classes, they can be imbued with functionality automatically (and you'll see a "naked" Python function used as a view later on for contrast). In this case, our `RecipeListAPIView` extends the `rest_framework.generics.ListCreateAPIView` class. This is important because that particular class tells Django that this view will handle both GET and POST requests for listing recipes and creating recipes, respectively. There are several classes you could extend here, and you'll see one or two more later, but it all comes down to what HTTP methods you want a given view class to handle.

That weird string you see with the three quotation marks after the class definition is called a *docstring*, and it's a literal string that can follow a function, method, class, or module definition. The three quotation marks in Python, as I mentioned briefly earlier, allow you to have a string that spans multiple lines, whether a docstring or not. Here, it's all on a single line, but because it follows the class definition, it's a docstring. As the name implies, a docstring is used to document code (usually for use by various tools, which in general is how they vary from regular # comments), and in our case, as you'll see a little later, they lead to a rather powerful mechanism. But for now, just notice how it documents what this function does.

The code inside the class (which will execute when an instance is constructed) is what does the work. By default, the code in the constructor like this will handle a GET request. The `Recipe.objects.all()` function returns a `QuerySet` that contains all the recipe records from the database. By setting the `serializer_class` variable to an instance of the `RecipeSerializer`, Django can serialize that `QuerySet` for us and will return the response as JSON automatically. It's because this class extends a view class provided by Django that Django knows how to do all of this, which allows us to write very little code to do what we need for this endpoint.

For creating a recipe, there's a little more work involved, so we'll need to write that code ourselves:

```
def post(self, request, *args, **kwargs):
    if serializer.is_valid():
        recipe = serializer.save()
        serializer = RecipeSerializer(recipe)
        return Response(serializer.data, status=status.HTTP_201_CREATED)
    return Response(serializer.errors, status=status.HTTP_400_BAD_REQUEST)
```

As you can see, the `post()` method is overridden. We have to do this for the same reason we needed to write code in the `Recipe` serializer: because of the one-to-many relationship. But, there's a bit less to do here because most of the work is done by the base class.

The `post()` method receives a reference to the class, the incoming request object, and various arguments. The first step is to ensure that the serializer was able to marshal the incoming JSON string into a Recipe object by calling the `is_valid()` method on it. Assuming it has, we ask the serializer to save the recipe to the database (handled by Django's ORM facilities). After that, we get a reference to that serializer, passing it the `Recipe` model object that was just created and saved. The serializer code that we looked at earlier will have already taken care of ensuring the ingredient records, if any were passed in as part of the recipe JSON, will be created in the database and will properly reference the recipe record, thereby creating the relationship. Finally, we just have to return the newly created recipe, since that's the contract our create endpoint provides. To do this, we return a new `Response` object, and during construction we pass it the `data` attribute of the serializer (which will take care of creating JSON for us automatically) and a suitable HTTP status code, 201 CREATED in this case. If for some reason the serializer couldn't marshal the incoming data, we return a 400 BAD REQUEST instead.

That takes care of listing recipes and creating recipes. What about updating and deleting recipes? It turns out, that's much easier:

```
class RecipeUpdateDeleteAPIView(rest_framework.generics.
RetrieveUpdateDestroyAPIView):
    """This endpoint allows for updating a recipe by passing in the ID to
    update"""
    queryset = Recipe.objects.all()
    serializer_class = RecipeSerializer
```

Yes, that's really all it takes! The base class – this time `RetrieveUpdateDestroyAPIView`, since it handles updates and deletes (and also retrieval of a single recipe, though we don't use that functionality in Fooderator, but there doesn't appear to be a base class for *only* updating and deleting at the time of this writing) – handles virtually everything for us. The only thing we have to do is provide a `QuerySet` for it to work against and the serializer class to use. After that, Django and its ORM magic know how to delete and update recipes from that `QuerySet`, so we're good to go!

Menu Items

Handling menu items is much easier because there's no nested data to worry about, so the base class will handle almost everything for us. We just have two bare-bones classes, beginning with this one:

```
class MenuItemListCreateAPIView(rest_framework.generics.ListCreateAPIView):
    """This endpoint lists all menu items in the database"""
    queryset = MenuItem.objects.all()
    serializer_class = MenuItemSerializer
```

As with recipes, a single class handles both listing menu items and creating new ones. All we need to do is again supply a `QuerySet` and the serializer class to use, and the rest is automatic.

Unlike with recipes, we can't update a menu item, so we just need a class for deleting:

```
class MenuItemDeleteAPIView(rest_framework.generics.DestroyAPIView):
    """This endpoint allows for deleting a menu item from the database by
    passing the ID to delete"""
```

```
queryset = MenuItem.objects.all()
serializer_class = MenuItemSerializer
```

The `DestroyAPIView` base class is just what we need. But, you may notice that this class is – base class aside – identical to the `MenuItemListCreateAPIView` class and wonder why they couldn't be a single class. In theory, they could be, but in practice, I couldn't find a base class that supports list and delete simultaneously, so we need two separate classes to get the job done.

There is a `GenericView` base class where you could in theory do all functions in a single class just by overriding the `get()`, `post()`, `delete()`, etc. methods. But, at that point, we're really not using Django and DRF to its full potential since the point is to write as little code as possible ourselves. But, it's an option if you have the need.

And that's it! We now have views that can handle all four CRUD operations for recipes and menu items!

Now, let's talk about the last REST API function we'll need to provide for our client in the next chapter.

A Special Case: The Shopping List

In order to show the user a shopping list, we have to do some calculations. They're simple: iterate the menu items in the database, and for each recipe they reference, collect all the unique ingredients across them all and the quantities of each. An ingredient is considered "unique" by the combination of name and ingredient unit (taking case differences out of the equation). In other words, a cup of carrots is considered a different ingredient than a pound of carrots. I did it this way because the user can enter units in freeform, and they may want to consider the ingredient to be a different thing based on those units (my wife, who is a professional chef, suggested it works this way, and I can barely work a microwave, so I listened!). This also means that "carrots" and "caruts" are different ingredients too, and those types of typos are entirely on the user.

The difference for this API function is that we don't actually need DRF for it, we need to write a function entirely on our own. And, this time, I actually do mean function, not class. I'm going to go through this bit by bit, but the following code is all one function:

```
def make_shopping_list(request):
    menuitems = MenuItem.objects.all()
```

So, we begin by defining a function, and the argument to it will be a request object, which Django will supply to us. Then, the first thing done in the function is to get a QuerySet of all menu items in the database.

Next, we create a dictionary:

```
dict_shopping_list = {}
```

A dictionary in Python is a key-value object, essentially the same as an object literal in JavaScript. This particular dictionary is where we're going to store the ingredients to show the user in the shopping list. Each item in the dictionary will be keyed by "<ingredient_name><amount_unit>", converted to lowercase, as previously discussed. The value of each entry will itself be an object that holds the name, amount unit, and amount of that ingredient.

Next, we begin to iterate over the menu items:

```
for menuitem in menuitems:
    print(menuitem)
    ingredients = Ingredient.objects.filter(recipe_id=menuitem.
    recipe_id)
    print(ingredients)
        print(ingredient)
        key = ingredient.name.lower() + ingredient.amount_unit.lower()
        if key in dict_shopping_list:
            print(dict_shopping_list[key])
            dict_shopping_list[key]["amount"] = dict_shopping_list[key]
            ["amount"] + ingredient.amount
        else:
            dict_shopping_list[key] = {
                "name": ingredient.name, "amount_unit": ingredient.
                amount_unit, "amount": ingredient.amount
            }
    print("dict_shopping_list", dict_shopping_list)
```

For each, we print() it (which uses the custom __str__ function we wrote on our model class) just for debugging purposes. Next, we construct the key of the ingredient in the dictionary as previously described. Python strings provide several functions, one of which is lower() to convert to lowercase.

The if statement after that checks to see if that key already exists in the dictionary. If it does, then the current value is print()'d (by retrieving the object from the dictionary by key using square bracket notation, just like in JavaScript), and then the amount is increased by the amount for the current ingredient being processed. If the key isn't found in the dictionary (the else block), then a new object is created, and that becomes the value for that key in the dictionary.

At the end of that iteration, the dictionary is print()'d so we can be sure everything is as we expect.

The last step is to create an array of objects to return to the client, since that's what our client code will need to display, as you'll see in the next chapter:

```
arr_shopping_list = []
for ingredient in dict_shopping_list:
    arr_shopping_list.append(dict_shopping_list[ingredient])
print("arr_shopping_list", arr_shopping_list)
```

A new array is created, and then we iterate the entries in the dictionary, using the append() method that Python arrays provide to add objects to it at the end.

Once that's done, we can easily return it to the client:

```
return HttpResponse(json.dumps(arr_shopping_list, indent=4))
```

Python provides a built-in json package that has several functions for dealing with transforming Python types to JSON, and dumps() is probably the most important. You simply feed it what you want converted to JSON, and optionally how many spaces to use to indent things (which is only important so that it's easier to read the JSON when debugging, the code that consumes it won't care either way), and it returns a string that is the resultant JSON. Here, we pass that to the HttpResponse function to return that JSON to the client (this differs from the earlier Response function because this is a "naked" HTTP response, not one that Django and DRF are creating for us). Note that the status code will be set automatically to 200, so nothing special needs to be done by the developer in terms of response status codes.

The last thing we need to do is add a way to access this function via a URL, because right now, we can't. To do that, we have to go back into the `fooderator/fooderator/urls.py` file and add an entry to `urlpatterns`:

```
from restapi.views import make_shopping_list

path("makeShoppingList/", make_shopping_list)
```

This isn't being handled by DRF, which is why it has to be added here and not in the `restapi` app itself. We also need to import the function, or else we can't reference it in the call to `path()`.

And with that, we have a full-featured (for what Fooderator needs at least) REST API ready to go! Now, let's talk about two more things related to it: documenting our API and testing our API.

Automatic Documentation Generation

One of the best things about using DRF with Django is that we can get some really nice documentation generated automatically for our REST API. More than just documentation, we can automatically get a page where we can interact with the API to test it easily.

To begin achieving these nifty things, we have to add a few things. First, in the `fooderator/fooderator/settings.py` file, we need to add a setting:

```
REST_FRAMEWORK = {
    'DEFAULT_SCHEMA_CLASS': 'rest_framework.schemas.coreapi.AutoSchema'
}
```

This tells DRF to use the `AutoSchema` class to introspect our views and generate documentation – an API schema, as it's called – for them. There are several parts to making this all work, but this setting is the only one we *must* specify to make it work; everything else is automatic with intelligent defaults (which you can, of course, override if you wish, even to the extent of providing a subclass of `AutoSchema` to do something entirely different, if you wish).

Once this is done and your app restarted, documentation will be generated, but we still need a way to access it. We can do that by adding an import and a new element to the urlpatterns array in the fooderator/fooderator/urls.py file. First, the new import:

```
from rest_framework.documentation import include_docs_urls
```

Then, the new element:

```
path("docs/", include_docs_urls(title="Fooderator REST API")),
```

What these together do is add a URL that Django will handle by sending the request to the include_docs_urls view, which is provided by DRF. The title specified is just a title to show on the documentation page, which is handy if you have multiple APIs in your project to document.

With all that done, the documentation page can be accessed via the URL http://127.0.0.1:8000/docs. What you get when you go there is what you see in Figure 13-5.

Figure 13-5. *The auto-generated API schema documentation page*

You can see the title we specified earlier on the left there, and I've expanded the recipe section and scrolled down a little bit to show the list and create endpoints. The other endpoints for both recipes and menu items are shown here (but note that the view for making a shopping list is not because remember that function isn't a DRF REST endpoint). As you can see, it shows you the URL to use and what HTTP method to use, and it also shows those docstrings you saw in the code earlier. In the case of creating a recipe, it shows you what the body content has to be too. This is some really nice documentation if you ask me!

What's even better is you can click those Interact buttons next to each endpoint. For example, look at Figure 13-6, where I've done so on the recipe list endpoint.

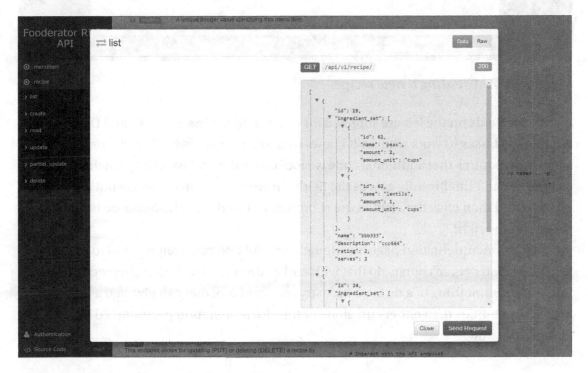

Figure 13-6. *Exercising the list endpoint*

I went ahead and clicked the Send Request button too, which is why you see the response on the right (don't worry about the actual data you see, this is just dummy data I was using while testing the code, so it doesn't really look like a proper recipe, at least none I'd like to eat!)

For the create endpoint, Figure 13-7 shows what it looks like for an endpoint that accepts data.

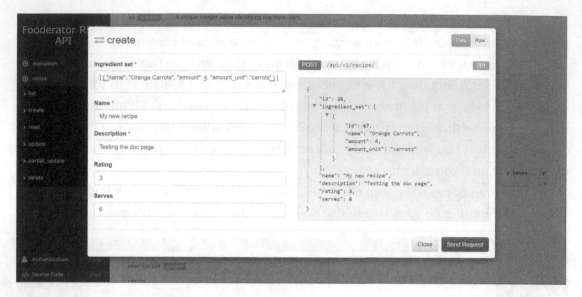

Figure 13-7. *Creating a new recipe*

All the fields on the left are supplied for us automatically since DRF and Django have the model classes to work with, so it knows what data is necessary. For the ingredient set, since that requires that additional code we looked earlier and isn't simply fields in the models, it can't intelligently give us the fields. However, we can manually put the proper JSON in and then click the Send Request button, as I've done. The response is again shown on the right.

So, this documentation page is extremely helpful and can even be used to test our REST API. You can, of course, do that with curl as discussed in earlier chapters as well. But, there's something of a de facto industry standard tool that can give you a bit more robust capabilities than either curl alone or this documentation page, and I'd like to discuss that now.

Use Postman to Test

Postman, which you can get at postman.com, is actually several things, but for our purposes here, the only one that matters is that it's a tool for working with APIs. Not just REST APIs, any API that can be called via HTTP can be used in Postman.

What does this app looks like? Well, on a Windows machine at least, it looks like Figure 13-8.

Figure 13-8. *Your first look at Postman*

Postman is another of those things that an entire book could be written for – there's no way I could cover everything here. But, I can point out some of the most crucial elements.

First, on the left, is your workspace. A workspace can have any number of collections, which are groups containing some number of requests. Conceptually, I tend to think of collections as projects I'm working on. A collection can have requests and folders underneath them, and you can organize things virtually any way you wish; there's no set rules. Here, you can see that I have several collections set up, one for some test requests I was working on to some lambda functions in Amazon Web Services. There's another for a secret hush-hush project of mine named "My App." There's the Postman Echo collection, which is one that should be there right after you install Postman automatically, and it allows you to mess around with an API provided by Postman itself to get familiar with the tool.

And, of course, there's Fooderator itself. Under it, you can see I have two folders, one for the requests associated with recipes and the other folder for those associated with menu items. I also have the request for making a shopping list there, not in a folder, which is a good example that proves you can have any request you like here, not just RESTful ones.

423

On the right, you can see that you can have multiple requests opened at a time, each becoming a tab. Here, I'm on the tab for the recipe list endpoint, and I've called the endpoint by clicking the Send button on the right. The results are shown below. You can view the response itself, as well as the Cookies and Headers on the response via the tabs above the JSON you see. The response itself can be viewed in its raw form, or in a "pretty," which is most typically how you'll want to see JSON.

Above the response, you see an area where you can enter query parameters or enter body content (if you change the HTTP method seen next to the URL to be used to something other than GET). It's also possible to add authorization data, headers, and cookies to the request by clicking through the tabs there below the URL. Each has a suitable entry section for you to enter your data in.

You can right-click the elements in the tree on the left, where you'll have options to create collections, folders, and requests. That's what I did for each of the endpoints in our API. Then, for each, you simply enter the URL, select the right HTTP method, provide query parameters, or body content as necessary, and you're good to go!

That already sounds pretty handy, but Postman can actually do quite a bit more. For example, it's possible to write test scripts in JavaScript and execute them against your API, so you can use Test-Driven Development methodologies when creating your APIs. You can create mock servers even, to simulate what your server-side code will eventually do. That's very handy if you want to work on your client-side code first without thinking too much about the server-side code until later.

And, here's perhaps the best part: all of this is stored in the cloud! You can move from machine to machine, and, so long as you created a Postman account, all your collections and configuration and everything can follow you from machine to machine!

This is really just a high-level introduction to Postman; there's a lot more that it can do for you. As I mentioned at the start, Postman is something of a de facto standard for this sort of tooling, but it's not the only option. Insomnia (`insomnia.rest`) is a similar tool to Postman that, as with Postman, offers a free tier and then several paid tiers if your needs require it. The functionality is similar, though my personal opinion is that Postman is a little bit more polished and robust. But, I've used Insomnia quite a bit over the last few years, and I never felt like it was lacking in any meaningful way.

In any case, these sorts of tools, while very helpful, are optional. There's always good 'ole curl there for you, and of course those DRF-generated documentation pages are pretty slick too. If you're a fan of VS Code – which a lot of people are these days – there are plenty of extensions for working with REST APIs (a quick search in the marketplace for "rest client" will find you the most popular at the time of this writing, and there are more to choose from). The point is there's lots of ways to test and develop your REST APIs; Postman is just one – though a very good one!

Serving Static Content Alongside the API

The next chapter is where we'll deal with the client code, but let's quickly talk about how you can serve static content, because up until now, we've only talked about building a RESTful API.

It turns out that Django is, out of the box, set up to serve static content. All you need to do is add a `static` directory under any of your app directories, under the `client` app directory in our case. Once you do that, you can access those files like so:

`http://127.0.0.1:8000/static/<filename>`

Yes, you've got yourself a little web server just that easy!

At this point, if you've downloaded the code for this book, you should be able to run the server (assuming you've installed Python itself, as well as Django, DRF, and Core API). Before moving on to the next chapter, make sure you can do so and preferably that you can talk to the API with Postman.

Suggested Exercises

I really only have three suggestions for the server side of Fooderator, but they should prove pretty challenging if you take them on and, more importantly, will force you to learn more about Django, Python, and DRF:

- Add the ability to store a number of guests for each menu item, and then calculate the shopping list amounts appropriately. Currently, we know how many people a given recipe serves, and that's great if that's always the exact number of dinner guests you have! It would be better though if you could say "20 people are coming for dinner" for a given menu item, and then the values are calculated appropriately so you buy enough food.

- While SQLite is a nice little database engine (and that's probably not giving it quite enough credit honestly), it's not generally something you'd use in a production environment. So, how about setting up something like a MySQL server and hooking Fooderator up to it? You'll have to do some research about how to configure a Django app to use a stand-alone database, but it absolutely can do that, and for the most part, it should just take some configuration changes; there likely won't be any code to change.

- Remember how there are some endpoints available that we don't actually need? Can you figure out how to configure a Django app to disallow those without breaking anything?

Summary

In this chapter, we built the server side of the Fooderator app, and in the process, you learned quite a bit, starting with a little bit of Python, the Django framework on top of it, how to build a RESTful interface with it plus DRF, and how to test that API with Postman.

In the next chapter, we will, naturally, build the client side of Fooderator, which comes with a batch of new knowledge as well!

CHAPTER 14

Feed Your Face: Fooderator, the Client

Now that we have a server and a REST API ready, willing, and able to service requests from a client, I guess it's about time to build that client, huh? In this chapter, we'll build the Fooderator client, and in the process, you'll learn more about React, including some "newer" ways to do things, along with two new libraries you can use in your projects, all while reinforcing what you've previously learned and creating a fully functional application for managing recipes, menus, and shopping lists.

Before we actually get to tearing into the Fooderator code though, there's a few topics I need to touch on, at least in brief, a few new things we're going to use, just so you aren't going in blind!

A New Component Library to Play With

For this project, we're going to put MUI aside and instead use a different component library: Ant Design. Ant Design (https://ant.design) is another popular choice among React developers because it supplies a huge set of components to choose from, all designed using a consistent and pleasing design language. In fact, the AntD (which is how I'll write it going forward) website's title shows a great deal of humorous self-awareness by calling it "The world's second most popular React UI framework." From a developer's standpoint, I also find its API to be very logical and consistent, which makes working with it a very pleasant experience.

© Frank Zammetti 2022
F. Zammetti, *Modern Full-Stack Development*, https://doi.org/10.1007/978-1-4842-8811-5_14

In Figure 14-1, you can see some of the AntD components available for layout, navigation, and a few general-purpose components.

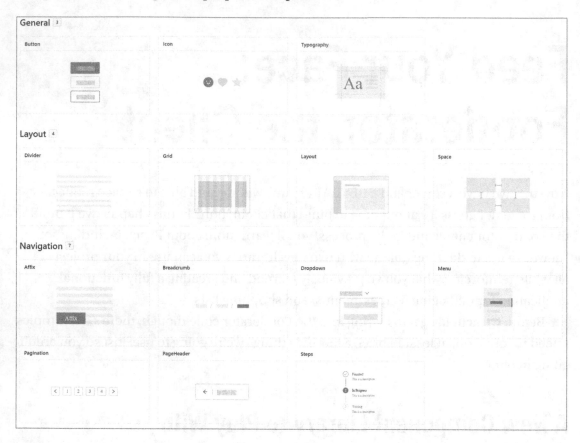

Figure 14-1. *Some of the general and navigation components AntD provides*

AntD also contains a rich set of components for entering data, as shown in Figure 14-2.

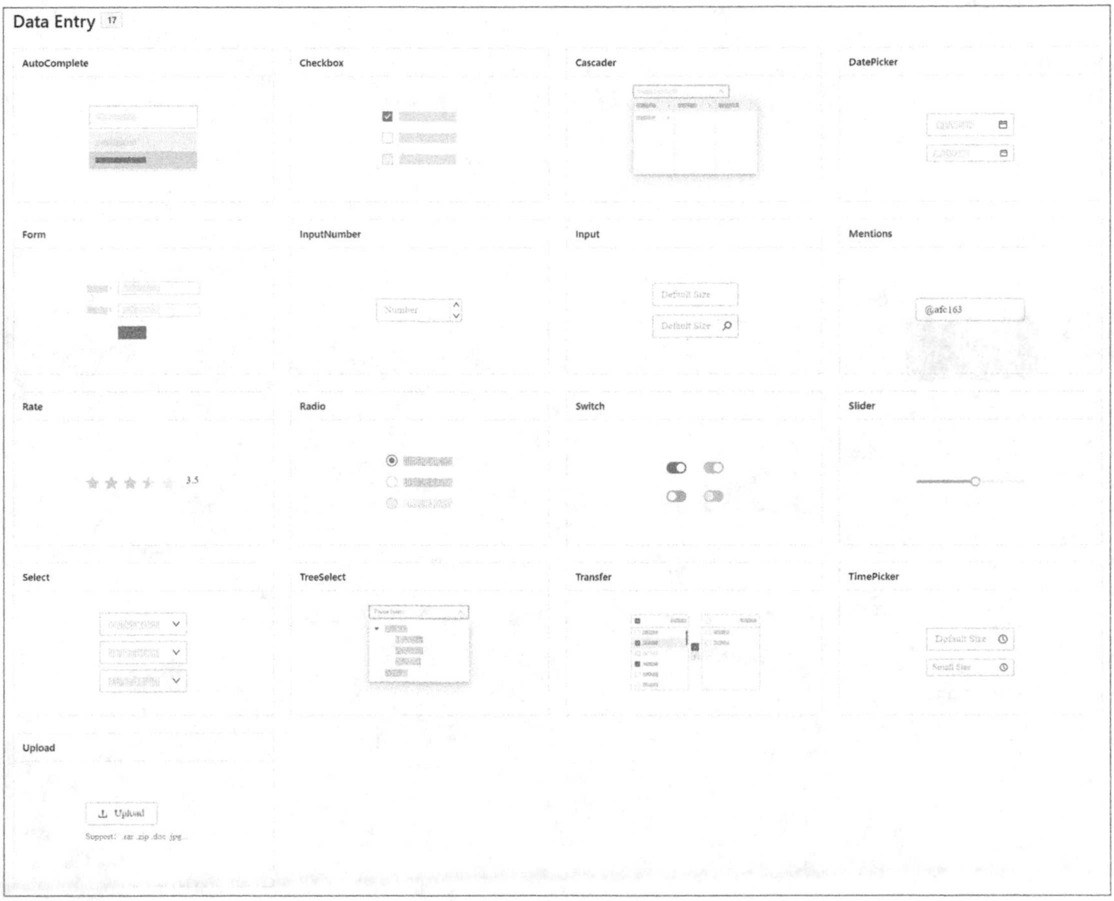

Figure 14-2. *The AntD data entry components*

Of course, what good would data entry components be without components for displaying and visualizing data? AntD has you covered there too, as you can see in Figure 14-3.

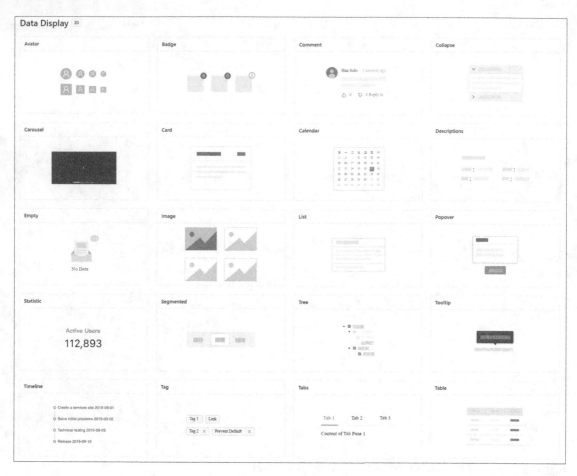

Figure 14-3. *AntD's data display components*

Finally, AntD offers several components for giving feedback to the user in numerous ways, plus a few "miscellaneous" components, which Figure 14-4 shows you.

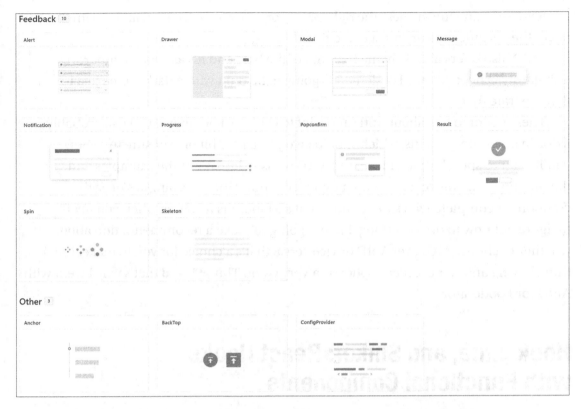

Figure 14-4. *Feedback components and a few miscellaneous "other" components*

AntD is free, though they also offer a paid tier which adds several "pro" components, which are enhanced versions of some of the other components you see here.

One of the things I really like about AntD is how logical and consistent things are. For example, need a button on your page? All you need is

```
import { Button } from "antd";
...later in your component code...
<Button type="text" onClick={handleClick}>Click Me</Button>
```

Couldn't be simpler, right? But, it's also very obvious, which means less time looking up documentation. As another example, what if you need a text field that accepts only numbers in a given range? It's easy:

```
import { InputNumber } from "antd";
...later in your component code...
<InputNumber min={10} max={20} />
```

See? You can almost guess the right props for a given component and the import you need; there's little mystery most of the time.

AntD also offers a dark theme right out of the box, and it's as easy as importing a single stylesheet. In fact, Fooderator is going to be built with a dark theme just to demonstrate that.

There's a lot to like about AntD and a lot to explore. Fooderator will use probably a dozen or so components, which should give you a nice bit of exposure to it. But, you'll want to spend some time on the AntD website looking at the examples and documentation. The documentation especially shows tons of examples of each component complete with source code, so it's a fabulous resource when you need to figure out how to do something. I'm not going to make a recommendation about whether to choose MUI over AntD or vice versa, that's a choice for you to make. But, I think having another excellent option is a Very Good Thing™, and that's why I went with AntD for Fooderator.

Hook, Line, and Sinker: React Hooks with Functional Components

A few chapters back, I spoke very briefly about the concept of functional components. When the first edition of this book was written, functional components were fairly new, so I chose primarily not to use them and went with class-based components instead. Since that time, functional components have come to dominate the React landscape. You can still use class-based components, but most developers are going the functional component route nowadays. However, you'll recall that I mentioned some limitations with functional components, namely, around lifecycle events and state. I also mentioned that the solution to that problem was something called hooks. Well, it's time to get into that a bit more!

Hooks were introduced in React version 16.8, with functional components having been introduced a few versions before that. Functional components have a few benefits over class-based components:

- They avoid some of the difficulty in reusing stateful logic between components (things like "wrapper hell" with render props).

- They make complex components easier to understand by avoiding "lifecycle spaghetti."

- Most developers simply find class-based components harder to read, and they're also a little more difficult for tooling to optimize.

Some of these may be debatable, but ultimately, most people tend to agree, most important the React team does, so functional components grew in popularity very quickly.

Hooks were added because certain things, most importantly state and lifecycle events, can't be done with functional components without them. There simply isn't a way without hooks. But hooks also arguably make code easier to read. Here's the classic example:

```
import React, { Component } from "react";
export default class Counter extends Component {
  constructor(inProps) {
    super(inProps);
    this.state = {
      count : 0
    };
  }
  render() {
    const myState: any = this.state;
    return (
      <div>
        <button
          onClick={() => this.setState({ count : myState.count + 1 })
          }>Bump Count</button>
        <br />
        The button has been pressed { myState.count } times
      </div>
    )
  }
}
```

It certainly isn't too difficult to understand. But, compare it with the functional version:

```
import React, { useState } from "react";
export default () => {
  const [ count, setCount ] = useState(0);
  return (
    <div>
      <button onClick={() => setCount(count + 1)}>Bump Count</button>
      <br />
      The button has been pressed: { count } times.
    </div>
  )
}
```

It's definitely shorter, isn't it? But, the bigger thing is that most people find that easier to read and understand. And, it's made possible by that useState thingy there, which, as it happens, is a hook! If you think it looks like a function, give yourself a point because that's exactly what it is! Hooks are just functions!

The useState Hook

As you just saw used in the functional component example, the useState hook is one of the two most-used hooks React offers and, as the name implies, allows you to add state to your functional components. When you call it, you are returned an array where the first element is a variable you use to access the current value of some state information, and the second argument is a function to use to change that value. The initial value of your state is passed to the useState hook function, and it can be anything you like: a number, a string, or an object with a whole bunch of stuff in it. In this instance, it's just a number. So, the typical way to deal with this returned array is to destructure it into two variables, count and setCount in this case (though you could name them however you wish). You can then use those variables anywhere in your functional code, as you see in the button's onClick handler.

Best of all, you can have as many useState hook calls in a single component as you wish! So, if you had a few dozen state values to deal with, you might decide it's better to organize them into two to three objects. You can then call useState two to three times, one per object, and you can then work with them individually as you see fit since you'll get back different variables and setter functions from each call.

And, really, that's just about all there fundamentally is to the useState hook, and really hooks in general. But, there's one more important hook that React offers that we should talk about before we conclude this section.

The useEffect Hook

In the earlier two projects, you saw how we needed to call the server to get some data when a component mounts. That need doesn't go away when using functional components, but we can't use componentDidMount from a functional component since it's a lifecycle event used in a class-based component paradigm. For these needs when using functional components, React now offers the useEffect hook.

The React developers consider such things to be "side effects," or just "effects" for short, because they can affect other components and can't be done during rendering with functional components. So, they came up with useEffect, which tells React to execute some code – your effect function – after flushing changes to the DOM (effectively that means when the component is mounted or when it is re-rendered).

As with useState, you can have multiple useEffect functions in your code, and each of them will execute after the initial component rendering and after any and all re-renders. This effectively allows you to hook into the React component lifecycle without using the old lifecycle event handlers like componentDidMount.

When we see useEffect used in the Fooderator code, I'll talk about a few more things related to it, but these are the basics of it that you need to know.

Other Hooks

As I mentioned at the start, one of the benefits of using hooks is the ability to share logic more easily. Remember, they're just functions after all, and you absolutely can write your own. You can then use your custom hooks in your components, thereby sharing that logic between them. It's not that you couldn't do any of this before, of course, but hooks make it a little more elegant.

It should be noted that hooks also don't block the browser from updating the screen, so React apps written exclusively with hooks are generally more performant and responsive than those that aren't. It should also be noted that, like most things in React, hook functions are scheduled, which means they may not *always* execute when you think they will. That *usually* won't matter, things will most of the time work as you expect, but every so often, this can bite you, so it's a good thing to keep in mind. This comes up much more with `useEffect` than most others though, if it's going to at all.

Third-party libraries also tend to add hooks that your app can use, and a fitting example of that is another new library we're going to use in Fooderator: Hookstate.

The (New) State of Things: Hookstate

In the previous two applications, the way state was handled was… a little weird… but for a reason.

As you'll recall, we had the `state.ts` file in each, with a `createState()` function. That function returned an object that contained all our state, `plus` functions to mutate it. This is one way to manage *global* state, which is what we needed: state that is shared across multiple components.

The alternative that new React developers tend to find first is to put their state in a component that is the parent of all other components and then pass that state down through the component tree as a prop. This is called *prop drilling*, and in smaller apps, it can work just fine. But, before long, it can become a huge mess. If a component ten components down in the component tree needs the state, but the eight between it and the top-level parent component that has the state don't, then those eight still need to pass the state prop down. As you can imagine, that can get messy in a large app.

That's why I did state the way I did in those two apps: it avoids prop drilling and gives us a centralized object where all our state is. But, while that avoids the prop drilling issue, so is better in that regard, it's a little bit odd to do state that way yourself. That's usually where third-party libraries come into the picture, since React doesn't really have a global state mechanism out of the box (there is something called `context` now, which can be used that way, but it's usually not the best approach, and as a result, I'm not covering it in this book). You'll hear the name Redux a lot, and for a long time, it was perhaps the most popular library available for state management in React. Several others exist as well, but the one I'm going to introduce here is one called Hookstate.

I actually feel like the way the Hookstate website (hookstate.js.org) describes it sums it up beautifully in one sentence:

> *The most straightforward, extensible, and incredibly fast state management that is based on React state hook.*

Or, to put it another way: it's a supercharged version of React's own `useState` hook.

As the name implies, it's completely hook-based. However, it can still actually be used with class-based components – or even in non-React code! – but primarily it's intended for functional React components. It can provide component-level state, as well as global-level state shared across multiple components. To create a global state, all you need to do is

```
import { createState } from "@hookstate/core";
const gs = createState(0);
export gs as globalState;
```

Put that code outside a component, like at the top of your entry point TypeScript file, and you've now got a state you can use in any component you wish (well, you'll also have to import `globalState` into any source file you need it in, of course), or even in code that isn't inside a component, functional or otherwise. As with React's own useState hook, you can create a Hookstate state with any primitive value or object you like, and you can have multiple state objects.

Inside your functional components, you can gain access to the state like so:

```
const state = useState(globalState);
```

That's it! From then on in your component code, you simply reference `state` and you're off to the races!

To mutate state, Hookstate offers several functions, but the simplest is just this:

```
state.set(1);
```

In the case of a primitive number type like this, that's all you need to do. It can get slightly more complex if you have nested values like in objects, but not much more, and you'll see that in Fooderator code later.

If you just need local state, you can simply call `useState()` in your component, passing it the initial value. And, you can have global state and local state in a single component, no problem. You can even use React's native `useState` hook to have React-provided local state plus Hookstate local state (and plus Hookstate global state if you want) all in one component. I'd suggest it's probably best to choose one or the other for local state, but the point is you *can* mix and match as you see fit.

Note that if you try to import useState from both React and Hookstate in the same source file, you'll need to alias one of them, so they don't conflict.

As I said, you'll see a little more of Hookstate when we get into the Fooderator code, but there's really not a whole lot more to see, it's pretty much that simple! And, before we finally get to the Fooderator code, there's one more bit of foundation laying I need to do, and that's about something called React Router.

Charting a Course with React Router

When you write an SPA, it is, obviously, a single page. It's a page whose content changes as things happen, but it's still a single page. That's a great paradigm for many use cases, but not always. Sometimes, you want something approaching a more traditional page-based website. There are several ways you could do this, but one popular option is by using a router, and React Router is one such router.

A router in general is a way to navigate between pages, where "pages" in this context means top-level React components. As you'll recall, every React app has a top-level component that is the parent to all others. Generally, everything that happens in a React app, and certainly when it's an SPA, happens within that parent component.

But what happens when, as you design your app, you realize that there really are several different pages, or views, as you might call them? For example, think of a message forum. There's the list of messages, then there's the message view where you can perhaps see all the replies to the message, and then there's probably an administrative view where you can delete messages and such. While they don't *have* to be, it probably makes sense to make those three separate pages, which means three separate top-level React components and component trees underneath them. But, you only ever render a single component to your page when a React app starts, so how do you do that?

A router can take care of that for you, and React Router is one of the most popular implementations of that idea.

Once you have the router setup, you can, just like in a plain old web app, create links. When clicked, the browser's address is changed to a new route, where a route corresponds to some React component. That component then re-renders the entire page as if it was loading for the first time.

The benefit to this is that browser history can be maintained, and you can use all the same facilities as in a normal app, things like query string parameters. As far as your browser is concerned, you're navigating between individual HTML pages, but at the code level, it's still all React components. You can also move between routes programmatically, as you'll see in Fooderator.

The details of how you work with React Router I think will make a lot more sense in context, so as we look at the Fooderator code, I'll get into those details. And, we're almost at the point of looking at that code, but, first, it would probably help to have some idea what we're building, at least in part, right? Here we go!

Your First Look at Fooderator

Fooderator is divided into four basic screens: the main menu, the recipe list (and the dialog for editing or adding a recipe), the menu list, and the shopping list screen. In Figure 14-5, you have your first glimpse of Fooderator, namely, the main menu.

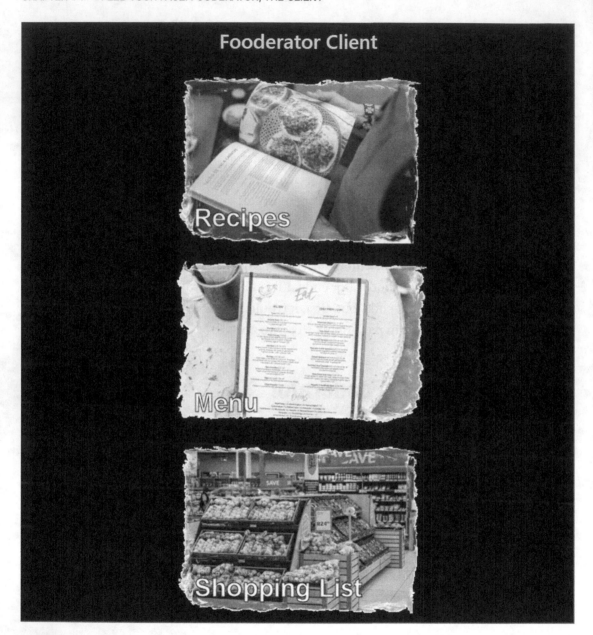

Figure 14-5. *The Fooderator main menu*

Each of the three images, when clicked, brings you to one of those other screens. For example, in Figure 14-6, you can see the recipe list screen.

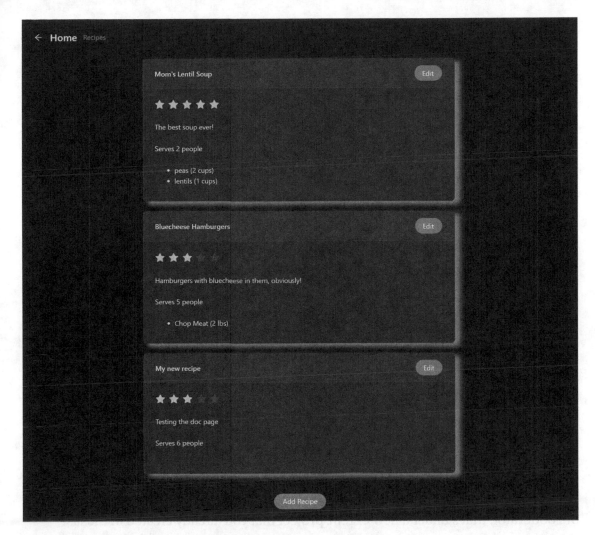

Figure 14-6. *The recipe list screen*

A couple of things to notice here. First, in the upper left, you have an arrow, which will bring you back to the main menu when clicked (and that destination is called out). Next to that is the name of the screen you're currently on. This paradigm is true on the other screens too.

Below that is a list of recipes, and I've styled things to kinda/sorta/maybe look like a recipe on an index card. You can start to see how the client relates to the server-side code here as you see the data presented on each card. A recipe can be edited (updated), and a new recipe added with the button on the bottom, and both lead to the same dialog, just empty in the case of adding a new recipe. I'll show you that dialog when we get to the point of discussing its code. Being a list, you can scroll to see more recipes, of course. Finally, as previously mentioned, this app uses a dark theme, just to be different!

441

The menu screen doesn't look too different from this given it's just another list of data elements. The shopping list screen is also similar, though each of those screens uses different components from AntD, so they do look a little different. Like with the recipe edit dialog, you'll see those screens when we get to their code a few sections from now.

Before that, let's talk about some basic setup and the overall structure of the Fooderator app.

At this point, I will assume that you've downloaded the code for this book. Once you do that, you'll need to go into the `fooderator/client/src` directory and execute the command `npm install` to get all your dependencies pulled down from the cloud and then execute the command `npm run build-prod` to build the code bundle and `index.html` file that will be talked about later (because it won't exist before you run these commands). Once that's done, start the server as described in the previous chapter, and then make sure Fooderator is accessible at `http://127.0.0.1/static/index.html`.

Setting Up the Basics

As you know from the previous chapter, the underlying structure of the project is based around Django. But, how does the client fit into that structure? Near the end of the last chapter, I mentioned that Django is set up by default to serve static content. All we need to do is add a `static` directory to an app under our project, and in the case of Fooderator, that's under a new `client` project that you already created in the last chapter. But, how does code get into that `static` directory in the first place? That's the part we have to do now because, being a React app, we know we need (or at least *want*) Webpack and so there will be a build step involved since we're writing our app in TypeScript. None of that changes because we're now serving our code with Django.

Client App Directory Structure

So, what we'll do is add another directory under the client directory named `src`. This will be the source code for our client and will also include the `package.json` file we know we need and the `node_modules` directory that will be present when dependencies are installed, as well as the `tsconfig.json` file for TypeScript configuration and `webpack.config.js` for

Webpack configuration. In other words, this `src` directory is not much different than from the previous two apps. The main difference is that when we build our code, the results will be put in the `fooderator/client/static` directory so that Django can serve our client to a browser. This is all created with a typical `npm init` command execution (because remember, as we build the client, the fact that it's under a Django app doesn't really enter into it, it's just a React app like we've built before).

Of course, we still need a place for the actual source code, and that place is going to be another directory named `src` inside the `src` directory. Slightly confusing, I know, but I think when you see Figure 14-7, which lays out the entire directory structure, it'll make more sense. Underneath that inner `src` directory is our `index.html` file where it all begins, and then we have a `code` directory, which is where all our actual application code is.

Figure 14-7. *The directory structure of the client project*

Inside that code directory, you find the main.tsx file, which is the main entry point and supplies the top-level component that is parent to all others, and the globalState.ts file that contains the global state for the app. We will, of course, look at these in turn. Below that is a components directory where all our individual components live, further broken down into screens corresponding to the three main menu images (and App.tsx, which is the main menu itself, since that's a screen too).

package.json

After initializing the project, it's time to add the scripts we'll need to package.json and of course any dependencies we need. Since the contents here are so similar to the past two projects, I'm just going to show the differences (and not counting the obvious things like the name and description attributes):

```
"scripts": {
  "dev": "webpack watch --mode development ",
  "build-prod": "webpack --mode production"
},
...
  "dependencies": {
    "@hookstate/core": "4.0.0-rc11",
    "antd": "4.21.4",
    "react-router-dom": "6.3.0"
  }
}
```

As far as dependencies go, Hookstate, AntD, and React Router are the new ones that we need; everything else is the same.

As for the scripts, there's two we need. The first, dev, is for doing development. During development, you'll need to start the Django project (manage.py runserver) and also execute the dev script here, which will take care of building the client code and putting it in /static and then monitoring for changes. In this way, you can work on the code and get live feedback as you do (note that the page won't automatically refresh on changes though). For a production build, we have a separate build-prod script so that when we're all set and development is done, we can produce properly minified and optimized client code.

Some Minor Webpack Changes

The webpack.config.js file for this project is almost the same as the previous two chapters as well. There's really just one important change:

```
output: {
  path : path.resolve("../", "static"),
  clean : false
}
```

That's to ensure that the output of a build goes into that static directory, which is one level up from the outer src directory, hence the ../ used. It's also important to set clean to false so that Webpack won't clear out the static folder on each build. That's because the images for the main menu are in there, and they would be deleted if we didn't do this, and our menu wouldn't work! An alternative approach would be to place those images in the src/src directory, probably in an img directory, and then add a step to have Webpack copy them in after the code is built. I decided to keep things simple though, hence this setting.

Into the Breach: index.html and main.tsx

Let's now finally start to explore the actual code of Fooderator, starting with two small files that form the foundation of the whole thing.

I've removed all log statements and comments from all code in this project and condensed it a bit to keep things as small as possible on these pages, but there are no substantive changes from what you'll get from the GitHub repo. One thing to note though: at the end of each source file is a console.log() statement. This is something I like to do because I can then quickly, at a glance in browser dev tools, see that each file loaded. It's a habit you may want to get into because it can sometimes save a lot of head-scratching if something doesn't work right.

---

index.html

As you know, you need some sort of main HTML page to start everything, and `index.html` is that page. But, just to save a little space, I'm not going to show it to you because you'll find that it's identical – save for the title – to the same file in the previous two projects. So, let's get on to more interesting things, shall we?

main.tsx

The main.tsx file is the main entry point of our app code, and it renders the top-level component. As always, we have some imports first:

```
import "normalize.css";
import "antd/dist/antd.dark.css";
import React from "react";
import { createRoot, Root } from "react-dom/client";
import { BrowserRouter, Routes, Route } from "react-router-dom";
import App from "./components/App";
import Menu from "./components/menu/Menu";
import Recipes from "./components/recipes/Recipes";
import ShoppingList from "./components/shoppingList/ShoppingList";
```

Normalize is again used as a CSS reset to ensure consistency across browsers. Next, the AntD stylesheet is imported, and in this case, the dark theme is used. After that, the basic React imports are done and then some imports related to React Router that we'll skip over for just a moment. Finally, of course, we need our own application code, or we won't get very far, so the four components that correspond to the three screens that the main menu images lead to – as well as the main menu itself in the App component – are imported.

Next, we create our root element as you've seen in the past:

```
const baseComponent: Root = createRoot(document.getElementById(
"mainContainer"));
```

Now, we can render the base component, and this is where React Router starts to come into the picture.

```
baseComponent.render(
  <BrowserRouter>
    <Routes>
      <Route path="/static/index.html" element={<App />} />
      <Route path="/static/index.html/recipes" element={<Recipes />} />
      <Route path="/static/index.html/menu" element={<Menu />} />
      <Route path="/static/index.html/shoppingList"
      element={<ShoppingList />} />
    </Routes>
  </BrowserRouter>
);
```

It begins with that `BrowserRouter` component. Everything else has to be a child of that; otherwise, React Router won't be able to do its job. Inside of it, we need to define the various routes through our app, which in the case of Fooderator means defining the four main screens. This all goes inside a `Routes` component, and then each route is its own `Route` component. Each of those requires that we tell it the path to the component that should be rendered for the route.

It probably makes sense to you why the first route, which is our main menu, uses the path it does. At least, the `/static/` part I think makes sense: that's where all our code is when built, after all. The `index.html` part might seem a little weird though. But, if you think about it, that really is the first URL that our application would use; that's the entry point to the app from the browser's perspective. And remember, React Router is working with the native browser URL and history mechanism, so we have to think about it from that perspective.

But, what about the other three? They seem weird - a path with `index.html` in it - doesn't it? Well, not really. If you think about the path of any resource on the Web accessed with HTTP, the path will contain all the intermediary stops between the domain and the target resource. In this case, the path is sort of artificial in that React Router is doing the actual navigation for the browser, in a sense. Because of that, since the main entry point is `index.html`, that effectively becomes the base location for any URL – you can think of it like the domain name in a website URL. Therefore, any resource path has to be relative to that starting point, hence why going to the Recipe screen starts in `static`, then goes *through* `index.html`, so to speak, and eventually lands on `recipes` to form the complete path.

Finally, the element prop of the Route components is literally the React component to render when this route is navigated to.

With those routes defined, we can begin to build the main menu and use them. But, before we get to that, let's see about that global state stuff since much depends on it!

The State of Things: globalState.ts

The globalState.ts file, naturally enough, is where our global state, courtesy of Hookstate, is built. This file will be imported anywhere else where a global state is needed. It begins with the import of Hookstate itself:

```
import { createState } from "@hookstate/core";
```

The createState() function is all we need from Hookstate, but before we can use it, given that we're using TypeScript here, we have some interfaces to create. The first of these is to represent a recipe:

```
export interface IRecipe {
  id?: number,
  name: string,
  description: string,
  rating: number,
  serves: number,
  ingredient_set: Array<IIngredient>
}
```

You should recognize this pretty quickly as matching up to the Recipe model class built in the last chapter. The only real consideration is that the id field has to be optional because when creating a recipe, we won't have that value on the client side until the recipe is saved on the server and we get it back with the generated id included.

Next comes the interface for an ingredient, which you'll note was referenced in the IRecipe interface already (order doesn't matter here):

```
export interface IIngredient {
  id?: number,
  name: string,
  amount: number,
```

```
  amount_unit: string,
  recipe_id?: number
}
```

Once again, it matches the Ingredient model class, and the id field again must be optional. In addition, the recipe_id field must also be optional for the same basic reason. We want to let the server always generate IDs during object creation, in both cases. The IDs are in a sense meant for the server side; they only really "bleed through" to the client code when doing updates or deletes since we have to tell the server code what ID to delete.

Next up is the rather simple interface for menu items:

```
export interface IMenuItem {
  id?: number,
  recipe: number
}
```

Remember that there's no information carried by a menu item except what recipe it references (and its own id, of course), so those are the only fields we need.

The final interface describes an object that is our global state itself:

```
export interface IGlobalState {
  initialLoadComplete: boolean,
  recipes: Array<IRecipe>,
  menuItems: Array<IMenuItem>
}
```

Now you can see why we had to define all those others: we need it here! The initialLoadComplete property will be used to indicate when we've loaded all the data from the server that is needed by the client at startup (more on this shortly). The recipes and menuItems are arrays of objects of type IRecipe and IMenuItem, respectively. Note that we don't store anything related to the shopping list because that's generated on the fly, so we don't need to. But, we do want to store all the recipes and menu items when the client starts up so that we don't have to constantly retrieve this data as the user does things; we just need to apply the necessary changes when needed (on both the client side and server side).

Finally, we're in a position now to create the actual global state:

```
const gs = createState({
  initialLoadComplete: false as boolean,
  recipes: [ ] as Array<IRecipe>,
  menuItems: [ ] as Array<IMenuItem>
} as IGlobalState);
export default gs;
```

As mentioned previously, Hookstate makes this easy: just a call to
createState(), passing it the initial state object. We start with empty arrays, and the
initialLoadComplete property obviously set to false since, indeed, we haven't loaded
any initial data yet! The gs variable is also exported as default so that we can import this
state anywhere we need, quick and easy.

There's one more bit of code in this source file, something tangentially related to
state, but which was needed in several places, so it made sense to add it here:

```
export const getIndexOfRecipeByID = (
  inID: number, inWhichArray: string): number => {
  if (inWhichArray === "recipes") {
    return gs.recipes.get().map(function(inItem) { return inItem.id;
    }).indexOf(inID);
  } else {
    return gs.menuItems.get().map(function(inItem) { return inItem.recipe;
    }).indexOf(inID);
  }
}
```

In several places in the code that you'll see later, there is a need to find a recipe or a
menu item in the arrays in global state, based on its ID. The problem is that being arrays,
we can't do a simple lookup, like we could if this was an object where the properties were
recipe or menu item IDs (and if we were to do that, most of the other code that needs
arrays of objects would be much more convoluted). So, this function takes in the ID to
search for, as well as which array to search, either "recipes" or "menuItems," which are
strings that you'll note matches the property names in the global state object.

With that, we can then get the recipe or menuItems array as appropriate and note
here that the get() method must be used, which is something Hookstate provides.
Because Hookstate monitors the attributes of your state object, it has to wrap them all

in some code of its own. So, if we just accessed attributes directly in the state object, we wouldn't get the real values. Calling get() on the attributes gets us the underlying values, which is what we want.

Once we do that, we have the proper array to search, and then the map() method is used. For each element in the array, its ID is returned as part of a new array (or, in the case of menu items, the associated recipe's ID is returned because the use case is finding the recipe object associated with a given menu item, not the menu item itself, since we'd already obviously have that). In other words, we now have an array of IDs. At that point, we can just return the value of a call to indexOf(), which will either be -1 if the recipe or menu item isn't found (which shouldn't ever happen) or the index in the array where the ID is. Since the IDs in the array are in the same order as the recipe or menu item array we're searching, that effectively also gives us the index of the object we want in those arrays.

When you see these in use, I think you'll find it's quite clear what's going on, but you may need to come back here and look at that code again when you have the context around it to be sure you understand what it's doing and why.

The Home Screen: App.tsx

Okay, so we have routes defined and we have some global state; let's put it to use! The first screen the user sees in Fooderator is the main menu, and that's housed in the App.tsx source file. As always, we have some imports at the top:

```
import React, { ReactElement, useEffect, useState } from "react";
import { Spin } from "antd";
import { Link } from "react-router-dom";
import { useHookstate } from "@hookstate/core";
import axios from "axios";
import globalState from "../globalState";
```

The typical React imports are there, as well as two hooks we'll need and that we'll see shortly. We then need a single component from AntD, the Spin component. This is used to show a spinning graphic that blocks the screen when we make calls to the server (a.k.a., a "spinner"), which we'll need to do here in order to load our list of recipes and menu items from the server. Then, the useHookstate hook is imported, which is how we'll make use of our global state. Axios, of course, you're already familiar with, and finally the globalState itself has to be imported so we can use it.

The Component Definition

After that, we begin a typical functional React component:

```
export default (): ReactElement => {
```

Since it's the only thing we need to export, we can do it inline like that.

Then, the first thing in the component is

```
const gs = useHookstate(globalState);
```

This gives us a gs variable that is a reference to our global state, managed by Hookstate, via the call to the useHookstate hook function. You'll see this used later.

In addition to the global state, we also have some local state using React itself:

```
const [ showSpinner, setShowSpinner ] = useState(false as boolean);
```

This will be used to determine when to show the AntD spinner.

useEffect Hook

Next up, we have a useEffect hook where we load the data from the server:

```
useEffect((): void => {
  if (gs.initialLoadComplete.get() === false) {
    setShowSpinner(true);
    (async () => {
      const responseRecipes: any = await axios.get("/api/v1/recipe/");
      const responseMenuItems: any = await axios.get("/api/v1/menuitem/");
      gs.recipes.merge([...responseRecipes.data]);
      gs.menuItems.merge([...responseMenuItems.data]);
      setShowSpinner(false);
      gs.initialLoadComplete.set(true);
    })();
  }
}, []);
```

You have to remember that a `useEffect` hook function can and will execute multiple times, so you have to deal with that somehow. See that empty array as the second argument to `useEffect()`? That's how you normally deal with it. That second argument is a list of dependencies. If any of them change, then the `useEffect` function will fire again, otherwise it won't. By passing an empty array, we're effectively telling React to only run our function once regardless of what changes since we're not giving it any dependencies to monitor, and this is a very common paradigm that makes `useEffect` work pretty much like `componentDidMount` does. As long as the component isn't completely destroyed, we can be sure our `useEffect` function only executes once.

The problem we have here though is that when we move between the screens in the app, this component will be re-created entirely, which means even with that empty array argument, the function can execute more than once. That's a problem because this function is all about loading data from the server, and we really don't want to do that more than once (for both efficiency reasons and because, as the code is written, you'd get doubles of all recipes and menu items). So, I've introduced the `initialLoadComplete` attribute in the global state. When `false`, we know we haven't loaded data from the server yet, so we can go ahead and do it; otherwise, the code does nothing. In this way, the `useEffect` function can execute all it wants, but we'll only ever load the data from the server once.

Now, assuming we *do* need to load the data from the server, that's where we get into the rest of the code. First, we mutate the local state by calling `setShowSpinner()` and passing it `true`. You'll see how that's used next, but I'm sure you can guess! After that, an IIFE is used, and that's because I wanted to use `await` for the server call (since I believe that syntax is just much cleaner than using Promise-based syntax), which must be inside an `async` function. But, we don't have an `async` function (and making a `useEffect` hook function `async`, while it works, isn't a good practice since it can impact render performance), but by using an IIFE, I can make *that* function `async` and then use `await` inside it. And, inside that function, two Axios calls are made, one to get recipes and one to get menu items. The response from each – an array – is merged into the arrays in global state using the `merge()` functions provided by Hookstate. This is one of several ways you can mutate arrays in a state object, and in this case, I think it's the simplest, and it's also why we have to make sure not to load data from the server twice: it would continually merge the recipes and menu items into the array and create duplicates. Finally, the spinner is hidden, and the flag is set in global state to ensure none of this happens again.

After that, it's time to return the actual React component:

```
return (
  <div style={{
    textAlign: "center", position: "relative", top: "50%", transform:
    "translateY(-50%)" }}>
    <Spin size="large" spinning={showSpinner}>
      <h1>Fooderator Client</h1>
      <div style={{ padding: "10px" }}>
        <Link to="recipes"><img src="/static/recipes.png" alt="Recipes" />
        </Link>
      </div>
      <div style={{ padding: "10px" }}>
        <Link to="menu"><img src="/static/menu.png" alt="Menu" /></Link>
      </div>
      <div style={{ padding: "10px" }}>
        <Link to="shoppingList"><img src="/static/shopping_list.png"
          alt="Shopping List" /></Link>
      </div>
    </Spin>
  </div>
);
```

The component itself is nothing too complex. The outer div provides us an element
that we can style to get the centering we want. The text-align setting takes care of
horizontally centering everything easily enough, but centering vertically requires the
last three attributes. Setting position to relative allows us to set the top attribute to
push all the content down to halfway on the page. Finally, the transform attribute then
in effect "counters" that by shifting it back up by half. The net effect is that everything is
centered vertically as well as horizontally in the viewport.

Next, we have the AntD Spin component, and as you can see, the spinning prop
is set to the value of our local state showSpinner variable. In this way, we can hide and
show the component via the call to setShowSpinner() as needed. Because we want the
screen to be blocked while the spinner is showing, we have to wrap everything else in it.

And, that "everything else" is simply an h1 element to show the title and then three divs with Link components inside of them, one for each image. The divs have some padding around them so the images don't bunch up, and then those Link components – provided by React Router – wrap a standard img tag, each referencing one of the images in the static directory. That makes them clickable, and because React Router knows what it's doing, all we need to tell it is which route a Link leads to – which component, from those we imported earlier – via the to prop.

Now that we have a main menu screen, let's see the first of the screens they lead to. However, I'm going to not go in order, so instead of looking at the Recipe screen first, we'll instead go to the Menu screen first.

The Menu Screen (Menu.tsx)

The menu screen is where the user sees the list of recipes they've added to the menu and can add and remove existing ones. Figure 14-8 shows this screen, and in it, I've clicked the Add Recipe button to show the list of recipes that can be added.

Figure 14-8. The menu screen, preparing to add a recipe

As you can see, each recipe has a Remove button next to it, and the Add Recipe button at the bottom shows a popup list of all the recipes that exist.

We begin with imports:

```
import React, { ReactElement, useState } from "react";
import { NavigateFunction, useNavigate } from "react-router-dom";
import { none, useHookstate } from "@hookstate/core";
import axios from "axios";
import { Button, Layout, PageHeader, List, Dropdown, Menu, notification,
MenuProps,
  Spin } from "antd";
const { Footer, Content } = Layout;
import globalState, { IMenuItem, IRecipe, getIndexOfRecipeByID }
  from "../../globalState";
```

You know all about the React imports, and here we need to specifically import some things from React Router. You'll see why shortly. Then, we have our Hookstate import, and this time there's something new: that none thing! This is something else you'll see used shortly, don't worry. Axios is brought in next, followed by a batch of AntD components. It makes more sense to talk about them as they are encountered, so let's skip to the next line, which is also AntD related. In some cases, you'll need to destructure something imported to get "subcomponents" out of it, so to speak. Such is the case with the Layout component. Under it are two other components, Footer and Content, and since we're going to need to reference them directly, this sort of destructuring must be done. This is fairly common when working with AntD. Finally, globalState is imported, and now we're also going to need two of our interfaces and that getIndexOfRecipeByID() function you saw earlier to make this screen work.

The Component Definition

After that, we start our component:

```
export default (): ReactElement => {

  const navigate: NavigateFunction = useNavigate();
```

The trick here is that as you saw in Figure 14-8, we want to have a header where we have a back arrow to get back to the main menu screen and to show the title of the current screen. To make that navigation work, we can't use the React Router's Link component because of how AntD requires us to do things, but what we *can* do is programmatically do the equivalent of that component. So, as you'll see later, when that arrow is clicked, we'll execute some code, and that code will use this navigate function that is using the React Router useNavigate() hook to get.

Next, we get a reference to global state:

```
const gs = useHookstate(globalState);
```

And again, we have local state for the spinner, since this screen will need to make a call to the server too:

```
const [ showSpinner, setShowSpinner ] = useState(false as boolean);
```

Now, normally, I try to explore the code in the order it appears in the source files, but in this case, I'm going to jump to the component definition first because I think it'll help you understand the flow a little better. But, note that there *are* a couple of functions before this, for handling various events, and we'll look at them after this.

```
return (
  <Spin size="large" spinning={showSpinner}>
    <Layout style={{ height: "100vh" }}>
```

We open with a spinner, as you've seen before, followed by a Layout component. This component allows you to define the overall layout of an entire page, typically providing things like a header and a footer. Most importantly for us, it supports a header area and a navigation arrow, plus some titling, all of which is embedded in a PageHeader component under the Layout component:

```
<PageHeader title="Home" subTitle="Menu"
  onBack={ (): void => { navigate("/static/index.html", { replace: true }
  ); } }></PageHeader>
```

As you can see, the title and subTitle props allow us to show the text we want. The navigation arrow is created automatically, but this is where that navigate function we got from the React Router useNavigate hook earlier come into the picture. By default, clicking the arrow does nothing; we need to have an onBack event handler to implement its functionality. In this case, we can call that navigate() function, giving it a path to the component (page) to navigate to. The URL passed to it should look pretty familiar since it matches up with the base HTML page to load for the app. The additional options argument after, and the replace: true setting, tells the React Router to completely replace the entire contents of the page, which we need it to in order to avoid everything breaking!

After that, we have another child of the Layout element, Content, which is where the main content of the page goes (in between any header or footer we might have):

```
<Content style={{
  color: "#ffffff", overflow: "auto", display: "flex", flexDirection:
  "column",
  justifyContent: "normal", alignItems: "center" }}>
  <List itemLayout="horizontal" dataSource={gs.menuItems.get()} style={{
  width: 640 }}
    renderItem={(inMenuItem, inIndex) => (
      <List.Item key={inMenuItem.id}
        actions={[<Button type="primary" shape="round"
          onClick={ (): void => { handleRemove(inMenuItem.id,
          inIndex); } }>
            Remove
          </Button>]}>
        <List.Item.Meta description={getRecipeForItem(inMenuItem.recipe).
        description}
          title={
            <Button type="text" style={{ paddingLeft: 0 }}>
              {getRecipeForItem(inMenuItem.recipe).name}
            </Button>
          } />
      </List.Item>
    )}/>
</Content>
```

The first thing done is to style this content so that it scrolls, and so everything is horizontally centered, and text is white.

After that, a List component is used, and just like with MUI, this is a list of items where each item is the result of rendering some component for an element in an array. In the case of an AntD list, that array is given through the dataSource prop, and here it's the MenuItems array in our global state object, and again we have to call get() on it so we can work with the actual array. You'll notice that we don't need to use map() or anything like that here to iterate the array as we do in other places, and that's because AntD is in effect doing it for us behind the scenes.

All we have to do in this case is provide a `renderItem` prop, and the value of it is some React component that will be rendered for each element in the array. For each, a `List.Item` component is rendered, where the key is the ID of the menu item. The `actions` prop provides a way for us to have buttons on the right of the item, the Remove button in this case. An AntD `Button` component, like its MUI cousin, offers many assorted styles and variations. Here, I want a round button with the "primary" color, which by default is blue. The `onClick` handler calls a `handleRemove()` function, which is one of those event handler functions you saw earlier. It passes that function both the ID of the menu item as well as its index in the `MenuItems` array, both of which we'll need, as you'll see soon.

In addition to the `List.Item` component, the `List.Item.Meta` component is supplied. This gives AntD some information to display, including the name of the recipe and its description. I want the name to be clickable, so it's surrounded by a `Button` component. And, since at this point we don't actually have the recipe's name or description, but we do have its ID, we need to use the `getIndexOfRecipeByID()` function, passing it the ID of the recipe, to get that information for both (you'll see this function soon; it's one of the functions I skipped over earlier).

Finally, we need to have a footer on the page where the Add Recipe button will go:

```
<Footer style={{ display: "flex", flexDirection: "column", alignItems:
"center" }}>
  <Dropdown placement="top" trigger={["click"]}
  arrow={{pointAtCenter: true}}
    overlay={
      <Menu onClick={handleAdd}
        items={gs.recipes.get().map(inRecipe => {
          return ({ key: inRecipe.id, label: inRecipe.name });
        })}/>
    }>
    <Button type="primary" shape="round">Add Recipe</Button>
  </Dropdown>
</Footer>
```

AntD knows how to build our page when we give it a `PageHeader`, `Content`, and `Footer` component, which is nice, and it of course knows to put the `Footer` at the bottom like we want. The styling done is simply to center the button. But, it's not just a `Button`, as you can see, there's a `Dropdown` component too. This is similar conceptually to a basic HTML select element, but it has much more flexibility. Here, I'm telling it to place the Dropdown above the triggering element (placement="top"), and I'm telling it to show the Dropdown on a client event of the child component it wraps (trigger={["click"]} – and note it's an array, so you can have multiple triggers if you wish) and to make the arrow point at the center of the triggering component (arrow={{pointAtCenter: true}}). That's much more than a simple select, right?

The overlay prop then defines the items to show in the list. This is actually another component, Menu, which can be used generically for creating little popup menus. You give it a function to call onClick and then the list of items to show. In this case, it's an array built from taking the recipes array in global state and returning an object for each that has the recipe's id as key and its name as label. When an item in the list is clicked, the handleAdd() event handler function will be called.

Finally, as a child of the Dropdown, we have a Button, and notice that there's no onClick prop for it. That's because being a child of the Dropdown, which AntD knows how to build, takes care of that.

Event Handler Functions

That completes the component itself. Now, we can go back and look at the event handler functions that I skipped over earlier, since now you've seen where they're called from. Let's start with handleAdd():

```
const handleAdd: MenuProps["onClick"] = ({ key }) => {
  if (typeof gs.menuItems.get().find(
    inRecipe => inRecipe.id === parseInt(key)
  ) !== "undefined") {
    notification.error({ message: "Duplicate",
      description: "That recipe is already on the menu" });
  } else {
    setShowSpinner(true);
    const menuItem: IMenuItem = { recipe: parseInt(key) };
    (async () => {
      const response: any = await axios.post("/api/v1/menuitem/", menuItem);
      gs.menuItems.merge([response.data]);
      setShowSpinner(false);
      notification.success({ message: "Recipe Added",
```

```
    description: "The recipe has been added to the menu" });
  })();
 }
};
```

This is the function called when an item from the Add Recipe button list is clicked. It's passed the key of the item, which you'll recall from the previous bit of code is the ID of the recipe. The first thing done is to see if this recipe is already on the menu. If we find the ID in the global state's menuItems array using the find() method, then the AntD notification.error() function is used to show a popup notification (if you jump ahead to Figure 14-10 a few pages hence, you can see what that looks like). There are several kinds of notification functions, all with different styling (icons and colors and such), error being one (others include warning(), info(), and success()).

If it's not a duplicate, then we get into the else block. There, the spinner is shown, and a new object is created based on the IMenuItem interface that has the ID of the recipe as the recipe attribute. Then, the IIFE async trick is used again to call the server, POST'ing the MenuItem to the right endpoint. The response we get back is the menu item that was saved to the database, so we merge() that into the global state object's MenuItems array, hide the spinner, and show a success() notification. At that point, the menu item is saved on the server side to the SQLite database as well as to our local global state, and the screen will automatically update as per the usual React state change re-render mechanism.

The next event handler function is for when a Remove button is clicked:

```
const handleRemove: Function = (inMenuItemID: number, inIndex: number) => {
  setShowSpinner(true);
  (async () => {
    const response: any = await axios.delete(`/api/v1/
    menuitem/${inMenuItemID}/`);
    gs.menuItems[inIndex].set(none);
    setShowSpinner(false);
    notification.success({ message: "Recipe Removed",
      description: "The recipe has been removed from the menu"
    });
  })();
};
```

In this case, we receive two pieces of information: the ID of the menu item and the index in the menuItems array. After the spinner is shown, a DELETE request is made to the server, passing the ID as part of the URL as per REST API semantics. This takes care of removing the menu item from the database. We then remove it from the menuItems array in global state, which is why we need the ID and the index. But, here's where that weird Hookstate none things come in! How do you delete an element from an array? In JavaScript, there are several ways, including splice() and slice(). But, remember how we always have to use get() when accessing things in a global state? As I mentioned earlier, that's because Hookstate has some code wrapped around it in order to be able to do its job. If you tried to delete an element using those typical JavaScript ways, you'd find that it didn't work because it in a sense "goes around" Hookstate. It won't see the change properly. Instead, you set the element to this special none value provided by Hookstate. Then, behind the scenes, Hookstate will take care of actually removing the element from the array. And note how you have to use set() here to change data, just like you have to use get() to retrieve data. This again ensures that Hookstate is aware of the change and does its work properly.

Once the global state is updated, we just need to hide the spinner and ask AntD to show a success() notification for us, and we're good to go.

That brings us to the final function, which isn't an event handler function, but it is one you saw used in a couple of spots earlier:

```
const getRecipeForItem: Function = (inRecipeID: number): IRecipe => {
  const indexOfRecipeInGSRecipes: number =
    getIndexOfRecipeByID(inRecipeID, "recipes");
  const recipe = gs.recipes.get()[indexOfRecipeInGSRecipes];
  return recipe;
};
```

The goal here is to return a reference to a recipe object from global state based on its ID. So, first, we need to find the index in the array of the recipe, so the getIndexOfRecipeByID() function that we imported from globalState earlier is used. Once we have the index, then it's a simple matter of getting a reference to that element in the recipes array in global state and returning it.

Now, I'm going to continue to jump around a bit, and we'll look at the Shopping List screen next, before we get to what is the biggest and most complicated of them all, the Recipe screen, and its related edit dialog.

The Shopping List Screen (ShoppingList.tsx)

Next, let's look at the Shopping List screen, which is where the user can see the list of ingredients they need to go buy. Figure 14-9 shows this screen.

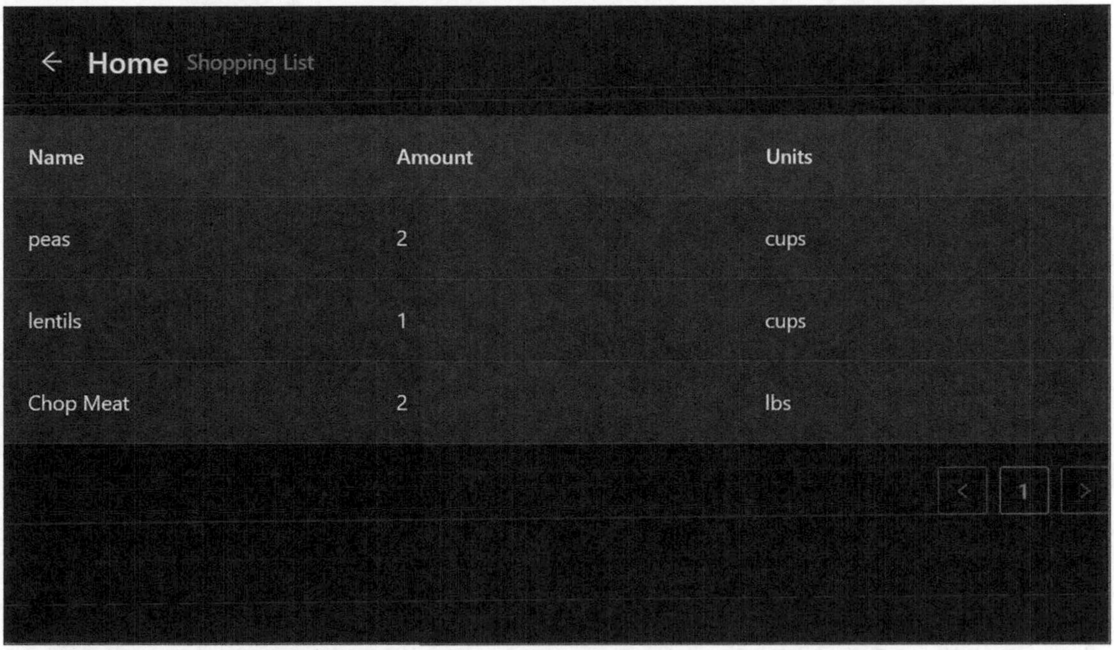
Home
Shopping List
Name
Amount
Units
peas
2
cups
lentils
1
cups
Chop Meat
2
lbs
1

Figure 14-9. *The shopping list screen*

Yep, that's it! This is a display-only screen; we just need a way to show what the server sends back to us; we don't even store this information on the client.

First up, some imports:

```
import React, { ReactElement, useEffect, useState } from "react";
import { NavigateFunction, useNavigate } from "react-router-dom";
import { Layout, PageHeader, Spin, Table } from "antd";
import axios from "axios";
const { Content } = Layout;
```

The only thing new here is the AntD `Table` component, which roughly mimics an HTML table, but with more functionality.

In order to make this work, we'll need an interface:

```
export interface IShoppingListItem {
  name: string,
  amount: number,
  amount_unit: string
}
```

This mimics the MenuItem model class on the server. This could have been placed in the `globalState.ts` file, alongside the other interfaces related to the data elements the app works with, but since this data doesn't get stored in state and in fact is only needed on this screen, it made more sense to put it here.

The Component Definition

Next up, we start our component, as always:

```
export default (): ReactElement => {

  const navigate: NavigateFunction = useNavigate();
```

We again have a header with the back arrow on it, so we again need the React Router code to implement that.

Then, we have some local state:

```
const [ showSpinner, setShowSpinner ] = useState(true as boolean);
const [ shoppingListItems, setShoppingListItems ] =
  useState([] as Array<IShoppingListItem>);
```

Since we're calling the server, we again need to deal with a spinner, and it's in the same way as in the Menu screen. Then, we of course need the data to actually display, and again, since it's only needed here, local state is a good choice.

useEffect Hook

Next, we have a useEffect hook:

```
useEffect((): void => {
  (async () => {
```

```
    const responseShoppingListItems: any = await axios.get
    ("/makeShoppingList");
    setShoppingListItems(responseShoppingListItems.data);
    setShowSpinner(false);
  })();
}, []);
```

That's pretty simple, right? It's just a GET request to the server's /makeShoppingList endpoint. Recall from the last chapter that this isn't a REST API, it's just a plain HTTP view handler function, so the response's data attribute provides the result we need, which you'll recall is the array of menu items in JSON form, which Axios has of course marshaled to an actual array for us, so we can pass that to our state setter function setShoppingListItems(), and that's all we need to do. Note the use of the empty array as the second argument to useEffect(), so we ensure this only happens once per component mount, and since the component will be completely destroyed and re-created if we navigate away and come back, that means we'll call the server every time we come to this screen, which is what we want, of course!

The Component Definition

Now, let's return the component itself, begin with this:

```
return (
  <Spin size="large" spinning={showSpinner}>
    <Layout style={{ height: "100vh" }}>
```

As before, we have a spinner, and the AntD Layout component is again used, specifying that it should fill the viewport's entire vertical space. We're not going to need a footer in this case, so the Layout will fill the entire screen.

We do have a header though, and that's next:

```
<PageHeader title="Home" subTitle="Shopping List"
  onBack={ (): void => {
    navigate("/static/index.html", { replace: true }); }
  }></PageHeader>
```

That's no different than on the Menu screen, so let's move on to the actual Content of the Layout:

```
<Content>
  <Table sticky={true} dataSource={shoppingListItems}
    rowKey={(inRecord) => inRecord.name}
    columns={[
      { title: "Name", dataIndex: "name", key: "name" },
      { title: "Amount", dataIndex: "amount", key: "amount" },
      { title: "Units", dataIndex: "amount_unit", key: "amountUnit" }
    ]}
  />
</Content>
```

Yes, that's really it! The Table component requires a dataSource prop, which is a reference to our array of menu items in local state. The sticky prop tells the table to make the headers "stick," meaning they won't scroll out of view if the table is large and the user scrolls. The rowKey prop ensures we have a unique key for each row, which is pretty typical in React any time you have multiple instances of any component, and, here, the key value is simply the name of the ingredient since we know that's unique as per the logic on the server. Finally, the column prop defines the actual columns in the table and what attribute of the objects in the dataSource array corresponds to each via the dataIndex prop. We also have to provide a key for the column, that is, a unique identifier for each column. This can be anything you like, but it made sense for them to match the column headers defined by the title prop (accepting case).

Now, let's move on to what is for sure the largest (in terms of code volume) and most complex of the screens, the Recipe.

The Recipe List Screen (Recipes.tsx)

The Recipe screen conceptually is broken into two parts: the list screen and the edit modal dialog. We'll start with the list screen, which is shown in Figure 14-10.

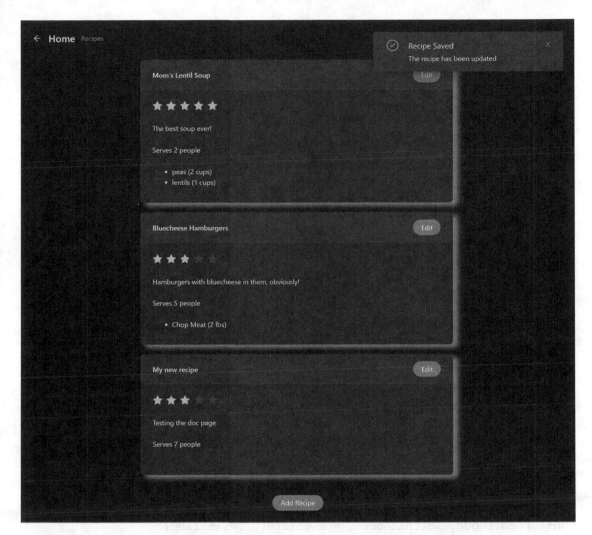

Figure 14-10. *The recipe list screen, also showing what a notification looks like*

I've tried to style this screen to roughly look like index cards with the recipes on them. Whether I succeeded or not is up to you, but for each, you can see the name, rating, description, and how many it serves. You can click the Edit button to modify existing recipes, and you can click the Add Recipe button to add a new one. Both of those buttons lead to the same modal dialog, but we'll be looking at that in the next section. So, for now, let's look at the imports we need for this screen:

```
import React, { MouseEventHandler, ReactElement, useState } from "react";
import { NavigateFunction, useNavigate } from "react-router-dom";
import { useHookstate } from "@hookstate/core";
```

```
import { Button, Card, Layout, PageHeader, Rate } from "antd";
const { Footer, Content } = Layout;
import globalState from "../../globalState";
import RecipesEdit from "./Recipes_Edit";
```

Most of those are things you've seen before or what you'd logically expect (the RecipesEdit is that modal dialog I mentioned, and it would be pretty hard to show that if we didn't import it!). One new thing is the MouseEventHandler. This is a React function type for handling mouse events. It will be used later when we type (in terms of TypeScript) one specific event handler, as you'll see.

The Component Definition

After the imports, as always, we start our component:

```
export default (): ReactElement => {

  const navigate: NavigateFunction = useNavigate();
```

Nothing new there; at this point, you know what this is all about. Similarly, you know what the next line is all about too:

```
const gs = useHookstate(globalState);
```

We need some local state in addition to global state after that:

```
const [ isEditVisible, setIsEditVisible ] = useState(false as boolean);
const [ editMode, setEditMode ] = useState("" as string);
const [ recipeID, setRecipeID ] = useState(-1 as number);\
```

The first is used to hide and show the edit dialog, much like we've done with the spinner in the past. Since that dialog can be used for both editing and adding a recipe, we're going to need a way to tell it which it is, so the editMode state variable will do that. Similarly, when editing a recipe, we'll naturally have to tell it which to edit, and that's what the recipeID variable will be used for.

Next up, we return the component to React:

```
return (
  <Layout style={{ height: "100vh" }}>
```

As with the Shopping List screen, we want to fill the entire viewport, hence the style setting. After that comes the modal edit dialog:

```
{isEditVisible &&
  <RecipesEdit editMode={editMode} recipeID={recipeID}
  setRecipeID={setRecipeID}
    isEditVisible={isEditVisible} setIsEditVisible={setIsEditVisible} />}
```

Here, you can see how those editMode and recipeID local state variables are handed to the dialog via props. We also need to give it the ability to mutate the recipeID variables, so we also pass its mutate functions. The dialog will also need to be able to hide itself, which again requires that it be able to mutate the state variable (isEditVisible) in this component, so we give it the setIsEditVisible() function as well. The value of isEditVisible is used to conditionally render the dialog, and that's how it can be "hidden" and "shown."

After that comes our PageHeader:

```
<PageHeader
  onBack={ (): void => { navigate("/static/index.html", { replace:
  true }); } }
  title="Home" subTitle="Recipes" />
```

And again, aside from the actual title itself, this is old hat at this point, so let's get into the Content itself:

```
<Content style={{
  color: "#ffffff", overflow: "auto", display: "flex", flexDirection:
  "column",
  justifyContent: "normal", alignItems: "center" }}>
```

The style settings here ensure that the content area will scroll (overflow set to auto) and that the individual recipes are all centered (the display, flexDirection, justifyContent, and alignItems attributes). I also set the text color to white across the board here.

Next, it's time to render our recipes:

```
{ gs.recipes.get().map(inRecipe => { return (
```

The recipes array in global state has them, of course, so we use map() to iterate the array and render some content for each. And, that content is as follows:

```
<Card type="inner" title={inRecipe.name}
  style={{ width: 640, margin: 10, borderRadius: "8px",
  boxShadow: "10px 6px 8px rgba(255, 255, 255, 0.5)" }} key={inRecipe.id}
  extra={<Button type="primary" shape="round"
  onClick={ (): void => { handleEdit(inRecipe.id); } }>Edit</Button>}>
  <Rate value={inRecipe.rating} />
  <br /><br />
  {inRecipe.description}
  <br /><br />
  Serves {inRecipe.serves} people
  <br /><br />
  <ul>
    { inRecipe.ingredient_set.map(inIngredient => {
      return (
        <li key={inIngredient.id}>
          {inIngredient.name} ({inIngredient.amount} {inIngredient.
          amount_unit})
        </li>
      );
    }) }
  </ul>
</Card>
```

The AntD Card component is a simple rectangular container for content, usually with a border. It can have some content in the upper-right corner via the extra prop; here, it's the Edit button. Then, any content nested under the component is rendered in the Card. Here, I've added some styling to the card to also give it a drop shadow (as well as a static width; otherwise, it would expand to fill the available width based on content and some padding to keep the content inside it away from the border). Since each Card is an item in a list, to keep React happy, we need to supply a key prop, and since the ID of a recipe is generated on the server and is always unique, that's a good choice for this.

Inside the card, it's a simple display of the attributes of a recipe taken from the inRecipe variable, which is the next recipe in the array passed to the function that map() executes. When we get to the ingredients, we again use map(), this time to iterate the ingredient_set attribute of inRecipe. For each, we return a list item (li) HTML element since we're creating an unordered (bullet, as it's frequently called) list (ul). Pretty straightforward, right?

Finally, we finish the Content component, and then we need a Footer on the page, so that we have a place to put the Add Recipe button:

```
    </Content>
      <Footer style={{ display: "flex", flexDirection: "column",
      alignItems: "center" }}>
        <Button type="primary" shape="round" onClick={handleAdd}>Add
        Recipe</Button>
      </Footer>
    </Layout>
  );
};
```

That's pretty much the same as the Add Recipe button on the Menu screen, so no surprises here, I expect.

Event Handler Functions

Now, we have two event handler functions to look at that I skipped over earlier, starting with the one for the Edit buttons:

```
const handleEdit: Function = (inID: number) => {
  setEditMode("Update Recipe");
  setRecipeID(inID);
  setIsEditVisible(true);
};
```

As you can see, the ID of the recipe is passed to it. The editMode local state variable is set, and note that the value it's set to is written in plain English, not a codeword or something, and that's because, as you'll see in the next section, it's used as the title for the dialog. Then, the ID of the recipe is saved in the recipeID local state variable, and, finally, the `isEditVisible` local state variable is set to `true`. That will cause a re-render, and this time the conditional rendering of the `RecipesEdit` component will occur, and we'll have a dialog shown to the user to edit the recipe.

Likewise, when the Add Recipe button is clicked, the `handleAdd()` function is called:

```
const handleAdd: MouseEventHandler = (): void => {
  setEditMode("Add Recipe");
  setRecipeID(-1);
  setIsEditVisible(true);
};
```

Here, because of how the button is used and rendered, the type of the function has to be `MouseEventHandler`, as opposed to plain old `Function` for the `handleEdit()` function before. Given what the code here does, it's just a small peculiarity we have to cope with to make TypeScript happy, it has no real bearing on what we're doing this time. But, since we want to try our best to always have real types for everything, we *do* have to deal with it by specifying the appropriate type even if it might not really matter to us in practice. Aside from that, the code is essentially the same as the Edit button's handler, and that makes sense since it leads to the same dialog. The only real difference is that there's no recipe ID yet since it hasn't been saved to the database, which is the point where the ID is generated. So, we'll use a value of `-1` so the code behind the dialog can differentiate an edit from an add.

It's a pretty simple screen, really. Most of the heavy lifting is actually in the dialog, which we can go look at right now!

The Recipe Edit Modal Dialog (Recipes_edit.tsx)

When editing or adding a recipe, the recipe edit modal dialog is shown, overlaid on top of the recipes list, as shown in Figure 14-11.

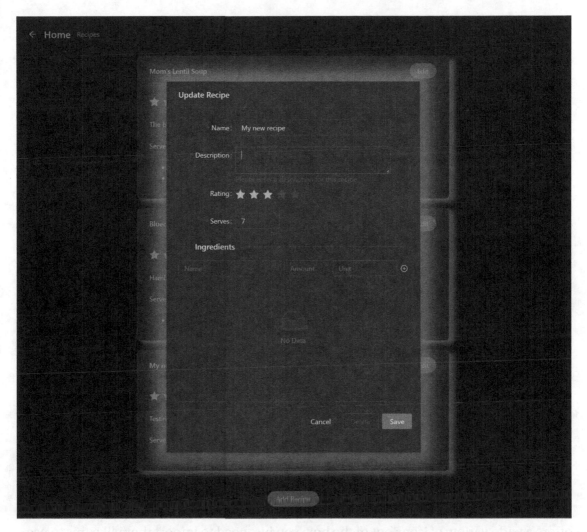

Figure 14-11. *The recipe new/edit modal dialog, showing required messages*

In this screenshot, you're seeing the dialog in edit (update) mode, as indicated by the title. I also took this opportunity to show you the field validation messages that AntD's form components provide automatically: you can see that the description is a required field because of the message that appears below it if you leave the field empty.

The basic structure of the screen is to have a few fields up top for name, description, rating (as shown with 1–5 stars), and how many the recipe serves. This is the basic information about a recipe, so to speak. Below that is a section for listing the ingredients. For that, we have three fields for name, amount, and unit (ounces, pounds, etc.), and the plus icon next to those adds it to the list section below (which, because there's currently no ingredients, automatically shows the "No data" icon). If you add an ingredient, there will be a minus icon next to it that allows you to remove it (but you cannot edit ingredients already added).

For the code, we start with our imports:

```
import React, { MouseEventHandler, ReactElement, useEffect, useState } from
"react";
import { Button, Divider, Form, Input, InputNumber, List, Modal,
notification, Popconfirm,
  Rate, Space, Spin
} from "antd";
import { PlusCircleOutlined, MinusCircleOutlined } from "@ant-
design/icons";
const { TextArea } = Input;
import { none, useHookstate } from "@hookstate/core";
import globalState, { IIngredient, IRecipe, getIndexOfRecipeByID }
  from "../../globalState";
import axios from "axios";
```

Most of it isn't new, just a few new AntD components, as you could have guessed. The names are, I'm sure, largely self-explanatory, save for maybe Popconfirm, Rate, and Space, but we'll get to all of them in turn. Note too that we have to use that destructuring trick to get the TextArea from the Input component since it's in effect a "subcomponent." That's for the description field, since it's not just a single line of text like the name is. Also, we have some icons imported from the AntD icons package. AntD offers a wide variety of icons out of the box; you just need to import them like this to use them as you would any other component.

Next, we begin our component:

```
export default (inProps): ReactElement => {

  const gs = useHookstate(globalState);
```

Nothing new there, but the next line has something new:

```
const [ form ] = Form.useForm();
```

Form.useForm() is an AntD-provided hook that gives us a way to get and manipulate the underlying data in the form, which all our components will be a part of here, much like in HTML how input elements are children of a <form> element.

Next, we need some local state:

```
const [ ingredients, setIngredients ] = useState([] as Array<IIngredient>);
const [ addIngredientData, setAddIngredientData ] =
  useState({ name: "", amount: 0, amount_unit: "" } as IIngredient);
const [ showSpinner, setShowSpinner ] = useState(false as boolean);
```

The ingredients variable is where we'll store the ingredients as we add and remove them. The addIngredientData is where we'll store the values of the three fields used to add an ingredient as the user edits them (you'll see how they are used shortly). As you can see from the useState() call, the initial value is an object that adheres to the IIngredient interface, and the initial values are what will be shown in the fields to start. Since we'll be calling the server, we'll need a spinner, so that the variable and setter function are present too.

Next up, we have a useEffect hook to look at:

```
useEffect((): void => {
  if (inProps.recipeID !== -1) {
    const indexOfRecipeInGSRecipes: number =
      getIndexOfRecipeByID(inProps.recipeID, "recipes");
    const recipe: IRecipe = gs.recipes.get()[indexOfRecipeInGSRecipes];
    form.setFieldsValue({
      name: recipe.name, description: recipe.description, rating:
      recipe.rating,
      serves: recipe.serves
    });
    setIngredients([...recipe.ingredient_set]);
  }
}, []);
```

Since we only want this to execute when the dialog component is mounted, we pass an empty array as the second argument. Then, in the function, we see what the ID of the recipe passed in via props is. If it's not -1, then we're editing a recipe. In that case, we use that indexOfRecipeInGSRecipes() function to get the index of the recipe, then get a reference to the recipe object itself. This has to be done because the fields on the screen need to reflect the current values of the recipe data. This is done with a call to the `form.setFieldsValue()` function. This is a method of the `form` object returned by the call to that `useForm()` hook earlier, and it simply takes in an object where the keys map to the name of form fields, and the values are literally the values to set in those fields. That takes care of the "basic" recipe data fields, which leaves the list of ingredients to deal with. For those, all we need to do is merge in the `ingredient_set` array from the `recipe` object using the `setIngredients()` state mutator method. As you'll see later, the AntD component used to list the ingredients will be re-rendered then, showing the ingredient list.

If this dialog is shown to add a recipe, none of this is required since all the fields already have proper starting values (meaning that, generally, they're blank), so we're good to go for that use case at this point.

Next, we begin returning our component:

```
return (
  <Modal title={inProps.editMode} visible={inProps.isEditVisible} centered
footer={null}
    destroyOnClose={true}
    style={{ boxShadow: "0px 0px 30px 20px rgba(255, 255, 255, 0.5)" }}
      closable={false}>
```

The `Modal` AntD component provides a modal dialog window, meaning it blocks what's behind it until dismissed in some way. You can see here how the `editMode` string that was set from the list screen becomes the `title` like I mentioned earlier. The `visible` prop maps to the local state variable from the list screen so this component can be hidden and shown as needed. The `centered` prop does exactly what you'd imagine: it centers the `Modal`! A `Modal` can have a `footer`, but in this case, it's not needed, so I've set it to `null` to hide it. Finally, the `destroyOnClose` prop is set to `true`, and this is done so that the `Modal` is re-created every time it's shown. This is necessary to ensure the `useEffect` hook fires each time and everything works as planned.

Everything else that follows is a child of that Modal component, beginning with the spinner:

```
<Spin size="large" spinning={showSpinner}>
```

A spinner is needed for when we call the server to save or delete a recipe, which you'll see when we get to the event handler functions after the component is complete.

Next up begins a form:

```
<Form name="editRecipe" labelCol={{ span: 6 }} wrapperCol={{ span: 16 }}
  preserve={false} form={form}
  initialValues={{ name: "", description: "", rating: 1, serves: 1 }}
  onFinish={handleSave} autoComplete="off" onFieldsChange={handleChanges}>
```

In this case though, it's not an HTML form, it's an AntD Form component. But, it serves the exact same purpose: it groups a bunch of data entry components into a single entity – a form – and allows us to address the Form as a whole for various things and allows for validation and error messages and all that sort of stuff. A Form has a name, so that you can have more than one at a time if needed. The labelCol and wrapperCol props define the layout of the form, labelCol for labels and wrapperCol for data entry components. The form gets divided into columns, so we're telling it how many of those columns the labels span, as well as how many the data entry components span. You can also set offsets if you don't want them to simply line up. The preserve prop set to false avoids a problem that can occur due to the adding and removing of ingredients later, since they are children of the Form too. Without this, ingredients wouldn't be removed properly. The form prop maps back to the form variable we got from the useForm() hook function so that we can access things through that variable later. The initialValues prop does exactly as the name implies: sets the initial values of the form fields. The onFinish prop tells the Form what function to execute when the form is submitted. Setting autoComplete to "off" disables the auto-completion your browser might normally do. And, finally, the onFieldsChange prop defines an event handler function to execute any time the form changes, and we'll get to that latter because it's key to making the ingredients section work.

Basic Recipe Info

Now that we have a form, we can begin to define data entry fields:

```
<Form.Item label="Name" name="name"
  rules={[{ required: true, message: "Please enter a name for this
  recipe" }]}>
  <Input />
</Form.Item>
```

Every element in a form is wrapped in a generic *Form.Item* component. This defines basic information that AntD needs, such as the *label* for the field, what its *name* is in the form, and *rules* to validate it with (here, specifying that it's *required* and what *message* to show if it's empty). Then, as a child of that *Form.Item* component, comes the actual data entry component. In this case, a basic Input component is used to provide a single-line text entry field. Most of the time, you won't need to specify any props at this level, though sometimes you may; it depends on what the component requires.

For the description, we use that TextArea that I mentioned when we looked at the imports:

```
<Form.Item label="Description" name="description"
  rules={[{ required: true, message: "Please enter a description for this
  recipe" }]}>
  <TextArea />
</Form.Item>
```

Otherwise, it's the same basic idea. And then, for the rating, it's just as simple:

```
<Form.Item label="Rating" name="rating" rules={[{ required: false }]}>
  <Rate />
</Form.Item>
```

In this case, the user isn't required to provide a rating (it will default to one star if not changed). The Rate component provides that star selection mechanism without us doing anything more. Pretty nice, right?

Finally, we have the number of people the recipe serves:

```
<Form.Item label="Serves" name="serves"
  rules={[{ required: true, message: "Please enter how many people this
  recipe serves" }]}>
  <InputNumber />
</Form.Item>
```

Since here we know we only want to accept a number, the InputNumber component is used because unlike the Input component that will allow any alphanumeric value to be entered, InputNumber only allows numbers.

The Ingredients Section

That takes care of the basic recipe information, so now we can begin the section where ingredients are entered. It starts with that divider you see:

```
<Divider orientation="left">Ingredients</Divider>
```

AntD provides the `Divider` component for this, generating a line with some text in it. The `orientation` prop tells AntD where to place the text.

Next up, we have the three data entry fields:

```
<Space align="baseline">
  <Form.Item name="addIngredient|name" rules=
    {[{ required: false, message: "Required" }]}>
    <Input value={addIngredientData.name} placeholder="Name" style={{
    width: 210 }} />
  </Form.Item>
<Form.Item name="addIngredient|amount"
  rules={[{ required: false, message: "Required" }]}>
    <InputNumber value={addIngredientData.amount} placeholder="Amount"
      style={{ width: 90 }} />
</Form.Item>
<Form.Item name="addIngredient|amount_unit"
  rules={[{ required: false, message: "Required" }]}>
    <Input value={addIngredientData.amount_unit} placeholder="Unit"
      style={{ width: 130 }} />
</Form.Item>
  <PlusCircleOutlined onClick={ handleAddIngredient } />
</Space>
```

All the fields are housed in an AntD `Space` component. This component lets us group other components together but doing so without them "sticking" together, by distributing space between them. This is usually in situations like this where you want to have components side by side. By setting the `align` prop to `"baseline"`, we're ensuring the alignment point of the components being aligned is aligned with the dominant baseline of the parent.

Then comes three Form.Item components, the first (name) with an Input child, the second (amount) with an InputNumber child, and the third (amount unit) again with an Input child. Note the name for each of these: the value "addIngredient", a pipe, and then what looks like a *real* name. This will come back into the picture when we get to the event handlers, but just keep it in mind for now.

In these cases, unlike the basic data fields, we actually *do* have some props to define at the data entry component level. Each of their value props are pointed to an attribute of the addIngredientData object. That ensures that as the user enters data here, that object will get updated. The placeholder prop allows us to show what would normally be a field label *inside* the field, something that's necessary due to these all being in a horizontal line and there not being space to label them otherwise. Finally, the width of each element is specified to ensure it all fits in a single line. At the end, we have a PlusCircleOutlined component, which is an AntD component from that icons package you saw imported earlier. When this is clicked, the handleAddIngredient function will be called.

That takes care of the UI needed to add an ingredient, but what about the list of existing ingredients? That comes next:

```
<div style={{ height: "210px", overflow: "auto" }}>
  <List itemLayout="horizontal" dataSource={ingredients}
    renderItem={(inIngredient: IIngredient, inIndex: number) => (
      <List.Item key={inIndex}
        actions={[
          <MinusCircleOutlined onClick={ (): void =>
          handleRemoveIngredient(inIndex) } />
        ]}>
        <List.Item.Meta title={
            `${inIngredient.name} ${inIngredient.amount} ${inIngredient.
            amount_unit}`
          } />
      </List.Item>
    )}
  />
</div>
<Divider orientation="left" />
```

It starts with a plain old HTML div, and inside of it goes an AntD List component. A List is simply a (usually) vertical rendering of the items in an array. In order to make the List scrollable, the containing div has a static height and overflow set to auto. The List itself is actually pretty similar to the Table component you saw earlier in that you provide it a dataSource prop, here our array of ingredients, tell it what orientation you want the list in (horizontal here), and then provide a function via the renderItem prop to execute for each item in the array, returning some component after all that. The component must be List.Item, and that's where your key must go. The actions prop, which is optional, provides a way to put some action control on the right, and here I'm using an AntD MinusCircleOutlined component, the other component imported from the icons package. That component has an onClick event handler that calls the handleRemoveIngredient function that you'll see soon. You then must provide a List.Item.Meta component, and here is where you specify some text to show. Here, I use the title prop to show the information that the user has entered for a given ingredient. At the end, another Divider is used so that we have lines before and after to separate the ingredient section visually.

The final piece of the puzzle is the buttons below the ingredients section.

```
<Form.Item wrapperCol={{ offset: 13, span: 16 }}>
  <Space>
    <Button type="text" onClick={ () => {
      inProps.setIsEditVisible(false); }
    }>Cancel</Button>
    <Popconfirm title="Are you sure to delete this recipe?"
      okText="Delete" okType="danger" cancelButtonProps={{ type: "text" }}
      cancelText="Cancel"
      onConfirm={handleDeleteConfirm}>
      <Button danger disabled={inProps.editMode === "Add
      Recipe"}>Delete</Button>
    </Popconfirm>
    <Button type="primary" htmlType="submit">Save</Button>
  </Space>
</Form.Item>
```

To get the alignment I want, I had to wrap those all in another Form.Item component so it would align according to how layout is defined on the Form, just like all the other fields on the form. Then, the offset prop is used to push the buttons over to the right. Then, like with the ingredient entry fields, I place the buttons in a Space component to get them aligned and spaced out well. The first button is Cancel, and if clicked, that simply hides the Modal via the local state mutator function passed in via props.

The Delete button is, well, seemingly not a button at all! In fact, it's an AntD Popconfirm component (see Figure 14-12). This is a component that provides a small popup with user-definable buttons to confirm an action. In this case, we of course want the user to confirm the deletion. The title prop lets us show the message text. There are basically two buttons always present, one that corresponds to yes, or ok, and one that corresponds to no, or cancel. We can define the text for each through the okText and cancelText props. Further, we can define a subtype for the buttons via the okType and cancelType props. In this case, I'm just using the okType to set that button to the "danger" type, which is red, so seems appropriate for a confirmation to delete a recipe. The cancelButtonProps prop is used to make the type of the cancel button "text", rather than a boxed-in button like Delete is. I did this just to make them stand apart from each other more. If the Cancel button is clicked, the Popconfirm simply goes away; nothing else happens. But if the Delete button is clicked, then the function specified by onConfirm is called to do the deletion. Finally, there is a Button component as a child of the Popconfirm. This is the component that will trigger the Popconfirm being shown (it therefore doesn't have to be a Button). Here again, I set the type to "danger", and also note that the button will be disabled if we're adding a new recipe since it doesn't have any function in that case.

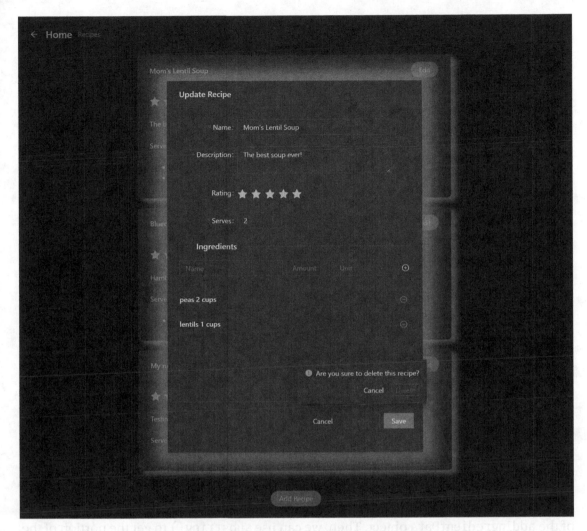

Figure 14-12. *What the popup confirm looks like when deleting a recipe*

The final Button is the Save button, and by this button being a child of the Form, and setting its htmlType to "submit", it will cause the Form to be submitted when clicked, and since we defined the onFinish event handler on the Form, clicking this button results in the handleSave() function being called.

Event Handler Functions

And now it's time to look at the event handlers I've passed over, starting with the handleChanges() handler:

```
const handleChanges = (changedFields, allFields): void => {
  const changedFieldName: string = changedFields[0].name[0];
  const locationOfPipe: number = changedFieldName.indexOf("|");
  if (locationOfPipe !== -1) {
    const aid: any = { ...addIngredientData };
    aid[changedFieldName.substring(locationOfPipe + 1)] =
    changedFields[0].value;
    setAddIngredientData(aid)
  }
};
```

Recall this was referenced by the onFieldsChange prop on the Form. This function will actually fire *any* time *any* field on the *entire* Form changes. The purpose of this function is to record what the user is entering in the add ingredient fields as they enter it, because otherwise we won't have a way to get this data later. So, we begin by getting the name of the field. Note that the changedFields argument is always an array, but it's always the first element we're interested in. Once we have the name, we check to see if it has a pipe character in it. Ah-ha! Remember that from earlier? That's how we tell if we need to do anything here! If there's no pipe, then it's not one of the add ingredient fields, and we ignore this event. If it *is* one of those fields though, the next step is to get a clone of the addIngredientData object. Then, we can use substring() to get the portion of the name after the pipe, which is the actual name of the changing field, which *also* happens to map to the attribute names in that addIngredientData object. Because of that, we can use bracket notation to update it, taking the value of the changing field. Finally, a call to setAddIngredientData(), passing it the new aid object, sets the entry in local state for later.

And "later" is actually right now because I'm going to jump to the handleAddIngredient() function now, which is called when that plus icon is clicked:

```
const handleAddIngredient: MouseEventHandler = (): void => {
  addIngredientData.name = addIngredientData.name.trim();
  setIngredients(ingredients.concat({ ...addIngredientData }));
```

```
setAddIngredientData({ name: "", amount: 0, amount_unit: "" })
form.setFieldsValue({ "addIngredient|name": "",
"addIngredient|amount": "",
  "addIngredient|amount_unit": "" });
};
```

First, the name value is `trim()`'d since that's used as a key value effectively when the shopping list is produced, so we don't want any leading or trailing spaces gumming up the works. Then, a call to `setIngredients()` is made, passing it a new array formed by merging in the new ingredient (stored in `addIngredientData`) using the `concat()` method of the `ingredients` array. The `addIngredientData` is cleared out so we start fresh if the user wants to add another ingredient, and a call to the `setFieldsValue()` method of the `form` reference allows us to pass an object with values for the three ingredient add fields to clear them out as well. That effectively resets the screen so it's ready to accept another ingredient, if the user so chooses, and the list of ingredients will automatically re-render to include the new ingredient thanks to the update of the `ingredients` array.

After that, we have the event handler function for when an ingredient is removed via a click of the minus icon:

```
const handleRemoveIngredient: Function = (inIndex: number): void => {
  const ing: Array<IIngredient> = ingredients.filter((v, i) => inIndex
  !== i );
  setIngredients(ing);
};
```

Yep, not much to it! We just need to get a new array via a `filter()` call that filters out the ingredient at the index specified by the `inIndex` argument, then set the `ingredients` local state to that new array.

Next up, we have the `handleSave()` function:

```
const handleSave = (inValues: any): void => {
  setShowSpinner(true);
  const recipe: IRecipe = {
    name: inValues.name,
    description: inValues.description,
    rating: inValues.rating,
```

```
    serves: inValues.serves,
    ingredient_set: ingredients.map((inIngredient) => { return {...
    inIngredient}; })
  };
```

This first part of the function, called when the Save button is clicked, of course, shows the spinner, since we'll be calling the server here, and then creates a new recipe object. The values are taken from the inValues passed in, which is provided by AntD, and are the values of the fields in the Form. The ingredient_set attribute is different though. There, we need to generate an array from the ingredients array that at this point has the list of ingredients for the recipe. Note that this is the case whether we're adding or editing a recipe. Recall on the server side that updating a recipe, as far as the ingredients go, is done by removing all ingredients and then adding whatever was passed in, so this works in either case with the same logic here.

Once that object is populated with data, we have to make a determination whether we're doing an add or an update:

```
if (inProps.recipeID === -1) {
  (async () => {
    const response: any = await axios.post("/api/v1/recipe/", recipe);
    gs.recipes.merge([response.data])
    notification.success({ message: "Recipe Saved",
      description: "The recipe has been saved" });
    inProps.setIsEditVisible(false);
  })();
```

When the recipeID passed in to the Modal component via props is -1, that means we're adding. In that case, it's pretty simple: we just need to use the IIFE trick to make an async call to the server via Axios, passing the recipe object in the body (Axios stringify()'s it to JSON and sticks it in the body of the request for us), then merge in the returned object to the recipes array in global state. That will cause the recipe list screen to update automatically. Then, the notification.success() function is called to inform the user everything went according to plan, and, finally, the Modal is hidden. Now the user is back on the recipe list screen, with the new recipe in the list.

For an update, we get into the `else` branch, and it is almost, but not quite, the same:

```
} else {
  recipe.id = inProps.recipeID;
  (async () => {
    const response: any = await axios.put(`/api/v1/recipe/${recipe.id}/`,
    recipe);
    const indexOfRecipeInGSRecipes: number =
      getIndexOfRecipeByID(inProps.recipeID, "recipes");
    gs.recipes[indexOfRecipeInGSRecipes].set(response.data);
    notification.success({ message: "Recipe Saved",
      description: "The recipe has been updated" });
    inProps.setIsEditVisible(false);
  })();
}
```

Since it's an update, we need to tell the REST endpoint the ID of the entity to update as part of the URL, so we pull that from the props and set it on the `recipe` object that was created earlier. After that, things proceed basically the same as for an add, except that after the response comes back from the server, we're of course not adding to the ingredients array, we're replacing the existing recipe object in it. Therefore, we have to get the index of the recipe with `indexOfRecipeInGSRecipes()`, then we can replace it with a `set()` call (because remember this is Hookstate we're dealing with). After that, a suitable message is shown, the `Modal` is hidden, and the recipe list screen is seen again, with whatever changes were made to the recipe reflected on the screen.

The very last event handler to look at is the one that is executed when the user confirms they want to delete a recipe via that `Popconfirm` from earlier:

```
const handleDeleteConfirm: MouseEventHandler = (): void => {
  setShowSpinner(true);
  (async () => {
    const response: any = await axios.delete(`/api/v1/recipe/${inProps.
      recipeID}/`);
    const indexOfRecipeInGSRecipes: number =
      getIndexOfRecipeByID(inProps.recipeID, "recipes");
    gs.recipes[indexOfRecipeInGSRecipes].set(none);
```

```
      const indexOfRecipeInGSMenuItems: number =
        getIndexOfRecipeByID(inProps.recipeID, "menuItems");
      gs.menuItems[indexOfRecipeInGSMenuItems].set(none);
    notification.success({ message: "Recipe Deleted",
      description: "The recipe has been deleted" });
    inProps.setIsEditVisible(false);
  })();
}
```

Once the spinner is shown, the server is called, a DELETE HTTP request, with the recipeID from props on the URL. Once that response comes back, the recipe is gone from the server, so now we have to deal with the data on the client. So, first, we get the index of the recipe in the global state recipes array. Then, we use the Hookstate-provided set() method, passing it the Hookstate-provided special none value. Hookstate will take care of literally removing it from the array. There's one more task we have to accomplish after that, and that's removing any menu item that might reference this recipe. That too will have been done on the server already, so we have to mirror it on the client. So, we use getIndexOfRecipeByID(), this time passing "menuItems" as the second argument for the first time. This does the same as always but gives us the index in the menuItems in global state instead of the recipes array. With that, we can set() the element to none again, show a notification, and hide Modal, and the menu item will be gone next time the user navigates to the Menu screen.

And with that, we've looked at all the code for Fooderator, both server side and client side!

Suggested Exercises

I'm sure you can think of several ideas to enhance this app already, but I have one to throw out for you, just to complete what was suggested in the previous chapter: implement the client side of the ability to specify a number of guests for a menu item. You'll need to modify the edit dialog appropriately, and you'll likely want to modify the list to show this information, and then you'll need to ensure you're passing that information to the server and that the server-side code is properly calculating the result. It's a relatively minor enhancement on the surface, but there's plenty to do to make it work – both client and server sides – so I think it's a good challenge for you that will promote your learning for sure.

Summary

In this chapter, you were introduced to several new things. You learned about hooks and how they allow you to use the React lifecycle in pure functional components. You got your first look at the AntD component library, saw a decent chunk of its components in action and saw how to build a UI with it. You were introduced to Hookstate, providing an (arguably) better way to handle state in a React app. You learned about React Router and how you can use it to allow your users to navigate through your apps in a new way. And, you used all of that together to build the client for the Fooderator REST API you built in the last chapter, finally putting all the pieces together to create a full, working (and maybe even useful, according to my wife!) app.

And with that, we've reached the conclusion of this book! I hope you've had a good time reading it, and I hope I've done a good job giving you a solid foundation in full-stack development using modern technologies and approaches. To be sure, there's still *tons* of stuff to learn, plenty of nooks and crannies even in what we explored together that wasn't touched on much (there's only so many pages my editor and publisher can allow me, after all!). But you've got an exciting road ahead of you as you dive deeper into the things we've discussed and learn what else these exciting technologies can do for you.

So, thank you very much for accompanying me on this journey, and I'll see you out there, among the stars... err, sorry, temporary lapse into sci-fi land. No, wait, you know what? I'm gonna stick with it! The sky's the limit with what you can start building now... and the stars are in the sky... so, yeah, let's do this:

I'll see you out there, among the (*modern full-stack development*) rock stars!

Index

A

addContact() method, 224, 257

addContactToList() state mutator
      method, 251

addMailboxToList() method, 249

AJAX, 252, 254, 295, 305

Android, 262, 275

AntD data, 429

anyMovesLeft() function, 354, 357

App.tsx source file, 451

    component, 452

    menu screen, 455, 456

        component, 456–460

        event handler, 460–462

    recipe edit modal dialog, 472, 474–478

        event handlers, 484–486, 488

        ingredients, 479–482

    Recipe screen, 466–468

        component, 468–471

        event handler, 471, 472

    Shopping List screen, 463, 464

        component, 464–466

    useEffect hook, 452–454, 464, 465

Atomicity, Consistency, Isolation, and
      Durability (ACID), 219

AutoSchema class, 419

Axios, 254–259, 295

B

Babel

    arrow function, 76

    .babelrc configuration file, 76, 77, 81

browsers, 77

installation, 75

npx babel test.js command, 76

npx command, 75

output, 76

plugins, 75, 81

presets

    env preset, 77

    react preset, 78

test.js file, 75

transpiler, 74

Babel loader, 167

BannerPlugin, 158

Base64-encoded, 154, 157, 295, 333

BaseLayout, 244, 270

BaseLayout component, 243, 247, 273,
      327, 343

BaseLayout.tsx, 244, 267

Basic Availability, Soft state, and
      Eventual (BASE), 219

BattleJong, 379

    Express library, 308

    game design, 308–310

    Mahjong Solitaire layout, 298, 299

    message, done, 312

    message, match, 311

    node modules, 303

    project setting up, 300

    requirements, 299

    server.ts, 304

    shuffling board, 316, 317

    tiles/board layouts, 314, 316

    tsconfig.json file, 301, 302

N

O

T

U

Printed in the United States
by Baker & Taylor Publisher Services